Orrery. January 2.ᵈ 1741-2.

These are the Books, from which I extracted my Remarks on the Life, and Writings of Doctor Swift. and therefore, there are many marks and notes throughout the volumes, that were only meant as assistant re:- :ferences for my own use...

G. Nº 8

dd. Shelf 4

Orrery's note on the verso of the first free endpaper of volume 1 of his copy of Faulkner's nine-volume set of Swift's works (1741-58), certifying that it was the copy he used in preparation of *Remarks on Swift*. Reproduced by permission of the Mortimer Rare Book Room, Smith College.

REMARKS ON THE LIFE
AND WRITINGS OF
DR. JONATHAN SWIFT

REMARKS ON THE LIFE AND WRITINGS OF DR. JONATHAN SWIFT

John Boyle, Fifth Earl of Cork and Orrery

Edited by João Fróes

DELAWARE

Newark: University of Delaware Press
London: Associated University Presses

©2000 by Associated University Presses, Inc.

PR
3726
.O77
2000

Associated University Presses
440 Forsgate Drive
Cranbury, NJ 08512

Associated University Presses
16 Barter Street
London WC1A 2AH, England

Associated University Presses
P.O. Box 338, Port Credit
Mississauga, Ontario
Canada L5G 4L8

The paper used in this publication meets the requirements of the American National Standard for Permanence of Paper for Printed Library Materials Z39.48-1984

Library of Congress Cataloging-in-Publication Data

Orrery, John Boyle, Earl of, 1707-1762.
Remarks on the life and writings of Dr. Jonathan Swift / John Boyle, Fifth Earl of Cork and Orrery; edited by João Fróes.
      p.   cm.
Includes bibliographical references and index.
ISBN 0-87413-651-2 (alk. paper)
    1. Swift, Jonathan, 1667-1745. 2. Authors, Irish--18th century--Biography. 3. Ireland--Intellectual life--18th century.
I. Fróes, João, 1965- . II. Title.
PR3726.077 2000
828'.509--dc21
[b]
          98-19295
          CIP

PRINTED IN THE UNITED STATES OF AMERICA

In Honor of Our Loving Mother the Blessed Virgin Mary, Queen of All Hearts, Coredemptrix, and Mediatrix of all Graces.

"O Mary, Conceived Without Sin, Pray for Us who have Recourse to Thee."

I also dedicate this book to the memory of my mother, Tereza Fróes.

CONTENTS

ACKNOWLEDGMENTS

In the course of preparing the present edition, Our Lord and Our Lady have blessed me with the help of many wonderful people and institutions. I wish to express my gratitude to Jesse Stevens, my typist, and to all at the English Department of the University of Southern Mississippi, especially Dr. David Wheeler, Dr. Noel Polk, and Dr. Michael Salda. My gratefulness also goes in a special way to Dr. A. C. Elias, Jr., Dr. Hermann Real, Dr. David Woolley, Dr. James Woolley, Dr. James May, and Dr. Randall McLeod. I am deeply grateful to all the librarians, curators, and staff of the libraries and institutions mentioned throughout this edition.

A very special "thank you" to my parents, Luiz and Tereza Fróes. All the love in the world to my wife, Sheila.

Manuscript notes in Houghton MS Eng 218.14 and 16423.3.4* are printed by permission of the Houghton Library, Harvard University, Cambridge, Massachusetts.

Manuscript notes in Williams.473 are printed by permission of Cambridge University Library.

Manuscript notes in Osborn pc 231 are printed by permission of the Beinecke Library, Yale University, New Haven, Connecticut.

I also gratefully acknowledge permission to print manuscript materials from the British Library; the Mortimer Rare Book Room, Smith College, Northampton, Massachusetts; Trinity College Library, Cambridge; Lilly Library, Indiana University; the University of Michigan Library; the Huntington Library; and the Bodleian Library.

The jacket illustration is reproduced by permission of the Master and Fellows of Trinity College Cambridge.

REMARKS ON THE LIFE
AND WRITINGS OF
DR. JONATHAN SWIFT

INTRODUCTION

A friend of Swift since 1732, John Boyle, fifth earl of Cork and Orrery, wrote the only book on Swift that became a best-seller in the eighteenth century, and that significantly influenced the views of later generations about Swift. Orrery's *Remarks on the Life and Writings of Dr. Jonathan Swift*, the earliest book-length study of Swift, also occasioned at least two books on Swift, by Patrick Delany and by Deane Swift (and probably Sheridan as well), which began the series of works on Swift, including those by the nineteenth-century biographers who always referred, either positively or negatively, to Orrery. Paul Korshin wrote that the nineteenth-century view of Swift "owes a great deal to Orrery,"[1] and A. C. Elias, Jr., mentioned that the *Remarks* "exerted a strong influence on Swift's reputation."[2] On the other hand, it was commonly known that Orrery had not been acquainted with Swift until late in the Dean's life (and Orrery himself admits it in the *Remarks*),[3] and this had caused some damage to the appreciation of the *Remarks*. But, as Phillip Sun has indicated, Orrery had access to trustworthy information on Swift.[4] In fact, as it will be seen, besides his direct contacts with Swift himself, Orrery had access to the then unpublished fragmentary autobiography *Family of Swift*, and relied on the testimonies of Deane Swift and Martha Whiteway, Swift's cousin and guardian.

Regarding Orrery's personal qualities, we have these words by Samuel Johnson, who personally knew Orrery: "His conversation was like his writings, neat and elegant, but without strength. He grasped at more than his abilities could reach; tried to pass for a better talker, a better writer, and a better thinker than he was."[5] However, not long after meeting Orrery, Swift wrote: "[Orrery] seems every way a most deserving Person, a good Scholar, with much wit, manners and modesty."[6] About nine months after Swift wrote those words, John Barber, Swift's friend and lord mayor of London, wrote: "My Lord Orrery's amiable qualities must make him the delight of all with you, as he is truly so with us, and when he comes over, your loss will be our gain, as the proverb says."[7] On 8 September 1743, William King (principal of St. Mary Hall, Oxford) delivered a speech on the occasion of Orrery's reception of the honorary degree of doctor in civil law, in which he says Orrery could not be praised too highly.[8] Orrery's close friendship with Pope is evident throughout Pope's letters, and in a note to Orrery (transcribed in a copy of Orrery's imitation of Horace *Odes* 1.5 [London edition], now at the Free Library of Philadelphia), Pope praises Orrery's version of Horace *Odes* 1.5.[9]

Still, the negative opinion about Orrery has prevailed. Lady Mary Wortley Montagu called Orrery "a dangler after wit."[10] Macaulay defined Orrery as "a most prodigious ass."[11] Harold Williams styled him "the pedantic Orrery,"[12] and A. C. Elias, Jr., who has made the most important researches on Orrery so far, once alluded to Orrery's lack of talent.[13] In the late 1940s, Mildred Prince came to Orrery's defense with a dissertation whose declared intention was to clear Orrery's name "of suspicions nearly two centuries old."[14] While Prince's dissertation is very useful, and in fact remains the only book-length study of Orrery, at least one scholar in the period was not impressed. At the end of the volume containing Prince's dissertation, which is at Smith College, we find a typewritten, four-page letter from James Clifford to Herbert Davis (then president of Smith College), dated 12 March 1948. In the letter's postscript, Clifford wrote that which is probably the best description of Orrery's status as a biographer and writer: "Orrery was an urbane, gentleman-scholar. It is a mistake to try to make him out to be a first-rate biographer and critic. He is excellent of his kind, and deserves more fame than he has received–that is certain. If Mrs. Prince brings him back to his proper place she will be doing a great service. If she tries to do too much more she will merely start the argument all over again."[15]

At any rate, the knowledge of some facts about Orrery will help us to understand better the *Remarks*, which has been so influential in Swift studies and, with the exception of A. C. Elias, Jr.'s two articles on the subject,[16] not as thoroughly studied by scholars as it should have been.

I

Orrery was born John Boyle on 2 January 1707, the only child of Charles Boyle, fourth earl of Orrery, and Elizabeth Cecil, daughter of the earl of Exeter. When the future biographer of Swift was born, his father was a shining public figure with little time for his son. Elizabeth Cecil died shortly after the birth of her son, so that the author of the *Remarks* never knew his mother. During the early years of John Boyle's life, his father was both a widower and a man of society. Spending most of his time in London, the fourth earl was the center of Christ Church men there, an active supporter of the Harley administration, an equally active member of "the Society" of Tories in the city, and a friend of Swift.[17] Swift had taken the fourth earl's side in the Phalaris controversy, and it is supposed that *The Battle of the Books* brought them together. References to social events in which both Swift and the fourth earl took part are seen in the *Journal to Stella*,[18] and one can only imagine how little parental attention was given to John Boyle while his famous father was engaged in affairs of importance, including his active part as envoy to Flanders in the negotiations preceding the signing of the Treaty of Utrecht.[19] Apparently, however, the fourth earl managed to make sure that his only child received a good early education. Elijah Fenton, later to be responsible for four books in Pope's *Odyssey*, had been secretary to the fourth earl in Flanders until he was dismissed in 1705. Fenton then went to Sevenoak, Kent, where he was a schoolmaster until, in 1714, he was invited back by the fourth earl to return as tutor to John Boyle.[20] Fenton taught the boy reading and Latin when the boy was between the ages of seven and thirteen.[21] Later in his life, the fifth earl would record his gratitude to Fenton, stating that Fenton and he remained friends until Fenton's death, in 1730. Orrery would later mention that he knew Fenton's contribution to Pope's *Odyssey* was larger than what was usually reckoned. He would also say that Pope "feared, rather than loved" Fenton, and that Fenton, "one of the worthiest and modestest men that ever adorned the court of Apollo," ended up becoming an alcoholic due to his past disillusions.[22]

John Boyle was sent to Westminster School, where he remained until 1720. In the early part of that decade, the fourth earl's fortunes began to decline. He was suspected of being implicated in Layer's plot and was thrown into the Tower in September 1722.[23] After six months in the Tower, the fourth earl was released on bail after Dr. Richard Mead (future friend of the fifth earl) certified that he would die if kept in the Tower any longer.[24] With the fourth earl's release from prison, the family situation seems to have returned to normal, and on 10 August 1723, John Boyle was matriculated in Christ Church, Oxford, his father's alma mater.[25] At Christ Church, John Boyle's tutor was John Fanshawe, a distinguished scholar who later became regius professor of Greek (1735-47).[26] However, unlike his famous father, John Boyle left Christ Church without taking a degree, in 1725.[27]

While at Westminster School and Christ Church, John Boyle dedicated some time to the writing of poetry. Among the Orrery Papers at the Houghton Library, there is a rough folio notebook bound in original sheepskin, shelf-mark MS Eng 218.11. The volume is entitled *Lusus Poetici*, and it contains a number of poems, all in John Boyle's hand. Although there is no identification of the author of these poems, they appear to be John Boyle's, perhaps as academic exercises, and include attempts at Latin and Greek poetry. The dates of composition of the poems in the volume are indicated by John Boyle's statement that one of the poems, entitled *On the Creation*, was written "in Colledge," and by the title of another poem, *Stanzas wrote some time after leaving Westminster School*,[28] which would place the date at around 1720. Since John Boyle's handwriting style in these two poems is identical with that seen in all other poems in the volume, perhaps they were all written between 1720 and 1725.

After John Boyle left Christ Church, he accompanied his father on a trip through the Continent, and on Christmas Day 1725, John Boyle wrote from Paris his earliest recorded letter.[29] Perhaps the fourth earl had to go to the Continent and wished his son to accompany him in order to enlarge the young man's view of the world, a common practice of parents in the century. But instead of broadening the young man's cultural values, the trip seems to have bored him, as he found himself languishing in the shadow of his father's fame and glory. Writing from Brussels on 18 February 1726, John Boyle says: "The Brusselians regard me comme le *Fils de Milord*; they seat me generally over against the Chimney and addressing themselves entirely to my noble Father, leave me to gaze at the Figures in the Fire."[30] To John Boyle's great relief, he was soon back in England, and he appears to have then spent most of his time in the family estate in Brittwell, Buckinghamshire, although the main property of the family was (and, unlike Brittwell, would remain so even after Orrery's death) Marston House, Frome, Somersetshire. In 1726 the young Boyle continued to flirt with literary projects, as may be seen in a previously unnoticed volume at the Clark Library of University of California at Los Angeles. The volume (shelf-mark MS B641 M3 C799 1726 Bound) contains a manuscript translation of a French novel entitled *Blanchia, or The Marriage of Revenge*, in John Boyle's hand throughout. The young Boyle himself wrote on the volume's first page: "Blanchia, A Novel. From the French: translated by Ld Boyle 1726." On the last page of the translation (actually a paraphrase), Boyle wrote: "John Boyle. 1726. Brittwell." As far as I could ascertain, this is the earliest extant manuscript document in John Boyle's hand.

In the subsequent months, John Boyle, to come of age in January 1728, began also to think of marriage, and the chosen lady was Henrietta (or Harriot) Hamilton, youngest daughter of the earl of Orkney; they were married on 9 May 1728. Although he was happy with his wife, John Boyle began to witness his father's friction with the earl of Orkney. It is not known why the two lords quarreled, but the hostility was open enough for John Boyle to notice it eight days before his wedding. On 1 February 1729, John Boyle mentioned the two lords' "state of War and Dissention,"[31] even though the happy occasion of the birth of John Boyle's first son on 27 January 1729 might have eased the situation a bit. The boy was named after the fourth earl, but if this had been an attempt to mollify the earl, it did not work. The tense family situation coexisted with John Boyle's increased attention to important family achievements. His early interest in literary matters now began to take the form of a strong interest in the works of his famous relations, including his estranged father. In the Orrery Papers at the Houghton Library is preserved a folio volume (shelf-mark MS Eng 218.13) featuring John Boyle's own copy of a play by his great-grandfather, the first earl of Orrery, entitled

Herod the Great. Preceding the play, John Boyle added a number of leaves, and wrote in them some remarks on the first earl of Orrery. The remarks are headed "John Boyle 1729" and feature an account of the first earl's life and character, as well as a eulogy of his poetry. John Boyle continued to work on this account for two years, as, on the last page of the remarks, he tells us the account was interrupted by his father's death in August 1731.

But the most revealing document about John Boyle's feelings toward his father during that period is a manuscript volume in the British Library (Add MS 10388). This is entirely in John Boyle's hand, and features his transcript of his father's translation of Plutarch's *Life of Lysander*, prepared by the fourth earl in his Christ Church days, under the guidance of his tutors Francis Atterbury and Robert Freind. Preceding the transcript of the *Life of Lysander*, John Boyle wrote some interesting notes that extend for eighteen numbered pages. The notes are headed "John Boyle 1730" and begin with an account of how the *Life of Lysander* was written and of the fourth earl's "victory" over Richard Bentley in the controversy about the *Epistles of Phalaris*. What follows is a sequence of poems by and to the fourth earl, carefully transcribed, and whose authors are identified by John Boyle. The most explicit statement by John Boyle regarding his estranged father is on Manuscript pages numbered 14-15:

what comes nearest my Heart, & I hope fills me with a just Emulation, as far as Those Parts which Heaven has been pleased to allot Me will admit, is, the great Reputation that my Father bears at this Day in the learned World. He began early to be distinguished for a rising Genius, & Dr Aldrich the learned Dean of Christ Church, in an Epitome of Logick which he wrote for him, & at his desire, calls him then *magnum hujus Aedis Ornamentum;* At that Colledge He translated this Life of Lysander, which, (to show the Honour I pay to any Thing, that is His) I have had taken from amongst the rest of Plutarch's Lives, and bound by Itself in this Manner.

Here we have an only child who was an aspiring man of letters, carefully and admiringly preserving the work of a father who was not on speaking terms with him, and who was also contemptuously treating his son's literary endeavors.

Even though John Boyle's second son, Hamilton, was born on 23 February 1730, the fourth earl remained cold and indifferent toward his son and grandchildren; only on Christmas Day 1730 did the fourth earl's resistance begin to melt away. On 8 May 1731, John Boyle recalls the event:

I was seized at Brittwell on Christmas Day, and growing worse and worse, my Father sent me to London in his Coach about three days after. As I still lost ground his uneasiness increased, and He came up in real agonies

to see me. I think verily his Sorrow gave me Pleasure, I am sure it gave
me Spirits. He attended my Bedside with the Constancy of a Nurse, and
the tenderness of an afflicted Parent. Ah! *sic Omnia fecisset!* The
remembrance affects me still so much that I can only in general terms
assure you that we are now in perfect amity; as seldom as possible asunder,
and as happy as possible when together; all his shyness is gone off, and all
my fears are banished. I imagined with my Recovery his Coolness might
have returned, but I judged wrong, He is still the same.[32]

In the words of Eustace Budgell (future secretary to the fifth earl), "the late
Lord Orrery now plainly saw all the Value of his Son, and was so much
pleased with him, that he could hardly be easy without him."[33]

At the same time, the fourth earl's health began to fail. After the
happiness of the birth of John Boyle's third child, Elizabeth, on 7 May 1731,
the family's concerns were directed toward the fourth earl's condition, and in
June 1731, John Boyle wrote that his father was determined to go to Ireland
and stay there for a month.[34] John Boyle also wrote that he did not believe
the trip would do his father's health any good,[35] and in early August, the
fourth earl was back in England with plans to go to France for his health. But
he did not even have time to leave England; he died on Saturday, 28 August,
and John Boyle reports that the fourth earl tried to say his son's name
immediately before expiring.[36] According to Eustace Budgell, John Boyle
was so shattered by his father's death that "it flung him into a Fit of Sickness,
which had like to have cost him his Life; and obliged him to go to the
Bath."[37] John Boyle's (now fifth earl of Orrery, and hereafter called
"Orrery") letters written in those days confirm Budgell's statement. Orrery
arrived in Bath on 15 October and on the next day, already noted the special
treatment he began to receive as a lord.[38]

Still, for all his honors, Orrery did not get what he probably wanted most
of all: his father's library. In his will, drawn on 6 November 1728, the fourth
earl bequeathed his valuable library, as well as some of his scientific
instruments, to Christ Church, leaving to Orrery only "the Journals of the
House of Lords, and such Books as relate to the English History and
Constitution."[39] The actual words in the will, expressing the fourth earl's
wish to leave his library to Christ Church, show a quite negative assessment
of Orrery's personality: "Having never observed that my own son hath showed
much taste or inclination either for entertainment or knowledge which study
and learning afford, I give and bequeath all my books and mathematical
instruments (with certain exceptions) to Christ-church College, in Oxford."[40]
Orrery appears to have been deeply hurt by his father's words. In Letter
XXIII of *Remarks on Swift*, Orrery refers to "the force of an arrow" which was
directed at him from his father's hand, and which considerably wounded
him.[41] Here, Orrery seems to refer to his father's words against him in the

will, and also tries to excuse his father, stating that the fourth earl acted "in a passion, and upon an extraordinary occasion."[42] In that same passage in Letter XXIII of the *Remarks*, Orrery claims that his father had directed "the remaining scar" (apparently the words in the will against Orrery) to be "entirely erased," but his "sudden death" prevented the removal of the unfavorable words in the will.[43] However, it is hard to believe that the clause could not have been changed even though the fourth earl really wanted it to be so. The implication in Orrery's words about the affair in Letter XXIII, that it was difficult and time-consuming to change the clause, is unpersuasive. Actually, Orrery himself was not sure that his father wanted to remove the clause from the will. In his letter to Counselor Kempe, dated 15 September 1731, Orrery wrote: "I am persuaded he [the fourth earl] intended to alter his last Will in my favour; *if He did not* [my emphasis], again I repeat to you, I forgive Him."[44] For someone like Orrery, who, as Johnson once said, aspired to be reputed as a man of letters who widely read and wrote,[45] the possession of the fourth earl's library would have been a valuable asset.[46] It is supposed that Orrery, to prove his father's words against him in the will were untrue, began to strive to acquire some recognition as a writer and a wit.[47] At any rate, it is certain that, after his father's death in 1731, Orrery began to be actively involved in literary affairs, and made the acquaintance of some eminent men of letters, the first of whom was Jonathan Swift.

II

Shortly before he met Swift, some important events took place in Orrery's life. On 7 March 1732, Orrery delivered his maiden speech in the House of Lords, during the debates regarding the Mutiny Bill.[48] Charles Ford later told Swift that Orrery was "extremely applauded" for that speech,[49] and Orrery moved that the troops should be limited to twelve thousand strong, a motion that reflects Orrery's lifelong aversion to standing armies. In spite of Orrery's eloquence, the motion failed by twenty-seven votes to eighty-eight. On 22 August 1732, almost exactly a year after his father's death, Orrery lost his wife. Orrery was again badly shaken, as may be seen in three unpublished letters at the Clark Library, UCLA. On 10 September 1732, Lord and Lady Orkney each wrote to Orrery, and both letters reveal that Orrery had retired somewhere and left his children with the Orkneys. Lord and Lady Orkney urged Orrery to submit to what had happened for the sake of the three children, who were now more than ever in need of a parent's help. The Orkneys also encouraged Orrery to take to himself the task of giving his children the best possible education, now that they would be deprived of a mother's presence. The third letter is from Eustace Budgell, dated London,

3 September 1732, and Budgell also urged Orrery to "submit to Fate" and to start thinking seriously about his children.

However, in the subsequent months, Orrery's thoughts were mainly directed toward literary matters. He had been in Ireland since 4 July 1732, and sometime after that date, Orrery first met Swift. Swift's earliest mention of Orrery is in his letter to Charles Ford dated 14 October 1732: "Ld Orrery stays here this winter. I meet him sometimes at dinners and he hath dined with me. He seems an honest man, and of good dispositions."[50] Also, in the autumn, Orrery began his correspondence with Pope, and since he had been "admitted to the number"[51] of Swift's friends, he wrote a poem to Swift on the Dean's birthday, 30 November 1732.[52] Orrery was obviously very proud of this poem, which he wrote on the first leaf of a notebook he gave Swift as a birthday gift.[53] He later printed it in the *Remarks*, and there is a neatly written manuscript copy, in his own hand, among the Piozzi Papers at the John Rylands University Library of Manchester.[54] In January 1733, Orrery wrote a poem on Pope's *Epitaph to Gay*, which was printed posthumously by John Duncombe,[55] and the manuscript of it, in Orrery's hand, is preserved in the Huntington Library.[56] This manuscript contains evidence that Orrery had sent it to Swift, probably for Swift's evaluation and criticism. The manuscript is endorsed by Swift himself;[57] apparently Orrery did not keep a copy for himself, since Swift arranged for another copy to be made for Orrery.[58] Also in 1733, Orrery went to the family's main estate, Marston House in Somersetshire, and acquired a new library, and also met Pope in London for the first time. Still in 1733, another event helped to further associate Orrery's name with the world of literature. Toward the middle of the year, the poet Mary Barber was preparing to publish her *Poems on Several Occasions* (London: C. Rivington, 1734), which may have been published either in 1733 or 1735, in spite of its imprint.[59] *Poems on Several Occasions* opens with a letter from Swift to Orrery dated Dublin, 20 August 1733,[60] in which Swift reports that Mary Barber had desired Swift's opinion as to the idea of dedicating the work to Orrery. Swift writes that those who knew Orrery would readily admit she was telling the truth in her planned eulogy of Orrery, but he feared Mary Barber would end up being listed in "the common Herd of Dedicators."[61] Swift believes it would not be proper for Mary Barber to offer Orrery such public praises, since she had received many favors from the earl, and he wished Orrery's character "should have a much stronger Support."[62] Swift then writes about the topics he imagined would be treated by Barber in her projected dedication to Orrery: Orrery's learning, genius, affability, generosity, patriotism, goodness, humility, condescension, agreeable conversation, and firm Christianity.[63] Swift approves of Barber's choice of a patron in Orrery, and finally highly recommends her poetry.[64] Swift's letter is followed by a letter from Barber to Orrery,[65] the first page of which bears Orrery's coat of arms.[66] Barber expatiates on Orrery's virtues, and is especially grateful for Orrery's help to her when she was "a Stranger in England" and for Orrery's continued generosity to her in Ireland when she was sick.[67] There follows Barber's preface to the work,[68] in which she calls Orrery "my great Patron and Benefactor."[69] The volume contains five poems by Barber addressed to Orrery.

Between 1737 and 1741, four poems by Orrery had appeared in print: a poem to the memory of the second duke of Buckingham;[70] imitations of Horace *Odes* 1.1[71] and 1.5;[72] and a poem to Mrs. Caesar (both Swift's and Orrery's friend).[73] We know that Swift both read and praised Orrery's imitations of Horace,[74] and Pope's praise of Orrery's imitation of Horace's *Odes* 1.5 has been mentioned.

On 30 June 1738, Orrery was married a second time. His bride was Margaret Hamilton, only daughter and heiress of John Hamilton, landowner of Caledon, county Tyrone, Ireland. By that marriage, Orrery "came to the acquisition" of an estate in Caledon that Orrery described as "a most delightful place."[75] Caledon was a welcome addition to the family's properties, since the estate in Brittwell and a house in Downing Street, London, had been sold a few years earlier. Caledon would become for Orrery the ideal place of retirement, and, besides Marston House in England, his favorite place, where he would spend a considerable amount of time whenever possible. Orrery stayed in Caledon in 1739 and 1740, returning to England in the winter of 1740, when he began to be close to Pope. The close friendship would last until Pope's death in May 1744. Orrery remained in England until 1746, and he divided his time between Marston and his home in Duke Street. He was also busy with more than just the publication of his poems. He was admitted as a member of the Royal Society in 1740, and on 21 November 1742, the first child of his second marriage was born and named Edmund. On 8 September 1743, Orrery received the honorary degree of doctor of civil law in Oxford, and his youngest daughter, Lucy, was born on 27 May 1744. Orrery returned to Ireland in 1746, to be in Caledon until June 1749, when he left for a short trip to England. Orrery was back in Ireland in October, having reached Dublin on 30 October. This time, the "Caledonian retirement" would last until the middle of August 1750. On 6 August 1750, Orrery arrived in his new London house in Leicester Fields. It was while he remained in Leicester Fields, until early January 1752, that Orrery would witness the appearance of his most controversial and commercially successful work: the *Remarks on Swift*.

III

"Other People may perhaps write fast: I shall always choose to write slow." This was how Orrery defined his method of writing to Andrew Millar on 12 July 1752,[76] at a time when both Millar and he were enjoying the great success of the *Remarks*. And these words seem to have been literally fulfilled in the case of the composition of the *Remarks*. Paul Korshin, like others before him, has stated that the *Remarks* had been written after Orrery's edition of the *Letters of Pliny*.[77] This seemed plausible enough from the fact that *Pliny* had first appeared in April 1751, and was addressed to Charles, Orrery's eldest son. The *Remarks* came out in November of that year and was addressed to Hamilton, Orrery's second son, and the last letter of the *Remarks* was dated 28 August 1751.[78] It appeared that Orrery had first conceived the idea of dedicating one work to his eldest son, and then decided to write something for Hamilton as well. In fact, this is what Orrery himself claims in Letter I of the *Remarks*.[79]   However, the *Remarks* affair was more complicated than that.

First, it is now possible to know that the *Remarks* was *not* written after, but *simultaneously* with *Pliny*. This fact had only been previously noticed by A. C. Elias, Jr., in a footnote in his pioneering article on the *Remarks*.[80] On 25 June 1751, shortly before the *Remarks* was published, Orrery told his friend Mr. Ferrebee:

> I have read many books to complete it [*Pliny*]. It was a siege of Troy; but at the same time I was carrying on another very different work, addressed to my second son, and which will be published next Winter. It shall be sent you, when I know how to convey it. There is time enough between this day, and its appearance to settle that point.[81]

Although it is not possible to determine the exact dates of the composition of the *Remarks*, Orrery's statement that it was written together with *Pliny* offers a great help. From Orrery's manuscript letters from Caledon to his friend the historian Thomas Birch, at the British Library,[82] we are able to know the dates of completion of practically all books of Orrery's *Pliny*. Judging from the dates of composition of *Pliny* given by Orrery in his letters to Birch, now at the British Library, we can say that the *Remarks* was being written as early as 1745, with possible interruptions for business transactions in 1747, and continued to receive Orrery's attention in 1747-51.

An indication of Orrery's work in preparation for the *Remarks* may be seen in Orrery's own copy of Faulkner's nine-volume set of Swift's works (1741-58), preserved at the Mortimer Rare Book Room, Smith College, with annotations and marks by Orrery.[83] In volume 1, on the verso of the first free endpaper, Orrery wrote:

> Orrery. January 2[d] 1741-2. These are the Books, from which I extracted my Remarks on the Life and Writings of Doctor Swift, and therefore there are many marks and notes throughout the volumes, that were only meant as assistant references for my own use. O.

Most of the notes and marks referred to have been discussed by Mildred Prince,[84] but a few facts need to be mentioned. Orrery was meticulous in marking even the table of contents for the works by Swift that interested him or suited the purposes of "moral teaching" of the *Remarks*. In volume 1, besides the above-mentioned note, Orrery wrote some queries on Swift's *A Discourse . . . . concerning Athens and Rome*, and the passages in Swift's prose tracts that are alluded to in the *Remarks* are duly marked, besides many other passages that attracted Orrery's attention. Volume 2 (Swift's poetry) has, on the first free endpaper, Orrery's account of a discussion as to the regularity of the lines in Swift's poem *The Petition of Frances Harris*, as well as a note stating that Bolingbroke used to call Swift "Frances Harris." On the opposite blank page, Orrery transcribed Swift's poem on Sir Thomas Prendergast, by whose motion in the House of Commons Faulkner was once arrested.[85] Again, he carefully marked the table of contents, and *Cadenus and Vanessa* is almost fully marked, especially the line on "the conscious Muse," which would receive Orrery's particular criticism in the *Remarks*. The rhymes in Swift's imitation of Horace *Epistles* 7.1, which Orrery considered to be bad ones in his interleaved copy of the *Remarks*, are marked as "Irish Rhymes."[86] The blanks in *The Author upon Himself*, regarding the duchess of Somerset and Thomas Thynne, are filled, and other passages throughout the volume are marked, which suggests Orrery's interest in Swift's poetry, in spite of his negative criticism of it in the *Remarks*.

We have another indication of Orrery's plans for some project about Swift in 1742. On 22 November, Martha Whiteway wrote to Orrery, reporting about Swift's condition, and it is evident that Orrery had asked her to send the account, which he included in Letter XI of the *Remarks*. On 19 November, Deane Swift sent Orrery an account of Swift's incident with Francis Wilson,[87] one of Swift's prebendaries, also at Orrery's request. On 4 December, Orrery wrote back to Mrs. Whiteway, saying she and Deane Swift had furnished him with "melancholy but ample materials for reflexion." Orrery then writes: "they were materials I wished for and desired."[88] Apparently, Orrery had wished to publish something related to Swift's affairs at once. On 29 December, William King wrote to Orrery, and in this letter, it may be seen that Orrery had sent him a copy of Deane Swift's letter of 19 November and proposed that King would make arrangements for its publication. King declines the proposal, saying its publication "would subject ye Printer to an action."[89] Significantly, although he printed Mrs. Whiteway's letter of 22 November in the *Remarks*,[90] Orrery did not include Deane Swift's account of 19 November in the book, but rather had it transcribed in one of his annotated copies of the *Remarks*,[91] to be discussed later. On 17 December 1743, Deane Swift wrote again to Orrery, giving an update on Swift's situation, and this was apparently written at Orrery's request.[92] Deane Swift would write again to Orrery about Swift on 4 April 1744 (letter included in the *Remarks*),[93] and once more it was at Orrery's request. Furthermore, Deane Swift wrote Orrery two other letters (dates unknown) about Swift, and both at Orrery's request. Portions of them are transcribed in the interleaves of Orrery's prepublication copy of the *Remarks*.[94] Those extant portions refer to *A Tale of a Tub*, and we see that Orrery had been trying to know for sure if Swift was really the author of the work, and decided to have recourse to Deane Swift once more.

Still regarding Orrery's work in preparation for the *Remarks*, it is possible to see that Orrery managed to have access to the manuscript of Swift's fragmentary autobiography, to be first published only in 1755 as an appendix to Deane Swift's *Essay upon the Life, Writings and Character of Dr. Jonathan Swift*. At the Pierpont Morgan Library (New York, New York), there is a transcript of Swift's autobiography in the hand of one of Orrery's scribes whose hand also appears in the Orrery Papers at Harvard.[95] There are marginal notes to the text, and those notes are also in the hand of Orrery's scribe, except for a note on manuscript page 7, which is in Orrery's hand. The marginal notes were printed by Herbert Davis in volume 5 of his edition of Swift's prose works,[96] but Davis neither identified the hand nor printed two of the marginal notes on manuscript pages 14-15. The first note describes a conversation between Swift and Orrery, about William III's offer to make Swift a captain of horse when Swift was a secretary to Sir William Temple. The second note features some observations by Orrery on Swift's poem *The Discovery*. Some of the marginal notes reveal that Orrery took time to inquire into some facts relating to Swift's ancestors,[97] that he had the transcript made from Swift's autograph copy,[98] and that he was hoping to locate "a fairer copy" of the autobiography, which he supposed John Lyon had.[99] In fact, in Letters I and II of the *Remarks*, there are noteworthy instances of Orrery's reliance on Swift's autobiography, and in two particular passages, Orrery repeats verbatim what Swift had written in the autobiography.[100]

Apparently, Orrery found a suitable frame within which to put whatever parts of the *Remarks* he had written up to 1748 when Hamilton, his second son, was matriculated in Christ Church on 8 June of that year.[101] Since he was already engaged in writing a book addressed to his eldest son, it must have seemed a good idea to write the life of Swift in the form of informal, morally instructive letters to Hamilton with the aim of aiding the young man in his "entrance into the world." As far as I could determine, Orrery was the first to write a biography in the form of letters.[102] At the same time, as James Clifford observed, Orrery's experiment was not very successful, in the light of later biographical theory and practice. Indeed, since Orrery's time, no author of biography has seen fit to use the epistolary form.[103] Clifford wrote that Orrery's only real claim to fame in writing a biographical work in the form of letters is "to have tried a special form which lies outside the mainstream of English biography."[104] As for Hamilton's reaction to

Orrery's numerous classical allusions in the *Remarks*, we may see that Hamilton's reading lists for the years 1749, 1750, and 1751 at Christ Church show he must have been comfortable enough with references to the classics.[105] An admirer of Horace and Virgil, Hamilton was once described by Orrery in these words: "under the modestest and gravest countenance imaginable, he has the most true humour of any youth I know."[106] Hamilton took his studies seriously, as he went on to receive his bachelor of arts degree in June 1754, and then proceeded to legal studies, becoming a faculty student (law) on 10 December 1762.[107]

Sometime after 8 June 1748, Orrery decided to send Hamilton that which is now Letter I of the *Remarks*, containing some of the material he had been writing since around 1746. As may be seen in the beginning of Letter II of the *Remarks*, Hamilton liked the idea and asked Orrery to send more letters. In the beginning of Letter III, we see that Hamilton sent Orrery his comments on Letter II, and was particularly moved by Orrery's account of Stella. From Letters III through VI, Orrery writes about Swift's life until the time of the *Drapier's Letters*, and in the beginning of Letter VII, we read that Hamilton was "impatient" to read about "all the works" of Swift. Orrery declines the request, since he considered a number of Swift's works to be negligible. Still, he goes on to write about Faulkner's edition of Swift's works and about Thomas Sheridan, and in the beginning of Letter VIII, we read that Hamilton had paid Orrery a surprise visit and asked his father to go on with the work as soon as possible. In Letter IX, Orrery gives his account of Swift's relationship with Vanessa, and in the beginning of Letter X, we read that Hamilton had written to Orrery on "the 24th instant." Hamilton was very pleased with the contents of Letter IX, and Orrery proceeds to give his remarks on Swift's poetry in general. In the remaining letters there are no more references to Hamilton's reactions or contacts with Orrery, but we may reasonably presume that the correspondence continued normally. However, it should not be assumed that the twenty-four letters were not altered and corrected by Orrery after he sent Hamilton his last letter, dated 28 August 1751, nor is it possible to know if Hamilton's responses were fictionalized by Orrery, since Hamilton's letters to Orrery have not survived.

In fact, it is probable that Orrery kept copies of the letters he sent to Hamilton, and continued working on them later. This is a point that is now impossible to determine, since no manuscript copies of the *Remarks* are extant, having been probably destroyed, as was the case with the manuscript of *Pliny*.[108] But there is one evidence that Orrery continued to work on the last three letters after the entire book had been printed. In his interleaved copy of the *Remarks*, Orrery wrote that he believed Letters I-XXI had been printed while he was still working on his theory that Virgil has represented Horace in the *Aeneid* by the character Creteas, which he printed in Letter XXIII.[109] As A. C. Elias, Jr., points out, it is likely that the twenty-four

letters had been printed while Orrery was revising the last three letters.[110]
Even if *only* the first twenty-one letters had then been printed, it is still true
that Orrery kept the printing house waiting. Orrery's choice of a publisher
and a printer in Dublin for the *Remarks* fell on Faulkner, and it was not until
13 August 1751 that Faulkner was able to add one of Orrery's afterthoughts
to the book. On that day, Orrery wrote to his friend Dr. Edward Barry, who
had offered criticisms of some of Orrery's poems in the past, saying he had
at last found a way to introduce Barry's name in the *Remarks*.[111] Barry's
name is mentioned in Letter XXIII, in a passage where Orrery flatteringly
compares Barry to Antonius Musa, Augustus's physician.[112]   On 30
November 1751, Faulkner would write that he did not "publish" the *Remarks*
until he had printed Orrery's inclusion of Barry's name.[113] Since Letter
XXIV is dated 28 August 1751, one wonders whether Faulkner still had to
wait a few more days to complete the printing of the whole work by the final
addition of Letter XXIV in late August 1751.

Whatever the case, the earliest edition of the *Remarks* is an odd affair that
shows Orrery's care with his work. This edition, a 204-page 12mo, hereafter
called FI, must have appeared sometime in September 1751, considering that
Faulkner "published" the *Remarks* only after the addition regarding Barry in
mid-August, and taking into account the date of Letter XXIV. Featuring
many misprints and readings that were later corrected by Orrery, FI does not
seem to have had a wide circulation. No publication date for it was found in
Faulkner's *Dublin Journal*, where one would expect it to be, nor is it
advertised in any other Dublin periodical. Considering the bad quality of its
text, and that Faulkner himself never mentioned it in his letters to Orrery, it
appears that FI was a sort of experimentation piece, as if Orrery first wanted
to test whether a printed version of the work would be of good quality before
launching it in a public manner.

IV

Orrery had been in his house in Leicester Fields since 6 August 1750, and
chose Andrew Millar as his London publisher of the *Remarks*.[114] In spite
of his mistakes in *Pliny*, James Bettenham was kept as printer.[115] Orrery
already had in hand a prepublication copy of the London first edition without
title page on 14 September 1751, and it has a number of passages in their
uncorrected form, as they appear in FI. From a manuscript note in this extant
prepublication copy (MS Eng 218.14, Houghton Library, Harvard University,
Cambridge, Massachusetts), which Orrery interleaved and annotated, we learn
that Orrery was applying to the edition printed in London the same tactics he
had used in the case of FI. He circulated some early printed copies among
"particular friends" and even sent about three copies to Ireland. We also learn
that those copies had a number of uncorrected passages that agreed with FI

and the prepublication copy itself. Orrery even decided to recall the copies he had given to his friends, and had one particular sheet reprinted, although he could not recover the copies he had sent to Ireland.[116] On 7 October 1751, Orrery already had with him a copy of the London first edition complete with title page. This particular copy, which is extant (Osborn pc 231, Osborn Collection, Beinecke Library, Yale University, New Haven, Connecticut), still featured thirty-one uncanceled passages, which Orrery meticulously marked out, stating they should be altered in "future editions."[117] However, for some unknown reason, those passages are still uncanceled in the London first edition, which appeared on Thursday, 7 November 1751. This first London edition had an initial printing of fifteen hundred copies, selling for 4*s*. each.[118] On Saturday, 9 November, Millar told Orrery that all fifteen hundred copies were sold, and that there was still a great demand for more. Millar put the printing house to work as fast as possible, and the public's demand was so great that Millar decided to have the new edition printed "in blue Paper" because the sheets were not dry enough to bear binding. Millar tried hard, and on Thursday, 23 November, he announced that his second edition would appear "next week." On Tuesday, 26 November, Millar said the new edition would come out "next Thursday," and it was finally published on Thursday, 28 November. Millar printed three thousand copies, and in less than a week, more than two thousand copies were sold.

Millar then applied to Orrery "for leave to begin another edition," as the demand continued to be great and it appeared that the second edition would be completely sold out soon. Millar put four presses to work, and on Saturday, 7 December, Millar announced that the third edition would be published "next week," "carefully corrected," which indeed proved to be the case. Millar also added these words to the advertisement: "The great Demand for these Book [*sic*] continuing, it is impossible to get them bound, without soiling the Beauty of the impression, they will therefore continue to be sold for 2*s*.6*d*. sew'd." In that same advertisement, Millar added a note saying he already had the fourth edition "in the Press" and that it would be published "with all convenient Dispatch." So, even before the third edition had come out, Millar was already foreseeing that the sales would continue to be high and began printing the fourth edition. On Tuesday, 10 December, the third edition was published, and in that day's advertisement, Millar repeated the claim that the fourth edition was "in the Press." Millar printed three thousand copies of the third edition, which also sold out. This means that, in a month, seventy-five hundred copies were sold. Millar's fourth edition was published on Saturday, 1 February 1752, and was available both in regular paper and "sew'd in blue Paper." On Thursday, 23 November 1752, it was announced that Millar's fifth edition would be published "next week." In the same advertisement, Millar said there were still some copies of his fourth edition available, which indicates the sales had diminished, but they were still steady enough to warrant the publication of a new edition. Millar's fifth edition appeared on Tuesday, 28 November 1752, and the advertisement for that day continued to appear until Saturday, 2 December, still mentioning that copies of the fourth edition were available. There were no more editions by Millar.

While the great sale of the London editions was going on, Faulkner appeared to have enjoyed success in Dublin, as well. On Tuesday, 12 November 1751, Faulkner announced in the *Dublin Journal* that, "in a few Days," he would publish Orrery's *Remarks*. The publication finally took place on Saturday, 23 November,[119] and on 26 November, Faulkner wrote to Orrery saying he had "sold more of them that day, and every day since" than he ever did "of any Book before."[120] In that same letter, we read that Orrery had "commanded" Faulkner to give away copies as gifts to certain persons. Dr. Edward Barry got "most of the Sheets" more than a week before the book came out, and Faulkner says Barry "had obliged" many of "his greatest patients" with those sheets. Faulkner gave the Duke of Dorset a bound copy three days before publication, and the Duke had been "entertained" by it "in the most agreeable manner" ever since. By post, Faulkner sent Lady Orrery a copy "sewed in blue paper," "several days before any one else could see it." Lady Orrery told Faulkner that she was pleased not only with her husband's work, but also with Faulkner's printing: "the paper is good, the print correct, and Type very clear." The Speaker of the Irish House of Lords was "ravished" with the *Remarks*, and "a clergyman" had visited Faulkner's shop on 25 November, saying the *Remarks* "was the best written book in the World, except the Bible." The "clergyman" also told Faulkner he would carry the *Remarks* "constantly in his pocket." Faulkner assured Orrery that, if he were to tell all he heard of the *Remarks*, he would have to write "an History" of every copy he sold.[121] According to Faulkner, the whole of Dublin was reading the *Remarks*, and Faulkner wrote again on 30 November,[122] saying the "amazing Demand" for the book continued. Faulkner said that "all the Judicious and Learned, as well as those that are unprejudiced," considered the *Remarks* to be "the finest and best written Piece in the English Tongue." Faulkner estimated his sale was "not inferior to Mr Millar's" and observed he had sold "above 300 in one Week, which is more than ever was known to be disposed of in so short a Time in Dublin."

Not all received the book so favorably, however. Faulkner mentions some were calling it "a Libel" against Swift, as well as accusing Faulkner of ingratitude toward Swift. Still, Faulkner maintains that all "Gentlemen of the best Taste and Learning in the Kingdom" agreed that the *Remarks* was "beyond any Work that they have seen." Faulkner proudly says that those "Gentlemen" also told him the *Remarks* was not only the best written, but also "the best printed Book that ever was done in Ireland." Faulkner repeats his claim that all Dublin is reading Orrery's "bewitching Book," while he expected "several Thrusts and Shots" made at him "in different Papers next week."[123]

In the last part of the letter, Faulkner alludes to one of the oddest incidents related to the *Remarks*. Faulkner thanks Orrery for having written to "Willson and Williamson" from whom Faulkner has not heard lately, but he supposes "they have dropped their Design." A few lines down, Faulkner says he did not think "Mr Bettenham to blame," for there might be "Sheets stolen" from Bettenham's Press, as there had been from Faulkner's.[124] Clearly, a piracy situation was being referred to, and as A. C. Elias, Jr., noted, Faulkner was referring to Peter Wilson and Matthew Williamson, two Dublin publishers who had been involved in piratical publications.[125] On 21 December 1751, Faulkner sent Orrery "three Packets" containing the "Design" he had mistakenly supposed was "dropped": a pirated *Remarks* entitled *Memoirs of the Life and Writings of Dr. Jonathan Swift, D.D., Dean of St. Patrick's, Dublin*, 12mo.[126] One must keep in mind that there was lack of copyright protection within the Irish book trade, and in fact, as Elias pointed out, "the Dublin book trade specialized in the quick, cheap reprint from London."[127] Normally, an "interloping publisher" in Ireland would advertise his wares "openly, brazenly proclaiming their superiority in type, cheapness, or accuracy."[128] However, in the case of the *Memoirs*, there had been an unusual attempt at secrecy, to disguise the altered text. As Elias remarked, the *Memoirs* removes the letter format of the *Remarks*, the more personalized passages, and all mention of Orrery's name. As Elias also observes, Orrery's long passages toward the beginning and the end of the *Remarks* had been dropped and short summaries put in their places. Some sentences are rearranged or altered, and Elias wrote that, for the Dublin of 1751, this was "an unusual little work indeed."[129] The *Memoirs* has for an imprint: "London: printed for J. Cooper in Pater-Noster Row," and as both Elias and M. Pollard have observed, this was done in order to hide the perpetrators' identities in Dublin.[130] As for how those responsible for the piracy had obtained the sheets of the *Remarks*, it is possible they had either been stolen from Bettenham's presses in London or taken from the prepublication copies of the London edition that Orrery had sent to Ireland and that he never recovered. In his letter of 21 December, Faulkner says he had learned "Peter Wilson and Oliver Neilson" were involved in the piracy, and Elias identified Oliver Nelson as another Dublin publisher involved in piratical editions.[131] Faulkner asks Orrery for directions on how to proceed on this affair, and Orrery answered in a postscript to one of his secretary's letters to Faulkner, saying it was not in his power "to resent the insult." Orrery recognizes that those responsible for the piracy had been "too cunning in the publication," and advises Faulkner to "revenge the affront" with "silence and contempt," as he himself would do.[132] On 2 January 1752, a London bookseller named Thomas Butler wrote to Orrery, saying that a correspondent in Dublin who regularly sends him "any new book published there" sent him a copy of the pirated version of the *Remarks*, which he offered to forward to Orrery.[133]

Butler asks for permission to reprint the pirated version in England, and Orrery replied on 6 January, declining to receive a copy of the pirated version from Butler, saying he had already seen it, evidently referring to the sheets Faulkner had sent him on 21 December. Orrery indicates he will legally defend Millar's rights to the *Remarks* and that if anyone publishes the piracy, they will do it "at their peril."[134] Not surprisingly, Butler dropped his idea.

In his letter to Orrery of 21 December 1751, Faulkner wrote that the edition he had published on 23 November was "out of print," and that he was going to publish his "duodecimo next Monday."[135] Accordingly, Faulkner's 339-page 12mo appeared on 30 December 1751, and Faulkner would also publish another 339-page 12mo with the words "The Second Edition, Corrected" on the title page, and the imprint 1752. It was followed by Faulkner's third edition, a 339-page octavo, imprint also 1752.[136] On 30 January 1752, Faulkner told Orrery about another favorable reception of the *Remarks*. The archbishop of Dublin was "in raptures" with the book, and had told Faulkner he thought Orrery was "the best Writer of the age" and that Orrery's observations were "superiour to any that he hath met with."[137] A fourth edition by Faulkner was never found, and a possible explanation appeared in Dobell's Catalogue no. 177 (1967), lot 340. That item is described as an edition by Faulkner with three lettering pieces on the spine, the center one reading "Fourth Edition." The copy's description also includes a note said to be "on the endpaper": "Mary Jesser's Book the Gift of the Right Hon. Earl and Countess of Cork, Sepr 3rd 1754." This particular copy was located at the Bodleian Library, where it is now preserved with the shelf-mark Don.f.500. The copy contains a note that identifies it as lot 340 in Dobell's 1967 Catalogue no. 177, and was received at the Bodleian on 27 June 1967. The uppermost lettering piece on the spine reads "Lord Orrery's Remarks on Swift," while the center one reads "Fourth Edition," and the third one reads "Dublin MDCCLII." The note on the first free endpaper certifying the copy as a gift from Orrery and his wife to Mary Jesser can still be seen. But the most interesting result of the examination of the copy is the discovery that it is not a "fourth edition," but rather, it is Faulkner's earliest printing, the 204-page 12mo that had appeared sometime in September 1751. And what is more amazing, the copy certainly had belonged to Orrery, who would have been able to correct the mistake, whether made deliberately or not. At any rate, the existence of this copy seems to indicate that a real fourth edition had never existed. It is significant that Faulkner's fifth edition does exist, and bears a 1757 imprint, being a 339-page 12mo.[138]

All Faulkner's editions have a few more luxuries than Millar's. As regards the footnotes included both in Faulkner's and Millar's editions, Faulkner alone included a footnote in Letter XXIII identifying Orrery's father as Charles, the fourth earl.[139] Also, Faulkner included an "Advertisement of the Editor" where he claims to have received the sheets from Orrery himself and took the liberty of adding footnotes to the book. As will be seen, Faulkner's early reception of the sheets did not help much toward the correctness of his texts. All of Faulkner's editions also have, on the first page of the text, an engraving showing Orrery's coat of arms and motto, something that is not found in Millar's editions. Lastly, Faulkner's editions have a half title including both a portrait of Swift and one of Orrery.

It might be proper to say a few words about the portraits of Swift in the different editions of the *Remarks*. The first thing to know about them is that they were not all prepared by the same engraver, although they were based on one single portrait: a pastel on paper, nearly life-size, painted soon after 1737 by Rupert Barber (son of Mary Barber, the poet).[140] As William LeFanu observed, Rupert Barber painted it when he came home to Dublin after studying in Bath,[141] and Sir Frederick Falkiner described it thus: "It is a fine, clean-cut sketch, apparently intended for a bust, for the throat and neck are bare, rising above the slight classic drapery, and this accounts for the disuse of the full-bottomed wig."[142] However, the engravings of Barber's portrait in the *Remarks* were far from being attractive. Falkiner believed that "the coarseness and the gloom" of the engravings were due to the "wretched art of the engraver."[143] Seumas O'Sullivan observed that, in Faulkner's editions, we have "the sunken cheeks, the frenzied eyes, and the shaggy eyebrows" in the engraving of Swift facing "the majestic brow, the nicely-placed ear, and the calm self-sufficiency" of Orrery in the engraving of his portrait.[144] O'Sullivan believed that Orrery wanted the engravings to be thus arranged so that Hamilton could compare "the face of a nobleman, a scholar, and a sane man" with the face of "a disordered man of genius."[145] O'Sullivan's argument is weakened by the fact that the London editions do not have the engraving of Orrery's portrait. In any case, the engraver of Barber's portrait of Swift in the London first and fourth editions, as well as in all of Faulkner's editions except the third, was Benjamin Wilson (1721-88), a painter who was also interested in science.[146] Wilson was responsible for many famous portraits, including a portrait of Shakespeare for the Stratford Town Hall in 1769,[147] and, as O'Sullivan observed, Wilson was "quite capable of giving us work quite different from what confronts us in the frontispiece to Orrery's book."[148] The engraver of Barber's portrait of Swift in the London second, third, and fifth editions was Simon Ravenet (1721?-74), a French engraver[149] who engraved Barber's portrait in reverse and portrayed an even uglier-looking Swift. As for Wilson's engraving in Faulkner's editions, it is somewhat darker and they are not enclosed in a circular frame (found in all London editions). The engraving of Barber's portrait in Faulkner's third edition was made by a Dublin engraver whose last name was Wheatley, who lived in Salutation Alley and later in Anglesea Street. Wheatley was responsible for the engravings of the maps in Charles Smith's *The Antient and Present State of the County and City of Waterford* (1746) and in Faulkner's

Ancient Universal History (1774). His engraving of Barber's portrait is probably the ugliest looking of all the engravings in the *Remarks*. Also, in all of Millar's and Faulkner's editions, immediately below the engraving of Swift's portrait there is this quotation from Pliny's Letters: *Cives aliquos virtutibus pares & habemus & habebimus, gloria neminem* (We have had other citizens of equal virtues, but we shall have no one with such glory). As for the engraving of Orrery's portrait in Faulkner's editions of the *Remarks*, it is not known who the engraver was, although it may be either Benjamin Wilson or John Faber, the younger (1695?-1756), who at around the time of the publication of the *Remarks* enjoyed a good reputation as an engraver.[150] The engravings of Orrery's portrait in Faulkner's third and fifth editions look different from the ones in the other editions by Faulkner.

Reviews of the *Remarks* appeared in the *Gentleman's Magazine* for November 1751 (pp. 483-86), December 1751 (pp. 531-35), and January 1752 (pp. 360-62); and in the *Monthly Review* for November 1751 (pp. 407-24), and December 1751 (pp. 475-87). These reviews are quite positive, and in the case of the *Monthly Review*, Orrery is praised for having obliged the "Republick of letters" with his "curious and entertaining performance."[151] Both periodicals, but especially the *Gentleman's Magazine*, print a good number of abstracts from passages in the *Remarks*, and if Orrery is negatively criticized at all, it is only for not having given more information in certain passages. It seems that while some persons disapproved of and attacked the *Remarks*–such as Lady Mary Wortley Montagu,[152] Mrs. Delany,[153] and two correspondents of Sir Charles Hanbury Williams[154]–the reaction of the general public was favorable. In fact, a German translation of the *Remarks* appeared as early as 1752.[155] In 1753, a French translation was published,[156] and the *Remarks* was already meriting a comment in a French work as early as 1752. In *Nouvelles Littéraires, &c. de France & Angleterre*, a correspondent writes from London to his friend in Paris on 25 January 1752, including a criticism of the *Remarks*.[157] The author announces the publication of the book and praises Orrery as a judicious critic, an impartial friend, and a noble writer. The author particularly admires Orrery's portrait of Stella, saying that Orrery did full justice to her and deploring Swift's behavior toward her and women in general.[158]

The *Remarks* also received a favorable review in the Dublin publication entitled the *Compendious Library* for January and February 1752, article 3, pages 113-28. The article offers an abstract of the work, with some commentary, always either favorable or lenient toward Orrery. On the first page of the article, the critic writes: "It is none of our Business to determine whether the noble Author acted a very kindly Part with Respect to his deceased Friend; but in Regard to the Publick, (the only View in which it concerns us to examine his Performance), he seems to have discharged that of a very able Writer, and has a Right to the Acknowledgments of all the

Lovers of Literature."[159] A volume containing the article with inscriptions by Orrery is extant among the Williams Collection at Cambridge University Library, shelf-mark Williams.542. In this volume, we see that Faulkner indeed tried to keep Orrery well informed about pieces written on the *Remarks*. Orrery signed and dated the volume: "Orrery. Marston house. April 19th 1752." Beneath this inscription, Orrery wrote: "Sent to me from Dublin, by M[r] Faulkner." Another note by Orrery beneath this note makes reference to the page numbers of the article. Orrery then added a note that is quite revealing of his own personality:

> There seems more candour, method, and judgement in the Critic on my Observations on Swift, than in most other of the writers, and cavillers, on that work. Abuse I despise too much to answer. But I with decent pleasure see my faults corrected & exposed in a manly gentleman like manner. One day or another perhaps I may review my performance, and alter & correct it in many places. O. Marston House. June 10th 1752.

Harold Williams added a note of his own, commenting on Orrery's disposition to "review, alter, and correct" the *Remarks*:

> So far as I know this is the most personal and candid observation on his book made, in writing, by Orrery; and suggests a more favourable view of his character than is commonly entertained. Harold Williams. 6 Dec 1932.[160]

Another odd episode regarding the *Remarks* was still to take place after Orrery's death. In 1783, a Dublin publisher named Charles Lodge reissued the *Remarks*. Lodge's edition is actually a faithful reissue of Faulkner's earliest printing, the 204-page 12mo of circa September 1751, except for the new title page and the absence of the frontispieces. Accordingly, the edition faithfully reproduces all the uncanceled readings that Orrery himself had corrected as early as September 1751, as well as the embarrassing misprints of Faulkner's first printing. Apparently, Faulkner had saved the remainder of his first printing (perhaps bound, perhaps in sheets), and, after his death, the stock was sold (one might suppose) to Charles Lodge. In our own century, the *Remarks* was reissued twice, in the form of facsimile editions. In 1968, Georg Olms published a facsimile reproduction of the London first edition of the *Remarks*, published on 7 November 1751, which has an incorrect text, although less so than Faulkner's earliest printing. Garland did the same in 1974.

V

The first problem faced by the editor of the *Remarks* is that the exact number of editions which existed, as well as their status, has not been previously known. The confusion was enhanced by the fact that three editions by Faulkner and one by Millar did not carry any identification in the title page, not to mention the fact that all editions but two (Faulkner's fifth edition, 1757, and Lodge's, 1783) carried the misleading imprint 1752. The first scholar to try to determine the exact number of editions the *Remarks* went through was Dr. Herman Teerink. In his bibliography of Swift, Teerink listed all of Millar's five editions, noticing there were "large and thick paper" copies of Millar's first and fourth editions, and that Millar's first edition presented a cancel on sig. L7.[161] While Teerink thus managed to draw up a list that identified all editions Millar had published, his researches on Faulkner's editions proved to be less successful. He could list only Faulkner's 339-page 8vo published on 23 November 1751, and Faulkner's 339-page 12mo published on 30 December 1751. Teerink observed there were "Large Paper copies" of Faulkner's 8vo, and that Faulkner's 339-page 12mo had exactly the same setting of type as his 8vo.[162] Teerink also wrote that Faulkner's 339-page 12mo had "no frontispiece portrait of Swift," which is a misleading statement, since some readers might think that all issues of the edition lacked the frontispiece. Actually, Teerink had examined the copy at Trinity College, Dublin, which indeed lacks the frontispiece, and his own, which evidently had the same defect. Although Teerink missed four other editions by Faulkner, he apparently tried hard to find them. In one of the British Library's copies of Faulkner's 339-page 8vo (shelf-mark 1488.g.17), after the preliminary "Advertisement of the Editor," a typewritten letter is inserted, which reads:

2, Morehampton Road
Dublin
11/11/48

Dear M.J.

Could you find time to let me have the details for which Dr Teerink asks in a letter which I received this week? He writes "As to Orrery's Remarks, 1752, what you say is partly new to me. In the first place, I have never heard of or seen a third Dublin edition, of which you say you have a copy. Could you give me full details? Title-page (differences from the first Dublin Edition), signatures, pagination, etc. In the first Dublin edition, besides L7 (pp. 157-8), K3 (pp. 133-4) is also a cancel. The letter concerns the alteration concave/convex on p. 134. How is this in the third Dublin edition?"

I am sorry to give you this trouble, but you have, I think, my copy of the third Dublin edition, and also I am a very bad hand at collating a book. I will look for you in The Pearl on Saturday at about 12-15 o'clock [illegible rubric].

Then there follows the answer, a typed transcript of the contents of sig. L7, and it may be seen that the copy examined by the typist has L7 in its uncanceled form. If "M.J." was indeed typing from a copy of Faulkner's third edition, this means he had a unique copy of that edition. All extant copies of Faulkner's third edition have sig. L7 in their canceled form, and even add one correction that had not been included in the canceled L7 sheets of Faulkner's 339-page 8vo and 12mo: the words "paid by him to Aristotle" are corrected from the reading "paid to him by Aristotle" seen in Faulkner's 339-page 8vo and 12mo. If then we are to trust "M.J.," he had a valuable copy that unfortunately has not come down to us.[163] The next scholar to work on the subject was A. C. Elias, Jr. Elias's valuable researches have shown that Faulkner's earliest edition was the 204-page 12mo, and Elias proved it by mentioning a number of uncanceled passages in the earliest printing, as compared to Faulkner's 339-page 8vo and 12mo, as well as Millar's first edition.[164] Elias's demonstration also included the fact that the break in the original printing of the *Remarks* in Letter XXI, while Orrery was working out his theory on Virgil's reference to Horace in the *Aeneid*, is reflected in the sheets of the 204-page 12mo.[165] Finally, Elias pointed out the fact that the earliest reading of the passage in Letter XXIII where Orrery refers to Horace's advice to Asinius Pollio (as seen in Orrery's interleaved copy) is present in the 204-page 12mo, while Faulkner's 339-page 8vo and 12mo present a corrected version.[166] Elias's work is the most important contribution to the study of the *Remarks* so far, but there was still more to be done. A number of copies of Faulkner's third and fifth editions were reported to exist, but were very little known. Faulkner's second and fourth editions were still missing. As we have seen, a copy of Faulkner's earliest printing at the Bodleian Library posing as "Fourth Edition" might explain the absence of a real fourth edition. However, I have found one copy of Faulkner's second edition, in the Beinecke Library, to be described later.

After I had determined the number of editions of the *Remarks*, the next step was to undertake a collation of as many copies of all editions as was possible. I have found that, indeed, as Millar's advertisements of 7 December and 10 December 1751 claimed, his third edition is the one that had been most carefully corrected. It is the edition that contains by far the greatest number of substantive variants, and an even greater number of accidentals. It seems that, after two London editions, Orrery decided to work seriously in correcting the readings he was not happy with even in the prepublication period of September-October 1751, readings that had been left uncorrected in Millar's first edition and, in some cases, even in Millar's second edition. However, Millar's fifth edition also proved to be a considerably corrected one. Although it was not as thoroughly corrected as Millar's third edition, Millar's fifth edition contained a number of new substantive variants representing corrections that could have come only from the author himself.   The substantives in Millar's fifth edition show that, even about a year after the book was first published in London, Orrery was still concerned about the correctness of its text and took time to make alterations. Therefore, the text of the present edition is that of Millar's third edition incorporating the substantive variants in Millar's fifth edition.   In the section featuring bibliographical descriptions of the different editions of the *Remarks*, I list all copies which I have located. Some of those copies were optically compared page for page with other copies, in either a Lindstrand or a McLeod Comparator.[167]   All copies of the *Remarks* in the following libraries were thus compared:

Houghton and Widener Libraries (Harvard); Baker Library (Harvard Business School); Beinecke and Sterling Libraries (Yale); Library of the Medical School (Yale); the Huntington Library; William Andrews Clark Library (University of California at Los Angeles); Kenneth Spencer Library (University of Kansas); New York Public Library; the Pierpont Morgan Library; Butler Library (Columbia University); Carl A. Kroch Library (Cornell University); Lilly Library (Indiana University); the University of Michigan Library, Ann Arbor; Van Pelt Library, University of Pennsylvania; Free Library of Philadelphia; the Library of Penn State University, University Park; William Allan Neilson Library (Smith College, Northampton, Massachusetts); the Lewis Walpole Library; Alderman Library (University of Virginia); John Hay Library (Brown University); the Library of the State University of New York at Stony Brook; the Milwaukee Public Library; the University of Florida Library; the University of Mississippi Library, and, also, A. C. Elias, Jr.'s personal copies.

I have also used the copies in the above-listed libraries for edition-to-edition comparisons.   Microfilms of the copies in the following libraries were examined:

The British Library; Cambridge University Library; the Bodleian Library (with photocopies of the copies' covers); the Folger Shakespeare Library; and the National Library of Wales.

I also examined photocopies of the copies of the London first edition at the College of the Holy Cross (Worcester, Massachusetts) and at the Trinity University Library (San Antonio, Texas), as well as a photocopy of the copy of Charles Lodge's reissue of Faulkner's earliest printing at the Pittsburgh

Theological Seminary. As for the copies in the institutions listed below, I received collations and/or bibliographical descriptions of them from the respective librarians, whom I thank for their cooperation:

Trinity College Library, Cambridge; John Rylands University Library of Manchester; Victoria and Albert Museum; the National Library of Scotland; Edinburgh University Library; Trinity College Library, Dublin; the Royal Irish Academy; the National Library of Ireland; the Gilbert Library, Dublin; Archbishop Marsh's Library, Dublin; the University of Chicago Library; the Newberry Library, Chicago; Northwestern University Library; Morris Library, Southern Illinois University; the University of Illinois Library; Harry Ransom Humanities Center, the University of Texas at Austin; Princeton University Library; the Bancroft Library, University of California at Berkeley; Rush Rhees Library, University of Rochester; Mills Memorial Library, McMaster University; the University of Minnesota Library; the Library of the University of Wisconsin at Madison; the University of Saint Thomas Library (Saint Paul, Minnesota); Stanford University Library; Library of Congress; the Library of the University of California at Santa Barbara; the University of Washington Library, Seattle; Seton Hall University Library; the Cleveland Public Library; and the Santa Clara University Library (Santa Clara, California). Also, from Maggs Bros. Limited, London (two copies of the London first edition in stock, Cat. 1132, lots 114-15), and from the Ehrenpreis Institute for Swift Studies (Münster, Germany).[168]

All copy-to-copy differences were noted, and the actual copy-text is one of the copies of the London third edition belonging to Dr. A. C. Elias, Jr.[169] The present edition is an old-spelling one, and I emended only the eighteenth-century practice of placing quotation marks at the start of each line of a quotation. Textual variants are printed at the bottom of the pages featuring the text of the *Remarks*, and the notes containing textual variants begin with a letter (given in the pertinent lines of the text). The original footnotes in the *Remarks*, as well as Orrery's errata and corrections in the annotated copy of the *Remarks*, Osborn pc 231 (Osborn Collection, Beinecke Library, Yale University), are also printed at the bottom of the pages of the text (notes beginning with a letter). Emendations from the London fifth edition (substantive, authorial corrections) are noted in the apparatus as well, also beginning with a letter. Notes with my commentary are printed as endnotes at the end of each Letter, and they begin with a number, given in the pertinent lines of the text.

Notes

1. Paul Korshin, "The Earl of Orrery and Swift's Early Reputation," *Harvard Library Bulletin* 16 (April 1968): 177.

2. A. C. Elias, Jr., "The First Printing of Orrery's *Remarks on Swift* (1751)," *Harvard Library Bulletin* 25 (July 1977): 310.

3. "He was in the decline of life when I knew him." In the present edition, p. 67.

4. Phillip S. Y. Sun, "Swift's Eighteenth-Century Biographies" (Ph.D. diss., Yale University, 1963), pp. 38-44.

5. James Boswell, *Boswell's Life of Johnson*, ed. George Birkbeck Hill, 6 vols. (Oxford: Clarendon Press, 1887), 5:238.

6. Swift to Charles Ford, 9 December 1732. Jonathan Swift, *The Correspondence of Jonathan Swift*, ed. Harold Williams, 5 vols. (Oxford: Clarendon Press, 1963-65), 4:91 (hereafter cited as *Correspondence of Swift*).

7. John Barber to Swift, 6 August 1733, ibid. 4:189.

8. "Tres Oratiunculae Habitae in Domo Convocationis Oxon.," in *Opera Gul. King, LL.D.* (no imprint, ca. 1760), p. 28.

9. John Boyle, fifth earl of Cork and Orrery, *Pyrrha: An Imitation of the Fifth Ode of the First Book of Horace* (London: Robert Dodsley, 1741), HOR.1741 M592, MS page 8, Free Library of Philadelphia, Philadelphia, Pennsylvania. For more information on Pope's note to Orrery, as well as its text, see João Fróes, "An Unpublished Note from Pope to Lord Orrery," *Scriblerian* 27 (spring 1995): 187-90.

10. Lady Mary to Lady Bute, 23 June 1754. Lady Mary Wortley Montagu, *The Complete Letters of Lady Mary Wortley Montagu*, ed. Robert Halsband, 3 vols. (Oxford: Clarendon Press, 1965-67), 3:56.

11. Copy of Orrery, *Remarks on Swift*, annotated by Lord Macaulay, C.45.c.13, p. 183, British Library.

12. Jonathan Swift, *The Poems of Jonathan Swift*, ed. Harold Williams, 2d ed., 3 vols. (Oxford: Clarendon Press, 1958), 1:xiii (hereafter cited as *Poems of Swift*).

13. A. C. Elias, Jr., "A Manuscript Book of Constantia Grierson's," *Swift Studies* 2 (1987): 51.

14. Mildred Prince, "The Literary Life and Position in the Eighteenth Century of John, Earl of Orrery" (Ph.D. diss., Smith College, 1948), p. 221 (hereafter cited as Prince, "The Literary Life and Position of Orrery").

15. James Clifford to Herbert Davis, 12 March 1948, ibid.

16. Elias, "First Printing of Orrery's *Remarks on Swift*," 310-21; A. C. Elias, Jr., "Lord Orrery's Copy of *Memoirs of the Life and Writings of Swift* (1751)," *Eighteenth-Century Ireland* 1 (1986): 111-25.

17. *Dictionary of National Biography*, s.v. "Boyle, Charles."

18. See Jonathan Swift, *Journal to Stella*, ed. Harold Williams, 2 vols. (Oxford: Clarendon Press, 1948), 1:99-100, 2:423, 431, 437, 505, 506, 512, and 514.

19. *Dictionary of National Biography*, s.v. "Boyle, Charles."

20. John Boyle, fifth earl of Cork and Orrery, *Letters from Italy, in the years 1754 and 1755*, ed. John Duncombe, 2d ed. (London: B. White, 1774), pp. [i]-ii (hereafter cited as Orrery, *Letters from Italy*).

21. Orrery to John Duncombe, 19 June 1756, [3], Orrery Papers, Autograph File, Houghton Library, Harvard University, Cambridge, Massachusetts (hereafter cited as Orrery Papers, Houghton Library , Harvard).

22. Orrery to John Duncombe, 19 June 1756, [3]-[4], ibid. See also Add MS 10388, MS pp. 17-8, British Library.

23. *Dictionary of National Biography*, s.v. "Boyle, Charles."

24. Ibid.

25. Information courtesy of John Wing, assistant librarian, Christ Church, Oxford.

26. Ibid.

27. Ibid.

28. *Lusus Poetici*, MS Eng 218.11, ff. 19r-19v, Orrery Papers, Houghton Library, Harvard.

29. John Boyle, fifth earl of Cork and Orrery, *The Orrery Papers*, ed. Emily Charlotte Boyle, countess of Cork and Orrery, 2 vols. (London: Duckworth, 1903), 1:42-43 (hereafter cited as *Orrery Papers*).

30. Ibid., 45-46.

31. Ibid., 83.

32. Ibid., 87.

33. Eustace Budgell, *Memoirs of the Life and Character of the Late Earl of Orrery*, 2d ed. (London: W. Mears, 1732), pp. 252-53 (hereafter cited as Budgell, *Memoirs of Orrery*).

34. *Orrery Papers* 1:88.

35. Ibid.

36. Ibid., 95.

37. Budgell, *Memoirs of Orrery*, pp. 255-56.

38. *Orrery Papers* 1:99.

39. Budgell, *Memoirs of Orrery*, p. 250.

40. Samuel Johnson claimed that the fourth earl's words against his son in the Will were occasioned by a quarrel between father and son. Johnson said the quarrel "arose from the son's not allowing his wife to keep company with his father's mistress." See Boswell, *Life of Johnson* 5:238 and n. 5. I have not found evidence to support Johnson's claim. See also *The Complete Peerage*, ed. G. E. Cokayne and Vicary Gibbs, 13 vols. (1910-40), 3:422 n.

41. In the present edition, p. 306.

42. Ibid.

43. Ibid.

44. *Orrery Papers* 1:95.

45. See Boswell, *Life of Johnson* 2:129, 3:183, and 5:238.

46. The Library of Christ Church still has the fourth earl's impressive collection of five thousand volumes, as well as his scientific instruments which, in 1992, were on loan to the History of Science Museum on Broad Street, Oxford.

47. Prince, "The Literary Life and Position of Orrery," p. 9.

48. For the text of the speech, see *Orrery Papers* 1: 110-11.

49. *Correspondence of Swift* 4:94-95.

50. Ibid., p. 77.

51. These are the words used by Orrery himself in the Remarks. See the present edition, p. 222.

52. *Poems of Swift* 2:609-10.

53. In the Sale Catalogue of Swift's Library, printed by Faulkner in 1745, the notebook is listed as lot 544: "Lord Orrery's fair Book, with his Verses; presented to Dr. Swift, on his Birth-day." In the catalogue's title page, it is mentioned that books marked with an asterisk have "Remarks or Observations on them in the Hand of Dr. *Swift*." The notebook is not marked with an asterisk, which means that Swift never wrote on it. See Harold Williams, *Dean Swift's Library* (Cambridge: University Press, 1932), pp. 26-27, and appendix with facsimile of the Sale Catalogue, p. 14.

54. Williams cited this manuscript copy, but did not mention that it is in Orrery's hand (*Poems of Swift* 2: 609).

55. Orrery, *Letters from Italy*, p. xii.

56. HM 14354, Huntington Library, San Marino, California.

57. Swift's endorsement reads "Orrery on Mr Pope Epitaph on Gay."

58. *Correspondence of Swift* 4:124.

59. Information courtesy of Dr. A. C. Elias, Jr.

60. Mary Barber, *Poems on Several Occasions* (London: C. Rivington, 1734), pp. iii-viii.

61. Ibid., p. iv.

62. Ibid., p. v.

63. Ibid., pp. v-vi.

64. Ibid., pp. vi-vii.

65. Ibid., pp. [ix]-xvi.

66. Ibid., p. [ix].

67. Ibid., p. xiv.

68. Ibid., pp. xvii-xxx.

69. Ibid., p. xxi.

70. John Boyle, fifth earl of Cork and Orrery, *A Poem, Sacred to the Memory of Edmund Sheffield, Duke of Buckingham, Duke and Marquis of Normanby, Earl of Mulgrave, and Baron of Butterwick* (London: J. Brindley, 1736). Announced as published in the *Gentleman's Magazine* and the *London Magazine*, March 1737. The Dublin edition was published by Faulkner in 1741, and the poem was also printed in the *Gentleman's Magazine*, June 1741, pp. 326-27. There had also been a privately printed version, which must have appeared sometime between November 1735 and June 1737, and a copy of it, annotated by Orrery, shelf-mark C107 bb 68, is in the British Library. A transcript of the poem in Orrery's hand is in MS Eng 218.2, VII, 27-31, Orrery Papers, Houghton Library, Harvard.

71. John Boyle, fifth earl of Cork and Orrery, *The First Ode of the First Book of Horace Imitated, and Inscribed to the Earl of Chesterfield* (London: C. Bathurst and G. Hawkins, 1741). Listed as published in the *Gentleman's Magazine* and in the *London Magazine*, April 1741. The Dublin edition, by Faulkner, appeared on Saturday, 11 April 1741.

72. John Boyle, fifth Earl of Cork and Orrery, *Pyrrha: An Imitation of the Fifth Ode of the First Book of Horace* (London: Robert Dodsley, 1741). Published on Thursday, 26 November 1741. The Dublin edition, by Faulkner, was published on Tuesday, 26 January 1742. There is a transcript of the

poem, in Orrery's hand, in MS Eng 218.2, VII, 41-43, Orrery Papers, Houghton Library, Harvard. Another transcript, Latin text in Orrery's hand, English text in Lady Orrery's hand, is in Add MS 4466, ff. 14-21, British Library. The poem also appears, with some variants, in the *London Magazine*, December 1737, p. 695.

73. Printed in the *Gentleman's Magazine*, June 1741, p. 325, and in the *Dublin Journal*, Tuesday, 23 June 1741. There are two transcripts in Orrery's hand: Rothschild 564, Library of Trinity College, Cambridge, and MS Eng 218.2, IV, 220-21, Orrery Papers, Houghton Library, Harvard.

74. Cf. Swift's praise of Orrery's imitation of Horace *Odes* 1.1, reported by Lady Orrery on 18 April and 23 April 1741 (MS Eng 218.26, Orrery Papers, Houghton Library, Harvard). See also Swift's praise of Orrery's imitation of Horace *Odes* 1.5 in *Correspondence of Swift* 4:406.

75. MS Eng 218.2, V, 9, Orrery Papers, Houghton Library, Harvard.

76. MS Eng 218.2, V, part iii, 82, ibid.

77. Korshin, "Earl of Orrery and Swift's Early Reputation," pp. 169-70.

78. In the present edition, p. 323.

79. In the present edition, p. 67.

80. Elias, "The First Printing of Orrery's *Remarks on Swift*," p. 319 n. 13.

81. MS Eng 218.2, V, part iii, 31, Orrery Papers, Houghton Library, Harvard.

82. Add MS 4303, British Library.

83. Shelf-mark 825 Sw5 (1741-58), Mortimer Rare Book Room, Smith College, Northampton, Massachusetts.

84. Prince, "The Literary Life and Position of Orrery," pp. 118-49.

85. See *Poems of Swift* 3:824-26.

86. Orrery uses this expression again in his interleaved and annotated prepublication copy of the *Remarks* (MS Eng 218.14, interleaf p. numbered 104, Houghton Library, Harvard).

87. Although the transcript of the account is dated 19 December in a copy of the *Remarks* annotated by Orrery, Williams Collection, Cambridge University Library, Williams.473, the correct date is 19 November. See *Correspondence of Swift* 5:209 n. 1.

88. In MS Eng 218.2, IV, 339-41, Orrery Papers, Houghton Library, Harvard.

89. Unpublished letters from William King to Orrery, MS.Eng.Hist.d.103, ff. 62r-62v, The Bodleian Library, Oxford.

90. In the present edition, pp. 177-78.

91. In copy of the *Remarks* annotated by Orrery, Williams.473, MS pages numbered 9-18, Williams Collection, Cambridge University Library.

92. Transcript in MS Eng 218.2, III, 71-72, Orrery Papers, Houghton Library, Harvard. Ehrenpreis quoted some lines of this letter, but its full text remains unpublished. See Irvin Ehrenpreis, *Swift: The Man, His Works, and the Age*, 3 vols. (Cambridge: Harvard University Press, 1962-83), 3:917 (hereafter cited as Ehrenpreis, *Swift*).

93. In the present edition, pp. 178-80.

94. Prepublication copy of the *Remarks*, interleaved and annotated by Orrery, MS 218.14, interleaf pages numbered 300-301, and 304-6, Houghton Library, Harvard.

95. Accession number MA 455, MS pages numbered 1-15, the Orrery Correspondence, Pierpont Morgan Library, New York City. It was offered as lot 734 during Christie's Orrery Sale (November 1905), and was then bought by the London dealer Frank T. Sabin who, in 1909, sold it to Mr. Pierpont Morgan, and it is still preserved at the Pierpont Morgan Library. I am indebted to Robert E. Parks, Robert H. Taylor Curator of Autograph Manuscripts at the Pierpont Morgan Library.

96. *The Prose Works of Jonathan Swift*, ed. Herbert Davis et al., 14 vols. (Oxford: Basil Blackwell and Mott, 1939-68), 5:352-56 (cited hereafter as *Prose Works of Swift*).

97. MA 455, MS pages numbered 2, 4, 7-8, Orrery Correspondence, Pierpont Morgan Library, New York City.

98. MA 455, MS pages numbered 4, 13, 14, ibid.

99. MA 455, MS page numbered 15, ibid.

100. For Orrery's use of Swift's autobiography in the *Remarks*, see João Fróes, "One of Orrery's Sources in *Remarks on Swift*: His Scribal Transcript of *Family of Swift*," *Swift Studies* 12 (1997): 36-44.

101. Information courtesy of John Wing, assistant librarian, Christ Church, Oxford.

102. See Prince, "The Literary Life and Position of Orrery," pp. v, 93.

103. James Clifford to Herbert Davis, 12 March 1948, in Prince, "The Literary Life and Position of Orrery."

104. Ibid.

105. The list for 1749 includes the *Iliad*, the *Aeneid*, and Cicero's treatise on Oratory. In 1750, Hamilton continued reading the *Iliad* and the *Aeneid*, and during that year was reading also three treatises by Cicero, as well as the Book of Genesis in Hebrew, together with the Acts of the Apostles and Saint Paul's Epistles to the Romans and Corinthians in Latin. In 1751, Hamilton was reading the *Iliad*, Lucretius, and Cicero's *Quaestiones Tusculane*, as well as the Book of Deuteronomy in Hebrew and Saint Paul's Epistle to the Galatians in Latin. All information about what Hamilton was reading at Christ Church in 1749-51 is taken directly from the Collection Book of Christ Church. I am grateful to Mr. John Wing, assistant librarian of Christ Church, for granting me access to that valuable document.

106. Orrery to Thomas Birch, 1 February 1748 (Add MS 4303, MS pp. 139-140, British Library).

107. Information courtesy of John Wing, assistant librarian, Christ Church, Oxford.

108. Orrery himself wrote that the manuscripts of *Pliny* were burned. See Add MS 4303, MS pp. 133-34, British Library.

109. Prepublication copy of the *Remarks* interleaved and annotated by Orrery, MS Eng 218.14, interleaf page numbered 126, Houghton Library, Harvard.

110. Elias, "First Printing of Orrery's *Remarks on Swift*," 317 n. 11.

111.   MS Eng 218.2, V, part iii, 37, Orrery Papers, Houghton Library, Harvard.

112.   In the present edition, p. 302.

113.   Faulkner to Orrery, 30 November 1751, Rothschild 836,   Library of Trinity College, Cambridge. A scribal transcript of the letter is in the annotated copy of the *Remarks*, 16423.3.4*, MS pages numbered 56-60, Houghton Library, Harvard. Interestingly enough, Faulkner's statement that he "did not publish" the *Remarks* until he had "printed D^r. Barry's Alteration" is omitted by the scribe in the copy of the *Remarks* 16423.3.4*, Houghton Library. Was the omission deliberate or not?

114.   As early as 12 November 1748, Philip Skelton (Orrery's friend from London) was telling Orrery that he thought Millar was "a very enterprizing bookseller" (MS Eng 218.2, V, 206, Orrery Papers, Houghton Library, Harvard). It appears as if Orrery was already considering prospective publishers for the *Remarks* at that time, and that he asked for Skelton's advice.

115.   Bettenham was the printer of Orrery's *Pliny* (Add MS 4303, MS p. 113, British Library). For Bettenham's mistakes in Orrery's *Pliny*, see Add MS 4303, MS pp. 117, 126, and 131, British Library.

116.   Prepublication copy of the *Remarks* interleaved and annotated by Orrery, MS Eng 218.14, interleaf pages numbered 137-138, Houghton Library, Harvard.

117.   Copy of the *Remarks* annotated by Orrery, Osborn pc 231, verso of first free endpaper, Osborn Collection, Beinecke Library, Yale University, New Haven, Connecticut.

118.   All information about the publication history of the five London editions by Millar is taken from: manuscript notes in prepublication copy of the *Remarks* interleaved and annotated by Orrery, MS Eng 218.14, Houghton Library, Harvard; copy of the *Remarks* (London first edition) annotated by Orrery, 16423.3.4*, Houghton Library, Harvard; copy of the *Remarks* (London second edition) annotated by Orrery, Williams.473, Williams Collection, Cambridge University Library; and, advertisements in the *London Evening Post* and the *Whitehall Evening Post* for the respective dates.

119.   Announced in the *Dublin Journal* for that date.

120. For the full text of the letter, see copy of the *Remarks* annotated by Orrery, 16423.3.4*, MS pages numbered 51-55, Houghton Library, Harvard.

121. For all these facts mentioned by Faulkner, see ibid.

122. Faulkner to Orrery, 30 November 1751, Rothschild 836, Library of Trinity College, Cambridge, and scribal transcript in copy of the *Remarks* annotated by Orrery, 16423.3.4*, MS pages numbered 56-60, Houghton Library, Harvard.

123. See copy of the *Remarks* annotated by Orrery, 16423.3.4*, MS pages numbered 56-60, Houghton Library, Harvard.

124. See ibid.

125. A. C. Elias, Jr., "Lord Orrery's Copy of *Memoirs of the Life and Writings of Swift* (1751)," *Eighteenth-Century Ireland* 1 (1986): 114-15. In this important article, Elias writes about a copy of the piracy now at the University of Pennsylvania Library, with extra leaves bound at the end featuring 11 pages of transcribed letters and notes in Orrery's hand regarding the letters. The letters are all about the piracy, and their text, as well as Orrery's notes about them, are printed in Elias's article, pp. 122-24.

126. Ibid., p. 112.

127. A. C. Elias, Jr., "Dublin at Mid-Century: The Tricks of *The Tricks of the Town* Laid Open," *Eighteenth-Century Ireland* 10 (1995): 110.

128. Elias, "Lord Orrery's Copy of *Memoirs of the Life and Writings of Swift*," p. 115.

129. Ibid., pp. 115-16.

130. Ibid., p. 115; M. Pollard, *Dublin's Trade in Books, 1550-1800* (Oxford: Clarendon Press, 1989), p. 176.

131. Elias, "Lord Orrery's Copy of *Memoirs of the Life and Writings of Swift*," p. 114.

132. Ibid., p. 123.

133. Ibid.

134. Ibid., pp. 123-24.

135. Ibid., p. 122.

136. As will be seen, only one copy of Faulkner's "second edition" is extant, and no publication dates for his second and third editions were found.

137. Copy of the *Remarks* annotated by Orrery, 16423.3.4*, MS pages numbered 122-23, Houghton Library, Harvard.

138. The exact publication date of this edition is unknown.

139. In the present edition, p. 305.

140. Rupert Barber was an eminent miniature painter and engraver. See *Dictionary of National Biography*, s.v. "Barber, Mary." See also Ehrenpreis, *Swift* 3:636; and *Poems of Swift* 2:477. As far as I could determine, there are four extant portraits of Swift by Rupert Barber. One is now at the Bryn Mawr College Library near Philadelphia, Pennsylvania; another one is owned by Professor Robert Folkenflik (University of California-Irvine); a third is still owned in Ireland by descendents of the original owner, according to Peter Rowan of P. & B. Rowan, rare book dealers in Belfast, Northern Ireland; and, there was one owned by William LeFanu, which may have been sold from LeFanu's estate after his death. I thank Dr. A. C. Elias, Jr., for having provided all this information.

141. William LeFanu, *A Catalogue of Books belonging to Dr Jonathan Swift, Dean of St. Patrick's, Dublin, Aug. 19. 1715* (Cambridge Bibliographical Society, 1988), frontispiece.

142. Sir Frederick Falkiner, "Of the Portraits, Busts and Engravings of Swift and Their Artists," in *The Prose Works of Jonathan Swift*, ed. Temple Scott, 12 vols. (London: George Bell and Sons, 1897-1908), 12:53.

143. Ibid.

144. Seumas O'Sullivan, "Jackal and Lion: A Note on Orrery's 'Remarks on Swift,'" in *The Rose and Bottle and Other Essays* (Dublin: Talbot Press, n.d.), pp. 56-57.

145. Ibid., p. 56.

146. See *Dictionary of National Biography*, s.v. "Wilson, Benjamin."

147. Ibid.

148. O'Sullivan, "Jackal and Lion," p. 55.

149. See *Dictionary of National Biography*, s.v. "Ravenet, Simon François."

150. See *Dictionary of National Biography*, s.v. "Faber, John, the younger."

151. *Monthly Review*, November 1751, p. 407.

152. See p. 14 in the present edition.

153. "The remarks of Lord Orrery on Dr. Swift are published, and have made me very angry: they are much commended, said to be very entertaining, but I am so angry at the unfriendly, ungenerous manner of Swift's being treated by one who calls him his friend, that it quite prejudices me against the book, and casts a cloud over all its merit." Mrs. Delany [Mary Granville], *The Autobiography and Correspondence*, ed. Lady Llanover, 3 vols. (London: R. Bentley, 1861), 3:64.

154. Henry Fox to Sir Charles Hanbury Williams, 19 November 1751 (CHW 54-10910, ff. 118r-118v, Lewis Walpole Library, Farmington, Connecticut); James Birt to Sir Charles Hanbury Williams, 5 March 1755 (CHW 60-10903, ff. 182r - 182v, Ibid.) In both instances, Orrery is negatively criticized as an author, and referred to as a detractor of Swift. I am grateful to Anna A. Malicka, library services assistant at the Lewis Walpole Library, for calling my attention to those documents.

155. *Des Grafen John von Orrery Vaterliche Briefe an seinem zu Oxford studirendem Sohn, Hamilton Boyle, in moralischen und kritischen Anmerkungen uber das Leben und die Schriften des beruhmten satyrischen Dechanten Dr. Jonathan Swift verfasset* (Hamburg und Leipzig: Georg Christian Grund und Adam Heinrich Holle, 1752).

156. *Lettres Historiques et Philologiques du Comte d'Orreri, sur la Vie et les Ouvrages de Swift* (A Londres, et se trouve à Paris: chez Lambert, 1753).

157. I am grateful to Dr. Hermann Real for kindly calling my attention to this piece, as well as furnishing me with a photocopy of it.

158. *Nouvelles Littéraires, &c. de France & d'Angleterre*, pp. 3-4.

159. *The Compendious Library*, January and February 1752, article 3, p. 113.

160.   This volume is mentioned in Harold Williams, "Swift's Early Biographers," in *Pope and His Contemporaries: Essays presented to George Sherburn*, ed. James L. Clifford and Louis A. Landa (Oxford: Clarendon Press, 1949), p. 120. I am grateful to Nicholas Smith, underlibrarian, Rare Books Dept. of Cambridge University Library, for providing me with photocopies of Orrery's notes, and for calling my attention to Williams's note on Orrery.

161. Herman Teerink, *A Bibliography of the Writings of Jonathan Swift*, ed. Arthur H. Scouten (Philadelphia: University of Pennsylvania Press, 1963), pp. 415-16.

162. Ibid., p. 416.

163. I could neither identify "M. J." nor the sender of the letter, although "M. J." may possibly be M. J. Craig, who in 1948 was publishing the catalogue of a Swift exhibition for St. Patrick's Hospital in Dublin. At the time I was writing this introduction, I learned Mr. Craig was still alive, but I was unable to contact him.

164. Elias, "First Printing of Orrery's *Remarks on Swift*," pp. 312-14.

165. Ibid., pp. 316-17.

166. Ibid., pp. 318-19.

167. I am grateful to Dr. Noel Polk, of the University of Southern Mississippi (Hattiesburg), for allowing me to use his Lindstrand Comparator. I also thank Dr. Randall McLeod (University of Toronto) for letting me use his McLeod Comparator.

168. I gratefully acknowledge the help of Mr. Edward Bayntun-Coward, and Dr. Hermann Real.

169. Dr. Elias has two copies of Millar's third edition. One of them has sig. F5 misnumbered F4. The actual copy-text of the present edition is the copy that does *not* have that error.

BIBLIOGRAPHICAL DESCRIPTION OF THE EDITIONS OF *REMARKS ON SWIFT*

LONDON EDITIONS

MI

–Millar's first edition, published 7 November 1751.

Title: REMARKS/ON THE/LIFE and WRITINGS/OF/Dr. *JONATHAN SWIFT*,/Dean of St. PATRICK'S, *Dublin*,/In a Series of/LETTERS/FROM/JOHN Earl of ORRERY/To his SON, the Honourable/*HAMILTON BOYLE*./[Quotation from Virgil *Aeneid* 3.461–2: *Haec sunt quae nostra liceat te voce moneri. Vade, Age.* "This it is whereof by my voice thou mayest be warned. Now go thy way."]/

Imprint: *LONDON*,/Printed for A. MILLAR, opposite to *Catharine-/ Street* in the *Strand*./MDCCLII.

Collation: 8vo; A^2 (-A1) $B-K^8 L^8$ ($\pm$ L7) $M-Z^8$

Frontispiece engraving of Swift's portrait, by Benjamin Wilson, 2 pp. (title and blank), [1]–339 (*Remarks*), [1] blank, [9] index, [1] blank.

Copies: British Library (C.45.c.13, 1509/1192); Cambridge U (Nn.49.38, Hib.5.752, and Williams.471); Bodleian (Godw. 8° 502); New York Public Library, Berg Collection (Swift-B); Houghton Library, Harvard (16423.3.4*); U of Illinois (X827 Sw5Yco 1752a); Cornell (PR 3726 C79 1752, 2 copies); McMaster U (B 317 8646); Columbia U (B 824 Sw5DC); Victoria and Albert Museum (Forster 8vo 6608, 2 copies); Lilly Library, Indiana U (PR 3726 C7); U of Michigan (Hubbard PR 3726 C79 1752, Asa Gray 828 S9770 c799 1752a); Beinecke Library, Yale (Ik Sw55 S752, 1986 343, and Osborn pc 231); Huntington (RB 113309, RB 375997, RB 94508); Clark Library, UCLA (PR 3726 C79); copies in stock at Maggs Bros. Ltd., London (Cat. 1132, lots 114–15); Stanford U (PR 3726 C7 1752a); Trinity College Dublin (77.gg.126); U of Kansas (C1610, C3660); Pierpont Morgan Library (PML 77498); U of Chicago (PR 3726 C82 1752 Rare); Princeton U (EX 3950.631); UC-Berkeley (Bancroft PR 3727 C67 1752L1); Library of Congress (PR 3726 C7); National

Library of Scotland ([Dav.1.].1.26); Edinburgh U (1 copy); U of Minnesota (Z824.Sw5.DC81); UC-Santa Barbara (PR 3726 C7 1752a); Newberry Library (E5.S97708); Northwestern U (824.5.S97Yo); U of Pennsylvania (PR 3726 .O77); Ehrenpreis Institute (1 copy); A. C. Elias, Jr. (2 copies); Trinity U, San Antonio, Texas (1 copy); U of Virginia (RBC PR 3726 C7 1752b); Trinity College Cambridge (Rothschild 1492); Mortimer Rare Book Room, Smith College (825 Sw5 Zco 1752, 825 Sw5 Zor 1752); Penn State-University Park (PR 3726 C7 1752b).

For the most part, MI preserves uncorrected passages found in Faulkner's 339-page 8vo and 12mo editions. And, as A. C. Elias, Jr., has pointed out, MI, like Faulkner's 339-page 8vo and 12mo editions, was set from corrected copies of the earliest printing of the work (FI). MI does correct, however, a number of specific passages that are corrected also in Faulkner's 339-page 8vo and 12mo: the passage where "concave mirrour" was changed into "convex mirrour" (Letter XI); the passage concerning the Battles of Arbella/Issus (Letter XIII); the passage concerning Horace's advice to Asinius Pollio (Letter XXIII); and "their eyes" to "his eyes" (Letter XX). The copy at the U of Michigan Hubbard PR 3726 C79 1752 has sig. L7 (the passage on Arbella/Issus) *both* as cancel and cancellandum. The cancellandum appears in its proper place, and is torn and stained halfway down the sheet. The cancel is inserted between the title page and page 1, and the stub is very visible. A similar occurrence is seen in one of Elias's copies, except that in it, sig. G1 is present in both states. Interestingly enough, there are no textual corrections in G1 as cancel, the text fully agreeing with the cancellandum. Elias's other copy is uncut, and has G1 as cancel only, although, again, there are no textual corrections. In fact, although all copies have G1 as cancel, *no* textual corrections appear in any of the canceled G1 sheets. The two copies offered in Maggs Bros. Catalogue 1132 (September 1991) as lots 114 and 115 are described as having cancels at sigs. B4, B5, and B8. Actually, in the copy offered as lot 115, sheets B4 and B5 are pinned to sheets B2 and B3, and sheet B8 is attached on the verso to a stub. No other copies of MI are known to have this arrangement, and there are no textual corrections in the respective sheets. It seems that those sheets were missed by the binder at the time of sewing and subsequently pinned in. Copy 2 at Cornell is a presentation copy from Orrery to one Lionel Seaman, and Orrery's inscription to Seaman may be seen. Also in this copy, Orrery corrects a passage in Letter VIII that reads "except in some few places, impartial" in all Dublin editions, as well as in the first, second, and third London editions. Orrery adds the words "the sentiments" beside the passage (p. 95), so that the corrected passage reads "except in some few places, the sentiments impartial." This is how the passage reads in the London fourth and fifth editions. This copy of MI with Orrery's correction at Cornell was used by Garland for its 1974 facsimile of the *Remarks*. The copy at the Ehrenpreis Institute had belonged to Ehrenpreis himself, and on the first free endpaper, we see Ehrenpreis's autograph and the date of purchase, 23 April 1946. The British Library copy C.45.c.13 is annotated by Lord Macaulay. The copies of MI at the Houghton and Beinecke Libraries are annotated by Orrery, and will be discussed later. There are copies of MI printed in large and thick paper, and their text fully agrees with that of regular copies.

MII

–Millar's second edition, published 28 November 1751.
Title: The same as MI, except for addition of "The SECOND EDITION, Corrected." and for "*Dublin*;"
Imprint: *LONDON*:/Printed for A. MILLAR, in the *Strand*./M.DCC.LII.
Collation: 12mo; A^2 (-A1), B – P^8
    Frontispiece engraving of Swift's portrait, by Ravenet, 2 pp. (title and blank), [1] – 214 (*Remarks*), [8] index.
Copies: British Library (615.c.10); A. C. Elias, Jr. (1 copy); Cambridge U (Hib.7.752.24, Williams.472, Williams.473); Bodleian (Vet. A5 f.1293); Widener Library, Harvard (16423.4); U of Illinois (X827 Sw5Yco 1752b); Gilbert Library, Dublin (GC5); Cornell (PR 3726 C79 1752a); McMaster U (B 10921 873); Victoria and Albert Museum (Dyce S8vo 7097); Lilly Library, Indiana U (PR 3726 C7 1752a); U of Michigan (PR 3726 C79 1752a); Sterling Library, Yale (Ik Sw55 S752c); Huntington (RB 314079, RB 374120); Clark Library, UCLA (PR 3726 C79 1752); Stanford U (PR 3726 C7 1752b); U of Kansas (B4206); Trinity College Dublin (198.s.102); National Library of Ireland (LO.SWIFT.294); Folger Shakespeare (PR 3726 C7 1752b Cage); U of Florida (Irish Coll.); UC-Berkeley (Bancroft PR 3727 C67 1752 L2); Library of Congress (PR 3726 C7 1752a); National Library of Wales (CD 8464); SUNY at Stony Brook (PR 3726 C7 1752a); U of Virginia (RBC PR 3726 C7 1752b); Ehrenpreis Institute (1 copy); Penn State-University Park (PR 3726 C7 1752c).

MII was set from corrected copies of MI, and was relatively well corrected by Orrery. A number of corrected readings from MI now appear, although there are still many uncorrected readings, which will be altered only in MIII. The copy at the National Library of Wales lacks the title page, but the examination of the copy soon proved it to be MII. The copy at the Lilly Library belonged to Orrery himself and contains this inscription in his hand: "Orrery. The Gift of Mr Andrew Millar." There are no other manuscript notes by Orrery in the copy, but, beneath Orrery's inscription, we read that this copy was given by Orrery to his youngest daughter, Lucy, on 1 May 1756. In turn, it was given by Lucy to her mother-in-law in April 1767. The copy at the British Library also belonged to Orrery, as it reads on the inner front cover: "Orrery. December 3^d 1751." The most important copy is the one at Cambridge, Williams.473, annotated by Orrery, to be discussed later.

MIII

–Millar's third edition, published 10 December 1751.
Title: Exactly the same as MII, except for "The THIRD EDITION, Corrected."
Imprint: *LONDON*:/Printed for A. MILLAR, in the *Strand*./M.DCC.LII.
Collation: 12mo; $B - P^8$

> Frontispiece engraving of Swift's portrait, by Ravenet, 2 pp. (title and blank), [1]–62, 65–214 (*Remarks*), [8] index, [2] advertisements.

Copies: British Library (1419.c.21, G.14903(1); A. C. Elias, Jr. (2 copies); Ehrenpreis Institute (1 copy); Cambridge U (Hib.8.752.9); Bodleian (2695 f.61); Widener Library, Harvard (16423.4.51); Cornell (PR 3726 C79 1752b); McMaster U (B856, B2792, B9712); Columbia U (Johnson K820 Sw54); U of Michigan (Hubbard PR 3726 C79 1752b); Library of the Medical School, Yale (1 copy); Lewis Walpole Library (53 Sw5 C81c); Huntington (RB 124624); Clark Library, UCLA (PR 3726 C79 1752b); John Hay Library, Brown U (HAY STAR YQH Sw5xco); Southern Illinois U (827.5 S977 Bcor 1752r3); Stanford U (PR 3726 C7 1752ba); U of Kansas (O'Hegarty B2352); National Library of Ireland (LO.Swift.266); U of Chicago (PR 3726 C8204 Rare); U of Florida (Irish Coll.); Free Library of Philadelphia (1 copy); UC-Berkeley (1 copy); National Library of Wales (1 copy); National Library of Scotland (Fin.160); John Rylands U Library of Manchester (R85191); UC-Santa Barbara (PR 3726 C7 1752b); Newberry Library (1 copy); Northwestern U (824.5 S97Yo 1752); U of Rochester (PR 3726 C79r 1752).

Set from MII, this is the most carefully corrected of all the editions, with many authorial, substantive variants. It is the copy-text of the present edition, which incorporates the substantive variants from Millar's fifth edition. All copies have an error in pagination, as page numbered 65 follows page numbered 62, although the text continues normally. One of Elias's copies and the one at the Ehrenpreis Institute have sig. F5 misnumbered F4. The British Library copy 1419.c.21 lacks Swift's portrait. The copy at the University of Kansas is one of the "blue-paper" copies announced by Millar in his advertisements of 7 December and 10 December 1751, which Millar had to print hurriedly due to the great demand. The papers are now more gray than blue. The University of Michigan copy is fully annotated in an unknown eighteenth-century hand. The notes quote extensively from Deane Swift's *Essay*, and seem to have been written by someone who wanted to compare Orrery's arguments with what was said elsewhere about Swift. The copy at the National Library of Scotland has a manuscript note beginning halfway down page 15, and is probably in the hand of Mary D'Ewes, niece to Mrs. Delany.

MIV

–Millar's fourth edition, published 1 February 1752.
Title: Exactly the same as MI, except for "The FOURTH EDITION."
Imprint: *LONDON,*/Printed for A. MILLAR, opposite to *Catharine-*/*Street* in the *Strand.*/M.DCC.LII.
Collation: 8vo; $B-N^8 O^8 (\pm O7) P-Z^8$
      Frontispiece engraving of Swift's portrait, by Wilson, title and blank, [1]–142, 127–321 (*Remarks*), [1] blank, [9] index, [3] blank.
Copies: British Library (633.h.11, 633.g.19); A. C. Elias, Jr. (1 copy); Cambridge U (7720.c.406); Bodleian (Vet. A5 e.2581); Houghton Library, Harvard (16423.3); U of Illinois (Nickell 469); Cornell (PR 3726 C79 1752c, PR 3726 C79 1752d); McMaster U (B 3680); Victoria and Albert Museum (Dyce 8vo 7098); U of Michigan (1 copy); Huntington (RB 65136); Southern Illinois U (827.5 S977 Bcor 1752r4); Stanford U (PR 3726 C7 1752c); Trinity College Dublin (Fag.c.5.49, Lecky A.7.23); U of Washington (RBC PR 3726 C7 1752); Seton Hall U (1 copy); National Library of Scotland (Milc.III.3); National Library of Ireland (THOM.92.ORR); U of Chicago (PR 3726 C8205 Rare); Library of Congress (PR 3726 C7 1752c); National Library of Wales (CT 808 S91); U of Wisconsin-Madison (SC PR 3726 C7); U of Minnesota (824 Sw5 DC81); College of the Holy Cross, Worcester, Massachusetts (1 copy); Cleveland Public Library (827 52 Z26); Santa Clara U, Santa Clara, California (PR 3727 07); U of Rochester (1 copy); Ehrenpreis Institute (1 copy); Mortimer Rare Book Room, Smith College (825 Sw5 Zor 1752c); U of Pennsylvania (EC75 C8137 752rd).

    This edition was set from MI, and O7 has the misleading appearance of a cancel, being glued to a stub. However, there are no textual corrections in the sheet, and the text fully agrees with that of MI for that particular section. The British Library copy 633.h.11 is a presentation copy from Orrery to his friend Thomas Birch, the historian, who had helped him with the printing of *Pliny*. On the first free endpaper, there is this note in Birch's hand: "Tho. Birch Febr 14 1752. From the Author." The British Library copy 633.g.19 lacks Swift's portrait, and all copies have an error in pagination. Numbers 127–42 are repeated, but the text continues normally. As in the case of MI, some copies of MIV were printed in large and thick paper, but their text fully agrees with that of regular copies.

MV

–Millar's fifth edition, published 28 November 1752.
Title: Same as MIII, with the exception of "The FIFTH EDITION."
      and "*Dublin,*"
Imprint: *LONDON,*/Printed for A. MILLAR, in the *Strand.*/M.DCC.LII.

Collation: 12mo; A^2-L^6

    Frontispiece engraving of Swift's portrait, by Ravenet, title and blank, [1]–240 (*Remarks*), [10] index.

Copies: British Library (20098.b.9, E/01398); Cambridge U (7720.d.1715); Bodleian (Douce B 559); Cornell (PR 3726 C79 1752f); Royal Irish Academy (1 copy); Victoria and Albert Museum (Forster 12mo 6609); U of Michigan (Hubbard PR 3726 C79 1752d); Huntington (RB 317043); Clark Library, UCLA (PR 3726 C79 1752d); John Hay Library, Brown U (HAY STAR YQH Sw5xco3, HAY LAMONT YQH Sw5yc); Trinity College Dublin (194.t.95); National Library of Ireland (LO); U of Chicago (PR 3726 C821); UC-Berkeley (1 copy); Library of Congress (PR 3726 C7 1752d); U of Minnesota (824 Sw5 DC81a); U of Pennsylvania (928 Sw5 O); U of Virginia (PR 3726 C7 1752a); A. C. Elias, Jr., (2 copies); SUNY at Stony Brook (1 copy); Penn State-University Park (PR 3726 C7 1752).

    Next to MIII, from which it is set, this edition is the one that contains the greatest number of substantive variants, all of them authorial. All substantive variants in this edition have been added to the text of the present edition, based on MIII.

DUBLIN EDITIONS

FI

–The earliest printing of the *Remarks*, published around early September 1751.

Title: REMARKS/ON THE/LIFE AND WRITINGS/OF/DR. *JONATHAN SWIFT*,/Dean of ST. PATRICK'S, DUBLIN,/In a SERIES of/LETTERS/FROM/JOHN EARL OF ORRERY,/To his SON, the HONOURABLE/*HAMILTON BOYLE*./[Quotation from Virgil*Aeneid* 3.461–62]/

Imprint: DUBLIN:/Printed by GEORGE FAULKNER, in *Essex-Street*./M DCC LII.

Collation: 12mo; B–H^{12} I–L^6 M3–M^8

    8 pp. preliminary leaves (frontispiece engraving of Swift's portrait, by Wilson, slightly different from the one in Millar's editions, half title with engraving of Orrery's portrait, blank and title), "Advertisement of the Editor," [1] blank, [1]-204, [9] index, [3] advertisements.

Copies: A. C. Elias, Jr., (1 copy); Bodleian (Don.f.500); UC-Berkeley (Bancroft PR 3727 B69 R3 1752); Cornell (PR 3726 C79 1752k); Beinecke Library, Yale (1990 114); Huntington RB (329816); Trinity College Dublin (R.mm.33); U of Kansas (B2353); U of Pennsylvania (PR 3726 .O77 1752); Pierpont Morgan Library (PML 77497); U of Florida (827.5 S977Yc); U of Wisconsin-Madison (RBD PR 3726 C7 1752a).

Textually speaking, this is the worst of all editions. It is the one that contains the greatest number of uncanceled readings, as well as numerous misprints. It is probable that it underwent limited circulation, which would explain the lack of advertisements for it. As the "Advertisement of the Editor" states, Orrery himself had delivered the sheets to Faulkner, and Faulkner added the footnotes. But judging from the textual quality of this edition, Orrery must have either given Faulkner a bad, uncorrected manuscript copy, or Faulkner's shop committed many blunders indeed. The Huntington copy was Faulkner's gift to Orrery, as we read in a note in Orrery's hand, on the first free endpaper: "Orrery the Gift of Mr George Faulkner. 1752." Beneath this note, we read that Orrery in turn gave this copy to his daughter Lucy, on 1 May 1756. The binding is typical of those used in presentation copies, with an elaborately designed spine lettering reading: "Earl of Orrery's Remarks on Swift. Dublin 1752." The Bodleian copy is the one previously described, with the center spine lettering identifying it as the "Fourth Edition." Elias's personal copy has the preliminary leaves arranged in a different order.

FIa

–Faulkner's 339-page 8vo, published 23 November 1751.
Title: Exactly the same as FI.
Imprint: DUBLIN:/Printed by GEORGE FAULKNER, in *Essex-Street.*/M DCC LII.
Collation: 8vo; A^2 B–I^8 K^8 (± K3) L^8 (± L7) M–X^8 (± X7, X8) Y–Z^8

8 pp. (preliminary leaves arranged as in FI), "Advertisement of the Editor," [1] blank, [1]-339, [1] blank, [8] index, [3] blank.

Copies: British Library (1488.g.17, 1488.g.23); Cambridge U (Williams.470); U of Illinois (X827 Sw5Yco 1752, NICKELL X827 Sw5Yco 1752a); Bodleian (Vet. A5 d.1484); New York Public Library, Berg Collection (Swift, J.-B); Baker Library, Harvard Business School (1 copy); U of Texas-Austin (PR 3726 C7 1752d); U of Wisconsin-Madison (SC PR 3726 C7 1752); U of St. Thomas, St. Paul, MN (1 copy); UC-Santa Barbara (PR 3726 C7 1752e); Royal Irish Academy (1 copy); McMaster U (B 4237, B 8647, B 10922); Lilly Library, Indiana U (PR 3726 C7 1752e); Trinity College Cambridge (Rw.2.27, Rw.2.28, Rw.10.1); U of Michigan (1 copy); Beinecke Library, Yale (Ik Sw55 S752b); Trinity College Dublin (S.k.15); Archbishop Marsh's Library, Dublin (1 copy); National Library of Ireland (LO.SWIFT.267/1); Clark Library, UCLA (PR 3726 C79 1752a); A. C. Elias, Jr. (2 copies); Milwaukee Public Library; U of Pennsylvania (PR 3726 .O77 1752b).

Set from corrected copies of FI, this edition seems to be the one Faulkner was most proud of, judging from the number of copies he gave away. It is also certain that Faulkner gave away copies of this edition to the prominent figures he mentioned in his letter to Orrery of 26 November (three days after this edition had appeared). Faulkner gave no fewer than three copies of this edition to Orrery, and all of them are extant. The copy in Trinity College Library, Cambridge, Rw.2.27 has this note in Orrery's hand, on the verso of the first free endpaper: "Orrery. The Gift of the Editor Mr Faulkner. 1752." On the inner front cover of the copy at the University of Michigan, there is this note in Orrery's hand: "Orrery 1752. The Gift of the Editor George Faulkner, from Dublin." On the first free endpaper, we have another note in Orrery's hand, thus: "Printed by Mr Faulkner on large superfine paper, for Presents." The copy at the Lilly Library has this note on the first free endpaper, in Faulkner's hand: "To the Earl of Orrery. The Gift of his Lordship's Much Obliged, Most Dutiful, Most Obedient, and Most humble Servant George Faulkner The Editor Dublin, January 29. 1752." On this same date, Faulkner gave a copy of FIa to Charles Boyle, Orrery's eldest son, which is the one at Trinity College Library, Cambridge, Rw.2.28, containing this note on the recto of the first free endpaper, in Faulkner's hand: "To the Lord Boyle. The Present of his Lordship's Most Dutiful, Most Obedient, and Most humble Servant George Faulkner The Editor Dublin, January 29. 1752." The other copy at Trinity College Library, Cambridge, Rw.10.1., has this note on the first free endpaper: "The Gift of the R^t Honble the Earl of Orrery to John Jesser. Ap 11th 1752." Presumably, this John Jesser is a relation of the Mary Jesser to whom Orrery and his wife gave the Bodleian copy of FI (Don.f.500). The copy in the Berg Collection, New York Public Library, had belonged to Edmund, Orrery's youngest son, as it contains his autograph on the first free endpaper. The copy at McMaster B 8647 has Orrery's signature on the first free endpaper, thus: "Corke & Orrery Marston House." The inclusion of the word "Corke" means the note was written sometime after December 1753, when the earldom of Cork passed to Orrery. On the copy's inner front cover, we also see Orrery's bookplate. The copy at the British Library 1488.g.17 still has K3 and L7 uncanceled, which means Faulkner must have already printed some copies before the respective corrections were made. In the other copy at the British Library 1488.g.23, the cancels are present, but the half title is missing. In all copies, page 80 is wrongly numbered as 78, and although X6 and X8 are cancels, there are no textual corrections in them. One of Elias's copies has twenty two lines of penciled verse on the first free endpaper. The copy at the Milwaukee Public Library also has a penciled poem, in the same place, containing a praise of Orrery and a condemnation of Swift's manners. Like MI and MIV, some copies of FIa were printed in large and thick paper, and their text fully agrees with that of regular copies.

FIb

–Faulkner's 339-page 12mo, published 30 December 1751.
Title: Exactly the same as FI and FIa.

Imprint: DUBLIN:/Printed by GEORGE FAULKNER, in *Essex-Street*./M DCC
LII.
Collation: 12mo; B – C^6 C^8-Q^8 (C7 misnumbered D3)
>8 pp. (preliminary leaves arranged as in FI and FIa), "Advertisement
>of the Editor," [1] blank, [1]–339 (*Remarks*), [1] blank, [9] index, [5]
>blank.
Copies: A. C. Elias, Jr. (2 copies); Bodleian (Vet. A5 f.1198, Vet. A5 f.2368);
U of Texas-Austin (PR 3726 C7 1752e, 2 copies); Cornell (PR 3726 C79
1752h); Folger Shakespeare (PR 3726 C7 1752 Cage).
>The text of this edition is identical with FIa, and the copy at the
Bodleian Vet. A5 f.1198 has G7 *both* as cancellandum and as cancel. The
copy at Cornell indicates that Orrery did a bit of promotion of his own book.
The copy is blind-stamped as an honor's prize from Charleville School, County
Cork, June 1752. We know that, around that time of the year, Charleville
School, of which Orrery was the main benefactor, conducted scholarship
contests (of which Orrery was also the patron), and the winner usually
received a prize that had to do with learning and/or education. It seems that
the winner for 1752 got the *Remarks* as a prize!

FII

–Faulkner's second edition, publication date unknown.
Title: Exactly the same as FI, FIa, and FIb, except for "The SECOND EDITION,
Corrected."
Imprint: DUBLIN:/Printed by GEORGE FAULKNER, in *Essex-Street*./M DCC
LII.
Collation: 12mo; A^2 B – P^{12} Q^8 (C7 signed D3, N5 signed N6)
>As for the rest, it agrees with FIb.
Copies: only one copy is extant, at the Beinecke Library, Yale (Ik Sw55 S752
Ck). On Tuesday, 21 November 1905, this copy was offered as part of lot 21
during Christie's Orrery Sale.

This is a reissue of FIb, with some retouching of the signatures.

FIII

–Faulkner's third edition, publication date unknown.
Title: Exactly the same as the previous editions, except for "The THIRD
EDITION, Corrected."
Imprint: DUBLIN:/Printed by GEORGE FAULKNER, in *Essex-Street*./M DCC
LII.
Collation: 8vo; A^2 (-A1) B – Z^8

8 pp. (preliminary leaves as in the previous editions, except that engraving of Swift's portrait is by Wheatley), "Advertisement of the Editor," [1] blank, [1]–339 (*Remarks*), [1] blank, [9] index, [3] advertisements.

Copies: Cambridge U (Hib.7.752.30, Williams.474); Bodleian (Vet. A5 e.2916); National Library of Wales (1 copy); Gilbert Library, Dublin (20G[221]); Library of the Medical School, Yale (1 copy); Trinity College Dublin (OLS 181.q.128); National Library of Ireland (LO.342/2, LO.Swift.342/1); U of Chicago (PR 3726 C82); Stanford U (PR 3726 C7 1752d); U of Mississippi (1 copy); Ehrenpreis Institute (1 copy).

Set from FIa, this edition includes a couple of corrections in the text, especially from Letters I–XIII. However, they are not substantive ones, and are not likely to be authorial. The copy at Cambridge Williams.474 is bound with the Swift sale catalogue of 1745.

No copies of Faulkner's fourth edition are extant. The Bodleian copy of FI, Don.f.500, with center spine lettering "Fourth Edition," may offer an explanation. See the section of the introduction discussing Faulkner's editions (p. 30 in the present edition).

FV

–Faulkner's fifth edition, publication date unknown.

Title: The same as in previous editions, except for "DUBLIN" and "The FIFTH EDITION, Corrected."

Imprint: DUBLIN:/Printed by GEORGE FAULKNER, in *Essex-Street*./M DCC LVII.

Collation: Same as FIb and FII, except for different signatures, and sig. D2 is repeated (although text continues normally).

Copies: A. C. Elias, Jr. (2 copies); Folger Shakespeare (PR 3726 C7 1757 Cage); National Library of Ireland (LO.Swift.295); Trinity College Dublin (198.s.105); Royal Irish Academy (MR 16); Widener Library, Harvard (16423.3.15); Cornell (PR 3726 C79 1757).

This edition is an interesting affair. Up to Letter XIII, it is a new edition, although sig. B is a line-for-line reprint of FIb. From Letter XIII to Letter XXIV, it is a reissue of FIb. As in the case of FIII, there are a couple of corrections in the text from Letter I to Letter XIII, not substantive and probably not authorial. It looks as if, in 1757, Faulkner decided to gather every sheet he could in order to publish a "new" edition. One of Elias's copies has G7 and L7 in their *uncancelled* form, while, in the other one, G7 and L7 are cancels.

Lodge's "Edition"

–Publication date unknown.

Title: REMARKS/ON THE/LIFE AND WRITINGS/OF/Dr. Jonathan Swift,/Dean of St. Patrick's, Dublin,/IN A SERIES OF/LETTERS/FROM/John Earl of Orrery,/To his SON, the Honourable/HAMILTON BOYLE./[Quotation from Virgil *Aeneid* 3.461–62] /

Imprint: *DUBLIN*:/Printed by CHARLES LODGE, NO. 22, *Church-Street.*/M,DCC,LXXXIII.

Collation: the same as in FI, without the preliminary leaves.

Copies: two copies are extant, one at the University of Virginia (PR 3726 .C7 1783) and the other at the Clifford E. Barbour Library, Pittsburgh Theological Seminary.

This is a reissue of FI, with a new title page added and all preliminary leaves taken away.

COPIES OF *REMARKS ON SWIFT* ANNOTATED
BY ORRERY

There are four extant copies of the *Remarks* annotated either by Orrery or his copyist. The notes in three of them are printed as separate sections in this present edition, and the notes in the copy at the Beinecke Library, Yale, which are actually Orrery's errata to his text, are presented in the textual notes (beginning with a letter) at the bottom of the pages featuring the text of the *Remarks*. Orrery's marginal headings in those annotated copies are not printed, since they merely give the topic of the particular passage in the text he is referring to.

The prepublication copy that Orrery had with him in London in early September 1751 is preserved at the Houghton Library, Harvard, shelf-mark MS Eng 218.14. It is interleaved and fully annotated by Orrery and occasionally by his copyist. The copy is dated by Orrery "Leicester Fields. September 14, 1751," and is without a title page or any other preliminary matter (except for the engraving of Orrery's portrait), having only the text of the twenty four letters and index. The interleaved text is preceded by some notes by Orrery, including a motto Orrery found to be a proper one for the book, and Orrery's declaration that he was responsible for the writing of all the notes in the copy. Orrery's note on interleaf pages numbered 17-19 is dated 9 November 1751, which indicates that he was still adding notes to this copy approximately two months after he first dated it. Also, Benjamin Wilson's letter to Orrery on the mistake concerning concave/convex mirrors (transcribed on interleaf pages numbered 135-36) is dated 2 November 1751, a further possible indication of the late inclusion of some notes. The notes on the interleaves consist of stories about Swift not included in the printed text, Orrery's correction of certain passages (which gives us his preferred readings in some cases), as well as quotations from books Orrery used as sources and, more importantly, pieces of evidence that Orrery indeed did some research before writing the *Remarks*. The account of Stella was based on reports by Mrs. Whiteway and Deane Swift, and Orrery even includes additional facts about Stella, which he left out of the printed text. Orrery also tells us of at least two instances where he learned about the subject he is referring to from direct contact with Swift himself. Finally, Orrery also includes some advertisements concerning the *Remarks*, and a considerable list of persons to whom he gave copies of the *Remarks*. All that is known about the copy's provenance is that it was received at Harvard on 17 October 1923.

The other annotated copy at the Houghton Library, Harvard, shelf-mark 16423.3.4*, was first offered in Dobell's Catalogue no. 6, September 1921, as lot 229. It was offered again in Dobell's Catalogue no. 10, January 1922, as lot 1170, and eventually found its way to the Houghton Library. It is a copy of MI, and is dated by Orrery "Leicester Fields, November 21, 1751." The notes, all in the hand of Orrery's copyist except for the transcript of Orrery's letter to the Reverend William Scott (in Orrery's hand), are found both before and after the printed matter. Before the printed matter, we find advertisements of the *Remarks*, together with commentaries on the publication of the work. After the last page of index, there are 144 pages of manuscript, containing transcripts of Orrery's correspondence related to the *Remarks*, part of some contemporary criticisms of the work, as well as a number of poems addressed to Orrery on the *Remarks*. The material included in these notes is highly informative and, in some instances, quite revealing, as far as the publication and contemporary reception of the *Remarks* are concerned. It also shows very clearly how Orrery was sensitive about criticisms of the work, in spite of the fact that he denied it often.

It terms of stories about Swift, the most interesting of all the annotated copies is the one now among the Harold Williams Collection, Cambridge University Library, shelf-mark Williams.473, a copy of MII, dated by Orrery "Leicester Fields, November 29, 1751." The earliest mention of this copy was in Henry Craik's preface to the first edition of his biography of Swift (1882), and Craik wrote that it was then "in the possession of Lord Cork." The copy was offered in the Orrery Sale at Christie's, London, on Wednesday, 22 November 1905, as lot 345. In September 1921, the copy was offered in Dobell's Catalogue no. 6 as lot 231, and Dobell offered it again in his Catalogue no. 10 (January 1922) as lot 1172. It was then purchased by one Charles Fitzgerald, of Sidmouth, who allowed Harold Williams to examine it. In an article in the *Times Literary Supplement* of Thursday, 24 May 1934 (p. 376), Williams gave a brief description of the volume and printed one of the pieces transcribed in this copy, Deane Swift's letter to Orrery of 19 November 1742, about the mistreatment Swift had received from Francis Wilson, one of Swift's prebendaries. Williams finally bought the copy from Fitzgerald, and upon Williams's death on 24 October 1964, it went to Cambridge, where it is now a part of the collection Williams bequeathed to his alma mater. As in the case of Houghton 16423.3.4*, this copy contains notes both before and after the printed matter. The notes are all in Orrery's hand, except for the transcripts of Deane Swift's letter to Orrery and the transcripts of the affidavits, as well as the commentary on the advertisements of the *Remarks*, which are in the copyist's hand. In the front leaves, we find advertisements on the publication of the *Remarks* with commentary and a short list of persons to whom Orrery gave copies of MII. Orrery also writes that due to the criticisms that he had treated Swift too severely in the book, he marked out with a pointing hand those passages that are "particularly in Swift's favour." In all, there are five passages marked out by Orrery, which, considering that the text of the second edition extends for 214 pages, shows that even Orrery himself had a hard time trying to find passages that are particularly friendly to Swift. After the printed matter, Orrery added 33 pages of manuscript text, a section featuring stories about Swift, and two of them are descriptive of moments when Swift and Orrery himself were together. On manuscript pages 28-29, Orrery mentions he had once seen a copy of Addison's *Freeholder* number 21 with marginalia by Swift. In a few instances, the stories are not much to Swift's credit, as in the incident where Swift recalled one of his servants who had left town some moments earlier, only to make him shut the door of his bedroom. Still, the stories are in general quite delightful to read, and are for the most part consistent with what we know about Swift's personality.

The last annotated copy is preserved at the Beinecke Library, Yale, shelf-mark Osborn pc 231, a copy of MI. This copy was first mentioned in Dobell's Catalogue no. 6 (September 1921), offered as lot 230. It was offered again by Dobell in his Catalogue no. 10 (January 1922) as lot 1171, and then passed into private hands. It was later purchased by James Cummins, Bookseller of New York City, from the daughter of a local private collector. Cummins sold it so fast that they had time to do only a brief description of the copy, which Cummins still has on computer but which was never published. Cummins sold it to Bernard Quaritch in June 1988, and in Quaritch's Catalogue no. 1103 (March 1989), it was offered, being then acquired by the Beinecke Library. On the verso of the first free endpaper, there is this inscription, in Orrery's hand: "Orrery. Leicester Fields. Octob^r 7 1751." Also on the verso of the first free endpaper, Orrery wrote: "In this book are the alterations that occurr to me, as proper for future editions." There follows a list of errata in Orrery's hand, which extends to the recto of the second free endpaper. In the text of the *Remarks*, there are a number of corrections in Orrery's hand, and also corrections in his hand on the first and seventh pages of the Index. Considering Orrery's dating of the copy, one may see that it was in Orrery's hands exactly a month before Millar's first edition appeared on 7 November 1751. The alterations listed by Orrery are *not* included in MI, and there are some possible reasons for their absence in MI. Orrery might have neglected telling Millar about the alterations because he wished to think over the matter, although he had already pointed to the need of some of those alterations in the prepublication copy dated 14 September 1751. If Orrery did tell Millar about the alterations, then someone (Bettenham?) must have been careless in the printing process, or it may be that Orrery was still thinking about some of those alterations a month later and Millar finally decided to wait no longer for Orrery's final word. As mentioned before, Orrery's errata, as well as his corrections in the text and index, are presented in the textual notes of the present edition.

LETTER I

To the Honourable
HAMILTON BOYLE,
Student of *Christ-Church* College
in *OXFORD*.

My dear HAMILTON,

I Want no motive to gratify your request of hearing often from me, especially as your letters always give me a particular pleasure. I read them over not only with the fondness of a father, but with the affection of a friend. They revive in my mind the agreeable hours which attend a studious life, in that elegant seat of the muses, from whence they are dated.[1] In such a situation, amidst the best Authors, and in a free conversation with men of letters, you will be able to adorn your mind, and give it a serene and a just way of thinking: And I shall have the happiness not only of seeing you forming yourself every day for public life, but rendered more capable of exerting your faculties, with dignity and advantage to your country, and with a rising reputation to yourself.

For my own part, early disappointments, the perplexed state of my affairs, indifferent health,[a] and many other untoward[b] incidents, all contributed to make me, even in my earliest part of life, too fond of retirement. Years have increased the inclination, and time rather confirms than corrects the error; however, I have not suffered my mind to be totally inactive: but by holding[c] as little connexion as possible with the living, I have employed myself in conversing, and forming an acquaintance with the dead: and have from thence

---

[a]indifferent health,] and indifferent state of health, FI; an indifferent state of health, FIa, FIb, FII, FIII, FV, MI

[b]many other untoward] many untoward FI, FIa, FIb, FII, FIII, FV, MI

[c]holding] having FI, FIa, FIb, FII, FIII, FV, MI

received more real satisfaction and improvement, than probably[d] might have attended me, had I been directed in the pursuit of fame, fortune, or ambition.

I am much pleased that you approve of my observations on PLINY's letters.[2] I engaged in that work, with a design of pointing out, to your brother Lord BOYLE,[3] the amiable qualities of that elegant Roman.[4] But I cannot rest satisfied unless I offer to you also some public token of my paternal affection: and therefore, I have lately been examining the works of Dr. SWIFT, with an intention of gathering materials for my future correspondence with you: and here, my dear HAMILTON, I dedicate to you those criticisms which have occurred to me; and shall mix with them such particulars of his life and character, as, I flatter myself, may tend at least to your entertainment, if not to your improvement.

Let me begin by giving you a short but general view of SWIFT's character. He[e] was in the decline of life when I knew him.[5] His friendship was an honour to me, and to say the truth, I have even drawn advantage from his errors. I have beheld him in all humours and dispositions, and I have formed various speculations from the several weaknesses to which I observed him liable. His capacity and strength of mind were undoubtedly equal to any task whatever. His pride, his spirit, or his ambition, call it by what name you please, was boundless: but, his views were checked in his younger years, and the anxiety of that disappointment had a visible effect upon all his actions.[6] He was sour and severe, but not absolutely ill-natured. He was sociable only to particular friends, and to them only at particular hours. He knew politeness more than he practised it. He was a mixture of avarice and generosity:[7] the former, was frequently prevalent, the latter, seldom appeared, unless excited by compassion. He was open to adulation, and could not, or would not distinguish between low flattery, and just applause. His abilities rendered him superior to envy. He was undisguised and perfectly sincere. I am induced to think, that he entered into orders, more from some private and fixed resolution, than from absolute choice:[8] be that as it may, he performed the duties of the church with great punctuality, and a decent degree of devotion.[9] He read prayers rather in a strong nervous voice, than in a graceful manner, and although[f] he has been often accused of irreligion, nothing of that kind appeared in his conversation or behaviour. His cast of

---

[d]probably] possibly FI, FIa, FIb, FII, FIII, FV, MI; Orrery's correction in Osborn pc 231: "possibly" to "probably."

[e]no new paragraph MV] new paragraph MIII

[f]although] altho' MI, MII, MIII, MIV, MV;
Orrery's correction in Osborn pc 231: "altho'" to "although."

mind induced him to think, and speak more of politics than of religion.[10] His perpetual views were directed towards power: and his chief aim was to be removed into *England*:[11] but when he found himself entirely disappointed, he turned his thoughts to opposition, and became the patron of *Ireland*, in which country he was born. Here it may not be improper to observe to you, that many of his friends imagined him a native of *England*, and many others, I know not whether to call them friends or enemies, were willing to suppose him the natural Son of Sir WILLIAM TEMPLE. Neither of these facts is[g] true. He was born in *Dublin*, *November* the thirtieth, in the year sixteen hundred and sixty seven, and was carried into *England* soon after his birth, by his nurse, who being obliged to cross the sea,[12] and having a nurse's fondness for the child at her breast, conveyed him on ship-board, without the knowledge of his mother or relations, and kept him with her at *Whitehaven* in *Cumberland*, during her residence three years at that place.[13] This extraordinary event made his return seem as if he had been transplanted to *Ireland*; rather than that he had owed his original existence to that soil.[14] But perhaps, he tacitly hoped to inspire different nations with a contention for his birth: at least in his angry moods, when he was peevish, and provoked at the ingratitude of *Ireland*, he was frequently heard to say, "I am not of this vile country, I am an Englishman." Such an assertion, although meant figuratively, was often received literally: and the report was still farther assisted by Mr. POPE,[15] who in one of his letters has this expression, "Tho' one or two of our friends are gone, since you saw your *native country*, there remain a few."[h 16]

But Dr. SWIFT, in his cooler hours, never denied his country: on the contrary, he frequently mentioned, and pointed out the house where he was born.[17] The other suggestion concerning the illegitimacy of his birth is equally false. Sir WILLIAM TEMPLE was employed as a minister abroad from the year sixteen hundred and sixty five, to the year sixteen hundred and seventy: first at *Brussels*, and afterwards at the *Hague*,[18] as you will find by his correspondence with the Earl of *Arlington*,[19] and other ministers of state: So that Dr. SWIFT's mother, who never crossed the sea, except from *England* to *Ireland*, was out of all possibility of a personal correspondence with Sir WILLIAM TEMPLE till some years after her son's birth.

I have already mentioned to you the exact place, and date of Dr. SWIFT's nativity; but the rules of biography make it necessary to give you some account of his family. It shall be as short as possible; since, although his ancestors

---

[g]is MV] are MIII

[h]Original footnote in the *Remarks*: "Letter LXXX. Mr. POPE to Dr. SWIFT, *March* 23, 1736–7." The numbering of the letter refers to the numbering in volume 7 of Faulkner's edition of Swift's works (1746).

were persons of very decent, and reputable characters, he himself has been the herald to blazon the dignity of their coat. His grandfather was the Reverend Mr. THOMAS SWIFT, Vicar of Goodridge near *Ross* in *Herefordshire*.[20] He enjoyed a paternal estate in that county, which is still in possession of his great grandson DEANE SWIFT, Esq;[21] He died in the year sixteen hundred and fifty eight, leaving six sons, GODWIN, THOMAS, DRYDEN, WILLIAM, JONATHAN and ADAM.[22] Two of them only, GODWIN and JONATHAN, left sons. The descendants of Godwin are mentioned in GUILLIM's heraldry.[23]   JONATHAN married Mrs. ABIGAIL ERICK of *Leicestershire*,[24] by whom he had one daughter[25] and a son. The daughter was born in the first year of Mr. SWIFT's marriage;[26] but he lived not to see the birth of his son,[i] who was called JONATHAN, in memory of his Father, and became afterwards the famous Dean of St. *Patrick*'s. The[j] greatest part of Mr. JONATHAN SWIFT's income had depended upon agencies, and other employments of that kind:[27] so that most of his fortune perished with him:[28] and the remainder being the only support that his widow could enjoy, the care, tuition, and expence of her two children devolved upon her husband's elder brother, Mr. GODWIN SWIFT,[29] who voluntarily became their guardian, and supplied the loss which they had sustained in a father.[30] Mrs. SWIFT, about two years after her husband's death, quitted *Ireland*, and retired to *Leicester*, the place of her nativity.[31]

The faculties of the mind appear and shine forth at different ages in different men. The infancy of Doctor SWIFT passed on without any marks of

---

[i]Original footnote in the *Remarks*: "Doctor SWIFT was born some months after his father's death." In MI and MII, the footnote reads: "Doctor SWIFT was born two months after his father's death." Orrery came to dismiss the validity of the statement as given in MI and MII, as we read in his manuscript note on interleaf pg. 9 in his interleaved and annotated prepublication copy of the *Remarks*, MS Eng. 218.14 (Houghton Library, Harvard University): "I have since heard, that Swift was born seven months after his father's death." Orrery adds: "The note may be altered in any future edition." As it turned out, "two months" was changed into "some months" in MIII, MIV, and MV (all of Faulkner's editions read "some months"). In a petition to the benchers of the King's Inns in Dublin, dated 25 April 1667, Mrs. Swift called herself a "disconsolate widow." Ehrenpreis says Swift's father died "in March or April" 1667 (Ehrenpreis, *Swift* 1:27). If Orrery is right, which seems to be suggested by the date of Mrs. Swift's petition (it must have been drawn shortly after Swift's father's death), Swift's father passed away in April, or, seven months before Swift's birth.

[j]no new paragaraph MV] new paragraph MIII

distinction. At six years old, he was sent to school at *Kilkenny*,[32] and about eight years afterwards, he was entered a student of Trinity College in *Dublin*.[33] He lived there in perfect regularity, and under an entire obedience to the statutes:[34] but the moroseness of his temper often rendered him very unacceptable to his companions; so that he was little regarded, and less beloved. Nor were the academical exercises agreeable to his genius. He held logic and metaphysics in the utmost contempt, and he scarce considered mathematics and natural philosophy, unless to turn them into ridicule.[35] The studies which he followed were history and poetry.[36] In these he made a great progress; but to all other branches of science he had given so very little application, that when he appeared as a candidate for the degree of Batchelor of Arts, he was set aside on account of insufficiency.[37]

You will be surprised at such an incident in his life: but the fact was undoubtedly true: and even at last he obtained his admission *speciali gratiâ:* a phrase which in that University carries with it the utmost marks of reproach. It is a kind of dishonourable degree,[38] and the record of it, notwithstanding Dr. SWIFT's present established character throughout the learned world, must for ever remain against him in the academical register at *Dublin*.[39]

Ambition, you will agree with me, could scarce have met with a severer blow. HERCULES found himself set aside for want of strength; or, if admitted among the wrestlers, admitted only by favour and indulgence; yet still he must be conscious, that he was HERCULES. Disappointments, the earlier they happen in life, the deeper impression they make upon the heart. SWIFT was full of indignation at the treatment which he had received in *Ireland*, and therefore resolved to pursue his studies at *Oxford*. However, that he might be admitted *ad eundem*, he was obliged to carry with him the *Testimonium* of his Degree.[40]

The expression *speciali gratiâ* is so peculiar to the University of *Dublin*, that, when Mr. SWIFT exhibited his Testimonial at *Oxford*, the members of the *English* University concluded, that the words *speciali gratiâ* must signify a Degree conferred in reward of extraordinary diligence, or learning. You may imagine, he did not try to undeceive them.[41] He was immediately admitted *ad eundem*,[42] and chose to enter himself of *Hart Hall*, now *Hartford College*,[43] where he constantly resided (some visits to his mother at *Leicester*, and to Sir WILLIAM TEMPLE at *Moore Park* excepted)[44] till he took his degree as Master of Arts, which, if I remember rightly, was in the year ninety-one.[45]

Having attended my friend SWIFT thus far in his road of life, let me rest a little before I proceed farther with him in the journey; and let me desire you to keep this letter, as I intend that it shall be followed hereafter by others of the same sort, and relating to the same person.

I am, my dearest HAMILTON,
your affectionate Father,

ORRERY.

Notes

1. Christ Church, Oxford. Hamilton had come up to Christ Church as a Westminster Student. He had won one of the studentships (roughly equivalent to scholarships) that were assigned to boys educated at Westminster School. He matriculated on 8 June 1748, and received his B.A. in June 1754. Hamilton then proceeded to legal studies, becoming a faculty student (law) on 10 December 1762.

2. Orrery himself defined his observations on Pliny's letters in a letter to William King, principal of St. Mary Hall, Oxford, dated Dublin, 27 August 1739: "to each Epistle I propose Notes, such as shall take in all Kinds of Learning, History, Humour, or agreeable Observations, so that the whole may be worth the Acceptance of the Publick" (*Orrery Papers* 1:265).

3. Charles Boyle, Orrery's eldest son, by Harriet Hamilton, his first wife. He was born on 27 January 1729. He was admitted at St. Mary Hall, Oxford, on 23 May 1745. When the earldom of Cork passed to Orrery in 1753, Charles Boyle took the courtesy title of Viscount Dungarvan, which was one of Orrery's titles. Charles Boyle was also M.P. for County Cork, 1756–59. He died in September 1759, predeceasing Orrery by approximately three years.

4. Cf. Orrery's remark on Pliny in his letter to William King from Dublin, 27 August 1739: "Pliny is an Author I have long studied, long admir'd and long lov'd: His Sentiments charm Me. He had a Soul that was an Honour to human Nature. He was learned and an Encourager of Learning. He was a fluent and a persuasive Orator: He was noble, generous and goodnatur'd" (*Orrery Papers* 1:265).

5. It is not known when exactly Orrery first met Swift, but Swift's earliest mention of Orrery is in his letter to Charles Ford, dated 14 October 1732 (*Correspondence of Swift* 4:77). In Letter XVI, before printing his poem to Swift on the Dean's birthday in 1732, Orrery says he decided to write that poem because Swift "had admitted" him as a friend. And, before telling the anecdote of Swift's *Death and Daphne*, in the *Remarks*, Orrery says it happened "soon after our [Swift and Orrery] acquaintance" which might mean some time in 1732 (Ehrenpreis, *Swift* 3:668 n. 3). On 9 December 1732, Swift told Charles Ford he often saw Orrery (*Correspondence of Swift* 4:91). Mildred Prince says Orrery and Swift met in Ireland in the autumn of 1732 ("The Literary Life and Position of Orrery," pp. iii and 13). In any case, Swift

must have been about sixty three years old when Orrery first met him. In *Pope and His Contemporaries: Essays Presented to George Sherburn*, ed. James L. Clifford and Louis A. Landa (Oxford: Clarendon Press, 1949), p. 115.

6. Cf. Swift's remark in his letter to Bolingbroke and Pope, dated Dublin, 5 April 1729: "I remember when I was a little boy, I felt a great fish at the end of my line which I drew up almost on the ground, but it dropt in, and the disappointment vexeth me to this day, and I believe it was the type of all my future disappointments" (*Correspondence of Swift* 3:329).

7. Instances of Swift's generosity include his establishment of a fund to make loans to weavers in 1721, and, in a letter to Pope dated 1 May 1733, Swift mentions that, every year, he used to set aside one-third of his income to charities (Ibid. 4:154).

8. Cf. Swift's words in *Family of Swift*: "Mr Swift lived with him [Temple] some time, but resolving to settle himself in some way of living, was inclined to take orders; however, although his fortune was very small, he had a scruple of entring into the Church meerly for support, and Sir William Temple then being Master of the Rolls in Ireland offered him an Employ of about £120 a year in that office, whereupon Mr Swift told him, That since he had now an opportunity of living without being driven into the Church for a maintenance, he was resolved to go to Ireland and take holy Orders" (Orrery's scribal transcript of *Family of Swift*, MA 455, manuscript pages 13–14, The Orrery Correspondence, Pierpont Morgan Library, New York City).

9. Cf. Delany's words on this point: "His [Swift's] cathedral of St. Patrick's, is the only church in that city, wherein the primitive practice of receiving the Sacrament every Lord's day, was renewed, and is still continued. And to the best of my remembrance, and belief, renewed in his time. At least, as he was Ordinary there; it could not be continued without his consent. And it is most certain that he constantly attended that Holy Office: consecrated and administered the Sacrament, in person. Nor do I believe he ever once failed to do so when it was in his power. I mean when he was not either sick, or absent, at too great a distance." In Patrick Delany, *Observations upon Lord Orrery's Remarks on the Life and Writings of Dr. Jonathan Swift* (London: W. Reeve, 1754), pp. 46-47 (hereafter cited as Delany, *Observations*).

10. Cf. these remarks in Swift's letter to Charles Ford dated 8 December 1719: "But as the world is turned, no cloister is retired enough to keep Politics out, and I will own they raise my passions whenever they come in my way" (*Correspondence of Swift* 2:330).

11. For Swift's constant inclination toward England, see his letter to Gay dated 8 January 1723 (*Correspondence of Swift* 2:441). See also his letter to Charles Ford dated 27 September 1714 (ibid. 1:132). The most explicit statement of Swift's desire to settle in England is in his letter to the earl of Peterborough dated 4 May 1711: "My ambition is to live in England, and with a competency to support me with honour" (ibid., p. 227).

12. According to Swift himself, the nurse was "under an absolute necessity of seeing one of her relations who was then extremely sick, and from whom she expected a Legacy" (Orrery's scribal transcript of *Family of Swift*, MA 455, manuscript page 9, Orrery Correspondence, Pierpont Morgan Library, New York City).

13. Cf. Swift's words on the subject: "and being at the ^{same} time extremely fond of the infant, she [Swift's nurse] stole him [Swift] on shipboard unknown to his Mother and Uncle, and carryed him with her to Whitehaven, where he continued for almost three years." Ibid.

14. Downie wrote that Swift's story of his being kidnapped by the nurse was indeed an attempt to extenuate his Irish birth. Downie also commented on the words by Orrery about the incident: "This is a reasonable assessment of the probable effect of Swift's alleged kidnapping on his infant mind. But he had a happy knack of altering his recollection of the past to fit in with his current prospect of things." In J. A. Downie, *Jonathan Swift, Political Writer* (London: Routledge & K. Paul, 1984), p. 5.

15. According to Spence, Swift told Pope he had been born "in the town of Leicester." James Osborn believes Swift may not have said this to Pope, but rather, that Pope might have misunderstood Swift when the Dean told him his mother finally retired to Leicester. See Joseph Spence, *Observations, Anecdotes, and Characters of Books and Men, Collected from Conversation*, ed. James M. Osborn, 2 vols. (Oxford: Clarendon Press, 1966), 1:52.

16. Pope to Swift, 23 March 1737 (*Correspondence of Swift* 5:16).

17. The exact address of Swift's birthplace is 7 Hoey's Court. By the time Swift was born, Hoey's Alley (also called Hoey's Court) was one of the best neighborhoods in Dublin, being close by St. Werburgh's Street, the busiest street in town and the place where famous lawyers lived. The parish church of St. Werburgh's was often frequented by prominent public figures, such as the lord lieutenants of Ireland. See Ehrenpreis, *Swift* 1:22–23.

18. Temple was invited to undertake a mission abroad in June 1665. After stopping a day in Brussels, he and his companion, Baron Wreden, arrived at Coesvelt on 4 July 1665. Temple was to see England in 1670 only, when he arrived in London on 29 September. See K. H. D. Haley, *An English Diplomat in the Low Countries: Sir William Temple and John de Witt, 1665–1672* (Oxford: Clarendon Press, 1986), pp. 53-276.

19. Temple's correspondent was Henry Bennett, earl of Arlington and secretary of state. He actually offered Temple the 1665 mission. Temple had been an admirer of Arlington, but the earl's foreign policy proved to be pro-French and against Temple's efforts on behalf of the Triple Alliance. See A. C. Elias, Jr., *Swift at Moor Park: Problems in Biography and Criticism* (Philadelphia: University of Pennsylvania Press), pp. 33–47 (cited hereafter as Elias, *Swift at Moor Park*). See also N. F. Lowe and W. J. McCormack, "Swift as 'Publisher' of Sir William Temple's *Letters* and *Miscellanea*," *Swift Studies* 8 (1993): 52–54.

20. Thomas Swift (1595–1658), vicar of Goodrich and rector of Bridstow, Herefordshire, who was the one ancestor Swift "venerated above all" (Ehrenpreis, *Swift* 1:4). Swift himself traced his family origin to Yorkshire (*Prose Works of Swift* 5:187), and Deane Swift repeated the claim, in his *Essay upon the Life, Writings and Character of Dr. Jonathan Swift* (London: Charles Bathurst, 1755), p. 7 (cited hereafter as Deane Swift, *Essay*). However, there were no real Yorkshire family ties (Ehrenpreis, *Swift* 1:4), and Thomas Swift's father (William Swift, 1566–1624), as well as his grandfather (Thomas Swyfte, 1535–1592) had been rectors of St. Andrew's, Canterbury. Thomas is said to have been disinherited by his mother for having robbed an orchard when he was a boy (*Prose Works of Swift* 5:187), and Deane Swift says he left the diocese of Canterbury in order to escape "the caprice, the severity, and the cruelty of an unnatural mother" (Deane Swift, *Essay*, p. 11). Thomas was then made vicar of Goodrich, Herefordshire, about two miles from Ross.

21. Swift says that "not above one half" of the estate came down to Deane Swift (*Prose Works of Swift* 5:188).

22. Besides the six sons mentioned by Orrery, Thomas Swift had five daughters: Maria, Aemilia, Elizabeth, Sarah, and Katherina. See "The Family of Swift's Father" in Ehrenpreis, *Swift* 1:267.

23. *A Display of Heraldrie*, by John Guillim (1565–1621), first published in 1610, and followed by a number of editions. Orrery owned a copy of the fifth edition "much enlarged," offered during Christie's Orrery Sale (November 1905) as lot 240. See *Catalogue of the Valuable and Extensive Library and*

Collection of Autograph Letters of the Rt. Hon. the Earl of Cork and Orrery (London: Christie, Manson & Woods, 1905) p. 33 (cited hereafter as *The Orrery Sale*).

24. In *Family of Swift*, Swift said his mother was from Leicestershire (Orrery's scribal transcript of *Family of Swift*, MA 455, manuscript page 8, Orrery Correspondence, Pierpont Morgan Library, New York City). Abigail Erick (Swift's mother) was the sister of Thomas Errick, vicar of Frisby-on-the-Wreake, Leicestershire, son of James Ericke, vicar of Thornton, Leicestershire. James Ericke married Elizabeth, daughter of William Imins of Ibstock, Leicestershire, on 16 October 1627, and was made vicar of Thornton in that same year. James and Elizabeth were thus Swift's maternal grandparents. In January 1634, James Ericke was accused of having held an unlawful conventicle, and, on 15 September, a sentence against him was passed. His daughter Mary was born on 18 September, and, sometime between September and November, James Ericke emigrated to Ireland. Swift's mother was then born in Ireland in 1640, and not in Leicestershire, as even Swift himself believed. Specifically, she is described as a Dublin spinster in her wedding licence. James Ericke died sometime before 1654, and Elizabeth, his wife, was buried on 4 September 1663, in St. John's Church, Dublin. See Ehrenpreis, *Swift* 1: 270–74.

25. Jane, Swift's sister, baptized on 1 May 1666. When Swift was still at Kilkenny School, Jane moved to Leicester with Mrs. Swift, although, around 1698, she was in Dublin, having got married there in 1699. Before Jane went back to Dublin, she had been with Swift at Moor Park, Sir William Temple's household, and she was to return to Moor Park to work for Temple's sister. Jane finally settled in England, and, although Swift and she had not seen each other for decades, he had paid her an allowance until her death, in 1736.

26. Actually, Swift's parents got married in the summer of 1664, and Jane was born in 1666.

27. Jonathan Swift, the elder, was actually assistant to Thomas Wale, steward of the King's Inns, Ireland's legal society. On Wale's death, he was made steward of the society (25 January 1666) and, on the next day, he was admitted as a member. Swift himself said that his father "had some employments and agencies" (Orrery's scribal transcript of *Family of Swift*, MA 455, manuscript page 8, Orrery Correspondence, Pierpont Morgan Library, New York City).

28. Cf. Swift's words on the matter in *Family of Swift*: "This marriage [Swift's parents'] was on both sides very indiscreet, for his wife brought her husband little or no fortune, and his death happening so suddenly before he could make a sufficient establishment for his family: and his son (not then born) hath often been heard to say, that he felt the consequences of that marriage not only through the whole course of his education, but during the greatest part of his life" (ibid., manuscript page 9).

29. Godwin, Thomas Swift's eldest son, born in 1628. He was admitted as a student in Gray's Inn in 1650, and married Elizabeth Wheeler, distantly related to the Marchioness of Ormond. He came over to Ireland with his brothers either at the Restoration or shortly before that. (Deane Swift says the migration to Ireland took place shortly after their father's death. See Deane Swift, *Essay*, pp. 14–15). In Ireland, Godwin obtained the positions of filacer in the Court of Common Pleas, and of attorney general of the county palatine of Tipperary, through the duke of Ormond's influence. Godwin had four wives in all, and Swift had described Godwin as "an ill Pleader, but perhaps a little too dextrous in the subtil parts of the Law" (Orrery's scribal transcript of *Family of Swift*, MA 455, manuscript page 7, Orrery Correspondence, Pierpont Morgan Library, New York City).

30. As Ehrenpreis notes, there is no conclusive evidence that Godwin had supported Swift in his studies, either at Kilkenny School or at Trinity College. It is more likely that William was the uncle who gave Swift the greatest help and support during Swift's years as a student. See Ehrenpreis, *Swift* 1:63–64; and Deane Swift, *Essay*, pp. 49–50.

31. Abigail Erick had apparently moved to Leicester while Swift was still at Kilkenny, which means sometime between 1673 and 1682. Ehrenpreis says this fact has not been proved (*Swift* 1:32). Leicester was not Abigail Erick's "place of nativity," as she was born in Dublin. Her ancestors were from Leicestershire.

32. Kilkenny Grammar School was one of the best in Ireland at that time. In spring and summer, the children had their first session of classes from six to ten in the morning. The second session was from noon to four in the afternoon. Morning and evening prayers, as well as a catechism, completed the strict discipline of the school. Students were required to know basic Latin before being admitted. See Ehrenpreis, *Swift* 1:34–42.

33. Swift entered Trinity College on 24 April 1682. He was then fourteen, having been admitted as a paying boarder.

34. Orrery is echoing Swift's own words in *Family of Swift*: "he [Swift] had lived with great Regularity and due Observance of the Statutes" (Orrery's scribal transcript of *Family of Swift*, MA 455, manuscript page 10, Orrery Correspondence, Pierpont Morgan Library, New York City). However, Swift was often fined for disciplinary offences such as missing chapel sessions and lectures on mathematics. In late 1688, Swift and five other students were punished for having insulted the junior dean and Swift was forced to kneel before the junior dean, and beg his pardon publicly. Ehrenpreis gives a full account of Swift's disciplinary fines (see *Swift* 1:67–70 and 284–85).

35. Cf. Swift's letter to his cousin Thomas, dated 3 May 1692: "To enter upon the causes of Philosophy is what I protest I will rather die in a ditch than go about" (*Correspondence of Swift* 1:11).

36. Cf. Swift's words in *Family of Swift*: "[Swift] turned himself to reading History and Poetry" (Orrery's scribal transcript of *Family of Swift*, MA 455, manuscript page 10, Orrery Correspondence, Pierpont Morgan Library, New York City).

37.   Orrery is again repeating Swift's own claim about his "Dullness and Insufficiency" (ibid.). However, Swift actually had a good performance in his studies at Trinity College, at least if we judge from his marks on the Easter term examinations for 1685. He received *male* in Aristotelian philosophy, *bene* in Greek and Latin, and *negligenter* in Latin theme. Other students, including Thomas, Swift's cousin, who were considered men of learning, had received either *male* or *mediocriter* in all three categories. *Negligenter* was the most common mark, and, of the 119 students taking those examinations, only Swift and six other students received *bene* in Latin and Greek. Swift did not receive *pessime*, the lowest mark, in any of the three categories.   See Ehrenpreis, *Swift* 1:57–62 and 279–83.

38. *Speciali gratiâ*, meaning "by special grace or favor," indeed indicated a degree conferred by the university's favor. However, it does not follow that Swift had been a bad student. Four students who were older than Swift and graduated with him also received that kind of degree, out of a class of thirty-eight. Degrees with the *speciali gratiâ* mark were also conferred to two students out of a group of thirty-eight (February 1685), to seven students out of thirty-one (February 1687), and to three students out of thirty-three (February 1688). See Ehrenpreis, *Swift* 1:62. Swift received his B.A. degree on 15 February 1686.

39. Cf. Swift's words in *Family of Swift*: "And this discreditable mark, as I am told, stands upon record in their College Registry." (Orrery's scribal transcript of *Family of Swift*, MA 455, manuscript page 10, Orrery Correspondence, Pierpont Morgan Library, New York City).

40. William Swift, Swift's uncle, had obtained this *Testimonium* from Trinity College for Swift. See Ehrenpreis, *Swift* 1:64.

41. Deane Swift tells how Swift himself had told him this story: "But I will tell you, said he [Swift], the best jest of it all was, when I produced my *Testimonium* at Oxford in order to be admitted *ad eundem*, they mistook *speciali gratiâ* for some particular strain of compliment, which I had received from the university of Dublin on account of my superior merit; and I leave you to guess, whether it was my business to undeceive them" (Deane Swift, *Essay*, p. 30).

42. On 14 June 1692.

43. Hart Hall was founded sometime in the thirteenth century, being incorporated as Hertford College in 1739. From Hertford College, it was transformed into Magdalen Hall, and a second time into Hertford College. See Christopher Brooke and Roger Highfield, *Oxford and Cambridge* (Cambridge: Cambridge University Press, 1988).

44. It is unlikely that Swift interrupted his activities at Oxford to visit either his mother or Temple. Swift's residence at Oxford lasted only three weeks.

45. Swift received his M.A. degree on 5 July 1692. No examination was required for the master's degree.

LETTER II

I Am happy, my dear HAMILTON, to find that the task which I have undertaken of placing together some memoirs of Dr. SWIFT's life, will be an acceptable present to you. In my last letter, you may remember, that I conducted Dr. SWIFT from his birth, in the year sixteen hundred and sixty seven, to his taking his degree of Master of Arts at *Oxford*, in the year sixteen hundred and ninety one.[1] Curiosity may induce you to know, in what manner he could subsist, or by what channel the springs of his revenue were supplied, at a time when both kingdoms, but particularly *Ireland*, were in great confusion.[2] You will almost tremble for him, when I tell you, that in the year of the Revolution,[3] his uncle GODWIN SWIFT had fallen into a kind of lethargy, or dotage, which deprived him by degrees of his speech and memory;[4] and rendered him totally incapable of being of the least service to his family and friends. But, in the midst of this distressful situation, as if it was ordained, that no incident should bereave mankind of such a genius, Sir WILLIAM TEMPLE (whose Lady was related to Dr. SWIFT's mother)[5] most generously stept in to his assistance, and avowedly supported his education at the University of *Oxford*.[6] Acts of generosity seldom meet with their just applause: Sir WILLIAM TEMPLE's friendship was immediately construed to proceed from a consciousness, that he was the real father of Mr. SWIFT, otherwise it was thought impossible, that he could be so uncommonly munificent to a young man, no ways related to him, and but distantly related to his wife. I am not quite certain, that SWIFT himself did not acquiesce in the calumny. Perhaps, like ALEXANDER, he thought the natural son of JUPITER would appear greater than the legitimate son of PHILIP.

But I must not omit to tell you, that another of his father's brothers, WILLIAM SWIFT, assisted him when at *Oxford*, by repeated acts of friendship and affection.[7] I have a letter now before me, which, tho' torn, and imperfect in several places, shews his gratitude and devotion to the uncle, whom I have just now mentioned, and whom he calls *the best of his relations*. I will transcribe this epistolary fragment; since at least it is so far curious, as it gives us a specimen of SWIFT's manner of writing and thinking, at that period of his life.

Moore Park, *Nov.* 29, 1692.[8]

SIR,

    My sister told me, you was pleased (when she was here) to wonder, I did so seldom write to you.[a] I —— [9] *been so kind, to impute it neither to ill mann* —— [10] *respect. I always* —— [11] *thought that sufficient from[b] one, who has always been but too troublesome to you: besides I knew your aversion to impertinence, and God knows so very private a life as mine can furnish a letter with little else: for I often am two or three months without seeing any body besides the family; and now my sister is gone,[12] I am likely to be more solitary than before. I am still to thank you for your care in my* Testimonium,[13] *and it was to very good purpose, for I never was more satisfied than in the behaviour of the University of* Oxford *to me. I had all the civilities I could wish for, and so many* —— [14] *favours, that I am ashamed to have been more obliged in a few weeks to strangers, than ever I was in seven years to* Dublin *College. I am not to take orders till the King gives me a Prebendary: and Sir* WILLIAM TEMPLE, *tho' he promises me the certainty of it, yet is less forward than I could wish; because, I suppose, he believes I shall leave him, and upon some accounts, he thinks me a little necessary to him* ——.[15] *If I were* —— [16] *entertainment, or doing you any satisfaction by my letters, I shall[c] be very glad to perform it that way, as I am bound to do it by all others. I am sorry my fortune should fling me so far from the best of my Relations, but hope that I shall have the happiness to see you some time or other. Pray my humble service to my good aunt, and the rest of my relations, if you please.*

    You do not see in these few lines the least symptoms of that peculiar turn of phrase, which afterwards appeared in all his writings; even in his most trifling letters.[17] Neither his learning, nor his genius were yet arrived to any degree of ripeness. Or perhaps the letter was rather the effect of duty than inclination; and in that case, the style of it must be elaborate, and void of all freedom and vivacity. It is dated from *Moore Park*, near *Farnham* in *Surry*, where Sir WILLIAM TEMPLE then resided.[18]

---

[a]write to you.] write   to you. FI

[b]from] for FI

[c]shall] should FI, FIa, FIb, FII, FIII, FV, MI, MII, MIV

SWIFT, as soon as he had quitted the University of *Oxford*, lived with Sir WILLIAM TEMPLE as his friend, and domestic companion. When he had been about two years at *Moore Park*,[19] he contracted a very long and dangerous illness, by eating an immoderate quantity of fruit.[20] To this surfeit I have often heard him ascribe that giddiness in his head, which with intermissions sometimes of a longer, and sometimes of a shorter continuance, pursued him[21] till it seemed to compleat its conquest, by rendering him the exact image of one of his own *Struldbruggs*,[22] a miserable spectacle, devoid of every appearance of human nature, except the outward form.

In compliance to the advice of his physicians, when he was sufficiently recovered to travel, he went into *Ireland*, to try the effects of his native air: and he found so much benefit by the journey, that in compliance to his own inclinations, he soon returned into *England*,[23] and was again most affectionately received by Sir WILLIAM TEMPLE,[24] who had now left *Moore Park*, and was settled at *Sheene*,[25] where he was often visited by King WILLIAM [26]. Here SWIFT had frequent opportunities of conversing with that Prince; in some of which conversations, the King offered to make him a captain of horse: an offer, which, in splenetic dispositions, he always seemed sorry to have refused;[27] but at that time he had resolved, within his own mind, to take orders;[28] and during his whole life, his resolutions, like the decrees of fate, were immoveable. Thus determined he again went over into *Ireland*, and immediately enlisted himself under the banner of the Church.[29] He was recommended by Sir WILLIAM TEMPLE to Lord CAPEL, then Lord Deputy,[30] who gave him the first vacancy, a prebend,[31] of which the income was about an hundred pounds a year.[32] SWIFT soon grew weary of this preferment: it was not sufficiently considerable, and was at so great a distance from the metropolis, that it absolutely deprived him of[d] that kind of conversation and society, in which he delighted. He had been used to very different scenes in *England*, and had naturally an aversion to solitude and retirement. He was glad therefore to resign his prebend[33] in favour of a friend,[34] and to return to *Sheene*,[35] where he lived domestically as usual, till the death of Sir WILLIAM TEMPLE,[36] who, besides a legacy in money,[37] left to him the care and trust of publishing his posthumous works.[38]

As during my friend SWIFT's residence with Sir WILLIAM TEMPLE, he became intimately acquainted with a Lady,[39] whom he has distinguished, and often celebrated in his works, under the name of STELLA;[40] I cannot think, my HAM, that it will be improper to give you at once her history; although, according to the rules of biography, I ought perhaps to have delayed the account, till we arrived at that period of his life, when he married her: but as I may have occasion to speak of her in various parts of SWIFT's Works, and

---

[d]of] from FI, FIa, FIb, FII, MI, MII

as his manner of living with her will shew you, how much he deviated from the common order of men, I shall fill up the rest of my letter with her extraordinary Story.

STELLA's real name was JOHNSON.[41] She was the daughter of Sir WILLIAM TEMPLE's steward,[42] and the concealed, but undoubted wife of Dr. SWIFT. Sir WILLIAM TEMPLE bequeathed her in his will one thousand pounds, as an acknowledgment of her father's faithful services.[43] I cannot tell how long she remained in *England*, or whether she made more journeys than one to *Ireland* after Sir WILLIAM TEMPLE's death;[44] but if my informations are right,[45] she was married to Dr. SWIFT in the year seventeen hundred and sixteen,[46] by Dr. ASHE then bishop of *Clogher*.[47]

STELLA was a most amiable woman, in mind, and person. She had an elevated understanding, with all the delicacy and softness of her sex.[e] Her voice, however sweet in itself, was still rendered more harmonious by what she said. Her wit was poignant without severity. Her manners were humane, polite, easy, and unreserved. Wherever she came she attracted attention and esteem. As virtue was her guide in morality, sincerity was her guide in religion. She was constant, but not ostentatious in her devotions. She was remarkably prudent in her conversation. She had great skill in music,[48] and was perfectly well versed in all the lesser arts that employ a lady's leisure. Her wit allowed her a fund of perpetual chearfulness: her prudence kept that chearfulness within proper limits. She exactly answered the description of PENELOPE in HOMER.

> *A woman loveliest of the lovely kind,*
> *In body perfect, and compleat in mind.*[49]

Such was STELLA: yet with all these accomplishments she never could prevail upon Dr. SWIFT to acknowledge her openly as his wife.[50] A great genius must tread in unbeaten paths, and deviate from the common road of life: otherwise, surely a diamond of so much lustre might have been publickly produced, although it had been fixed within the collet[51] of matrimony: but the flaw, which in Dr. SWIFT's eye reduced the value of such a jewel, was the servile state of her father, who, as I said[f] before, was a menial servant to Sir WILLIAM TEMPLE. Ambition and pride will, at any time, conquer reason and justice; and each larger degree of pride, like the larger fishes of prey, will

---

[e]sex.] own sex. MI, MII

[f]as I said MV] as has been said MIII

devour all the less: thus the vanity of boasting of such[g] a wife was suppressed by the greater vanity of keeping free from a low alliance.

Dr. SWIFT and Mrs. JOHNSON continued the same oeconomy of life after marriage, which they had pursued before it. They lived in separate houses; he remaining at the deanery, she, in lodgings at a distance from him, and on the other side of the river *Liffy*.[52] Nothing appeared in their behaviour inconsistent with decorum, or beyond the limits of platonic love. They conversed like friends; but they industriously took care, to summon witnesses of their conversation: a rule to which they adhered so strictly, that it would be difficult, if not impossible, to prove they had ever been together without some third person.[53]

A conduct so extraordinary in itself always gives room for various comments and reflections: but, however unaccountable this renunciation of marriage rites[h] might appear to the world, it certainly arose[i] not from any consciousness of too near a consanguinity between him and Mrs. JOHNSON, although the general voice of fame was willing to make them both the natural children of Sir WILLIAM TEMPLE.[54] I am persuaded, that Dr. SWIFT was not of that opinion; because, the same false pride that induced him to deny the legitimate daughter of an obscure servant, might have prompted him to own the natural daughter of so eminent a man as Sir WILLIAM TEMPLE. There[j] are actions of which the true sources will never be discovered. This perhaps is one. I have told you the fact, in the manner I have received it from several of SWIFT's friends and relations,[55] and I must leave you to make your own observations upon it.

You may imagine, that a woman of STELLA's delicacy must repine at such an extraordinary situation. The outward honours, which she received, are as frequently bestowed upon a mistress, as a wife.[k] She was absolutely virtuous, and yet was obliged to submit to all the appearances of vice, except in the presence of those few people, who were witnesses of the cautious manner in which she lived with her husband, who scorned, my HAMILTON, even to be married like any other man.

---

[g]boasting of such MV] boasting such MIII

[h]rites] rights FI

[i]arose] rose FI

[j]new paragraph FI

[k]as a wife.] as upon a wife. FI, FIa, FIb, FII, FIII, FV

Inward anxiety affected by degrees the calmness of her mind, and the strength of her body. She began to decline in her health in the year seventeen hundred and twenty-four;[56] and from the first symptoms of decay, she rather hastened, than shrunk back in the descent, tacitly pleased, to find her footsteps tending to that place, where *they neither marry, nor are given in marriage.*[57] She died towards the end of *January*, seventeen hundred and twenty-seven, or eight,[58] absolutely destroyed by the peculiarity of her fate: a fate, which perhaps she could not have incurred by an alliance with any other person in the world.

My paper, my time, and every circumstance, put me in mind of assuring you, my dear HAMILTON, that I am,

Your most affectionate Father,
ORRERY.

Notes

1. Swift received his master's degree on 5 July 1692.

2. Cf. Deane Swift's words on this subject: "I am inclined to believe, that if not the whole, the greater part of that money which supplied all his occasions, whether at Oxford, Moore-Park, or any where else, from the year 1688 until he was presented by the Lord Capel to the prebend of Kilsoot [*sic*] about the latter end of the year 1694, were remittances that he received from his uncle William Swift, and particularly from his cousin german Willoughby Swift, who was in those times a very considerable merchant at Lisbon; whose paternal kindness, liberality and affection to a great number of his relations, and particularly to Dr. Swift among the rest, as well as to all the numerous progeny of his father, can never be sufficiently praised or acknowledged by the family" (Deane Swift, *Essay*, pp. 49-50). Willoughby was the eldest son of Godwin Swift by Elizabeth Wheeler, Godwin's first wife. Swift himself acknowledges Willoughby's help to him in a letter to Deane Swift (Swift's cousin, father of Swift's biographer, and Godwin's son by his third wife), dated 3 June 1694 (*Correspondence of Swift* 1:15-16). Deane Swift also prints these words from a letter from Mrs. Swift to his father, where she reckons Willoughby's help to her son: "Pray be pleased to present my best service to my good nephew Swift [Willoughby] and tell him I always bear in my heart a grateful remembrance of all the kindness he was pleased to shew to my son" (Deane Swift, *Essay*, p. 53).

3. The Revolution affected the course of Swift's studies in Trinity College. In the college register of 19 February 1689, it was stated that the university authorities were allowing students to leave "for their security." In March, St. George Ashe (Swift's tutor) and nine other fellows left for England. In September, a regiment of foot was quartered in the college. In his letter of recommendation on Swift's behalf to Sir Robert Southwell, secretary of state for Ireland, Sir William Temple says: "he [Swift] was forced away by the desertion of that Colledge upon the calamitys of the Country" (*Correspondence of Swift* 1:1). Swift would have completed his master's degree requirements in April.

4. According to Deane Swift, Godwin had a stroke, "a sort of lethargy," in 1688 (Deane Swift, *Essay*, p. 36). The fact that Godwin was deprived of his "speech and memory" suggested to Margaret Hamilton (Orrery's second wife) the idea that Swift's disease, whose symptoms were similar to Godwin's, was hereditary: "a case [Godwin's illness] so similar to that of poor Dr. Swift that we might almost imagine there was something hereditary in that dreadful disorder which first attacked the Uncle then the nephew" (Lady Orrery to Orrery, 8 January 1753, in *Orrery Papers* 2:254).

5. As Ehrenpreis observes, the connection between Mrs. Swift and Dorothy Osborne, Temple's wife, has not been traced. Still, on Temple's death, Mrs. Swift received an allowance for mourning. See Ehrenpreis, *Swift* 1:4.

6. All we know for sure is that Swift, after leaving Ireland in late 1688 or early 1689, went to his mother's house in Leicester. From there, he went to Surrey and joined Temple's household. See ibid., pp. 92 and 102. Swift must have been welcomed with kindness by Temple. See Jonathan Swift, *Journal to Stella*, ed. Harold Williams, 2 vols. (Oxford: Clarendon Press, 1948), 1:xi-xii (cited hereafter as Swift, *Journal to Stella*). See also Elias, *Swift at Moor Park*, pp. 128-32.

7. William Swift's role as Swift's most helpful uncle is described in Deane Swift, *Essay*, pp. 49-50. See Ehrenpreis, *Swift* 1:64.

8. Orrery's *Remarks* remains the earliest published source of this letter. Harold Williams printed it while giving conjectural readings within brackets for the defective passages. See *Correspondence of Swift* 1:11-12.

9. "hope you have" (Williams)

10. "manners or want of" (Williams).

11. "have" (Williams).

12. Jane Swift had apparently left for Ireland. See Ehrenpreis, *Swift* 1:174.

13. For William Swift's care of Swift's *testimonium*, see ibid., p. 64.

14. "showed me" (Williams).

15. "at present" (Williams).

16. "affording you" (Williams).

17. In the *Gentleman's Magazine*, April 1752, one "J. W." writing from "W——l, Staffordshire" on 11 March, criticizes these observations by Orrery on Swift's letter to his uncle William. "J. W." states that, upon reading these comments by Orrery on Swift's letter, he remembered he had an earlier letter by Swift: "I recollected that I had a letter in my possession of a somewhat earlier date than that which Lord Orrery has published, and withall more perfect; in which his Lordship (if he reads your Magazine) may see, that Dr. Swift was much the same man, with regard to the peculiarity of his turn of sentiment and phrase, at five and twenty, as he was, when his Lordship conversed with him, bating his improvements in the after part of his life" (*GM*, April 1752, p. 157). After the comments by "J. W.," there follows the text of that earlier letter (ibid., pp. 157-58), from Swift to John Kendall, vicar of Thornton, Leicestershire, dated 11 February 1691, printed in *Correspondence of Swift* 1:2-5, and which is actually Swift's earliest recorded letter. "J. W." claims the letter is "genuine," and that he had transcribed it "some years ago, from the original under the dean's own hand." Harold Williams printed the text of the letter from a transcript in the Leicester Museum, and did not mention, or did not know, that the letter had been printed in the *Gentleman's Magazine* for April 1752.

18. Swift left Ireland either in late 1688 or early 1689, and then proceeded to his mother's house in Leicester. From there, Swift went to Surrey, but it is not certain whether he arrived at Moor Park or Sheene. Swift must have joined Temple's household for the first time by the summer of 1689 or by the end of the year. Swift then began to feel the symptoms of Ménière's disease, and, upon his physicians' recommendation, went to Ireland again. He returned to England about August 1691, staying with his mother through the autumn. Swift was back at Moor Park around Christmas 1691. Swift was absent for three weeks to take his master's degree at Oxford in the summer of 1692, but rejoined Temple after taking his degree. Swift would leave Moor Park again in early May 1694, and went to his mother's in Leicester. From

Leicester, he went to Dublin to receive holy orders. He would return to Moor Park for the last time in May 1696. See Ehrenpreis, *Swift* 1:102-8, and 142-49.

19. In *Family of Swift*, Swift also wrote he stayed at Moor Park "for about two years" before leaving it for the first time (Orrery's scribal transcript of *Family of Swift*, MA 455, manuscript page 11, Orrery Correspondence, Pierpont Morgan Library, New York City).

20. The origin of Ménière's disease, Swift's lifelong illness, is still unknown. See Irvin Ehrenpreis, *The Personality of Swift* (London: Methuen, 1958), p. 119. The "surfeit of fruit" which Swift mentions as the cause of his disease may have taken place in Sheene (*Correspondence of Swift* 3:32).

21. Cf. Swift's own words in *Family of Swift*: "this disorder pursued him with intermissions of two or three years to the end of his Life" (Orrery's scribal transcript of *Family of Swift*, MA 455, manuscript page 11, Orrery Correspondence, Pierpont Morgan Library, New York City).

22. Cf. Mrs. Pilkington's words: "he [Swift] lived to be a Struldbrugg, helpless as a Child, and unable to assist himself." In Laetitia Pilkington, *Memoirs of Mrs. L. Pilkington*, 3 vols. (London: R. Griffiths, 1748-54), 3:160-61 (cited hereafter as Pilkington, *Memoirs*). Mrs. Pilkington's volume 3 appeared in 1754 (information courtesy of Dr. A. C. Elias, Jr.).

23. Cf. Swift's words in *Family of Swift*: "Upon this occasion he returned to Ireland by advice of Physicians, who weakly imagined that his native air might be of some use to recover his Health. But growing worse, he soon went back to Sir William Temple" (Orrery's scribal transcript of *Family of Swift*, MA 455, manuscript page 11, Orrery Correspondence, Pierpont Morgan Library, New York City). Swift's trip to Ireland for his health also was intended to be a possible occasion for preferment. Temple wrote a letter of recommendation for Swift to Robert Southwell, secretary of state for Ireland (*Correspondence of Swift* 1:1-2), to suggest either a place for Swift or a fellowship at Trinity College. Neither of those alternatives took place. Temple then invited Swift back to his household. See Ehrenpreis, *Swift* 1:106-7.

24. For a discussion of Swift's position in the Moor Park household, and Temple's possible opinions about his young secretary, see Elias, *Swift at Moor Park*, pp. 140-54.

25. Temple was at Moor Park at that time. See Homer Woodbridge, *Sir William Temple: The Man and his Work* (New York: Modern Language Association of America, 1940), p. 222.

26. Swift wrote that William III "visited his old Friend [Temple] often at Sheen, and took his advice in affairs of greatest consequence" (Orrery's scribal transcript of *Family of Swift*, MA 455, manuscript page 11, Orrery Correspondence, Pierpont Morgan Library, New York City).

27. Cf. Orrery's marginal note in his scribal transcript of *Family of Swift* (the note is in the hand of Orrery's scribe): "The Dean has told me, that K. William once offered to make him a Captain of Horse; which, as far as I dared, between jest and earnest, I used to blame him for not accepting of, considering the state of his fortune at that time, and the uncertainty of rising by merit to any Eminence in the Church: and I remember, he was so far from being displeased with what I said to him, that I was almost tempted to think, he repented that he did not accept of the Commission" (ibid., manuscript pages 14-15).

28. Writing to his cousin Deane Swift from Leicester, 3 June 1694, Swift says he designed "to be ordained September next," and to do "what Endeavours" he could "for something in the Church" (*Correspondence of Swift* 1:16). Swift had left Temple in early May, and he tells Deane Swift what happened: "He [Temple] was extream angry I left him, and yet would not oblige Himself any further than upon my good Behaviour, nor would promise any thing firmly to Me at all; so that every Body judged I did best to leave Him" (ibid.).

29. Swift had to wait for a few months to be ordained. On 3 June 1694, Swift said he would leave Leicester in four days for Ireland (ibid., p. 15). Upon arriving in Dublin, Swift learned he had to produce a letter of reference from someone, as canon law required proof of the candidate's integrity of life during the three years before ordination. This requirement was even more strictly enforced in Swift's case, as it had been some years since he had taken his degree, which caused suspicions. Swift had to perform the embarrassing task of writing to Temple (whom he had lately angered with his departure), requesting a letter of reference. Surprisingly, though, Temple did send a letter in time for Swift to be ordained deacon on 28 October 1694, and priest on 13 January 1695. See Ehrenpreis, *Swift* 1:150-53.

30. Henry, Lord Capel of Tewkesbury. He was made a lord justice of Ireland in 1693, and, in 1695, was installed Lord Deputy. With this title, he became sole governor of Ireland. Capel died while in office, on 30 May 1696.

31. The prebend of Kilroot was presented to Swift on 28 January 1695, fifteen days after his priestly ordination, and he was installed on 15 March. Kilroot, on the northern side of Belfast Lough, consisted of the vicarages of Kilroot and Templecorran, as well as the rectory of Ballynure. The church of Kilroot

was then in ruins, although the churches of Templecorran and Ballynure were still in use. See Ehrenpreis, *Swift* 1:153; and *Correspondence of Swift* 1:19.

32. Swift also wrote that Capel "gave him a Prebend in the North worth about £100 a year" (Orrery's scribal transcript of *Family of Swift*, MA 455, manuscript page 14, Orrery Correspondence, Pierpont Morgan Library, New York City).

33. After receiving, in the spring of 1696, an invitation from Temple to come back to Moor Park, Swift left Kilroot in mid-May 1696, and, as usual, stopped in Leicester to see his mother. After passing through London, he finally reached Moor Park. Swift had decided to resign Kilroot while he was still in Ireland, but the resignation was effected in January 1698. See Ehrenpreis, *Swift* 1:170-71; and *Correspondence of Swift* 1:25.

34. This is John Winder, rector of Carnmoney, a vicarage in the Kilroot area, who came to earn Swift's friendship. There are two recorded letters from Swift to Winder, and Winder had once transcribed some of Swift's sermons at Kilroot. It was through Swift's efforts that Winder was installed as Swift's successor at Kilroot. Winder was installed on 15 March 1698, and continued to hold the prebend of Kilroot until his death in 1717. See *Correspondence of Swift* 1:25-31; and Ehrenpreis, *Swift* 1:171.

35. Swift returned to Moor Park.

36. Temple died on 27 January 1699, at 1:00 P.M., and, four months later, Swift's sister wrote from Dublin to her cousin Deane Swift, saying: "My poor brother has lost his best friend Sir William Temple, who was so fond of him whilst he lived, that he made him give up his living in this country to stay with him at Moore-Park, and promised to get him one in England; but death came in between, and has left him unprovided both of friend and living" (Deane Swift, *Essay*, p. 66; *Correspondence of Swift* 1:32). After Temple died, Swift continued at Moor Park for four or five weeks, settling the final financial accounts of the household. Swift may have left by March 9 (Elias, *Swift at Moor Park*, pp. 97 and 255-56).

37. One hundred pounds. Swift's legacy was mentioned in a codicil added to Temple's last will.

38. Swift was responsible for the following publications of Temple's writings: *Letters written by Sir William Temple, Baronet and other Ministers of State*, in two volumes (1699); *Miscellanea, the Third Part* (1701); *Letters to the King, the Prince of Orange, the Chief Ministers of State, and Other Persons* (1703) and

Memoirs Part III (1709). This last work caused a quarrel with Lady Giffard, Temple's sister, who accused Swift of publishing it without authorization. See Ehrenpreis, *Swift* 2:339-43. See also N. F. Lowe and W. J. McCormack, "Swift as 'Publisher' of Sir William Temple's *Letters* and *Miscellanea*," *Swift Studies* 8 (1993): 46-57.

39. Stella, or, Esther Johnson. Swift first met her when he joined Temple's household for the first time. Stella was then eight years old, although Swift says she was six (*Prose Works of Swift* 5:227). It is not certain when Swift first began to call her "Stella," but he refers to her by this name in his first birthday poem to her (1719).

40. Besides the *Journal to Stella*, Swift wrote twelve poems to Stella, *On the Death of Mrs. Johnson*, *Bons Mots de Stella*, prayers for her during her times of sickness, and there are two extant letters from Swift to Stella outside the *Journal*.

41. The parish register records Stella's christened name as "Hester," although she always wrote her first name as "Esther."

42. Stella was born in Richmond, Surrey, on 13 March 1681 (baptized in the Richmond parish church on 20 March), and was thus fourteen years younger than Swift. Her parents were Edward Johnson ("younger brother of a good family in Nottinghamshire," according to Swift in *Prose Works of Swift* 5:227) who had been Temple's steward, and Bridget, Temple's housekeeper.

43. Stella was identified in Temple's will as "servant to my sister," and received the lease of some lands in Morristown, county Wicklow, Ireland. Actually, Temple had drawn several wills, the last of which was dated 8 March 1695, and a codicil was added to it on 2 February 1698. Stella's mother received twenty pounds and half a year's wages, and she continued to work for Temple's sister. According to Swift, at the time of Temple's death, Stella's fortune "was in all not above fifteen hundred pounds" (*Prose Works of Swift* 5:228). Stella also had some property at Trim, Ireland, and received an annuity from Temple's sister (Swift, *Journal to Stella* 1:xxviii).

44. After Temple's death, Stella spent about two years at Moor Park or Farnham. Swift says he then convinced Stella and Rebecca Dingley (Stella's lifelong companion) "to draw what money they had into Ireland," where they could get an interest rate of ten per cent and "all necessaries of life at half the price" (*Prose Works of Swift* 5:228). Stella and Mrs. Dingley moved to Ireland either in 1700 or 1701. We know of only one trip of Stella and Mrs. Dingley to England after they moved to Ireland, and this was in 1708. Deane Swift

dates Stella's trip to England in 1705, but he is probably mistaken. He might be correct in the length of their stay, "five or six months" (Deane Swift, *Essay*, p. 90). On 22 January 1708, Swift told Archdeacon Walls that Stella and Mrs. Dingley planned to leave for Ireland in the spring (*Correspondence of Swift* 1:66). See Swift, *Journal to Stella* 1:xviii and xxviii.

45. Maxwell Gold commented on these words: "Orrery, in his use of the phrase 'if my informations are right,' shows a laudable exactness in his unwillingness to specify without qualification the exact date of the ceremony, since his principal informant, Mrs. Whiteway, was herself indefinite regarding it." In Maxwell B. Gold, *Swift's Marriage to Stella* (New York: Russell & Russell, 1967), p. 73.

46. Referring to Orrery's account of the marriage, Delany wrote: "Your [Orrery's] account of the marriage, is, I am satisfied, true" (Delany, *Observations*, pp. 52-53). Deane Swift admits the marriage took place ("I am thoroughly persuaded," p. 92), and gives his own conjecture about its motives (*Essay*, pp. 94-95). Ehrenpreis is positive in saying he does not believe Swift and Stella were ever married (Ehrenpreis, *Swift* 3:405). Maxwell Gold wrote that Swift and Stella were probably married in the circumstances mentioned by Orrery. See Gold, *Swift's Marriage to Stella*, pp. 26-67, for an examination of evidence against the marriage, and pp. 67-116 for an examination of evidence supporting the marriage.

47. St. George Ashe (ca. 1658-1718), Swift's tutor at Trinity College. He was successively appointed bishop of Cloyne, Clogher, and Derry.

48. Deane Swift says Stella was "totally unacquainted with musick" (*Essay*, p. 80).

49.   Oh, woman! loveliest of the lovely kind,
        In body perfect, and complete in mind!
                      (Pope, *Odyssey* 18.291-92)

50. Mrs. Pilkington claimed Swift *did* wish to acknowledge Stella as his wife (Pilkington, *Memoirs* 3:56-57). Delany wrote that Stella was the one who rejected the idea, because "the Dean's temper was so altered, and his attention to money so increased" that she "could not take upon herself the care of his house and economy" (Delany, *Observations*, p. 56). Deane Swift says Swift never acknowledged Stella as his wife for fear of his enemies ("half-mankind" in 1716) who could publicize "the obscurity" of Stella's birth and education (*Essay*, pp. 83-85). Sheridan wrote that, shortly before Stella died, she asked Swift "in the most earnest and pathetic terms" to acknowledge her as his wife.

Stella would have asked this in order to avoid slander over her name in the future. Swift would have walked out of the room without giving Stella an answer. In Thomas Sheridan, *The Life of the Rev. Dr. Jonathan Swift, Dean of St. Patrick's, Dublin*, 2d ed. (London: J. F. and C. Rivington et al., 1787), pp. 311-12, Sheridan claims to have received the story from his father, Swift's friend. Maxwell Gold fully discusses the question of the acknowledgment of the marriage, and states that, three months before Stella's death, Swift had offered to acknowledge it.   Stella refused it on account of the acknowledgment's inconsequentiality at that point. See Gold, *Swift's Marriage to Stella*, pp. 124-25.

51. In the *OED*, 2d ed., 20 vols., this sentence by Orrery featuring the word *collet* is quoted (3:483), and this particular meaning of *collet* is given: "The circle or flange in a ring in which the stone is set; also the setting for a precious stone in a piece of jewellery," in the figurative sense.

52. Harold Williams described this behavior of Swift and Stella, and wrote that both had always "observed an almost exaggerated propriety." Williams also wrote: "Whether at Dublin or Laracor the ladies were free of his lodgings, or house, only when Swift was away. In Dublin, upon his return, they removed elsewhere; or, when he was in the country, they found rooms in Trim, occupied a little cottage at Laracor, or were the guests of Dr. Raymond. Further, Swift hardly allowed himself at any time to be left alone in the same room with Stella" (Swift, *Journal to Stella* 1:xxix). The river mentioned by Orrery is the Liffey, which crossed Dublin from west to east, emptying into the Bay of Dublin.

53. A frequent companion of Swift and Stella might have been Rebecca Dingley, whose grandmother was Temple's aunt. She had been waiting woman to Temple's sister when Swift was at Moor Park. She became Stella's lifelong companion, and outlived Stella by fifteen years, dying in 1743. Swift had apparently paid her an annuity of fifty guineas by quarterly installments. See *Correspondence of Swift* 5:244-45.

54. This theory was defended by "C.M.P.G.N.S.T.N.S.," the anonymous author of an article in the *Gentleman's Magazine*, November 1757, 487ff. By suggesting that Stella and Swift were Temple's illegitimate children, the author tried to refute Orrery's charges about Swift's pride and "cruelty" to Stella. He thus explained the strange behavior of Swift and Stella as caused by fear of incest, which would prevent their marriage. See David French, "The Identity of C.M.P.G.N.S.T.N.S.," in *Jonathan Swift: Tercentenary Essays*, University of Tulsa Department of English Monograph Series, no. 3 (Tulsa, Okla.:

University of Tulsa Press, 1967), 1-9. The theory has been attacked by most biographers.

55.   Mainly Mrs. Whiteway.   See prepublication copy of the *Remarks* interleaved and annotated by Orrery, MS Eng 218.14, interleaf pages numbered 21-28, Houghton Library, Harvard.

56. Stella had been a sickly girl until she was fifteen, and Swift wrote about her state of health some years before her death: "For some years past, she had been visited with continual ill-health; and several times, within these two years, her life was despaired of. But, for this twelve-month past, she never had a day's health; and, properly speaking, she hath been dying six months, but kept alive, almost against nature, by the generous kindness of two physicians, and the care of her friends" (*Prose Works of Swift* 5:228).

57. Matt. 22:30, Mark 12:25, and Luke 20:35.

58. Stella died on Sunday, 28 January 1728, at about 6:00 P.M. In her will, she left Swift a strongbox with a hundred fifty pounds in gold. Stella's will, dated 30 December 1727, is signed "Esther Johnson, Spinster." Stella's will was destroyed in the fire of the Four Courts, Dublin, in 1922. A photograph of one page of the will may be seen in the *Lady of the House*, a Dublin magazine, Christmas number, 1908. For a facsimile of Stella's will, see Sir William Wilde, *The Closing Years of Dean Swift's Life* (Dublin: Hodges and Smith, 1849), pp. 97-101.

LETTER III

I Join with you entirely in thinking STELLA one of the most unfortunate of her sex. Her catastrophe was such as might have drawn pity from a breast less susceptible of that passion than yours. Injurious treatment, disappointed love, a long lingering illness, were all circumstances of the melancholy kind. Be not surprized, my HAMILTON, when I tell you, that he never spoke of her without a sigh: for such is the perverseness of human nature, that we bewail those persons dead, whom we treated cruelly when living. But, I am making reflections, when I intended to write memoirs. Let us return to SWIFT.

Upon the death of Sir WILLIAM TEMPLE he came to *London,* and took the earliest opportunity of delivering a petition[a] to King WILLIAM, under the claim of a promise made by his Majesty to Sir WILLIAM TEMPLE, "That Mr. SWIFT should have the first vacancy, which might happen among the prebends of *Westminster* or *Canterbury.*"[1] The promises of kings are often a kind of chaff, which the breath of a minister bloweth, and scattereth away from the face of a court. The petition[b] had no effect. It was either totally forgotten, or drowned amidst the clamours of more urgent claims.[2] From this first disappointment, may probably be dated that bitterness towards kings, and courtiers, which is to be found so universally dispersed throughout his works.

After a long and fruitless attendance at *Whitehall,* SWIFT reluctantly gave up all thoughts of a settlement in *England.*[3] He had dedicated Sir WILLIAM TEMPLE's works to the king.[4] The dedication was neglected, nor did his Majesty take the least notice of him after Sir WILLIAM TEMPLE's death. What then was to be done? honour, or, to use a properer word, pride hindered him from staying long in a state of servility and contempt. He complied therefore with an invitation from the Earl of BERKLEY[5] (appointed one of the Lords Justices in *Ireland*) to attend him as his chaplain and private secretary. Lord

---

[a]petition] memorial FI, FIa, FIb, FII, FIII, FV

[b]petition] memorial FIa, FIb, FII, FIII, FV

94

BERKLEY landed near *Waterford*;[6] and Mr. SWIFT acted as secretary during the whole journey to *Dublin*. But another of Lord BERKLEY's attendants, whose name was BUSH,[7] had, by this time, insinuated himself into the Earl's favour, and had *whispered* to his Lordship,[8] that the post of secretary was not proper for a clergyman, to whom only church preferments could be suitable or advantageous. Lord BERKLEY listened perhaps too attentively to these insinuations, and making some slight apology to Mr. SWIFT, divested him of that office, and bestowed it upon Mr. BUSH.[9] Here again was another disappointment, and a fresh object of indignation. The treatment was thought injurious, and SWIFT expressed his sensibility of it in a short, but satyrical copy of verses entitled *The Discovery*.[10]

However, during the government of the Earls of BERKLEY and GALWAY,[11] who were jointly Lords Justices of *Ireland*, two livings, *Laracor* and *Rathbeggan*, were bestowed upon Mr. SWIFT.[12] The first of these rectories was worth about two hundred, and the latter about sixty pounds a year;[13] and they were the only church preferments that he enjoyed, 'till he was appointed Dean of St. *Patrick*'s, in the year seventeen hundred and thirteen.

As soon as he had taken possession of his two livings, he went to reside at *Laracor*,[14] and gave public notice to his parishioners, that he would read prayers on every Wednesday and Friday. Upon the subsequent Wednesday the bell was rung, and the Rector attended in his desk, when after having sat some time, and finding the congregation to consist only of himself, and his clerk ROGER, he began with great composure and gravity, but with a turn peculiar to himself, "*Dearly beloved* ROGER, *the Scripture moveth you and me in sundry places*." And then proceeded regularly through the whole service.[15] I mention this trifling circumstance only to shew you, that he could not resist a vein of humour, whenever he had an opportunity of exerting it.

As I have given you a particular example of his humour, let me give you a particular instance of his pride: especially as it comes in properly enough in point of time.

Whilst SWIFT was chaplain to Lord BERKLEY, his only sister, by the consent and approbation of her uncles and relations, was married to a man in trade,[16] whose fortune, character, and situation, were esteemed, by all her friends, suitable for her in every respect.[17] But, the marriage was entirely disagreeable to her brother. It seemed to interrupt those ambitious views, which he had long since formed: He grew outragious at the thoughts of being brother-in-law to a tradesman.[18] He utterly refused all reconciliation with his sister,[19] nor would he even listen to[c] the entreaties of his mother, who

---

[c]nor would he even listen to] nor ever would listen to FI, FIa, FIb, FII, MI

came over to *Ireland*, under the strongest hopes of pacifying[d] his anger,[20] having, in every other instance, found[e] him a dutiful, and an obedient[f] son: but his pride was not to be conquered,[21] and Mrs. SWIFT finding her son inflexible hastened back to *Leicester*, where she continued till her death.[22]

During his mother's life-time, he scarce ever failed to pay her an annual visit.[23] But his manner of travelling was as singular as any other of his actions. He often went in a waggon; but more frequently walked from *Holyhead* to *Leicester, London*, or any other part of *England*. He generally chose to dine with waggoners, hostlers, and persons of that rank; and he used to lye at night in[g] houses where he found written over the door *Lodgings for a penny*. He delighted in scenes of low life. The vulgar dialect was not only a fund of humour for him, but I verily believe was acceptable to his nature; otherwise I know not how to account for the many filthy ideas, and indecent expressions (I mean indecent in point of cleanliness and delicacy) that will be found throughout his works.[24]

I need not tell you, that a strict residence at *Laracor*, was not in the least suitable to his disposition. He was perpetually making excursions not only to *Dublin*, and other parts of *Ireland*, but into *England*, especially to *London*. So rambling a disposition occasioned to him a considerable loss. The rich deanery of *Derry* became vacant at this time,[25] and was intended for him by Lord BERKLEY; if Dr. KING, then Bishop of *Derry*, and afterwards Archbishop of *Dublin*,[26] had not interposed, entreating with great earnestness, that the deanery might be given to some grave and elderly divine, rather than to so young a man;[27] "because (added the Bishop) the situation of *Derry* is in the midst of presbyterians; and I should be glad of a clergyman, who would[h] be of assistance to me.[28] I have no objection to Mr. SWIFT. I know him to be a sprightly ingenious young man; but instead of residing, I dare say, he will be eternally flying backwards and forwards to *London*; and therefore I entreat, that he may be provided for in some other place."[29]

---

[d]under the strongest hopes of pacifying] under almost a certainty of pacifying FI, FIa, FIb, FII, MI

[e]in every other instance, found] in all other respects, ever found FI, FIa, FIb, FII, MI; in every other instance found MII

[f]and an obedient] and obedient FI

[g]in MV] at the MIII

[h]would] could FI, FIa, FIb, FII, MI, MII

SWIFT was accordingly set aside on account of *youth*; but, as if his stars had destined to him a parallel revenge, he lived to see the Bishop of *Derry* afterwards set aside on account of *age*. That Prelate had been Archbishop of *Dublin* many years, and had been long celebrated for his wit and learning, when Dr. LINDSEY, the Primate of *Ireland*,[30] died. Upon his death Archbishop KING immediately made claim to the Primacy, as a preferment to which he had a right from his station in the see of *Dublin*, and from his acknowledged character in the church. Neither of these pretensions were prevalent.[31] He was looked upon as *too far advanced in years* to be removed. The reason alledged was as mortifying as the refusal itself: but the Archbishop had no opportunity of shewing his resentment, except to the new Primate Dr. BOLTER,[32] whom he received at his own house, and in his dining parlour, without rising from his chair, and to whom he made an apology, by saying, in his usual strain of wit, and with his usual sneering countenance, "My Lord, I am certain your Grace will forgive me, because, *You know I am too old to rise.*"

In the year 1701, SWIFT took his Doctor's degree,[33] and towards the latter end of that year, or according to our absurd way of reckoning, in the year 1701/02[34] King WILLIAM died.[35] Queen ANNE's reign will open a new scene, and will probably afford me materials for more letters than one. The more the better, when in each of them I can assure you, that your behaviour, as well as my own inclinations, oblige me to be

Your affectionate Father,
ORRERY.

Notes

1. Cf. Swift's words on this matter: "Upon this Event Mr Swift moved to London, and applyed by Petition to King William, upon the claim of a Promise his Majesty had made to Sir William Temple that he would give Mr Swift a Prebend of Canterbury or Westminster." In Orrery's scribal transcript of *Family of Swift*, MA 455, manuscript page 14, Orrery Correspondence, Pierpont Morgan Library, New York City.

2. Cf. Swift's words on this point: "The Earl of Rumney who professed much friendship for him [Swift] promised to Second his Petition, but as he was an old vitious illiterate Rake without any sense of Truth or Honour, said not a word to the King." Ibid.

3. In *Family of Swift*, Swift used the same words: "And Mr Swift after long attendance in vain . . . " (ibid.)

4. The edition of Temple's letters in two volumes, edited by Swift, was advertised in the *Post Boy*, and the *Flying Post,* 3 June 1699, as well as in the *London Gazette*, 8 June 1699. They were being sold by 30 November 1699.

5. Charles, second earl of Berkeley (1649-1710). He had been an envoy extraordinary at the Hague (1689-94), where he had Matthew Prior for his secretary. When Swift took the "unattractive post" of Berkeley's private chaplain, the earl was fifty years old and suffered from the gout. See Ehrenpreis, *Swift* 1:261.

6. Berkeley received sudden instructions to leave for Ireland and assume his new office. He briefly visited his castle in Gloucestershire, and, in the meantime, Swift took leave of Moor Park and went to see his mother at Leicester. It is not known when Swift joined the group, but Ehrenpreis believes it was at "an early part in the expedition." The group reached Wales in August, and, after a two-week delay, moved on to Bristol. Sailing from Bristol, they landed at the south coast port of Waterford on 17 August 1699. After disembarking, Berkeley proceeded north to Kilkenny, where the group had a reception. Then the group went forth to Dublin. See ibid., 2:6.

7. Arthur Bushe, who held an office in the Irish customs. Some months before Berkeley's trip, Bushe had unsuccessfully tried to obtain the position of commissioner of the revenue. In order to get the appointment held by Swift, Bushe went to Dublin before the group arrived, and met them outside the city. Older and more experienced than Swift, Bushe ended up getting the job, although, as Ehrenpreis notes, "there is no sign that he measured himself against the young chaplain" (ibid., pp. 6-7).

8. Orrery is alluding to the following lines in Swift's poem *The Discovery*, which refer to Berkeley and Bushe:

> Imagine now My L-d and Bu-sh
> Whisp'ring in Junto most profound,
> (lines 21-22)
> Enrag'd to see the World abus'd
> By two such whisp'ring Kings of Branford.
> (lines 47-48)

See *Poems of Swift* 1:63-64.

9. Cf. Swift's words on this matter in *Family of Swift*: "And Mr Swift after long attendance in vain; thought it better to comply with an Invitation given him by the Earl of Berkeley to attend him to Ireland as His Chaplain and private Secretary; His Lordship having been appointed one of the Lords Justices of that Kingdom. He attended his Lordship, who landed near Waterford, and Mr Swift acted as Secretary the whole journey to Dublin. But another Person, had so far insinuated himself into the Earl's favour, by telling him, that the Post of Secretary was not proper for a Clergyman, nor would be of any advantage to one who aimed only at Church-preferments, that his Lordship after a poor Apology gave that office to the other." In Orrery's scribal transcript of *Family of Swift*, MA 455, manuscript pages 14-15, Orrery Correspondence, Pierpont Morgan Library, New York City.

10. *Poems of Swift* 1:61-64. There is a manuscript transcript, in the hand of one of Orrery's scribes, in MS Eng 218.2, III, pages numbered 112-14 (Williams mistakenly gives the volume's shelf-mark as MS Eng 218.14), Orrery Papers, Houghton Library, Harvard.

11. William III appointed three lords justices to govern Ireland, after Henry Sidney had been made earl of Romney and Capel had died in office. Berkeley was one of them. Galway was born Henri de Massue, a French expatriate who served the English army with some distinction. William III then gave him the title of earl of Galway and forty thousand acres of land in Ireland. He served as lord justice for two years, and later became lord justice of Ireland again for a short time (1715-16). The third lord justice was Edward Villiers, earl of Jersey, who actually just collected fees.

12. Swift got whatever was left of Dr. John Bolton's livings after Bolton accepted the bishopric of Derry and kept Ratoath. Swift kept those livings until his death. On 22 March 1700, by a patent dated 20 February 1700, Swift received the small rectory of Agher, the vicarage of Rathbeggan, and the large vicarage of Laracor. All of them were located "less than half a day's journey from Dublin," and Laracor and Agher adjoined one another, whereas Rathbeggan was at some miles' distance from them. After paying £117 on fees and curates in the first year, Swift enjoyed an income of £230 a year from those three parishes, collectively known as "Laracor." On 28 September 1700, he was collated to the Saint Patrick's prebend of Dunlavin, and was installed in Saint Patrick's Cathedral on 22 October 1700. See Ehrenpreis, *Swift* 2:12-15.

13. Swift claimed that the livings he then received were "not worth above a third part" of the coveted deanery of Derry, and "at this present time [sometime between 1727-1729], not a sixth." See Orrery's scribal transcript of

Family of Swift, MA 455, manuscript page 15, Orrery Correspondence, Pierpont Morgan Library, New York City.

14. Actually, Swift remained close to Dublin Castle and Berkeley's family. Swift became a close friend to the family, and, in particular, to Berkeley's second daughter, Elizabeth, later Lady Betty Germain (1680-1769). Lady Betty remained Swift's friend and correspondent in later years. Swift's poem *The Humble Petition of Frances Harris* dates from that period (early 1701). It was handed about in manuscript for nine years until it first appeared in print in 1709. Although the poem is not mentioned in the *Remarks*, Orrery wrote these words about it in the front free endpaper of volume 2 of his own copy of Faulkner's edition of Swift's works, used in preparation for the writing of the *Remarks*, now in the Mortimer Rare Book Room, Smith College: "I heard a dispute once in company, whether *Frances Harris*, were written all in the same manner. Some affirmed that every line contained the same number of beat, or syllables; others affirmed, the contrary. Upon trial the latter were in the right. O. Lord Bolingbroke particularly admired the Poem of *Frances Harris*, and used to call the Dean by that name."

15. Deane Swift repeats the story (*Essay*, pp. 116-17).

16. Jane Swift married Joseph Fenton in December 1699. Jane had been living with her uncle, William Swift, in Bride Street, Dublin, where Fenton apparently lived. See Ehrenpreis, *Swift* 2:17.

17. At that time, Jane was over thirty three years old, and could offer very little dowry (ibid.). Deane Swift says Jane was "of a middle size, finely shaped, and rather beyond what is called the agreeable throughout her whole person" (*Essay*, pp. 101-2). Deane Swift also mentions she was "at that time worth 300 l." and Deane Swift says Fenton was "an insolent, brutal fellow" who abused Swift after he had learned about Swift's opinion on the marriage (ibid., p. 349). Fenton is described by Harold Williams as "a worthless character" (Swift, *Journal to Stella* 1:101).

18. Fenton was either a tanner or a currier, and Deane Swift admits and justifies Swift's dislike of Fenton's profession (*Essay*, pp. 103-4). However, one should consider other aspects of Fenton's life that might have constituted the true reason for Swift's objection. Fenton had been married before, and had at least two children (Ehrenpreis, *Swift* 2:17), and Deane Swift mentions Fenton had a bad temper (*Essay*, p. 349). On 25 September 1711, Swift told Stella: "I pity poor Jenny [Jane, Swift's sister]–but her husband is a dunce, and with respect to him she loses little by her deafness" (Swift, *Journal to Stella* 1:368).

19. Swift was indeed unwilling to see Jane on some occasions (Swift, *Journal to Stella* 1:366, 2:532-33; Ehrenpreis, *Swift* 2:560). In a letter to Benjamin Motte dated 25 October 1735, Swift said he did not care "one Straw" what happened to his sister (*Correspondence of Swift* 4:411). But, as Ehrenpreis observes, it is wrong to think Swift ignored or neglected his sister after her marriage. Swift used his influence on her behalf (Swift, *Journal to Stella* 1:101-2), and he paid her a regular allowance of probably fifteen pounds since at least the time of her husband's death (Delany, *Observations*, p. 72; Ehrenpreis, *Swift* 2:18).

20. Actually, it seems that Mrs. Swift did not like Joseph Fenton at all. Writing to Stella on 1 January 1711, Swift mentioned his mother had left some money to Jane (and entrusted it to Swift) on condition that it was "not to come to her [Jane's] husband" (Swift, *Journal to Stella* 1:150).

21. Joseph Fenton seems to have died around 1720. Twelve years after her marriage, Jane went to Sheene to work for Lady Giffard, Temple's sister. Jane remained in Surrey after Lady Giffard's death, and died in Guildford in 1736. Swift put on mourning for her. See Ehrenpreis, *Swift* 2:18.

22. Swift's mother died on 24 April 1710, at about ten in the morning. Swift was notified of her death on 10 May. According to him, she had been "ill all winter, and lame, and extremely ill a month or six weeks before her death" (*Prose Works of Swift* 5:196).

23. Indeed, Swift's visits to his mother were frequent (for some instances, see Ehrenpreis, *Swift* 1:44, 107, 2:44, 112, 195, and 338).

24. According to Delany, Swift's "indecency" began with his visits to Pope in 1726. Delany's words are: "the defilement became much more conspicuous, upon his return from his first long visit to Mr. Pope: and that in all the time I had the honour to be known to him, antecedent to this era, his ideas, and his style throughout the whole course of his conversation, were remarkably delicate and pure; beyond those of most men I ever was acquainted with" (*Observations*, p. 75).

25. Coote Ormsby, dean of Derry ("one of the best endowed deanships in Ireland"), died in late January 1700. See Ehrenpreis, *Swift* 2:9.

26. William King (1650-1729), future archbishop of Dublin and Swift's friend.

27. Cf. Swift's words in *Family of Swift*: "The Excuse presented was his being too young, although he were then thirty years old." In Orrery's scribal transcript of *Family of Swift*, MA 455, manuscript page 15, Orrery Correspondence, Pierpont Morgan Library, New York City.

28. See *A Great Archbishop of Dublin, William King, D.D., 1650-1729*, ed. Sir Charles Simeon King (London: Longmans, Green, 1908), p. 35.

29. What actually happened is that, upon Dean Ormsby's death, King wrote to Narcissus Marsh (then Archbishop of Dublin), drawing up a list of five state chaplains who would suit him. Swift's name is not included in the list, which featured the names of three men later to be involved in dealings with Swift: Dr. John Bolton of Ratoath and Laracor; Dr. Edward Synge, vicar of Christ Church, Cork; and Dr. John Stearne, then rector of Trim. John Bolton, who was one of Berkeley's state chaplains, and had been in holy orders for twenty two years, was the preferred candidate. However, Bolton was reluctant to accept the remote deanery of Derry and give up his livings near Dublin. When Bolton refused the appointment, the lords justices offered the deanship to Edward Synge, who also turned it down, because his widowed mother did not want him to move from Cork. Upon Synge's refusal, Archbishop Marsh asked the lords justices to let Bolton keep the valuable living of Ratoath along with the deanship of Derry. This arrangement was agreed to, and Bolton accepted the enlarged conditions. See Ehrenpreis, *Swift* 2:10-11.

30. Thomas Lindsay, the Tory archbishop of Armagh, primate of Ireland, appointed to that office by Queen Anne. See ibid., pp. 717-18.

31. For Archbishop King's problems in trying to get the primacy, see Louis Landa, *Swift and the Church of Ireland* (Oxford: Clarendon Press, 1954), pp. 171-77.

32. Hugh Boulter (1672-1742), archbishop of Armagh (primate of Ireland), succeeding Thomas Lindsay. For his character, see Ehrenpreis, *Swift* 3:284-85, and 544-45.

33. Swift received his degree of doctor of divinity on 16 February 1702, at Trinity College, Dublin. Swift then paid £44 in "fees and treat" (ibid., 2:76).

34. Here, Orrery may be making a plug for the coming calendar reforms of 1752.

35. William III died on 8 March 1702. He had fallen from his horse on 21 February.

LETTER IV

UPON the death of King WILLIAM, and the accession of Queen ANNE, Dr. SWIFT came into *England.*[1] It cannot be denied, that the chief ministers of that Queen, whether distinguished under the titles of Whigs or Tories, of High Church or of Low Church, were, from the beginning to the end of her reign, encouragers of learning, and patrons of learned men. The wits and poets of that aera were numerous and eminent. Amidst the croud, yet shining above the rest, appeared Dr. SWIFT.

> *Ipse ante alios pulcherrimus omnes,*
> *Infert se socium Aeneas, atque agmina jungit.*[2]

It will be impossible, in mentioning the reign of this Princess, or in writing memoirs of Dr. SWIFT, to avoid the frequent use of those cant words Whig and Tory, *"two creatures,* says a modern author,[a] *who are born with a secret antipathy to each other, and engage as naturally when they meet, as the elephant and rhinoceros."*[3] In a mixture of these two jarring animals consisted the first ministry of Queen ANNE; but the greater share of the administration was committed to the Whigs, who, with indefatigable industry, soon engrossed the whole;[4] enclosing their Sovereign within their own fortifications, and keeping her captive within their own walls. The Queen, whose heart was naturally inclined towards the Tories,[5] remained an unwilling prisoner several years to the Whigs; till Mr. HARLEY,[6] with a Tory army, undermined all the whiggish fortresses, levelled their works to the ground, seized their[b] Princess, and during the remainder of her life, surrounded and defended her with a new set of troops under the command of the Duke of ORMOND.[7]

---

[a]Original footnote in the *Remarks*: "See the Spectator, No. 50."

[b]their] the FI, FIa, FIb, FII, FIII, FV, MI, MII

Dr. SWIFT was known to the great men of each denomination: and although he soon attached himself openly to the Tories, it is certain he had been bred up, and educated with Whigs; at least with such, who, in the Lexicon of Party, may be found ranged under that title. His motives for quitting the lower vallies of Whiggism for the higher regions of Torism appear throughout his works. The persons who had now signalized themselves as Whigs, had renounced those principles by which the old Whigs were denoted, and had embraced several of those tenets of which their forefathers had either a real, or a pretended, abhorrence. The effects of power and ambition are extraordinary and boundless, they blind our faculties, they stagger our resolution, and they subvert our nature. Not all the metamorphoses of OVID can produce a parallel equal to the change that appears in the same man, when from a Patriot he becomes a Courtier: yet it may be asserted, and will redound to the honour of Dr. SWIFT, that when he rose into the confidence and esteem of those great men, who sat at the helm of affairs during the last years of Queen ANNE's reign, he scarce ever lost himself, or grew giddy by the plenitude of power, and the exalted station of frequently appearing in the confidence, and favour of the reigning minister. He may have been carried away by inconsiderate passion; but he was not to be swayed by deliberate evil. He may have erred in judgment, but he was upright in intention. The welfare and prosperity of these kingdoms were the constant aim of his politics, and the immediate subject of his thoughts and writings. But, as HAMLET says, "Something too much of this."[8] Let us continue therefore to trace the footsteps of his life; in which scarce any circumstance can be found material from the year seventeen hundred and two, till the change of the ministry in the year seventeen hundred and ten.[9] During this interval, he had worked hard within those subterraneous passages, where, as has been hinted before, the mine was formed that blew up the whiggish ramparts, and opened a way for the Tories to the Queen. SWIFT was to the Tories, what CAESAR was to the Romans, at once a leader of their armies, and an historiographer of their triumphs. He resided very much in *England*:[10] his inclinations were always there. His intimacy with Lord OXFORD commenced, as far as may be deduced from his works, in *October* 1709.[11] In a poem written in the year 1713,[12] he says,

> *'Tis (let me see) three years and more*
> (October *next it will be four*)
> *Since* HARLEY *bid me first attend,*
> *And chose me for an humble friend.*[13]

And again in another poem written in the same year,[14]

> *My Lord would carry on the jest,*

> *And down to* Windsor *take his guest.*
> SWIFT *much admires the place and air,*
> *And longs to be a Canon there.*
> *A Canon! that's a place too mean,*
> *No, Doctor, you shall be a Dean.*[15]

By this last quotation, and by numberless other instances in his works, it seems undeniable that a settlement in *England* was the unvaried object of Dr. SWIFT's ambition: so that his promotion to a deanery in *Ireland*, was rather a disappointment than a reward.[16] In a letter to Mr. GAY, he says, *"The best and greatest part of my life, untill these last eight years, I spent in* England. *There I made my friendships, and there I left my desires. I am condemned for ever to another country:"*[c] [17] and in answer to a letter from Mr. POPE,[18] who had offered incense to him, as to a tutelar saint in a state of separation, he writes thus. *"You are an ill catholic, or a worse geographer; for I can assure you,* Ireland *is not paradise; and I appeal even to a Spanish divine, whether addresses were ever made to a friend in hell or purgatory?"*[d] [19] I shall cite no other quotations; but you will find in his letters many expressions to the same purport.

Among the various branches, into which SWIFT's expansive genius spread itself, those peculiar talents of levelling his writings to the lowest, and sustaining their dignity to the highest capacity, were probably the original motives that attracted the Earl of OXFORD's friendship to him.[20] In the year 1709, the character of Dr. SWIFT, as an author, was perfectly established:[21] he had shewn abilities equal to those attributed by HOMER to ULYSSES: he could appear a beggar among beggars, and a king among kings.[22]

From the year 1710, to the latest period of Queen ANNE, we find him fighting on the side of the ministers, and maintaining their cause in pamphlets, poems, and weekly papers.[23] In one of his letters to Mr. POPE he has this expression, *"I have conversed in some freedom with more ministers of state, of all parties, than usually happens to men of my level; and I confess, in their capacity as ministers, I look upon them as a race of people whose acquaintance*

---

[c]Original footnote in the *Remarks*: "Letter 5. Vol. 7." The letter's number refers to the numbering in volume 7 of Faulkner's edition of Swift's works (1746).

[d]Original footnote in the *Remarks*: "Letter 4. Vol. 7." The letter's number refers to the numbering in volume 7 of Faulkner's edition of Swift's works (1746).

no man would court otherwise than on the score of vanity, or ambition."[e] [24]
Lord OXFORD, as a gentleman, and a scholar, might be open and unreserved
to Dr. SWIFT, as far as his Lordship's nature would permit; but as a minister
of state he ever appeared mysterious and aenigmatical, delivering his oracles,
like the Delphian Deity, in occult terms and ambiguous expressions.[25]

A man always appears of more consequence to himself, than he is in reality
to any other person. Such perhaps was the case of Dr. SWIFT. He found
himself much indulged by the smiles, and conversation of the Earl of
OXFORD. He knew how useful he was to the administration in general: and
in one of his letters (I think the same which I have last quoted) he mentions,
that the place of historiographer was intended for him;[26] but I am apt to
suspect that he flattered himself too highly: at least it is very evident, that he
remained without any preferment till the year 1713, when he was made Dean
of St. *Patrick*'s.[27] In point of power and revenue, such a deanery might be
esteemed no inconsiderable promotion;[28] but to an ambitious mind, whose
perpetual aim was a settlement in *England*, a dignity in any other kingdom
must appear (as perhaps it was designed) only an honourable, and profitable
banishment.[29]

But, my HAMILTON, I will never hide the freedom of my sentiments from
you. I am much inclined to believe that the temper of my friend SWIFT might
occasion his *English* friends to wish him happily and properly promoted, at a
distance. His spirit, for I would give it the softest name, was ever untractable.
The notions[f] of his genius were often irregular. He assumed more the air of
a patron, than of a friend. He affected rather to dictate than advise. He was
elated with the appearance of enjoying ministerial confidence. He enjoyed the
shadow: the substance was detained from him. He was employed, not trusted;
and at the same time that he imagined himself a subtil diver, who dextrously
shot down into the profoundest regions of politics, he was suffered only to
sound the shallows nearest the shore, and was scarce admitted to descend
below the froth at the top. Perhaps the deeper bottoms were too muddy for
his inspection.[30]

By reflexions of this sort we may account for his disappointment in an
English bishoprick. A disappointment which, he imagined, he owed to a joint
application made against him to the Queen by Dr. SHARPE, Archbishop of

---

[e]Original footnote in the *Remarks*: "Letter 4. Vol. 7." The letter's number
refers to the numbering in volume 7 of Faulkner's edition of Swift's works
(1746). Actually, the reference to the letter's number in the footnote in the
Remarks is wrong: the letter alluded to is Letter 5 in volume 7 of Faulkner's
edition of Swift's works (1746).

[f]notions] motions FI, FIa, FIb, FII, FIII, FV, MI, MII

York,[31] and by a Lady of the highest rank and character.[32] Archbishop SHARPE, according to Dr. SWIFT's account, had represented him to the Queen, as a person who was not a Christian; the great Lady had supported the aspersion; and the Queen, upon such assurances, had given away the bishoprick, contrary to her Majesty's first intentions. SWIFT kept himself indeed within some tolerable bounds, when he spoke of the Queen: but his indignation knew no limits, when he mentioned the Archbishop, or the Lady.

Business and ceremony, (two commanders, that I hope you will list under much more willingly than I can) call me away from my letter, although nothing can ever call away my thoughts from you, or interrupt the tenderness with which I am, dear HAMILTON,

Your[g] *affectionate Father,*
ORRERY.

---

[g]Your] Your most MIV

Notes

1. William III's successor, Queen Anne, soon proved to be favorable to the Anglican establishment, by means of two measures: the creation of a fund from ecclesiastical fees to improve poor benefices, and the rising of John Sharp, the high-church archbishop of York, in the Crown's favor. Discerning the favorable moment for the clergy, Swift left Ireland in late April 1702. Swift stopped to see his mother at Leicester, and arrived in London in May 1702. See Downie, *Jonathan Swift, Political Writer*, pp. 73-75, and 80-85.

2. "Aeneas himself, goodly beyond all others, advances to join her [Dido] and unites his band with hers" (Virgil *Aeneid* 4.141-42).

3. *Spectator*, no. 50 (27 April 1711).

4. Downie writes thus on the subject: "Queen Anne's first ministry was a coalition of Tory and Country party elements, led by the Duke of Marlborough as Captain-General and Sidney, Lord Godolphin as Lord Treasurer. Whigs were largely excluded from the Cabinet and from high office." In *Jonathan Swift, Political Writer*, p. 80.

5. On 7 November 1710, Swift says he had seen Queen Anne walking "with all Tories about her; not one Whig" (Swift, *Journal to Stella* 1:84). On 18 February 1711, Swift mentions that the Queen had realized how much she had been "used" by the former Whig ministry (ibid., p. 195). But on 8 December 1711, the day after Parliament had rejected a peace without Spain, Swift expressed doubts about the sincerity of her attachment to the Tories (ibid., 2:433). Queen Anne was "reconciled" to the Tories on 29 December 1711, when she created twelve new lords of Tory principles (ibid., pp. 449-50). Two days later, she dismissed the duke of Marlborough from his employments, which completed the renewal of the Tories' confidence in her (ibid., p. 452).

6. Robert Harley, first earl of Oxford (1661-1724). Swift and Harley had first met each other on 4 October 1710, when Swift said that Harley received him "with the greatest respect and kindness imaginable" (ibid., 1:41). At that time, Harley had been chancellor of the exchequer since Lord Godolphin's dismissal as lord treasurer in August. He was created Lord Oxford and made Lord Treasurer on 29 May 1711.

7. James Butler, second duke of Ormond (1665-1745), Lord Lieutenant of Ireland (1703-07). He got the regiment of foot guards after Marlborough's dismissal in late 1711. He was also appointed general in Flanders and made efforts to end the war in the Continent.

8. *Hamlet*, 3.2.72.

9. Actually, during this period, Swift launched some of his major prose tracts such as *A Letter concerning the Sacramental Test, Argument Against Abolishing Christianity, Project for the Advancement of Religion*, and the Bickerstaff papers. Swift's poetic productions between 1703 and 1710 (*Poems of Swift* 1:78-127) include important pieces such as *Baucis and Philemon, A Description of the Morning*, and *A Description of a City Shower*.

10. From 1701 to 1709, these were the periods when Swift stayed in England: April-September 1701, April-October 1702, November 1703-May 1704, November 1707-June 1709. See Swift, *Account Books*, pp. 1-94.

11. Swift first met Harley on 4 October 1710 (Swift, *Journal to Stella* 1:41).

12. The reference is to *An Imitation of the Sixth Satire of the Second Book of Horace*, lines 1-132 by Swift and lines 133-221 by Pope. Swift's part was written in July 1714, and completed about 1 August. See *Poems of Swift* 1:197-98.

13. *An Imitation of the Sixth Satire of the Second Book of Horace*, lines 63-66. Orrery is following Faulkner's dating of about 1713, which causes the mistake in his dating the beginning of the "intimacy" between Swift and Harley.

14. Swift's *Part of the Seventh Epistle of the First Book of Horace Imitated: and Address'd to a Noble Peer*, published on 23 October 1713 in London by A. Dodd, quarto. The poem was written on Swift's return to England after being installed as dean of St. Patrick's (*Poems of Swift* 1:170).

15. Swift's *Part of the Seventh Epistle of the First Book of Horace Imitated: and Address'd to a Noble Peer*, lines 81-87.

16. Cf. Swift's remarks to Stella on 18 April 1713, the day when it was announced Swift was to be dean of St. Patrick's: "neither can I feel Joy at passing my days in Ireland: and I confess I thought the Ministry would not let me go; but perhaps they can't help it" (Swift, *Journal to Stella* 2:662).

17. Swift to Gay, 8 January 1723 (*Correspondence of Swift* 2:441-42).

18. Pope to Swift, 20 June 1716 (ibid., p. 211).

19. Swift to Pope, 30 August 1716 (ibid., p. 214).

20. For the reasons of the development of the Swift-Harley friendship, see Jonathan Swift, *Swift vs. Mainwaring: The Examiner and the Medley*, ed. Frank Ellis (Oxford: Clarendon Press, 1985), pp. xxvi-xxviii (cited hereafter as Swift, *The Examiner*).

21. Cf. these remarks by Harold Williams on Swift's fame around 1709: "It is therefore a mistake to imagine Swift as at this time a wholly unknown country clergyman from Dublin. He could count on the acquaintance of men of rank and position, and on their regard for his intellectual ability, and he had won a reputation on equal standing within the circle of the wits who graced the reign of Queen Anne" (Swift, *Journal to Stella* 1:xiv).

22. Homer *Odyssey* 13.464-470, 500-509.

23. See Swift, *The Examiner* pp. xxxi-xxxiii; and, David Woolley, "The Canon of Swift's Pamphleteering, 1710-1714, and *The New Way of Selling Places at Court*," *Swift Studies* 3 (1988): 96-117. See also David Woolley, "'The Author of the *Examiner*' and the Whiggish Answer-Jobbers of 1711-12," *Swift Studies* 5 (1990): 91-111.

24. Swift to Pope, 10 January 1721 (*Correspondence of Swift* 2:370).

25. Cf. Swift's words on Harley in *The Character of Robert Harley*: "However, it must be allowed, that an obstinate love of Secrecy in this Minister, seems at distance to have some Resemblance of Cunning; for he is not onely very retentive of Secrets, but *appears* to be so too; which I number among his Defects. He hath been blamed by his Friends for refusing to discover his Intentions, even in those Points where the wisest man may have need of advice and assistance: and some have censured him upon that account, as if he were jealous of Power; to which he hath been heard to answer, that he seldom did otherwise without cause to repent" (*Prose Works of Swift* 7:179).

26. Swift to Pope, 10 January 1721 (*Correspondence of Swift* 2:367).

27. Swift tells Stella of a complaint he made about his lack of preferment on 13 April 1713: "At noon, Lord Treasurer [Oxford] hearing I was in Mr. Lewis' [Erasmus Lewis, Oxford's secretary] office, came to me, and said many things too long to repeat. I told him I had nothing to do but go to Ireland immediately; for I could not, with any reputation, stay longer here, unless I had something honourable immediately given to me" (Swift, *Journal to Stella* 2:660). Five days later, Swift was made dean of Saint Patrick's.

28. Actually, Swift had some expenses when installed dean: £800 for his house, £150 for first-fruits, and the expense of the patent itself, which made Swift's total expenditure amount to £1,000. See Ehrenpreis, *Swift* 2:667, 675-77, and 3:3-6. See also Delany, *Observations*, pp. 200-201, and 207-209; and, Louis Landa, "Swift's Deanery Income: A New Document," in *Pope and His Contemporaries: Essays Presented to George Sherburn*, ed. James L. Clifford and Louis A. Landa (Oxford: Clarendon Press, 1949), pp. 159-70.

29. On 30 April 1713, Swift referred to his appointment as "a banishment": "I am condemned to live again in Ireland, and all that the Court and Ministry did for me, was to let me chuse my station in the country where I am banished" (*Correspondence of Swift* 1:345-46).

30. The question of Swift's true influence with the Tory ministry of 1710 has always been a controversial one. David Woolley and J. A. Downie offered the first important pieces of evidence in favor of Swift's involvement with the ministry's affairs. From the Harley papers in the British Library, Woolley and Downie could authenticate the fact that Swift had seen Queen Anne's speech of 9 April 1713, and corrected it. Woolley and Downie also disclosed evidence of Swift's involvement in the composition of the queen's speech of 2 March 1714. See J. A. Downie and David Woolley, "Swift, Oxford, and the Composition of the Queen's Speeches, 1710-1714," *British Library Journal* 8 (1982): 121-46. Also, Downie has revealed the manuscript of a bill sent by John Barber (the London printer of the *Examiner*) to Oxford, mentioning Oxford's purchase of one hundred copies of numbers 5 to 50 of the *Examiner*, which cover Swift's contributions. More importantly, the bill's last article has a note referring "the truth of it" to Swift. Downie's conclusion is that there is enough evidence "to accept that he [Swift] bore considerable responsibility for the production and distribution of ministerial propaganda from 1711 onwards." See J. A. Downie, "Swift and the Oxford Ministry: New Evidence," *Swift Studies* 1 (1986): 2-8.

31. John Sharp (1645-1714), archbishop of York since 1691, who had been dean of Canterbury in 1689. In his *Political and Literary Anecdotes* (pp. 60-61), William King, principal of St. Mary Hall, says Bolingbroke did not believe Sharp worked against Swift's promotion, claiming it was Oxford's invention to make Swift content with the deanery of St. Patrick's. Ehrenpreis doubts Bolingbroke's claim, believing it just reflects Bolingbroke's "old hatred of Oxford" (*Swift* 2:632). On 23 April 1713, after the Queen had signed the warrant for Swift's appointment as dean of St. Patrick's, Swift told Stella that Sharp, his "mortal enemy," wished to see him (Swift, *Journal to Stella* 2:665). On 26 April Swift mentioned Sharp said he would never more speak against Swift (ibid., p. 667). Swift called Sharp "a crazy prelate" in line 2 of *The*

Author upon Himself (*Poems of Swift* 1:193), and mentioned him in lines 47-52 of the poem:

> *York* is from Lambeth sent, to shew the Queen
> A dang'rous Treatise writ against the Spleen;
> Which by the Style, the Matter, and the Drift,
> 'Tis thought could be the Work of none but S——
> Poor *York*! the harmless Tool of others Hate;
> He sues for Pardon, and repents too late.

(ibid., p. 195).

32.   Elizabeth Percy (1667-1722), daughter of the fifth earl of Northumberland, and friend of Lady Giffard, Temple's sister. On 30 May 1682, Elizabeth married the sixth duke of Somerset, thus becoming duchess of Somerset. When Lady Giffard accused Swift of publishing *Memoirs Part III* without her authorization, the duchess took Lady Giffard's side, saying Swift was "a man of no principle either of honour or religion" (Ehrenpreis, *Swift* 2:340-41). On 23 December 1711, Swift said he had written his verse attack on the duchess, *The Windsor Prophecy*, which was printed the next day (Swift, *Journal to Stella* 2:444). On the twenty sixth, Lady Masham advised Swift not to publish it (ibid., p. 446), and Swift said it was only "given about," a claim he repeated on 4 January (ibid., p. 454). In spite of Swift's claims, the poem was published on 24 December. See *Poems of Swift* 1:145-48.

LETTER V

MOST people, my dear HAM, are fond of a settlement in their native country: but Dr. SWIFT had little reason to rejoice in the land where his lot had fallen: for, upon his arrival in *Ireland* to take possession of the deanery,[1] he found the violence of party raging in that kingdom to the highest degree.[2] The common people were taught to look upon him as a Jacobite; and they proceeded so far in their detestation, as to throw stones and dirt at him as he passed through the streets.[3] The chapter of St. *Patrick*'s, like the rest of the kingdom, received him with great reluctance. They thwarted him in every point that he proposed. He was avoided as a pestilence. He was opposed as an invader. He was marked out as an enemy to his country. Such was his first reception as Dean of St. *Patrick*'s.[4] Fewer talents, and less firmness, must have yielded to so outragious an opposition, *sed contra audentior ibat.*[5] He had seen enough of human nature, to be convinced, that the passions of low, self-interested minds, ebb and flow continually. They love they know not whom, they hate they know not why: they are captivated by words: guided by names: and governed by accidents. SACHEVERELL[6] *and the Church* had been of as great service to one party in the year 1710, as *Popery and Slavery* were to the other in the year 1713.[7] But, to shew you the strange revolutions in this world, Dr. SWIFT, who was now the detestation of the *Irish* rabble, lived to be afterwards the most absolute monarch over them that ever governed men.

His first step was to reduce to reason and obedience his reverend brethren the chapter of St. *Patrick*'s: in which he succeeded so perfectly, and so speedily, that in a short time after his arrival, not one member of that body offered to contradict him, even in trifles.[8] On the contrary, they held him in the highest respect and veneration; so that he sat in the Chapter-house, like JUPITER in the Synod of the Gods. Whether fear or conviction were the motives of so immediate a change, I leave you to consider, but certain it is

Viro Phoebi chorus assurrexerit omnis[9]

SWIFT made no longer a stay in *Ireland*, in the year 1713, than was requisite to establish himself as Dean, and to pass through certain customs and formalities,[10] or to use his own words,

> *Through all vexations,*
> *Patents, Instalments, Abjurations,*
> *First Fruits, and Tenths, and Chapter-Treats,*
> *Dues, Payments, Fees, Demands, and-Cheats.*[11]

During the time of these ceremonies he kept a constant correspondence with his friends in *England:*[12] all of whom were eminent, either in birth, station, or abilities. Among these, let me begin with the name of Mr. POPE. The world has already seen a long series of their correspondence: but a remarkable letter of Mr. POPE's having been lately communicated to me, and bearing date at the latter end of the year 1713, as I cannot part with the original, I will send you a very faithful copy of it.[13] I should first say, that it is in answer to one from SWIFT, wherein he had jocosely made an offer to his friend of a sum of money, *ex causâ religionis,*[14] or, in plain english, to induce Mr. POPE to change his religion.[15] The wit of the letter itself will excuse all further[a] commentaries.

Binfield, *December*[b] 8, 1713.

SIR,

NOT to trouble you at present with a recital of all my obligations to you, I shall only mention two things, which I take particularly kind of you: your desire that I should write to you, and your proposal of giving me twenty guineas to change my religion, which last you must give me leave to make the subject of this letter.

Sure no clergyman ever offered so much out of his own purse for the sake of any religion. 'Tis almost as many pieces of gold, as an Apostle could get of silver from the priests of old, on a much more valuable consideration.[16] *I believe it will be better worth my while to propose a change of my faith by subscription, than a translation of* HOMER. *And to convince you, how well disposed I am to the reformation, I shall be content, if you can prevail with my Lord Treasurer, and the ministry, to rise to the same sum, each of them, on this pious account, as my Lord* HALLIFAX *has done on the profane one.*[17] *I am afraid there's no being at once a poet and a good Christian, and I am very much straitened between two, while the Whigs seem willing to contribute as much, to continue me the one, as you would, to make me the other. But, if you can*

---

[a]further MV] farther MIII

[b]*December*] Dec. MIV

move every man in the government, who has above ten thousand pounds a year, to subscribe as much as yourself, I shall become a convert, as most men do, when the LORD turns[18] it to my interest. I know they have the truth of religion so much at heart, that they'd certainly give more to have one good subject translated from popery to the church of England, than twenty heathenish authors out of any unknown tongue into ours. I therefore commission you, Mr. DEAN, with full authority, to transact this affair in my name, and to propose as follows. First, that as to the head of our church, the Pope, I may engage to renounce his power, whensoever I shall receive any particular indulgences from the head of your church, the Queen.

As to communion in one kind, I shall also promise to change it for communion in both, as soon as the ministry will allow me.[19]

For invocations to saints, mine shall be turned to dedications to sinners, when I shall find the great ones of this world as willing to do me any good, as I believe those of the other are.

You see I shall not be obstinate in the main points; but there is one article I must reserve, and which you seemed not unwilling to allow me, prayer for the dead. There are people to whose souls I wish as well as to my own; and I must crave leave humbly to lay before them, that though the subscriptions abovementioned will suffice for myself, there are necessary perquisites and additions, which I must demand on the score of this charitable article. It is also to be considered, that the greater part of those, whose souls I am most concerned for, were unfortunately heretics, schismatics, poets, painters, or persons of such lives and manners, as few or no churches are willing to save. The expence will therefore be the greater to make an effectual provision for the said souls.

Old DRYDEN, though a Roman Catholic, was a poet; and 'tis revealed in the visions of some ancient saints, that no poet was ever saved under some hundred of masses. I cannot set his delivery from purgatory at less than fifty pounds sterling.

WALSH[20] was not only a Socinian,[21] but (what you'll own is harder to be saved) a Whig. He cannot modestly be rated at less than an hundred.

L'ESTRANGE,[22] being a Tory, we compute him but at twenty pounds, which I hope no friend of the party can deny to give, to keep him from damning in the next life, considering they never gave him sixpence to keep him from starving in this.[23]

All this together amounts to one hundred and seventy pounds.

In the next place, I must desire you to represent, that there are several of my friends yet living, whom I design, GOD willing, to outlive, in consideration of legacies; out of which it is a doctrine in the reformed church, that not a farthing shall be allowed to save their souls who gave them.

There is one **** who will dye within these few months, with ******* one[24] Mr. JERVAS,[25] who hath grievously offended in making the likeness of *almost all things in heaven above and earth below; and one Mr.* GAY, *an unhappy youth, who writes pastorals during the time of divine service, whose case is the more deplorable, as he hath miserably lavished away all that silver he should have reserved for his soul's health, in buttons and loops for his coat.*[26]

I can't pretend to have these people honestly saved under some hundred pounds, whether you consider the difficulty of such a work, or the extreme love and tenderness I bear them, which will infallibly make me push this charity as far as I am able. There is but one more whose salvation I insist[c] *upon, and then I have done: but indeed it may prove of so much greater charge than all the rest, that I will only lay the case before you and the ministry, and leave*[d] *to their prudence and generosity, what sum they shall think fit to bestow upon it.*

The person I mean, is Dr. SWIFT; *a dignified clergyman, but one, who, by his own confession, has composed more libels than sermons. If it be true, what I have heard often affirmed by innocent people, That too much wit is dangerous to salvation, this unfortunate gentleman must certainly be damned to all eternity. But, I hope his long experience in the world, and frequent conversation with great men, will cause him (as it has some others) to have less and less wit every day. Be it as it will, I should not think my own soul deserved to be saved, if I did not endeavour to save his; for I have all the obligations in nature to him. He has brought me into better company than I cared for, made me merrier when I was sick than I had a mind to be, and put me upon making poems on purpose, that he might alter them &c.*

I once thought I could never have discharged my debt to his kindness, but have lately been informed, to my unspeakable comfort, that I have more than paid it all. For, MONSIEUR DE MONTAGNE *has assured me, "that the person who receives a benefit obliges the giver:"*[27] *for since the chief endeavour of one friend is to do good to the other, he who administers both the matter and occasion, is the man who is liberal. At this rate it is impossible Dr.* SWIFT *should be ever out of my debt, as matters stand already: and, for the future, he may expect daily more obligations from*

his most faithful, affectionate
humble servant
A. POPE.

I have finished the Rape of the Lock,[28] *but I believe I may stay here till* Christmas, *without hindrance of business.*

---

[c]insist] assist MIV

[d]Orrery's correction in Osborn pc 231: "lay" to "leave."

In the beginning of the year 1714, SWIFT returned to *England*.[29] He found his *great* friends, who sat in the seat of power, much disunited among themselves.[30] He saw the Queen declining in her health, and distressed in her situation:[31] while faction was exerting itself, and gathering new strength every day. The part which he had to act upon this occasion, was not so difficult, as it was disagreeable. He exerted the utmost of his skill to reunite the ministers,[32] and to cement the apertures of the state. I could descend into very minute particulars, were I to tell you what I have heard him say upon this occasion: but, my dearest HAM, let me speak to you with my usual sincerity. We are at present too near that aera, and have had too many unexpected consequences from it, either to judge impartially, or to write undauntedly, of those tempestuous times. Be contented if I tell you, that as soon as SWIFT found his pains fruitless, his arguments unavailing,[33] and his endeavours, like the stone of SISYPHUS,[34] rolling back upon himself, he retired to a friend's house in *Berkshire*,[35] where he remained till the Queen died.[36] So fatal a catastrophe put a final period to all his views in *England*, and made him return, as fast as possible, to his deanery in *Ireland*, loaded with those agonizing passions, grief and discontent. I am sorry to leave him in so uneasy a situation, but I must hasten to subscribe myself,

Your affectionate Father
ORRERY.

Notes

1. Swift arrived in Dublin on Wednesday, 10 June 1713, at 9 P.M., and was installed dean of Saint Patrick's on the thirteenth (Ehrenpreis, *Swift* 2:666).

2. Writing from Trim on 16 July 1713, Swift says all in Dublin are "Party-mad" (*Correspondence of Swift* 1:376).

3. Harold Williams referred to these words by Orrery and wrote: "There is little reason to accept this story. His [Swift's] health was poor, he was little abroad, and within two weeks he left for Laracor" (ibid., p. 372).

4. According to Delany, Swift's reception in Ireland in June 1713 was "as kind, and honourable as he could wish." Delany also says Swift was "remarkably caressed, and received with very distinguished respect, wherever he came" (*Observations*, pp. 87-88).

5. "But go forth to face them more boldly" (Virgil *Aeneid* 6.95).

6. The slogan "Sacheverell and the Church" is related to some incidents with Henry Sacheverell (ca. 1674-1724), clergyman of St. Saviour's Church, Southwark. On 5 November 1709, Sacheverell preached a sermon entitled "The perils of false brethren" at St. Paul's, and the sermon was published on 25 November 1709. The printer was examined by a parliamentary committee, and Sacheverell was tried from 27 February to 23 March 1710. On 7 March Sacheverell made his defense in Westminster Hall, stating that the prosecutors were trying to tell the clergy "what doctrines they are to preach or not." Sacheverell also accused his prosecutors of twisting the meaning of passages in his sermon in order to incriminate him, and declared he supported the Hanoverian succession, pleading nonguilty. On 23 March, Sacheverell was found guilty of treason, but his sentence was actually only a prohibition from preaching for three years. Those who supported Sacheverell then used the slogan "Sacheverell and the Church," and the Whig administration appeared to the public opinion as "anti-Church." See F. F. Madan, *A Critical Bibliography of Dr. Henry Sacheverell*, ed. W. A. Speck, University of Kansas Publications Library Series, no. 43 (Lawrence: University of Kansas Press, 1978), pp. 17-100.

7. In his *A Preface to the Bishop of Sarum's Introduction to the Third Volume of the History of the Reformation of the Church of England*, Swift refers to the Whig politicians' campaign of "Popery and Slavery," as exemplified by the *Introduction* of Gilbert Burnet, the Whig bishop of Salisbury: "He [Burnet] then goes on describing the condition of the Kingdom after such a manner as if Destruction hung over us by a single Hair; as if the *Pope*, the *Devil*, the *Pretender*, and *France*, were just at our Doors" (*Prose Works of Swift* 4:61). In the *Examiner*, no. 40, Swift refutes the Whigs' claim that the Tory ministry was working for the pretender and for the restoration of Catholicism, and he ironically argues that the victory of the pretender and of "Popery" would be more likely under a Whig administration (Swift, *The Examiner*, pp. 399-407).

8. Louis Landa referred to this passage, as well as to Orrery's account of Swift's first reception as dean, as "gross exaggeration." In Landa, *Swift and the Church of Ireland*, p. 74.

9. "All the choir of Phoebus rose to do him honour" (Virgil *Eclogues* 6.66).

10. Swift stayed in Ireland from Wednesday, 10 June, to Saturday, 29 August 1713. See Swift, *Account Books*, pp. 156-59. However, the formalities and official visits to Swift lasted only for fifteen days after Swift's installation on 13 June. Swift then went away to Laracor on Thursday, 25 June (ibid., p. 156).

11. Swift, *Part of the Seventh Epistle of the First Book of Horace Imitated: and Address'd to a Noble Peer*, lines 101-4.

12. Actually, there are no recorded letters from or to Swift during the fifteen days between his installation and departure to Laracor. Between the time of Swift's trip to Laracor (25 June 1713) and 29 August 1713 (when Swift left for England), Swift's correspondents were: Joshua Dawson (undersecretary at Dublin Castle), Vanessa, Erasmus Lewis (Oxford's secretary), Charles Ford, Archbishop William King, Bishop Atterbury, Matthew Prior, Thomas Walls (archdeacon of Achonry), and the earl of Dartmouth. See *Correspondence of Swift* 1:367-86.

13. There is a manuscript transcript of this letter, in the hand of one of Orrery's scribes, in MS Eng 218.2, III, pages numbered 123-29, Orrery Papers, Houghton Library, Harvard. The transcript is headed "Mr Pope to Dr Swift, in Answer to a Letter from the D^r persuading Mr Pope to change his Religion." In the margin of the letter's heading at the Houghton volume, someone wrote down "copied." The *Remarks* is the earliest published source of this letter's text, but, as George Sherburn observes, the Houghton transcript offers a better text. In Alexander Pope, *The Correspondence of Alexander Pope*, ed. George Sherburn, 5 vols. (Oxford: Clarendon Press, 1956), 1:198-99. Both Sherburn and Williams print the letter's text from Orrery's transcript at the Houghton Library (ibid., pp. 198-201; *Correspondence of Swift* 1:412-15).

14. "For the sake of religion."

15. Swift's letter to Pope in which Swift made Pope an offer of twenty guineas to change his religion has not survived.

16. An ironic allusion to Judas Iscariot's betrayal of Christ and the amount he received for it, thirty pieces of silver. The amount is specified only in Matt. 26:15.

17. Halifax had subscribed for ten sets of Pope's *Iliad*, at six guineas per set.

18. Orrery's transcript in MS Eng 218.2, III, page numbered 124, Orrery Papers, Houghton Library, Harvard, reads "when the Lords turn."

19. Orrery's transcript adds some words to this paragraph, thus: "As to Communion in one Kind, I shall also promise to change it for Communion in both, as soon as the Ministry will allow me wherewithal to eat, and to drink" (ibid., page numbered 125).

20. William Walsh (1663-1708), critic and poet, for whom see *Dictionary of National Biography*, s.v. "Walsh, William."

21. Someone who belonged to a sect founded by two Italian theologians of the sixteenth century named Laelius and Faustus Socinus who denied the divinity of Christ. In Pope's day, Socinianism was quite relevant, considered by the church to be a growing threat to orthodox Christianity.

22. Sir Roger L'Estrange (1616-1704), Tory journalist, for whom see *Dictionary of National Biography*, s.v. "L'Estrange, Sir Roger."

23. In the article about L'Estrange in the *Dictionary of National Biography*, we read that these words by Pope do not "seem wholly justifiable." But the author of the article admits L'Estrange "had to depend for his livelihood mainly on his pen, and the hackwork that he did for the booksellers as a translator only brought him a precarious income." See ibid.

24. Orrery's transcript omits the asterisks, thus: "There is One, who will dye within these few Months, with one Mr. Jervas, . . ." (MS Eng 218.2, III, page numbered 127, Orrery Papers, Houghton Library, Harvard).

25. Charles Jervas (or Jarvis), ca. 1675-1739, Irish painter and friend of Swift, Pope, Arbuthnot, Addison, and others, for whom see *Dictionary of National Biography*, s.v. "Jervas or Jarvis, Charles."

26. Cf. these lines in Gay, *The Shepherd's Week* (published in April 1714), in the prologue addressed to Bolingbroke:

> I sold my sheep and lambkins too,
> For silver loops and garment blue.

27. Montaigne, *Essays*, "Of Friendship," 1:27.

28. The enlarged version, in five cantos, published on 4 March 1714.

29. Swift actually arrived in England on Monday, 31 August 1713, and reached London on 9 September. See Swift, *Account Books*, pp. 159-60. As Swift himself describes it, he was recalled to England "by a hundred letters" asking him to use his endeavors to reconcile Oxford and Bolingbroke (*Correspondence of Swift* 5:45).

30. Swift himself describes the situation he found when he arrived in England, as well as his efforts to reunite Oxford and Bolingbroke: "When I returned to England, I found their Quarrels and Coldness increased; I laboured to

reconcile them as much as I was able; I contrived to bring them to my Lord Masham's, at St. James's. My Lord and Lady Masham left us together. I expostulated with them both, but could not find any good Consequences. I was to go to Windsor next day with my Ld. Treasurer; I pretended Business that prevented me; and so I sent them to Windsor next day, which was Saturday, in the same coach: expecting they would come to some éclaircissement, But I followed them to Windsor; where my Lord Bolingbroke told me (for I followed them) that my scheme had come to nothing. Things went on at the same Rate, They grew more estranged every day" (Swift to the second earl of Oxford, 14 June 1737, (ibid., pp. 45-46).

31. On the night of 23 December 1713, Queen Anne had a violent ague, from which she recovered a few days later. Still, concerns about her health and the succession increased. See Ehrenpreis, *Swift* 2:698.

32. In early 1714, Swift was often at court, while Oxford and Bolingbroke were secretly trying to convince the pretender to turn Protestant and thus ascend to England's throne. Seeing that the ministry was rapidly collapsing, Swift still remained at court only for the sake of the disposal of four bishoprics in Ireland. No agreement was ever reached between the two ministers, although Swift even managed to have Oxford and Bolingbroke by themselves in the same coach on a four-hour trip to Windsor. See ibid., pp. 728-29.

33. Cf. Swift's words in *Enquiry into the Behavior of the Queen's Last Ministry*: "And two Nights after sitting with Him [Oxford] and Lord Bolingbroke in Lady Masham's Lodgings at St. James's for some Hours, I told the Treasurer, that having despaired of any Reconciliation between them, I had only stayed some time longer to forward the Disposal of those Bishopricks in Ireland, which since His Lordship told me was out of his Power, I now resolved to retire immediately, as from an Evil I could neither help to redress nor endure the Sight of." In Jonathan Swift, *An Enquiry into the Behavior of the Queen's Last Ministry*, ed. Irvin Ehrenpreis (Bloomington: Indiana University Press, 1956), pp. 55-56.

34. The legendary founder of Corinth, doomed to roll a huge rock up a hill. As soon as it reached the summit, it rolled down the slope and Sisyphus had to roll it up again.

35. Swift left London on Monday, 31 May 1714, and arrived in Oxford on that same day. Swift stayed in Oxford three days, leaving on Thursday, 3 June. Swift then went on to the house of John Geree (1672-1761), Swift's friend from the time of Moor Park. Geree was a graduate of Corpus Christi

College, Oxford, and had obtained the rectory of Letcombe Bassett, a small village in Berkshire, where he also had a school. In the quiet of that rural area, and in the company of the "sober, taciturn" Geree, Swift could "plan to sort out his accumulated papers, write a few things he had in mind, keep clear of exasperations, and finally proceed to Ireland rested and in good health" (Ehrenpreis, *Swift* 2:730).

36. Queen Anne died in the morning of Sunday, 1 August 1714. Swift left Letcombe Bassett on 16 August, riding to Chester and then to Holyhead. Swift arrived in Dublin on 24 August. He was to see England again twelve years later.

LETTER VI

WE are now, dear HAMILTON, no longer to behold Dr. SWIFT of any importance in *England*: his hopes there are crushed for ever: his ministerial friends are degraded, banished, or imprisoned.[1] Indecent rage, sanguinary zeal, and ill-tempered loyalty revelled at large throughout the three kingdoms, especially in *Ireland*,[2] where duels were fought almost every week, and where the pest was so universal, that the ladies were as violent as the gentlemen. Even children at school quarrelled for Kings, instead of fighting for apples.

As SWIFT was known to have been attached to the Queen's last ministry, to have written against the Whigs, and "*to*[a] *have oiled many a spring which* HARLEY *moved*,"[3] he met with frequent indignities from the populace, and indeed was equally abused by persons of all ranks and denominations.[4] Such a treatment soured his temper, confined his acquaintance, and added bitterness to his style: and, since the future part of his life and writings is to differ, in all circumstances, so widely from the past, since his studies and companions, his politics and his customs, are now to be altered and exchanged for new habits, new friends, new ambition, and a new world, suffer me, my HAM, to take a general review of him as an author.

If we consider his prose works, we shall find a certain masterly conciseness in their style, that has never been equalled by any other writer. The truth of this assertion will more evidently appear by comparing him with some of the authors of his own time. Of these Dr. TILLOTSON,[5] and Mr. ADDISON, are to be numbered among the most eminent. ADDISON has all the powers that can captivate and improve: his diction is easy, his periods are well turned, his expressions are flowing, and his humour is delicate. TILLOTSON is nervous, grave, majestic, and perspicuous.[6] We must join both these characters together to form a true idea of Dr. SWIFT: yet as he outdoes ADDISON in humour, he excels TILLOTSON in perspicuity. The Archbishop indeed confined himself to subjects relative to his profession:[7] but ADDISON and

---

[a]"*to*] italics om. MIV

SWIFT are more diffusive writers. They continually vary in their manner, and treat different topics in a different style. When the writings of ADDISON terminate in party, he loses himself extremely, and from a delicate, and just comedian, deviates into one of the lowest kind.[b] Not so Dr. SWIFT; he appears like a masterly gladiator. He wields the sword of party with ease, justness and dexterity: and while he entertains the ignorant and the vulgar, he draws an equal attention from the learned and the great. When he is serious, his gravity becomes him. When he laughs, his readers must laugh with him. But, what shall be said for his love of trifles, and his want of delicacy and decorum? Errors, that if he did not contract, at least he encreased in *Ireland*. They are without a parallel. I hope they will ever remain so. The first of them arose meerly from his love of flattery, with which he was daily fed in that kingdom: the second proceeded from the misanthropy of his disposition, which induced him peevishly to debase mankind, and even to ridicule human nature itself. Politics were his favourite topic, as they gave him an opportunity of gratifying his ambition, and thirst of power: yet even in[c] this road, he seldom[d] continued long in one particular path.[e] He has written miscellaneously, and has chosen rather to appear a wandering comet, than a fixed star. Had he applied the faculties of his mind to one great, and useful work, he must have shined more gloriously, and might have enlightened a whole planetary system in the political world.

The poetical performances of Dr. SWIFT ought to be considered as occasional poems written[f] either to please, or vex some particular persons.[8] We must not suppose them designed for posterity: if he had cultivated his genius in that way, he must certainly have excelled, especially in satir. We see fine sketches, in several of his pieces: but he seems more desirous to inform, and strengthen his mind, than to indulge the luxuriancy of his imagination. He chooses to discover, and correct errors in the works of others, rather than to illustrate, and add beauties to his own. Like a skilful artist, he is fond of probing wounds to their depth, and of enlarging them to open view. He prefers caustics, which erode proud flesh, to softer balsamics, which give more

---

[b]Original footnote in the *Remarks*: "See the papers entitled the Freeholder."

[c]yet even in] yet in FI, FIa, FIb, FII

[d]he seldom] he has seldom FI, FIa, FIb, FII, MI, MII

[e]one particular path.] one path. FI, FIa, FIb, FII, FIII, FV

[f]written] framed FI, FIa, FIb, FII

immediate ease. He aims to be severely useful, rather than politely engaging: and as he was either not informed,[g] or would not take pains to excel in poetry, he became, in some measure, superior to it; and assumed more the air and manners of a critic, than of a poet. Had he lived in the same age with HORACE, he would have approached nearer to him, than any other poet: and if we may make an allowance for the different course of study, and different form of government, to which each of these great men was[h] subject, we may observe, in several instances, a strong resemblance between them.[9] Both poets are equally distinguished for wit and humour. Each displays a peculiar felicity in diction: but of the two, HORACE is the more elegant and delicate: while he condemns, he pleases. SWIFT takes pleasure in giving pain: the dissimilitude of their tempers might be owing to the different turns in their fortune. SWIFT early formed large views of ambition, and was disappointed. HORACE, from an exiled low state[10] rose into affluence, and enjoyed the favour and friendship of AUGUSTUS.[11] Each poet was the delight of the principal persons of his age. *Cum magnis vixisse*[12] was not more applicable to HORACE, than to SWIFT. They both were temperate: both were frugal; and both were of the same Epicurean taste, HORACE had his LYDIA,[13] SWIFT had his VANESSA. HORACE had his MAECENAS[14] and his AGRIPPA.[15] SWIFT had his OXFORD, and his BOLINGBROKE. HORACE had his VIRGIL, SWIFT had his POPE.

After the great names, which I have just now mentioned, it is matter of astonishment to find the same person, who had enjoyed the highest, and the best conversation, equally delighted with the lowest and the worst: and yet it is certain, from[i] SWIFT's settlement in *Dublin* as Dean of St. *Patrick's*, his choice of companions in general,[j] shewed him of a very depraved taste.[16]

From the year seventeen hundred and fourteen, till he appeared in the year twenty a champion for *Ireland* against WOOD's halfpence,[17] his spirit of politics, and of patriotism, was kept almost closely confined within his own breast. Idleness and trifles engrossed too many of his hours: fools and sycophants too much of his conversation. However, let me observe to you, that the treatment which he received, after the death of Queen ANN, was almost a sufficient reason to justify a contempt, if not an abhorrence, of the human race. He had bravely withstood all hostile indignities, during the life

---

[g]informed MV] formed MIII

[h]was MV] were MIII

[i]certain, from] certain, that from FI, FIa, FIb, FII

[j]Orrery's correction in Osborn pc 231: "in general" to "in general,"

time of that Princess; but when the whole army of his friends were not only routed, but taken prisoners, he dropt his sword, and retired into his fortification at *Dublin*, from whence he seldom stirred beyond the limits of his own garden, unless in great indulgence to some particular favourites.

His attendance upon the public service of the church was regular and uninterrupted: and indeed regularity was peculiar to him in all his actions, even in the greatest trifles. His hours of walking, and reading, never varied: His motions were guided by his watch, which was so constantly held in his hand, or placed before him upon his table, that he seldom deviated many minutes, in the daily revolution of his exercises and employments. His works, from the year 1714, to the year 1720, are few in number, and of small importance. Poems to STELLA, and trifles to Dr. SHERIDAN,[18] fill up a great part of that period.

In the year 1720, he began to re-assume, in some degree, the character of a political writer. A small pamphlet *in defence of the Irish manufactures*, was, I believe, his first essay (in *Ireland*) in that kind of writing:[19] and to that pamphlet, he owed the turn of the popular tide in his favour.[k] His sayings of wit and humour had been handed about, and repeated from time to time among the people. They had the effect of an artful preface, and had pre-engaged all readers in his favour. They were adapted to the understanding, and pleased the imagination of the vulgar: and he was now looked upon in a new light, and distinguished by the title of THE DEAN.

The flux and reflux of popular love and hatred are equally violent. They are often owing to accidents, but sometimes to the return of reason, which, unassisted by education, may not be able to guide the lower class of people, into the right track[l] at the beginning, but will be sufficient to keep them in it, when experience has pointed out the road. The pamphlet, proposing the universal use of *Irish* manufactures *within the kingdom*, had captivated all hearts.[20] *Some little pieces of poetry to the same purpose* were no less acceptable and engaging. The attachment which the Dean bore to the true interest of *Ireland*, was no longer doubted. His patriotism was as manifest as his wit. He was looked upon with pleasure and respect, as he passed through the streets: and he had attained so high a degree of popularity, as to become an arbitrator in the disputes of property among his neighbours: nor did any man dare to appeal from his opinion, or to murmur at his decrees.

But the popular affection, which the Dean had hitherto acquired, may be said not to have been universal, till the publication of the DRAPIER's *letters*,[21] which made all ranks, and all professions unanimous in his

---

[k]Original footnote in the *Remarks*: "See Letter 16th."

[l]track] tract FI, FIa, FIb, FII, FIII, FV, MI, MII

applause. The occasion of those letters was a scarcity of copper coin in *Ireland*,[22] to so great a degree, that for some time past the chief manufacturers throughout the kingdom were obliged to pay their workmen in pieces of tin, or in other tokens of supposititious value. Such a method was very disadvantageous to the lower parts of traffic, and was in general an impediment to the commerce of the state. To remedy this evil, the late King granted a patent to WILLIAM WOOD,[23] to coin, during the term of fourteen years, farthings and halfpence in *England* for the use of *Ireland*, to the value of a certain sum specified.[24] These halfpence and farthings were to be received by those persons, who would voluntarily accept them.[25] But the patent was thought to be of[m] such dangerous consequence to the public, and of such exorbitant advantage to the patentee, that the DEAN, under the character of M.B. DRAPIER, wrote a letter to the people, warning them not to accept WOOD's halfpence and farthings as current coin. This first letter was succeeded by several others to the same purpose, all which are inserted in his works.

At the sound of the DRAPIER's trumpet, a spirit arose among the people, that, in the eastern phrase, was *like unto a tempest in the day of the whirlwind*.[26] Every person of every rank, party, and denomination, was convinced, that the admission of WOOD's copper must prove fatal to the commonwealth. The Papist, the Fanatic, the Tory, the Whig, all listed themselves volunteers under the banner of M.B. DRAPIER, and were all equally zealous to serve the common cause.[27] Much heat, and many fiery speeches against the administration, were the consequence of this union: nor had the flames been allayed, notwithstanding threats and proclamations,[28] had not the coin been totally suppressed, and had not WOOD withdrawn his patent.[29]

This is the most succinct account that can be given of an affair, which alarmed the whole *Irish* nation to a degree that in a less loyal kingdom must have fomented a rebellion: but the stedfast loyalty of the *Irish*, and their true devotion to the present royal family is immoveable: and although this unfortunate nation may not hitherto have found many distinguishing marks of favour and indulgence from the throne; yet it is to be hoped, in time they may meet with their reward.

The name of AUGUSTUS was not bestowed upon OCTAVIUS CÆSAR with more universal approbation, than the name of THE DRAPIER was bestowed upon THE DEAN. He had no sooner assumed his new *cognomen*, than he became the idol of the people of *Ireland* to a degree of devotion, that in the most superstitious country scarce any idol ever obtained.[30] Libations to his health, or, in plain english, bumpers were poured forth to the DRAPIER as

---

[m]thought to be of] thought of FI, FIa, FIb, FII, FIII, FV

large and as *frequent* as *to the*[n] *glorious and immortal memory of K.*[o] WILLIAM *the third.* His effigies was[p] painted in every street in *Dublin.* Acclamations and vows for his prosperity attended his footsteps wherever he passed. He was consulted in all points relating to domestic policy in general, and to the trade of *Ireland* in particular: but he was more immediately looked upon as the legislator of the weavers,[31] who frequently came in a body, consisting of fifty or sixty chieftains of their trade, to receive his advice, in settling the rates of their manufactures, and the wages of their journeymen. He received their addresses with less majesty than sternness, and ranging his subjects in a circle round his parlour, spoke as copiously, and with as little difficulty and hesitation, to the several points in which they supplicated his assistance, as if trade had been the only study and employment of his life. When elections were depending for the city of *Dublin,* many corporations refused to declare themselves, till they had consulted his sentiments and inclinations, which were punctually followed with equal chearfulness and submission. In this state of power, and popular love and admiration, he remained till he lost his senses: a loss which he seemed to foresee, and prophetically lamented to many of his friends.[q]

I have now conducted the Dean through the most interesting circumstances of his life to the fatal period, wherein he was utterly deprived of reason. If your curiosity leads you to enquire into the particulars of that misfortune, it must be the subject of some future letter: for, at present, I think it is time to indulge myself in assuring you, that I am with an inexpressible warmth of heart, my dear HAMILTON,

Your most affectionate Father
ORRERY.

---

[n]*to the*] italics om. FI, FIa, FIb, FII, FIII, FV, MI

[o]*K.*] *King* FI, FIa, FIb, FII, FIII, FV

[p]was] were FI, FIa, FIb, FII

[q]Original footnote in the *Remarks*: "See Letter XXI."

Notes

1. Oxford was removed from office on Tuesday, 27 July 1714, and upon the proclamation of George I, Oxford and Bolingbroke were insulted by the mob in London (*Correspondence of Swift* 2:102-3). After Queen Anne's death, Oxford remained in London, hoping to get a place in the new king's councils, which did not happen. A Parliament mostly made up of Whigs met in March 1715. On 9-10 June 1715, the report of the Committee of Secrecy (chaired by Robert Walpole), on treason by Tory leaders, was read in the House of Commons, and Oxford, Bolingbroke, Ormond and Strafford were impeached. Bolingbroke had already fled to France on 27 March 1715, but Oxford, who had remained in the country, was confined in the Tower on 9 July. Bolingbroke had been dismissed from office on 31 August 1714. Ormond fled to France on 20 July, and joined Bolingbroke there.

2. The Irish Parliament of George I first met on Saturday, 12 November 1715, and appointed the Duke of Grafton and Lord Galway as lords justices, as well as William Conolly as Speaker. Suspected Jacobites and active Tories were arrested and mistreated. See Ehrenpreis, *Swift* 3:20-21.

3. Swift, *The Author upon Himself*, line 40.

4. One such instance is the incident between Swift and the seventh Lord Blayney (1693-1733), an Irish peer. In the winter of 1715-16, Swift was returning to Dublin, after a ride to Howth, with two mounted servants. A chaise then began to race up to Swift from behind, without passing him. Swift finally got over to the side of a ditch, and reproached the men in the chaise. One of them was Blayney, who supposedly threatened to shoot with his pistol. After the incident, Swift sent a petition to the Irish House of Lords, protesting against Blayney's conduct and asking for protection. See Ehrenpreis, *Swift* 3:21-22; and *Prose Works of Swift* 5:199-200 and xxiv.

5. John Tillotson (1630-94), archbishop of Canterbury, for whom see *Dictionary of National Biography*, s.v. "Tillotson, John."

6. Tillotson was "the only primate who took first rank in his day as a preacher, and he thoroughly believed in the religious efficacy of the pulpit" (ibid.).

7. Besides his sermons, Tillotson had written discourses on religious subjects, most notably *The Rule of Faith*.

8. Williams wrote about the value of Swift's poetic productions, "undeservedly overshadowed" (*Poems of Swift* 1:xiii-xvii). The first book-length study of Swift's poetry was Maurice Johnson, *The Sin of Wit: Jonathan Swift as a Poet* (Syracuse, N. Y.: Syracuse University Press, 1950).

9. Caroline Goad wrote that Orrery, while pointing to the external likeness depending upon circumstances and opportunities, does not perceive "the deep, underlying dissimilarity in the genius" of Swift and Horace. In Caroline Goad, *Horace in the English Literature of the Eighteenth-Century* (New Haven: Yale University Press, 1918), p. 482.

10. Horace's father had been a slave and a foreigner, possibly Greek. See Horace *Satires* 1.6.45-46. In that same Satire, Horace mentions his father had been a tax collector (89-97).

11. Horace's last poems are all dedicated to Augustus: the fourth book of *Odes*, the *Saecular Hymn*, and the second book of *Epistles*.

12. "To have lived with great persons."

13. For Horace's addresses to Lydia, see *Odes* 1.8, and 1.13.

14. Horace's Satires were written at Maecenas's instigation, and the following works by Horace are directly addressed to Maecenas: *Odes* 1.1 and 20; *Odes* 2.12 and 17; *Odes* 3.29; *Odes* 4.11; *Epodes* 14; and *Epistles* 1.1, 7, and 19.

15. Horace addressed *Odes* 1.6 to Agrippa.

16. Delany answered this passage (*Observations*, pp. 90-99), mentioning the virtues of some of Swift's Irish friends, including the Grattans and John Worrall (d. 1751), dean's vicar and vicar choral of St. Patrick's.

17. An error, since the controversy about Wood's halfpence did not begin until after 12 July 1722, when Wood's patent was issued. See Jonathan Swift, *The Drapier's Letters to the People of Ireland*, ed. Herbert Davis (Oxford: Clarendon Press, 1935), pp. xxiii and lxix-lxxi (cited hereafter as Swift, *The Drapier's Letters*).

18. For the trifles exchanged between Swift and Sheridan, see *Poems of Swift* 3:965-1052.

19. *A Proposal for the Universal Use of Irish Manufactures* was published shortly before 28 May 1720. Swift's earliest tract specifically dedicated to Irish affairs had been *The Story of the Injured Lady* (probably written in 1707), and Swift might have added some words to it in 1720. See *Prose Works of Swift* 9:ix-xi.

20. There were some contemporary reactions to *A Proposal for the Universal Use of Irish Manufactures*. Already in 1720, there appeared a tract entitled *An Answer to the Proposal for the Universal Use of Irish Manufactures*. In that same year, it appeared again with the title *A Defence of English Commodities* (Dublin printed, London reprinted: J. Roberts, 1720). There was also a piece entitled *A Letter to the Reverend Dr. Swift Dean of St. Patrick's Dublin; Relating to the present State of the Manufactures of Ireland* (Dublin: C. Carter, 1721), by Roger Kendrick, who would be made verger of St. Patrick's on 5 May 1732. See Oliver Ferguson, *Jonathan Swift and Ireland* (Urbana: University of Illinois Press, 1962), p. 59.

21. For accounts of *The Drapier's Letters*, see: Swift, *The Drapier's Letters*, pp. ix-xcv; and Ehrenpreis, *Swift* 3:187-318.

22. There was indeed a shortage of small change in Ireland, but silver was more urgently needed than copper. Swift stated that £10,000 worth of halfpence would be enough to remedy the shortage. See Ehrenpreis, *Swift* 3:188-92; and Swift, *The Drapier's Letters*, p. xi.

23. William Wood (1671-1730), an ironmaster from Woolverhampton, Staffordshire, for whom see *Dictionary of National Biography*, s.v. "Wood, William"; and J. M. Treadwell, "William Wood and the Company of Ironmasters of Great Britain," *Business History* 16 (1974): 97-112.

24. The indenture between Wood and the Crown gave Wood "full, free, sole, and absolute power, privilege, license, and authority" to coin 360 tons of copper halfpence and farthings for fourteen years, thus: "100 tons only were to be coined in the first year, and twenty tons in each of the last thirteen." The indenture further specified: "one avoirdupois pound weight of copper should not be converted into more farthings and halfpence than would make thirty pence by tale; all the said farthings and halfpence to be of equal weight in themselves, or as near thereunto as might be, allowing a remedy not exceeding two farthings over or under in each pound." At the rate of 30*d.* to the pound weight of pure copper, the total value of currency to be issued by Wood amounted to £100,800. Also, Wood could lower that rate (already lower than the English one) even further, as well as coining for as long as he liked, since the patent did not provide specific penalties regarding the time

period. See Ehrenpreis, *Swift* 3:192-93.

25. The indenture's words are: "to pass and to be received as current money, by such as shall or will, voluntarily and willingly, and not otherwise, receive the same, within the said kingdom of Ireland and not elsewhere." No one could be forced to take Wood's money because, by law, only gold and silver could be legal tender. As Ehrenpreis observes, the consequence was that "if the people could be made to refuse the money, they would defeat the whole scheme" (ibid., p. 194).

26. Amos 1:14.

27. Ehrenpreis observes that, by the winter of 1723-24, all Irish leaders "now stood like a Roman square against Wood's patent" (Ehrenpreis, *Swift* 3:207).

28. For the text of the Proclamation against the Drapier of 27 October 1724, see Swift, *The Drapier's Letters*, pp. 265-66.

29. On 16 December 1724, Lord Carteret, then lord lieutenant of Ireland, suggested the dropping of the patent and the payment of a compensation to William Wood (ibid., p. lvi). Wood agreed to surrender his patent for a pension of £24,000 for eight years. On 19 August 1725, the lords justices of England wrote to Carteret, notifying the surrender.

30. In mid-April 1725, leading citizens of Dublin put forward a motion to confer the city's freedom on Swift. Their first attempt to pass the motion was unsuccessful, due to the influence of John Rogerson, the recorder of Dublin, who had presented the indictment against Swift's *Seasonable Advice*. But, in their second attempt, Rogerson was absent, and the motion passed. In Ehrenpreis's words, "Swift was now installed as a father of his country; and the health, opinions, and activities of the dean began to receive public comment as matters of great interest" (*Swift* 3:298).

31. Cf. Ehrenpreis's words: "Because Ireland had ample supplies of excellent raw wool, and because the Dean of St. Patrick's knew at first hand the plight of his neighbours the weavers, Swift gave special attention to woollen manufactures. The weavers knew of his concern and would often ask him to advise them." (ibid., 2:614).

LETTER VII

My dear HAMILTON,

YOU seem not only desirous, but impatient, that I should pass critically through[a] all the works of my friend SWIFT. Your request is unreasonable if you imagine, that I must say something upon every individual performance. There are many[b] pieces that I despise, others that I loath, and others again that delight[c] and improve me.[d] These[e] last shall be discussed particularly. The former are not worthy of your notice. They are of no farther use than to shew us, in general, the errors of human nature; and to convince us, that neither the height of wit, nor genius, can bring a man to such a degree of perfection, as vanity would often prompt him to believe.

In a disquisition of the sort which you require, I shall avoid as much as possible any annotations upon that kind of satir, in which the Dean indulged himself against particular persons: most of whom it is probable had provoked[f] his rage by their own misconduct, and consequently owed to their own rashness the wounds which they received from his pen: but I have no delight in those kind of writings, except for the sake of the wit, which, either in general, or in particular satir, is equally to be admired. The edge of wit will

---

[a]through MV] thorough MIII

[b]many] some FI, FIa, FIb, FII, MI

[c]and others again that delight] but many more that delight FI, FIa, FIb, FII, MI; and others that delight FIII, FV, MII

[d]me.] me again. MII

[e]These] and these FI, FIa, FIb, FII, MI; again these FIII, FV

[f]probable had provoked] probable provoked FI, FIa, FIb, FII, MI, MII

always remain keen, and its blade will be bright and shining, when the stone, upon wh:ch it has been whetted, is worn out, or thrown aside and forgotten. Personal satir against evil magistrates, corrupt ministers, and those giants of power, who gorge themselves with the entrails of their country, is different from that personal satir, which too often proceeds merely from self-love, or ill-nature: the one is written in defence of the public; the other in defence of ourselves. The one is armed by the sword of justice, and encouraged not only by the voice of the people, but by the principles of morality: the other is dictated by passion, supported by pride, and applauded by flattery. At the same time that I say this, I think every man of wit has a right to laugh at fools, who give offence, or at coxcombs, who are public nusances. SWIFT indeed has left no weapon of sarcasm untried, no branch of satir uncultivated: but while he has maintained a perpetual war against the mighty men in power, he has remained invulnerable, if not victorious.

Upon a review of the Dean's writings, it cannot be sufficiently lamented, that there is no just, or perfect edition of his works. FAULKNER's edition,[1] at least the four first volumes of it (for there are now eight)[2] were published, by the permission and connivance, if not by the particular appointment of the Dean himself.[3] But the several pieces are thrown together without any order or regularity whatever: so that like the ancient chaos which contained an immense collection of various treasures, they remain in their state of confusion *rudis indigestaque moles:*[4] and yet the incoherency of situation is perhaps one of the most excusable faults in the collection: for the materials are of so different, and so incongruous a nature, that it seems as if the author, (who was in reality the editor,) imagined the public under an absolute necessity of accepting the basest coin from the same hand, that had exhibited the purest. Surely the idle amusements of a man's private and domestic life, are not to be sent forth as sufficient entertainments for the witty or the learned. Posthumous works indeed are often worthless and improper, from the ill judged zeal of ignorant executors, or imprudent friends: but, a living author remains without excuse, who either wilfully, or wantonly imposes upon the world.

The English edition of SWIFT's works I have scarce seen;[5] and I have had little inclination to examine it, because I was acquainted with the Dean, at the time when FAULKNER's edition came out, and therefore must always look upon that copy as most authentic; well knowing that Mr. FAULKNER had the advantage of printing his edition, by the consent and approbation of the author himself. The four first volumes were published by subscription, and every sheet of them was brought to the Dean for his revisal and correction. The two next were published in the same manner. The seventh volume was printed from a number of surreptitious letters published in *England:*[6] and the eighth volume did not come out till after the Dean's death.[7] In the publication of the six first volumes, the situation and arrangement of each particular piece, in verse and prose, was left entirely to the editor. In that point, the Dean either could not, or would not give him the least assistance. The dates were often guessed at, and every scrap was thrust into the parcel that might augment the collection. Such a conduct has been productive of a confusion that offends the eye, and misleads the understanding. We have less pleasure in looking at a palace built at different times, and put together by ignorant workmen, than in viewing a plain regular building composed by a masterly hand in all the beauty of symmetry and order. The materials of the former may be more valuable, but the simplicity of the latter is more acceptable. For health and exercise who would not chuse rather to walk upon a platform than in a labyrinth? or, who does not wish to see an edition of SWIFT's works becoming the genius, and dignity of the author? When such an edition is undertaken, I should hope that all the *minutiae* of his idle hours might be entirely excluded; or at least placed, like out[g] buildings, at a distance from the chief edifices of state.

SWIFT was naturally fond of seeing his works in print, and he was encouraged in this fondness by his friend Dr. SHERIDAN,[8] who had the *cacoethes scribendi*[9] to the greatest degree, and was continually letting off squibs, rockets, and all sorts of little fireworks from the press, by which means he offended many particular persons, who, although they stood in awe of SWIFT, held SHERIDAN at defiance.[10] The truth is, the poor Doctor, by nature the most peaceable, inoffensive man alive,[11] was in a continual state of warfare with the minor poets,[12] and they revenged themselves, or, in the style of Mr. BAYS,[13] often gave him *flash for flash*, and *singed his feathers*. The affection between THESEUS and PIRITHOUS[14] was not greater than the affection between SWIFT and SHERIDAN: but the friendship that cemented the two ancient heroes probably commenced upon motives very different from those which united the two modern divines.[15] As in a former letter, I drew a picture of SWIFT's wife,[h] let me here give you some sketches of SWIFT's friend.[16]

Dr. SHERIDAN was a schoolmaster, and, in many instances, perfectly well adapted for that station.[17] He was deeply versed in the Greek and Roman languages;[18] and in their customs and antiquities. He had that kind of good-nature, which absence of mind, indolence of body, and carelessness of fortune

---

[g]Orrery's correction in Osborn pc 231: "out" to "detached." This correction was never made in any of the editions of the *Remarks*.

[h]Original footnote in the *Remarks*: "Letter II. page 14." in MII, MIII, and MV. "Letter II. page 22." in FI, FIa, FIb, FII, FIII, FV, MI, and MIV. The page numbers refer to the location of the section alluded to by Orrery in the different editions.

produce; and although not over strict in his own conduct, yet he took care of the morality of his scholars, whom he sent to the University remarkably well founded[i] in all classical learning,[19] and not ill instructed in the social duties of life. He was slovenly, indigent, and chearful. He knew books much better than men: and he knew the value of money least of all.[20] In this situation, and with this disposition, SWIFT fastened upon him, as upon a prey with which he intended to regale himself, whenever his appetite should prompt him. SHERIDAN therefore was kept constantly within his reach: and the only time he was permitted to go beyond the limits of his chain, was to take possession of a living in the county of *Corke*, which had been bestowed upon him by the then Lord Lieutenant of *Ireland*, the present Earl of *Granville*.[21] SHERIDAN, in one fatal moment, or by one fatal text, effected his own ruin.[22] You will find the story told by SWIFT himself, in the fourth volume of his works:[j] [23] so that here I need only tell you, that this ill-starred, good-natured, improvident man returned to *Dublin*, unhinged from all favour at court, and even banished from the castle.[24] But still he remained a punster, a quibbler, a fiddler, and a wit. Not a day passed without a rebus, an anagram, or a madrigal. His pen and his fiddle-stick were in continual motion; and yet to little or no purpose, if we may give credit to the following verses,[25] which shall serve as the conclusion of his poetical character,

> With music and poetry equally bless'd
> A bard thus APOLLO most humbly address'd,
> Great author of poetry, music, and light,
> Instructed by thee I both fiddle and write:
> Yet unheeded I scrape, or I scribble all day,
> My tunes are neglected, my verse flung away.
> Thy substitute here VICE-APOLLO[k] disdains
> To vouch for my numbers, or list to my strains.
> Thy manual sign he refuses to put
> To the airs I produce from the pen, or the gut.
> Be thou then propitious, great PHOEBUS, and grant
> Relief; or reward to my merit, or want.

---

[i]founded] grounded FI

[j]Original footnote in the *Remarks*: "Page 289. In a pamphlet entitled, A Vindication of his Excellency JOHN Lord CARTERET from the charge of favouring none but Tories, High Churchmen, and Jacobites." "Page 289" refers to the page number in Faulkner's volume 4.

[k]Original footnote in the *Remarks*: "Dr. SWIFT."

Tho' the DEAN and DELANY[l] transcendently shine,
O! brighten one solo, or sonnet of mine.
Make one work immortal; 'tis all I request;
APOLLO look'd pleas'd, and resolving to jest
Replied, honest friend, I've consider'd your case,
Nor dislike your unmeaning and innocent face.
Your petition I grant, the boon is not great,
Your works shall continue, and here's the receipt,
On *Roundos*[m] hereafter your fiddle-strings spend,
Write verses in circles; they never shall end.

In the course of my correspondence, my dear HAM, you may possibly observe some seeming contradictions, as I am pursuing the Dean through the mazy turnings of his character. But, they will easily be reconciled, when you consider, that, of all mankind, SWIFT perhaps had the greatest contrasts in his temper. He often put me in mind of that wild opinion, which PLUTARCH says was entertained by the sages of old, "That we are subject to the influence of two principles, or deities, who are in constant opposition to each other: the one directing us to the right hand, and through the right road, the other driving us astray, and opposing us from pursuing the track[n] pointed out by his adversary."[26] The Manichean heresy, you know, was[o] built upon this hypothesis:[27] and it is not impossible (as the doctrine itself was propagated before the time of MANES)[28] that some antient speculative philosopher may have invented such a kind of mythology, merely to solve the various contradictions which he found fluctuating within his own breast.

You will possibly expect from me a collection of apophthegms, which the Dean may have uttered upon various occasions. But, the witty records of table-talk in my mind seem too minute and over curious; at least I must wish to treat with you upon subjects of more importance. I mean such subjects as will teach you to follow some moral virtue, or to shun some moral evil.

---

[l]Original footnote in the *Remarks*: "Now Dean of *Downe*." Delany was appointed dean of Down in 1744.

[m]Original footnote in the *Remarks*: "A song, or peculiar kind of poetry, which returns to the beginning of the first verse, and so continues in a perpetual rotation."

[n]track] tract FI, FIa, FIb, FII, FIII, FV, MI

[o]was] has been FI, FIa, FIb, FII, MI, MII

Forgive me too, if I am now and then guilty of repetitions. In reviewing the same person so often, the same thoughts, if not the same expressions, will inevitably occur. But, excuses for this kind of errors, are, I hope, unnecessary. Candour and truth are the chief points that I have had in view, knowing them to be coincident with your own manner of thinking.

You are now sufficiently prepared for that particular edition of SWIFT's works, which I intend to pursue: and I shall undertake the performance with great pleasure and alacrity; because I flatter myself it may be acceptable to you, as it comes from

your most affectionate Father
ORRERY.

Notes

1. For an account of the history of Faulkner's edition of Swift's works, see Ehrenpreis, *Swift* 3:779-90.

2. Volumes 1, 3, and 4 of Faulkner's edition were ready on 26 November 1734. Volume 2 came out only on 6 January 1735. Volumes 5 and 6 were published sometime between April and August 1738. In 1741, a volume of *Letters* was published without the identification "volume 7" on the title page. In 1746, this volume of *Letters* was provided with a new title and called volume 7. Volume 8 appeared in 1746. See Teerink, *A Bibliography of the Writings of Jonathan Swift*, pp. 22-24, and 47.

3. On this subject, Ehrenpreis observed: "Systematic collations have shown that Swift did not in fact supervise the edition as carefully as Faulkner claims. But they also show that the corrections made were due either to Swift directly or to his instructions, which Faulkner followed only too thoroughly. Certainly, Faulkner made extraordinary efforts to gather together manuscript copies of Swift's unpublished works held by various persons in Ireland and England; and the delay in the appearance of the volumes was due in part to this desire for completeness. As the bookseller put it, he collected 'as many original pieces as were possible to be got of the supposed author's from his friends in England, which we found great difficulty in procuring'. The notes, on the other hand, often sound like the immediate work of Swift rather than Faulkner's composition" (Ehrenpreis, *Swift* 3:784).

4. "A rough, unordered mass of things" (Ovid *Metamorphoses* 1.7).

5. An edition of Swift's works was published in London in 1751. See Teerink, *A Bibliography of the Writings of Jonathan Swift*, p. 78.

6. For the complicated dealings regarding the printing and publication of the Swift-Pope correspondence, see: Maynard Mack, "The First Printing of the Letters of Pope and Swift," *Library* 19 (March 1939): 465-85; Vinton A. Dearing, "New Light on the First Printing of the Letters of Pope and Swift," *Library* 24 (June, September 1943): 74-80; and, A. C. Elias, Jr., "The Pope-Swift *Letters* (1740-41): Notes on the First State of the First Impression," *Papers of the Bibliographical Society of America* 69 (1975): 323-43.

7. As mentioned before, volume 8 came out in 1746.

8. For an account of Sheridan's life, see Jonathan Swift and Thomas Sheridan, *The Intelligencer*, ed. James Woolley (Oxford: Clarendon Press, 1992), pp. 6-16 (cited hereafter as Swift, *The Intelligencer*).

9. "The itch for writing" (Juvenal *Satires* 7.52).

10. Cf. James Woolley's words on the subject: "Yet Sheridan thrived on controversy; hardly anything he wrote failed to elicit a reply or rejoinder, not even his grammar, his Persius, or his sermon on St. Cecilia's day. We have a lampoon against him, 'Upon Mr. Sheridan's turning Author, 1716', though we have nothing he wrote in 1716" (Swift, *The Intelligencer*, pp. 17-18).

11. In *The History of the Second Solomon*, Swift says Sheridan "has no ill-design upon any person but himself, and he is the greatest deceiver of himself on all occasions" (*Prose Works of Swift* 5:223).

12. James Woolley calls Sheridan "an incessant versifier" (Swift, *The Intelligencer*, p. 17).

13. See *The Rehearsal*, by George Villiers, second duke of Buckingham (1628-87), first printed in 1672.

14. Orrery is referring to the legendary friendship between Theseus, an Attic hero, and Pirithous, a hero of the Lapiths (a Thessalian people).

15. See James Woolley, "Thomas Sheridan and Swift," *Studies in Eighteenth-Century Culture* 9 (1979): 93-114.

16. Orrery was acquainted with Sheridan. See Thomas Sheridan, *The Poems of Thomas Sheridan*, ed. Robert Hogan (Newark: University of Delaware Press, 1994), pp. 409-10.

17. See Swift's praise of Sheridan's performance as a schoolmaster, Sheridan's "chief shining quality" (*Prose Works of Swift* 5:216).

18. As early as 1714, Sheridan had published a Latin grammar, and its preface, as James Woolley points out, indicates he had been teaching for some time (Swift, *The Intelligencer*, p. 8). Swift observes Sheridan was "a great master of the Greek and Roman languages" (*Prose Works of Swift* 5:216).

19. Cf. James Woolley's words: "A conventional measure of Sheridan's success as a teacher is the number of students he enrolled in Trinity College. During the ten-year period 1718-29, he was conspicuously the college's greatest source of new students. In one year (1720-1), thirty-six schoolmasters sent eighty-six new students; Sheridan alone was responsible for fifteen of them. A 1725 class list preserved in one of his notebooks shows, when compared with *Alumni Dublinenses*, that twenty out of the twenty-four boys in his top three classes entered TCD—a very high proportion" (Swift, *The Intelligencer*, p. 9).

20. See Swift's narrative of Sheridan's financial blunders in *Prose Works of Swift* 5:223-24. See also Woolley's words about Sheridan's income (Swift, *The Intelligencer*, p. 11).

21. John, Lord Carteret.

22. On 1 August 1725, the anniversary of the Hanoverian Succession, Sheridan preached a sermon on the verse "Sufficient unto the day is the evil thereof" (from Matt. 6:34). See Swift, *The Intelligencer*, pp. 11-12; and *Prose Works of Swift* 12:162-64.

23. That is, Faulkner's volume 4.

24. After the incident on 1 August 1725, Lord Carteret removed Sheridan from the list of his domestic chaplains and forbade Sheridan the Castle, although Carteret could not remove Sheridan from the living to which he had been instituted. Archdeacon Russell then gave Sheridan a lease of the manor of Drumlane, worth £250 per year. See Swift, *The Intelligencer*, p. 12.

25. *On Dr. Sheridan's Circular Verses*, by George Rochfort (ca. 1682-1730), Irish M.P. The poem was printed by Williams in *Poems of Swift* 3:1027-28. Delany says Orrery printed "an imperfect copy" of the poem (*Observations*, p. 108), and indeed, Orrery omitted lines 15-16, which are given by Delany:

With them, I'm content, thou should'st make thy abode:

> But visit thy servant, in jig, or in ode.
>
> (ibid., p. 109)

Williams printed the full version of the poem, including the lines omitted by Orrery (*Poems of Swift* 3:1028).

26. In Plutarch *Moralia*, "Isis and Osiris," 5.369-71.

27. Manichaeism, a Christian heresy, teaches the duality of two uncreated principles, Light-Darkness or Good-Evil.

28. The belief in dualism, or two primeval powers active in the universe, had been stated by Zoroaster, who lived sometime between 1000 and 600 B.C. Manes, or Mani, the founder of Manichaeism, lived A.D. 216-76.

LETTER VIII

I Was very glad to be interrupted, by your unexpected visit. The sight of you, and the happiness which I constantly receive in your company, are recollected by me in your absence, with such a kind of inexpressible pleasure, as the warmest affection and the truest tenderness inspire: and as I am always earnest to comply with your requests, I take the earliest opportunity of going on with a plan, that hitherto has received the encouragement of your filial partiality.

The first volume of FAULKNER's edition consists of various tracts jumbled together, without any regularity or order. The first treatise in this volume is intitled, *A discourse of the contests and dissensions between the nobles and commons in* Athens *and* Rome.[1] It was written in the year 1701,[2] towards the latter end of King WILLIAM's reign, and at a time, when that Prince was made extremely uneasy, by the violence with which some of his ministers, and chief favourites were pursued.[3] However bright the crown of *England* might have glittered in the eyes of the Prince of *Orange*, he found it, when placed upon his head, a crown of thorns. The longer he wore the diadem, the bandelet still became more tight and irksome. Complaints, and enquiries arose in the senate. Feuds, and unchristian animosities, in the convocation. Nor had foreign affairs a more propitious aspect. LEWIS the fourteenth was making large strides towards universal monarchy. Plots were carrying on at St. GERMAIN's. The *Dutch* had acknowledged the Duke of ANJOU as King of SPAIN: and EUROPE in general seemed pregnant of fire, and ready to burst into flames.[4] Thus began the year 1701. King WILLIAM in hopes to dispel this sulphureous body of clouds, which seemed to threaten some future thunder of extraordinary violence, had made several changes in his ministry, and had removed some of his faithfullest servants from places of the highest trust and dignity.[5] The alteration proved of little or no effect. The animosity of the house of commons could not be appeased. They looked upon the loss[a]

---

[a]loss] deprivation FI, FIa, FIb, FII, MI, MII

143

of lucrative employments, as an insufficient punishment for high crimes and misdemeanours: and they began first by impeaching the Earl of PORTLAND;[b][6] and then proceeded to the impeachments of Lord SOMERS,[c][7] the Earl of ORFORD,[d] and the Earl of HALLIFAX.[e][8]

These were all great men; and the three last were of remarkable abilities and experience. Lord SOMERS was the general patron of the *literati*, and the particular friend of Dr. SWIFT.[9] The Earl of ORFORD had been considered in a manner as lord high admiral; the whole affairs of the navy having been committed to his charge.[10] Lord HALLIFAX had a fine genius for poetry, and had employed his more youthful part of life in that science. He was distinguished by the name of MOUSE MOUNTAGUE, having ridiculed, jointly with MAT PRIOR, Mr. DRYDEN's famous poem of the Hind and Panther.[11] The parody is drawn from HORACE's fable of the City Mouse and Country Mouse,[12] and begins,

> *A milk white mouse, immortal and unchang'd,*
> *Fed on soft cheese, and o'er the dairy rang'd.*[13]

But afterwards, upon Mr. MOUNTAGUE's promotion to the chancellorship of the Exchequer, PRIOR, with a good humoured indignation at seeing his friend preferred, and himself neglected,[14] concludes an epistle written in the year 1698, to FLEETWOOD SHEPHERD, Esq;[15] with these three lines,

> *My friend CHARLES MOUNTAGUE's prefer'd,*
> *Nor wou'd I have it long observ'd,*
> *That one Mouse eats, while t'other's starv'd.*[16]

---

[b]Original footnote in the *Remarks*: ""WILLIAM BENTINCK, Earl of PORTLAND, Groom of the stole."

[c]Original footnote in the *Remarks*: "JOHN SOMERS, Baron SOMERS of *Evesham*. First, Lord Keeper: afterwards, Lord High Chancellor."

[d]Original footnote in the *Remarks*: "EDWARD RUSSEL, Earl of ORFORD. Treasurer of the Navy, and one of the Lords Commissioners of the Admiralty."

[e]Original footnote in the *Remarks*: "CHARLES MOUNTAGUE, Earl of HALLIFAX, appointed one of the Commissioners of the Treasury; and afterwards made Chancellor of the Exchequer."

You will find the characters of the four impeached lords described under *Athenian* names. PHOCION is the Earl of PORTLAND. ARISTIDES is Lord SOMERS. THEMISTOCLES is the Earl of ORFORD. PERICLES is the Earl of HALLIFAX.[17]   In parallels of this sort, it is impossible that every circumstance should tally with the utmost exactness: but the whole treatise is full of historical knowledge, and excellent reflexions. It is not mixed with any improper sallies of wit, or any light airs of humour; and in point of style and learning, is equal, if not superior, to any of his political works.

Subsequent to *the discourse concerning Athens and Rome* is a paper written in the year 1703,[18] in derision of the style and manner of Mr. ROBERT BOYLE.[19]   To what a height must the spirit of sarcasm arise in an author, who could prevail upon himself to ridicule so good a man as Mr. BOYLE? The[f] sword of wit, like the scythe of time, cuts down friend and foe, and attacks every object that accidentally lies in its way.   But,[g] sharp and irresistible as the[h] edge of it may be, Mr. BOYLE will always remain invulnerable.

The sentiments of a church-of-England-man, with respect to religion and government, was written in the year 1708.[20] It is adapted to that particular period. The style of the whole pamphlet is nervous, and, except in some few places, the sentiments impartial.[i] The state of *Holland* is so justly, and, at the same time, so concisely delineated, that I cannot help transcribing it. Speaking of the *Dutch*, the author says, "*They are a commonwealth founded on a sudden, by a desperate attempt in[j] a desperate condition, not formed or digested into a regular system by mature thought and reason, but huddled up under the pressure of sudden exigencies; calculated for no long duration, and hitherto subsisting by accident in the midst of contending powers, who cannot yet agree about sharing it amongst them.*"[21] This tract is very well worth your reading and attention: and it confirms an observation which will perpetually occur, that SWIFT excels in whatever style or manner he assumes. When he is in earnest, his strength of reason carries with it conviction. When in jest, every competitor in the race of wit is left behind him.

---

[f]The] But, the FI, FIa, FIb, FII, FIII, FV, MI

[g]But,] However, FI, FIa, FIb, FII, MI

[h]irresistible as the] irresistible the FI

[i]the sentiments impartial. MV] impartial. MIII

[j]in] on FI, FIa, FIb, FII, FIII, FV, MI, MII

The argument against abolishing Christianity[22] is carried on with the highest wit and humour. Graver divines threaten their readers with future punishments: SWIFT artfully exhibits a picture of present shame. He judged rightly in imagining that a small treatise, written with a spirit of mirth and freedom, must be more efficacious, than long sermons, or laborious lessons of morality. He endeavours to laugh us into religion, well knowing, that we are often laughed out of it. As you have not read the pamphlet, excuse a quotation, to which may be prefixed the old proverb *ex pede Herculem.*[23] *"I would fain know* (says the Dean) *how it can be pretended, that the churches are misapplied. Where are more appointments and rendezvouses of gallantry? Where more care to appear in the foremost box with greater advantage of dress? Where more meetings for business? Where more bargains driven of all sorts? And where so many conveniencies or incitements to sleep?"*[24]

The papers which immediately follow are entirely humorous, and relate to PARTRIDGE the almanac maker:[25] and although they are not only temporary, but local, yet by an art peculiar to SWIFT himself, they are rendered immortal, so as to be read with pleasure, as long as the English language subsists.

To these succeeds *A project for the advancement of religion, and the reformation of manners,* written in the year 1709,[26] and dedicated to the Countess of BERKLEY.[27] The author appears in earnest throughout the whole treatise, and the dedication, or introduction, is in a strain of serious panegyric, which the Lady, to whom it is addressed, undoubtedly deserved. But as the pamphlet is of the satirical kind, I am apt to imagine, that my friend the Dean put a violence upon himself, in chusing to appear candidly serious, rather than to laugh silently[k] under his usual mask of gravity.[28] Read it, and tell me your opinion: for methinks, upon these occasions, I perceive him writing in shackles.

The tritical essay on the faculties of the mind,[29] will make you smile.

The letter to the Earl of Oxford *for correcting, improving, and ascertaining the* English *tongue*[30] might have been a very useful performance, if it had been longer, and less eclipsed by compliments to the noble person to whom it is addressed.[31] It seems to have been intended as a preface to some more enlarged design: at the head of which such an introduction must have appeared with great propriety. A work of this kind is much wanted, as our language, instead of being improved, is every day growing worse, and more debased. We bewilder ourselves in various orthography; we speak, and we write at random; and if a man's common conversation were to be committed to paper, he would be startled *for to* find himself guilty in *a few* sentences, of so many solecisms and such false English. I believe we are the only people

---

[k]laugh silently] smile FI, FIa, FIb, FII, MI

in the Christian world, who repeat the Lord's Prayer, in an ungrammatical manner: and I remember to have heard, that when a motion was made in the Convocation to alter the word [which] for the word [who] the proposition was rejected by the majority. This instance may shew you of what sort of men, the most learned, and even the most reverend assemblies, are sometimes composed. But let us consider the conduct of a neighbouring nation. How industrious have the French been to improve their language? and to what a state of perfection have they brought it? *Rome*, by her conquests, made her dialect universal: *France*, by her policy, has done the same. By policy, I mean the encouragement of arts and sciences; which will often render a nation more powerful than arms. Nothing has contributed so much to the purity and excellence of the French tongue, as the noble academies established for that purpose:[32] and, until some public work of the same kind is undertaken in *England*,[33] we cannot flatter ourselves with any hopes of amending the errors, or ascertaining the limits of our style. I shall not presume even to whisper to you, that I think a design of this sort is sufficiently momentous to attract the consideration of our legislative powers. Their thoughts are otherways employed, and their faculties otherways applied. But I will venture to say, that if to our hospitals for lunatics, an hospital was added for the reception, and support of men of sense and learning, it would be of the highest honour to the present age, and of no less advantage to posterity. I call it an hospital, because I suppose it to be erected for the benefit of such persons, whose infirm fortunes, or diseased revenues, may have rendered the strength and abilities of their minds weak and useless to the public: for I entirely agree with ARISTOTLE, where he says, in the words of his scholiast. *Eum praeclara et magna vix posse exequi et praestare, cui facultates desunt: quoniam per amicos et civilem potentiam veluti per instrumenta necesse est pleraque effici.*[34] The reflexions, that arise from this theme, I find, are driving me beyond the bounds of a letter: therefore I shall only add, that I heartily wish you may think an attention to your native language as useful, and improving a study, as can be pursued, in whatever station of life Providence may allot you.

There are two other letters in this volume extremely worthy of your notice. The one is, *To a young gentleman lately entered into holy orders.*[35] The other is, *To a young lady on her marriage.*[36] The former ought to be read by all the young clergymen in the three kingdoms, and the latter by all the new married women. But, here again is the peculiar felicity of SWIFT's writings; the letters are addressed only to a young clergyman[37] and a young lady,[38] but they are adapted to every age and understanding. They contain observations that delight and improve every mind; and they will be read, with pleasure and advantage, by the oldest, and most exemplary divines, and by the most distinguished, and most accomplished ladies.

The rest of the volume is filled up with short tracts, and papers of various sorts: mostly humorous, and entertaining. You will laugh at the story in one of the *Intelligencers*, of *Whisk* and *Swobbers:*[39] and you will wish *the Tatler* on those inferior duties of life, called *Les petites Morales*,[40] hung up in every 'squire's hall in *England*. I am, my dearest HAMILTON,

Your most affectionate Father
ORRERY.

Notes

1. *Prose Works of Swift* 1:195-236. Swift arrived in London on 15 April 1701, with Lord Berkeley, who had been recalled from Ireland on 28 March. Swift then arranged for the publication of two works: one was Temple's *Miscellanea The Third Part*, announced in the *Post Angel* in July as "soon to be published," entered in the Stationers Register on 28 July, and published in mid-October. The other was *A Discourse*, announced as "Tomorrow will be published" in the *Flying Post* for 21-23 October, and also advertised in the *Post Boy* for 21 October.

2. Swift himself says he wrote *A Discourse* "in a few weeks" after he arrived in London on 15 April. See *Prose Works of Swift* 1:119.

3. In September 1697, the Treaty of Ryswick was signed, ending the nine-year war between France, on one side, and the English, the Austrians, and the Dutch. The Whig Junto, responsible for that inconclusive peace (which did not determine who was to succeed the childless Charles II as king of Spain), began to collapse when the second earl of Sunderland (Temple's friend, and from whom Swift hoped for preferment) was removed from his position as lord chamberlain toward the end of the year. In August 1698, the general election returned a majority of Tories, and in May 1699, three Whig politicians were dismissed: Edward Russell, earl of Orford (first lord of the admiralty), Charles Montagu (chancellor of the exchequer), and Charles Talbot, duke of shrewsbury (secretary of state). See Jonathan Swift, *A Discourse of the Contests and Dissentions between the Nobles and Commons in Athens and Rome*, ed. Frank Ellis (Oxford: Clarendon Press, 1967), pp. 14-16 (cited hereafter as Swift, *A Discourse*).

4. On 20 October 1700, Charles II (king of Spain) died, and in his latest will, declared the six-year-old Philip, duke of Anjou (grandson of Louis XIV), heir to the Spanish empire. Louis XIV then renounced the Second Partition Treaty, which had determined that Archduke Charles (younger son of

Emperor Leopold I) was to be heir to the throne of Spain, and declared the duke of Anjou to be king of Spain. War between England and France now appeared inevitable. To complicate matters, the exiled James II died in France on 5 September 1701, and Louis XIV proclaimed James II's son, the thirteen-year-old James Frances Edward, Prince of Wales, to be king of England as James III. William III recalled the English ambassador from France, and on 20 September, the French ambassador in England was declared persona non grata, being expelled from England on 23 September.

5. Following the dismissal of Orford, Montagu, and Shrewsbury (first lord of the admiralty, chancellor of the exchequer, and secretary of state, respectively), all their places were filled by Tories. In May 1700, the commissions of the three lords justices of Ireland were revoked. In June, William III appointed the high churchman and Tory Lawrence Hyde, earl of Rochester, as lord lieutenant of Ireland. William III then began to form a new ministry around Rochester, Godolphin, and Robert Harley. But the Tories were not satisfied with those concessions. Harley was to be elected speaker of the House of Commons.

6. On 1 April 1701, the House of Commons considered a motion to impeach the earl of Portland "for high crimes and misdemeanors in negotiating the Second Treaty of Partition." The motion passed almost unanimously. See Swift, *A Discourse*, p. 47.

7. After the motion for Portland's impeachment was carried out, a motion to impeach Somers was defeated. On 14 April, the Commons continued with their investigations on Somers, and at 8 P.M., Somers made his defense. In spite of Somers's good defense, the motion for his impeachment passed 198-188. See ibid., pp. 47-49.

8. The impeachments of Orford and Montagu were "carried by increasingly large majorities" after the motion to impeach Somers had passed. See ibid., p. 49.

9. On 10 May 1704, Swift published *A Tale of a Tub* with a "long-delayed and hopeful dedication to Lord Somers," whose "political fortunes were again in the ascendant." See ibid., p. 180.

10. Orford was first lord of the admiralty.

11. *The Hind and the Panther, Transvers'd to the Story of the Country Mouse and the City Mouse* (London: W. Davis, 1687).

12. In Horace *Satires* 2.6.

13. In *The Literary Works of Matthew Prior*, ed. H. Bunker Wright and Monroe K. Spears (Oxford: Clarendon Press, 1959), p. 40.

14. Actually, by 1698, Prior was both secretary of the English embassy in Paris, and secretary to the lords justices in Ireland. See Ehrenpreis, *Swift* 1:247-48.

15. *To Mr. Fleetwood Shepherd*, published in Curll's volume *Poems on Several Occasions* (end of January 1707), under the title of "A Second Epistle to Sir Fleetwood Sheppard." For the text of the poem, see Prior, *Literary Works*, pp. 83-85.

16. *To Mr. Fleetwood Shepherd*, lines 64-66.

17. Frank Ellis points to the brilliancy of Swift's classical parallelism in *A Discourse*, pp. 156-62. Ellis also makes the same identifications pointed to here by Orrery (ibid., pp. 134-35). However, Downie has demonstrated that the parallelism is neither neat nor accurate. See J. A. Downie, "Swift's *Discourse*: Allegorical Satire or Parallel History?" *Swift Studies* 2 (1987): 25-32. Orrery himself was confused while trying to determine who was who in Swift's parallelism. In his copy of volume 1 of Faulkner's edition of Swift's works, used in preparation for the writing of the *Remarks* (at the Mortimer Rare Book Room, Smith College), Orrery wrote these queries about the parallels:

Queries

Page 17. Nicias, Lymachus, and Alcibiades. Who are they?
Page 15. Swift says he shall take notice only of six. I do not find which are the six. The names are

1. Miltiades
2. Aristides
3. Themistocles
4. Pericles

Then he mentions the three above [word struck out] and gives only the character of Alcibiades.

18. *A Meditation upon a Broomstick* (*Prose Works of Swift* 1:239-40) was probably written during Swift's visit to the Berkeleys at their castle in

Gloucestershire, in August 1702 (Ehrenpreis, *Swift* 2:91 n. 2). Faulkner gives 1703 as the date when Swift wrote the piece.

19. Robert Boyle (1627-91), author and natural philosopher, was Orrery's distant relative. In *A Meditation*, Swift particularly satirizes Boyle's *Occasional Reflections upon several Subjects with a Discourse touching occasional Meditations*, published in 1665.

20. *Prose Works of Swift* 2:1-25. *The Sentiments* was first published in 1711.

21. Ibid., p. 7.

22. Ibid., pp. 26-39. It was probably written in mid-1708, and published in 1711.

23. "To know Hercules by the foot." This proverb is related to a legend concerning the death of Hercules (the Latin name of the Greek mythological figure named Heracles). According to that legend, Hercules made his final arrangements by building a funeral fire and climbing onto it. Philoctetes, one of Hercules' servants, set fire to the wood, and Hercules made Philoctetes promise not to reveal the location of the bonfire to anybody. When Philoctetes was subsequently questioned, he refused to speak, but went to the site and kicked the ground with his foot in a significant way. He was then punished by receiving a severe wound in the offending foot. See Pierre Grimal, *The Dictionary of Classical Mythology*, trans. A. R. Maxwell-Hyslop (Oxford: Basil Blackwell, 1986), p. 207. Orrery means that, in the same way that one could recognize the punishment of Hercules by looking at Philoctetes' wounded foot, one could recognize Swift's style by reading the passage Orrery is quoting from *Argument against Abolishing Christianity*.

24. *Prose Works of Swift* 2:31.

25. For Swift's satirical tracts on John Partridge, see *Prose Works of Swift* 2:141-70. For John Partridge (1644-1715), almanac maker and astrologer born at East Sheen, see *Dictionary of National Biography*, s.v. "Partridge, John"; and George Mayhew, "The Early Life of John Partridge," *Studies in English Literature* 1 (1916): 31-42.

26. *Prose Works of Swift* 2:43-63. It was advertised as published "this day" in the *Daily Courant* of 9 April 1709.

27. Elizabeth, countess of Berkeley (1655-1719), wife of the second earl of Berkeley.

28. Delany quoted this passage, and told Orrery, "with great submission," that the *Project* "is not properly of the satirical kind" (*Observations*, p. 279). Ehrenpreis mentions how some scholars "have thought it [the *Project*] a parody" (*Swift* 2:276).

29. *Prose Works of Swift* 1:246-51. The work is dated 6 August 1707.

30. Ibid., 4:5-21. The work is signed and dated by Swift "February 22, 1712." It was published on 17 May 1712.

31. Cf. Herbert Davis's remarks: "In fact, the lengthy panegyric of Harley, the praise of him as one who saved his country from 'ruin by a *foreign War*, and a *domestick Faction*,' as well as other matters, is obviously partisan. It could not conceivably have been interpreted otherwise by contemporaries; nor could Swift have been unaware of the provocative impact on the Whigs" (ibid., p. xii).

32. The French Academy was founded in 1635.

33. Johnson's *Dictionary* appeared on 15 April 1755, and Orrery gave a copy of it to the *Academia della Crusca* in Florence.

34. "Those whose faculties have been weakened can only perform and present important or illustrious actions at a great cost; because they perform them with the help of friends and the civil power who act as instruments." Aristotle *Nicomachean Ethics* 1.8.15-16. The "scholiast" referred to by Orrery is Nicomachus, Aristotle's son, who was probably the editor of *Nicomachean Ethics*. Cicero believed that Nicomachus might have been the author of the work. See Aristotle, *Nicomachean Ethics*, Loeb Classical Library (London, 1926), p. xvii.

35. *Prose Works of Swift* 9:61-81. It was first published in Dublin by Edward Waters in 1720, with the title *A Letter from a Lay-Patron to a Gentleman Designing for Holy Orders*. The English edition has the title *A Letter to a Young Gentleman Lately Enter'd into Holy Orders*, and was published on 3 January 1721, being dated 9 January 1720 at the end of the text.

36. Ibid., pp. 83-94. It was first published in *Miscellanies, the First Volume* (1727). The fair manuscript copy in Swift's hand in the Huntington Library (HM 1599) has no title and is dated at the end "Deanry – House, Febr. 11th, 1722-3."

37. Herbert Davis wrote that the work "was probably never addressed to any particular person, but intended to answer the general need of the young clergy, in a manner rather different from the series of such Letters, Directions and Advice addressed to young Divines on the subject of writing and delivering sermons, which had appeared not infrequently during the previous fifty years" (ibid., pp. xxii-xxiv).

38. Deborah Staunton (1703-37), wife of John Rochfort, Irish M.P. and Swift's friend. For an account of her life, see George P. Mayhew, *Rage or Raillery: The Swift Manuscripts at the Huntington Library* (San Marino, Calif.: Huntington Library, 1967), pp. 47-51.

39. In *The Intelligencer*, no. 5, by Swift, dated probably Saturday, 8 June 1728 (Swift, *The Intelligencer*, p. 80; see p. 32 for its dating).

40. In the *Tatler*, no. 20, 6 March 1710 (*Prose Works of Swift* 2:184-87).

LETTER IX

WE are now come, my dear HAMILTON, to the second volume of SWIFT's works. It is filled with poetry: but the poems in general are short and satirical. The poem of the greatest length, and, I believe, the longest ever composed by Dr. SWIFT, is of a very extraordinary nature, and upon a very extraordinary subject. It is called CADENUS and VANESSA.[1] As a poem, it is excellent in its kind, perfectly correct, and admirably conducted. SWIFT, who had the nicest ear, is remarkably chaste and delicate in his rhymes. A bad rhyme appeared to him one of the capital sins in poetry; and yet it is a sin into which some of our greatest poets have fallen. DRYDEN frequently: POPE sometimes. The former was embarassed with a wife and family, and was often under such necessitous circumstances as to be obliged to publish, or to want subsistence. The latter was in a less confined, and in a much more easy situation: he was naturally judicious, and uncommonly attentive to maintain the dignity of his character. Although his body was weak, his mind was equal to the weight of his laurel crown; and he wore it not only with ease, but majesty. Take him as a poet, *we shall not see his like again.*[2] But why do I keep you in suspense? you are impatient, I dare say, to know some particulars of VANESSA. Her real name was ESTHER VANHOMRIGH.[a][3] She was one of the daughters of BARTHOLOMEW VANHOMRIGH, a Dutch merchant of *Amsterdam*, who, upon the revolution, went into *Ireland*, and was appointed, by King WILLIAM, a commissioner of the revenue.[4] Her mother, whose name I forget, was born in *Ireland*, of very mean extraction.[5] The Dutch merchant, by parsimony and prudence, had collected a fortune of about sixteen thousand pounds:[6] he bequeathed an equal division of it to his wife and his four children, of which two were sons, and two were daughters.[7] The sons, after the death of their father, travelled abroad.[8] The eldest died

---

[a]Original footnote in the *Remarks*: "The name is pronounced VANNUMMERY."

154

beyond sea, and the youngest surviving his brother only a short time,[9] the whole patrimony fell to his two sisters, ESTHER and MARY.[10]

With this increase of wealth, and with heads and hearts elated by affluence, and unrestrained by foresight or discretion, the widow VANHOMRIGH and her two daughters quitted the illuxurious soil of their native country for the more elegant pleasures of the English court.[11] During their residence at *London,* they lived in a course of prodigality that stretched itself far beyond the limits of their income, and reduced them to great distress;[12] in the midst of which the mother died,[13] and the two daughters hastened in all secrecy back to *Ireland,* beginning their journey on a Sunday, to avoid the interruption, and importunities of a certain fierce kind of animals called bailiffs,[14] who are not only sworn foes to wit and gaiety, but whose tyranny, although it could not have reached the deified VANESSA, might have been very fatal to ESTHER VANHOMRIGH. Within two years after their arrival in *Ireland,* MARY the youngest sister died,[15] and the small remains of the shipwreckt fortune centered in VANESSA.[16]

Vanity makes terrible devastation in a female breast. It batters down all restraints of modesty, and carries away every seed of virtue. VANESSA was excessively vain. The character given of her by CADENUS is fine painting, but, in general, fictitious. She was fond of dress: impatient to be admired: very romantic in her turn of mind: superior, in her own opinion, to all her sex: full of pertness, gaiety, and pride:[17] not without some agreeable accomplishments, but far from being either beautiful or genteel: ambitious, at any rate, to be esteemed a wit; and, with that view, always affecting to keep company with wits:[18] a great reader, and a violent admirer of poetry:[19] happy in the thoughts of being reputed SWIFT's concubine: but still aiming and intending to be his wife. By nature haughty, and disdainful, looking with the pity of contempt upon her inferiors, and with the smiles of self-approbation upon her equals: but upon Dr. SWIFT with the eyes of love. Her love was founded in vanity, or, to use a more fashionable phrase, *in taste.* His own lines are the best proof of my assertion.

> CADENUS *many things had writ;*
> VANESSA *much esteem'd his wit,*
> *And call'd for his poetic works;*
> *Mean time the boy[b] in secret lurks,*
> *And while the book was in her hand,*
> *The urchin, from his private stand,*
> *Took aim, and shot with all his strength*
> *A dart of such prodigious length;*

---

[b]Original footnote in the *Remarks*: "CUPID."

It pierc'd the feeble volume thro',
And deep transfix'd her bosom too.
Some lines, more moving than the rest,
Stuck to the point that pierc'd her breast;
And borne[c] directly to her heart
With pains unknown encreas'd the smart.
VANESSA, not in years a score,
Dreams of a gown of forty four;
Imaginary charms can find,
In eyes, with reading, almost blind:
CADENUS now no more appears
Declin'd in health, advanc'd in years:
She fancies music in his tongue,
Nor further looks, but thinks him young.[20]

The poem itself is dated in the year 1713,[21] when SWIFT was in his meridian altitude; favoured by the courtiers; flattered, feared, and admired by the greatest men in the nation.

By the verses which I have already recited, it may be presumed, that the lady was first smitten with the fame and character of CADENUS, and afterwards with his person. Her first thoughts pursued a phantom. Her latter[d] passion desired a substance. The manner in which she discovered her inclinations, is poetically described in these lines.

She own'd the wand'ring of her thoughts,
But he must answer for her faults.
She well remember'd, to her cost,
That all his lessons were not lost.
Two maxims she cou'd still produce,
And sad experience taught their use:
That virtue, pleas'd by being shown,
Knows nothing which it dare not own:
Can make us, without fear, disclose
Our inmost secrets to our foes:
That common forms were not design'd
Directors to a noble mind.
Now, said the nymph, to let you see,
My actions with your rules agree;

---

[c]borne] born MI, MII

[d]latter MV] later MIII

> *That I can vulgar forms despise,*
> *And have no secrets to disguise,*
> *I knew, by what you said and writ,*
> *How dang'rous things were men of wit;*
> *You caution'd me against their charms,*
> *But never gave me equal arms:*
> *Your lessons found the weakest part,*
> *Aim'd at the head, and reach'd the heart.*[22]

Supposing this account to be true, and I own to you, my HAM, I can scarce think it otherwise, it is evident, that the fair VANESSA had made a surprising progress in the philosophic doctrines, which she had received from her preceptor. His rules were certainly of a most extraordinary kind. He taught her, that vice, as soon as it defied shame, was immediately changed into virtue. That vulgar forms were not binding upon certain *choice spirits*, to whom either the writings, or the persons of men of wit were acceptable. She heard the lesson with attention, and imbibed the philosophy with eagerness. The maxims suited her exalted turn of mind. She imagined that if the theory appeared so charming, the practice must be much more delightful. The close connexion of soul and body seemed to require, in the eye of a female philosopher, that each should succeed the other in all pleasurable enjoyments. The former had been sufficiently regaled, why must the latter remain unsatisfied? "Nature, said VANESSA, abhors a *vacuum*, and nature ought always to be obeyed." She communicated these sentiments to her tutor, but he seemed not to comprehend her meaning, nor to conceive the *distinctio rationis*[23] that had taken rise in his own school. He answered her in the *non-essential modes*. He talked of friendship, of the delights of reason, of gratitude, respect and esteem.[24] He almost preached upon virtue, and he muttered some indistinct phrases concerning chastity.

So unaccountable a conduct in CADENUS may be thought rather to proceed from defects in nature, than from the scrupulous difficulties of a tender conscience. Such a supposition will still appear more strong, if we recollect the distant manner in which SWIFT cohabited with STELLA, colder, if possible, after, than before, she was his wife: and I now recollect some of his own lines that seem to confirm the surmise, as they contain an insinuation against VANESSA, not perhaps so much intended to wound her reputation, as to save his own.

> *But what success VANESSA met*
> *Is to the world a secret yet.*
> *Whether the nymph, to please her swain,*
> *Talks in a high romantic strain;*
> *Or whether he at last descends,*

To act with less seraphic ends;
Or to compound the business, whether
They temper love and books together,
Must never to mankind be told,
Nor shall the conscious muse unfold.[25]

It is impossible to read this cruel hint without great indignation against the *conscious muse*, especially as it is the finishing stroke of a picture, which was already drawn in too loose a garment, and too unguarded a posture. In this instance, I am afraid the Dean must remain inexcusable.

VANESSA, in some time after the death of her sister, retired to *Selbridge*,[26] a small house and estate that had been purchased by her father, within ten or twelve miles of *Dublin*.[27] Spleen and disappointment were the companions of her solitude. The narrowness of her income, the coldness of her lover, the loss of her reputation, all contributed to make her miserable, and to encrease the frenzical disposition of her mind. In this melancholy situation she remained several years, during which time CADENUS visited her frequently.[28] Their particular conversation, as it passed without witnesses, must for ever remain unknown: but, in general, it is certain, that she often pressed him to marry her. His answers were rather turns of wit than positive denials; till at last, being unable to sustain her weight of misery any longer, she writ a very tender epistle to CADENUS, insisting peremptorily upon as serious an answer, and an immediate acceptance, or absolute refusal of her, as his wife. His reply was delivered by his own hand. He brought it with him when he made his final visit at *Selbridge:* and throwing down the letter upon her table, with great passion hastened back to his horse, carrying in his countenance the frowns of anger and indignation.[29]

Dr. SWIFT had a natural severity of face, which even his smiles could scarce soften, or his utmost gaiety render placid and serene: but when that sternness of visage was encreased by rage, it is scarce possible to imagine looks, or features, that carried in them more terror and austerity. VANESSA had seen him in all tempers, and from his outward appearance she guessed at the inward contents of his letter. She read it with as much resolution as the present cruelty of her fate, and the raging pride of her heart, would permit. She found herself entirely discarded from his friendship and conversation.[30] Her offers were treated with insolence and disdain. She met with reproaches instead of love, and with tyranny instead of affection. She had long thrown away the gentle lenitives of virtue; which, upon this occasion, might have proved healing ingredients to so deep, and so dangerous a wound. She had preferred wit to religion,[31] she had utterly destroyed her character, and her conscience: and she was now fallen a prey to the horror of her own thoughts.

Tum vero infelix fatis exterrita Dido

Mortem orat: taedet caeli convexa tueri.[32]

She did not survive many days the letter delivered to her by CADENUS, but, during that short interval, she was sufficiently composed, to cancel a will made in SWIFT's favour, and to make another,[33] wherein she left her fortune[34] (which, by long retirement, was in some measure retrieved) to her two executors, Dr. BERKLEY, the present Bishop of CLOYNE,[35] and Mr. MARSHAL, one of the King's Serjeants at law.[36] She had chosen Mr. MARSHAL, not only as he had an excellent character, but as he was her relation.[37] She had little personal acquaintance with Dr. BERKLEY: his virtues, and his genius, were universally known: yet other motives perhaps induced her to appoint him a joint executor: in such an appointment, she probably designed to mortify the pride of Dr. SWIFT, by letting him see, that, in her last thoughts, she preferred a stranger before him.[38]

Thus perished, at *Selbridge*, under all the agonies of despair, Mrs. ESTHER VANHOMRIGH;[39] a miserable example of an ill-spent life, fantastic wit, visionary schemes, and female weakness.

My paper scarce allows room for the affectionate name of

ORRERY.

Notes

1. *Poems of Swift* 2:683-714. First published in Dublin around 19 April 1726.

2. *Hamlet*, 1.2.187-88.

3. Esther (or Hester) Vanhomrigh was born on 14 February 1688, and was the eldest daughter of the Dutch merchant Bartholomew Vanhomrigh and Hester Stone, daughter of a commissioner of the Irish revenue. Swift and Vanessa had first met each other as early as 1708 in Dunstable (Swift's stop between Leicester and London). On that occasion, Vanessa would have spilled coffee in the fireplace at Dunstable (*Correspondence of Swift* 1:366 and 2:356). It is also possible that Swift and Vanessa had first met each other even earlier than that date. Swift may have first met the family in Ireland, before the family moved to London in December 1707 (ibid., 5:240).

4. Bartholomew Vanhomrigh was already living in Dublin before the time of William III. He got married in 1686, and became an alderman. He left Ireland during the troubles that took place by the time of the Revolution, and went to England. When he came back from England, Bartholomew was a commissary-general to the army in Ireland. After the conflicts in Ireland

following the Revolution, Bartholomew sat in the Irish Parliament and was also appointed as commissioner of the revenue. In 1697, Bartholomew was nominated lord mayor of Dublin.

5. Deane Swift wrote that Hester Stone, Vanessa's mother, had been born "in Dublin of English parents" and was sole heiress to her father's fortune, which "did not amount to about five hundred pounds." Deane Swift also states that Hester Stone "appears to have been a woman of politeness and good-breeding." See Deane Swift, *Essay*, pp. 257-59.

6. Bartholomew Vanhomrigh died on 29 December 1703, and left his family the "ample fortune" of £16,000 (Ehrenpreis, *Swift* 2:311).

7. The Vanhomrighs' eldest son was Bartholomew, who entered Christ Church, Oxford, as a student on 15 April 1708, and died in the summer of 1715. The two other children were: Mary ("Molkin" or "Moll"), born in 1694 and baptized on 7 September 1694, for whom Swift had a warm affection (ibid., 2:312 and 3:94, 385-87), and Ginkel, the youngest child (born ca. 1694), who died in the autumn of 1710, being buried in St. James's Church, London, on 8 October 1710.

8. Bartholomew went to France in 1713, and spent the spring and summer there. Writing to Swift from Paris on 8 April 1713, Matthew Prior says he could not find Bartholomew since he had received Swift's letter to him from Bartholomew (*Correspondence of Swift* 1:341). Writing again to Swift on 16 August 1713, Prior says Bartholomew "has run terribly here into Debt and being in durance has sent to his Mother upon pecuniary concerns" (ibid., p. 381). It is not known whether Ginkel traveled abroad, and since he was around sixteen when he died, it seems unlikely that he did so.

9. This is incorrect. Bartholomew, the eldest son (born in 1693) died in the summer of 1715, whereas Ginkel, the youngest child (born ca. 1694) died in the autumn of 1710.

10. In 1714, Bartholomew drew up his will, and, in it, he bequeathed to his sisters a life interest in his estate. Upon his death in 1715, Vanessa and Mary took possession of that bequest (ibid., 2:148 n. 1).

11. Orrery speaks as if Bartholomew and Ginkel were already dead by the time the Vanhomrighs moved to London in December 1707. But Ginkel died in 1710, and Bartholomew died in 1715.

12. Freeman describes Mrs. Vanhomrigh's life by the time the family moved to London: "Mrs. Vanhomrigh was at this time a widow with four children, Hessy or Esther, aged twenty, and three others, the eldest of whom was fifteen. She was comfortably off, but preferred to live as if she were rich, and did so live as far as credit with the local tradesmen allowed her, fond of society, ambitious, and of sufficiently youthful appearance for the gossips to whisper that she was engaged to be married a second time." In Jonathan Swift, *Vanessa and Her Correspondence with Jonathan Swift*, ed. A. Martin Freeman (London: Selwyn & Blount, 1921), p. 8 (cited hereafter as Freeman, *Vanessa and Swift*).

13. Mrs. Vanhomrigh died in January 1714, and appointed Vanessa sole executrix (Ehrenpreis, *Swift* 2:748).

14. Regarding this point, Freeman wrote: "There is no evidence to support the statement of Orrery, that Esther and Mary Vanhomrigh left London because they could not otherwise avoid imprisonment for debt. The motive was no doubt that London, now that their mother was dead and Swift had gone away, held little attraction. Moreover, in Ireland they would be able to live on their own property and look into their law affairs, which, though they could wait indefinitely while Swift was in London, would, with Swift in Dublin, appear to demand immediate attention" (Freeman, *Vanessa and Swift*, pp. 28-29). Williams wrote that, probably on the occasion of her mother's death, Vanessa borrowed £50 at 5 percent from Benjamin Tooke. The interest was never paid, and Vanessa assumed some of Mrs. Vanhomrigh's debts. Those debts included payment for coffee supplied from the St. James's Coffee-house, and £33.7s.6d. to one Katherine Hill. Before leaving London in October 1714, Vanessa pawned some jewels to John Barber. See *Correspondence of Swift* 2:56 n. 1, and 360. Barber sold the jewels nearly three years after Vanessa's death.

15. Mary Vanhomrigh died on Monday, 22 February 1721, and was buried on Friday, 3 March 1721, in the churchyard of St. Andrew's, Dublin.

16. Mary Vanhomrigh's will was proved on 11 May 1721. In it, all her property was left to Vanessa.

17. Cf. Freeman's words on Vanessa: "For she was a young woman of an unusual type, or of a type considered unusual by her friends, with no taste for cards or entertainments, or for parties, little even for dress; intelligent and receptive, interested in the things of the mind, yet too idle to study, petulant, self-willed but not strong-willed, delighting in reasonable conversation as much

as she hated tattle, and withal very childish" (Freeman, *Vanessa and Swift*, p. 9).

18. Vanessa's acquaintances included Charles Ford, William King (archbishop of Dublin), Theophilus Bolton (bishop of Clonfert and Elphin, and archbishop of Cashel), Robert Lindsay (justice of the common pleas of Ireland), and Benjamin Pratt (provost of Trinity College, Dublin, and later dean of Down). See Ehrenpreis, *Swift* 3:392.

19. Vanessa wrote *A Rebus* on Swift (*Poems of Swift* 2:715-17), and there are three other poems attributed to Vanessa: *To Love*, *Ode to Spring*, and *Ode to Wisdom* (ibid., pp. 717-20).

20. Swift, *Cadenus and Vanessa*, lines 510-31.

21. In a letter dated 19 April 1726, Swift mentioned that the poem was written "at Windsor near fourteen years ago" (*Correspondence of Swift* 3:130), a statement he repeats on 7 July 1726 (ibid., p. 137). This means it was written sometime between August and September 1712, when Swift was at Windsor. On line 525 of the poem, Swift stated he was then forty four, and indeed this was his age at that time. On the other hand, Swift was at Windsor in the autumn of 1713, and Williams wrote that, after returning to England from his stay in Ireland in the summer of 1713, Swift, "embarrassed but unwilling" to end the relationship with Vanessa, "found an outlet" by writing the poem at Windsor in the autumn of 1713. See *Poems of Swift* 2:684-85.

22. Swift, *Cadenus and Vanessa*, lines 602-23.

23. "A distinction made by reason." This is a conventional expression in logics, opposed to *distinctio realis* or a distinction based on reality, independent of reason.

24. Cf. lines 780-89 of Swift, *Cadenus and Vanessa*:

> But Friendship in its greatest Height,
> A constant, rational Delight,
> On Virtue's Basis fix'd to last,
> When Love's Allurements long are past;
> Which gently warms, but cannot burn;
> He [Cadenus] gladly offers in return:

(*Poems of Swift* 2:711)

25. Swift, *Cadenus and Vanessa*, lines 818-27.

26. Vanessa had already gone to Celbridge with Mary in the summer of 1720 (Ehrenpreis, *Swift* 3:96).

27. Celbridge is located in county Kildare, eleven miles west of Dublin, where Vanessa owned "an imposing house and a handsome estate left by her father" (ibid., p. 93). Celbridge was built by Vanessa's father, and it came to be owned later by the Marlay and Grattan families. Today, Celbridge is owned by the St. John of God Brothers.

28. Williams pointed out that a paragraph in Swift's letter to Vanessa dated 15 October 1720 indicates Swift had visited Vanessa at Celbridge sometime before the letter was written (*Correspondence of Swift* 2:359 n. 3). Ehrenpreis wrote that "we know Swift kept visiting Vanessa" except for periods of Swift's absence in 1721 and 1722 (Ehrenpreis, *Swift* 3:385). Ehrenpreis also wrote that, after Mary Vanhomrigh's death, "while Vanessa lodged in Dublin, they could meet (weekly, perhaps!) at the home of a close-mouthed sympathizer, as they had done at Barber's house in London, years before" (ibid., p. 387).

29. Without mentioning his source, Sheridan gave a similar account. See Thomas Sheridan, *The Life of the Rev. Dr. Jonathan Swift, Dean of St. Patrick's, Dublin*, 2d ed. (London: J. F. and C. Rivington et al., 1787), p. 285.

30. Ehrenpreis speculated that Swift foresaw Vanessa's death, and, fearing to "preside over her death," curtailed his visits to her. See Ehrenpreis, *Swift* 3:388.

31. Cf. these words by John Evans, bishop of Meath, on 27 July 1723: "'Tis generally believed she [Vanessa] lived without God in the world. When Dean Price (the minister of her parish) offered her his services in her last minutes: she sent him word no Price no prayers with a scrap out of the Tale of a Tub . . . and so she died" (ibid., p. 390).

32. "Then, indeed, awed by her doom, luckless Dido prays for death; she is weary of gazing on the arch of heaven" (Virgil *Aeneid* 4.450-51).

33. Vanessa made her will on 1 May 1723. See the text of Vanessa's will in Freeman, *Vanessa and Swift*, pp. 186-89.

34. £5,000.

35. George Berkeley (1685-1753), philosopher and bishop of Cloyne.

36. Robert Marshall (d. 1774) was the lawyer who had advised Vanessa before her death.

37. Sheridan also mentions that Marshall was Vanessa's "relation." See Sheridan, *The Life of the Rev. Dr. Jonathan Swift*, p. 286.

38. Berkeley did not expect to be constituted executor to Vanessa ("a lady to whom I was a perfect stranger, having never in the whole course of my life, to my knowledge, exchanged one single word with her"). See Ehrenpreis, *Swift* 3:390.

39. Vanessa died on Sunday, 2 June 1723, at night. On the next day, her will was opened, and proved on 6 June.

LETTER X

My dear HAMILTON,

I Have received yours of the 24th instant. You seem so much pleased with the commentaries relating to VANESSA, and you have expressed so much satisfaction in my account of STELLA, that probably you wish SWIFT to have had as many wives and mistresses as SOLOMON,[1] in order to furnish me with perpetual materials for the history of a Lady. It is true, my friend the Dean kept company with many of the fair sex, but they were rather his amusement than his admiration. He trifled away many hours in their conversation,[2] he filled many pages in their praise, and by the power of his head, he gained the character of a lover, without the least assistance from his heart. To this particular kind of pride supported by the bent of his genius, and joined by[a] the excessive coldness of his nature, VANESSA owed the ruin of her reputation, and from the same causes, STELLA remained an unacknowledged wife. If we consider SWIFT's behaviour, so far only as it relates to women, we shall find, that he looked upon them rather as busts, than as whole figures. In his panegyrical descriptions, he has seldom descended lower than the center of their hearts: or if ever he has designed a compleat statue, it has been generally cast in a dirty, or in a disagreeable mould: as if the statuary had not conceived, or had not experienced, that justness of proportion, that delicacy of limbs,[b] and those pleasing, and graceful attitudes which have constituted the sex to be the most beautiful part of the creation. If you review his several poems to STELLA, you will find them fuller of affection than desire, and more expressive of friendship than of love. For example,

Thou, STELLA, *wert no longer young,*

---

[a]by MV] to MIII

[b]limbs, MV] limb, MIII

> *When first for thee my harp I strung;*
> *Without one word of* CUPID's *darts,*
> *Of killing eyes, or bleeding hearts:*
> *With friendship and esteem possest*
> *I ne'er admitted Love a guest.*[3]

Most of the poems, which are absolutely addressed to STELLA, or which describe her in a variety of attitudes, turn upon her age:[4] a kind of excuse perhaps for SWIFT's want of love.

I began one of my former letters, my dear HAMILTON, by a declaration that it was impossible for me to pass a very minute comment upon the various pieces that he has written; and I must renew the same declaration in regard to his poems. They are not only mingled improperly, in points of dates, and subjects,[5] but many, very many of them, are temporary, trifling, and I had almost said puerile. Several of them are personal, and consequently scarce amusing; or at least, they leave a very small impression upon our minds. Such indeed as are likely to draw your attention, are exquisite, and so peculiarly his own, that whoever has dared to imitate him in these, or in any of his works, has constantly failed in the attempt. Upon a general view of his poetry, we shall find him, as in his other performances, an uncommon, surprizing, heteroclite genius, luxurious in his fancy, lively in his ideas, humorous in his descriptions, and bitter, exceeding bitter in his satir. The restlessness of his imagination, and the disappointment of his ambition, have both contributed to hinder him from undertaking any poetical work of length or importance. His wit was sufficient to every labour: no flight could have wearied the strength of his pinions: perhaps if the extensive views of his nature had been fully satisfied, his airy motions had been more regular, and less sudden. But he now appears, like an eagle that is sometimes chained, and at that particular time, for want of nobler, and more proper food, diverts his confinement, and appeases his hunger, by destroying the gnats, butterflies, and other wretched insects, that unluckily happen to buzz, or flutter within his reach.[6]

While I have been reading over this volume of his poetry, I have considered him as an *Aegyptian* hieroglyphic, which, though it had an unnatural, and frequently an indecent appearance, yet it always contained some secret marks of wisdom, and sometimes of deep morality. The subjects of his poems are often nauseous, and the performances beautifully disagreeable.

The Lady's Dressing Room[7] has been universally condemned, as deficient in point of delicacy, even to the highest degree.[8] The best apology that can be made in its favour, is to suppose, that the author exhibited his CELIA in the most hideous colours he could find, lest she might be mistaken as a goddess, when she was only a mortal. External beauty is very alluring to youth and inexperience; and SWIFT, by pulling off the borrowed plumes of his harpy, discovers at once a frightful bird of prey, and by making her offensive, renders her less dangerous and inviting. Such, I hope, was his design;[9] but let his views and motives have been ever so beneficial, his general want of delicacy and decorum must not hope to find even[c] the shadow of an excuse; for it is impossible not to own, that he too frequently forgets that politeness and tenderness of manners, which are undoubtedly due to human kind. From his early, and repeated disappointments, he became a misanthrope. If his mind had been more equal and content, I am willing to believe, that he would have viewed the works of nature with a more benign aspect. And perhaps, under a less constant rotation of anxiety, he might have preserved his senses to the last scene of life, and might have enjoyed that calm *exit* from the stage, for which his friend HORACE so earnestly supplicates APOLLO.

> *Frui paratis et valido mihi*
> *Latoë dones, et, precor, integrâ*
> *Cum mente, nec turpem senectam*
> *Degere, nec cithorâ carentem.*[10]

I have already told you, that his pride was so great as scarce to admit any body to the least share of his friendship, except such who could amuse him, or such who could do him honour. To these two different classes we owe many of his poems. His companions and humble followers find themselves immortalized by the insertion of their names in addresses to STELLA,[11] or in other miscellaneous pieces written in an easy, although not in a careless manner. His more exalted friends, whose stations and characters did him honour, are treated in a different style: and you will perceive a real dignity, and a most delicate kind of wit in all his poems to Lord OXFORD,[12] Lord PETERBOROUGH,[13] Lord CARTERET,[d] [14] Mr. PULTNEY,[e] [15] and I think I may particularly add, in a poem to the Countess of WINCHELSEA,[f] [16] and another to Mrs. BIDDY FLOYDE.[17] These names abetted him in his pursuit of fame. They reflected back the glory which he gave. But, still I cannot recollect one poem, nay, scarce a couplet, to his noble patron Lord BOLINGBROKE.[18] In that instance he has been as silent, as VIRGIL has been to HORACE,[19] and yet he certainly had not a grain of envy in his composition.

---

[c]to find even] even to find FI, FIa, FIb, FII, FIII, FV, MI, MII

[d]Original footnote in the *Remarks*: "Now Earl of GRANVILE."

[e]Original footnote in the *Remarks*: "Now Earl of BATH."

[f]Original footnote in the *Remarks*: "Under the name of ARDELIA."

I think I can discern a third kind of style in his poems addressed to Mr.
POPE,[20] Mr. GAY,[21] Dr. DELANY,[22] and Dr. YOUNG.[23]   When he
writes to them, there is a mixture of ease, dignity, familiarity, and affection.
They were his intimate friends, whom he loved sincerely, and whom he wished
to accompany into the poetical regions of eternity.[24]

I have just now cast my eye over a poem called *Death and Daphne*,[25]
which makes me recollect an odd incident relating to that nymph.[26] SWIFT,
soon after our acquaintance, introduced me to her, as to one of his female
favourites.[27] I had scarce been half an hour in her company, before she
asked me, if I had seen the DEAN's poem upon *Death and Daphne*. As I told
her I had not, she immediately unlocked a cabinet, and bringing out the
manuscript, read it to me with a seeming satisfaction, of which, at that time,
I doubted the sincerity. While she was reading, the Dean was perpetually
correcting her for bad pronunciation, and for placing a wrong emphasis upon
particular words.[28] As soon as she had gone thorough the composition, she
assured me smilingly, that the portrait of DAPHNE was drawn for herself: I
begged to be excused from believing it, and protested that I could not see one
feature that had the least resemblance, but the Dean immediately burst into
a fit of laughter. "You fancy, says he, that you are very polite, but you are
much mistaken. That Lady had rather be a DAPHNE drawn by me, than a
SACHARISSA[29] by any other pencil."[30] She confirmed what he had said,
with great earnestness, so that I had no other method of retrieving my error,
than by whispering in her ear, as I was conducting her down stairs to dinner,
that indeed I found

"Her hand as dry and cold as lead."[31]

You see the command which SWIFT had over all his females; and you would
have smiled to have found his house a constant seraglio of very virtuous
women, who attended him from morning till night, with an obedience, an awe,
and an assiduity, that are seldom paid to the richest, or the most powerful
lovers; no, not even to the Grand Seignior[32] himself.

To these Ladies SWIFT owed the publication of many pieces, which ought
never to have been delivered to the press. He communicated every
composition as soon as finished, to his female senate, who, not only passed
their judgement on the performance, but constantly asked, and almost as
constantly obtained, a copy of it. You cannot be surprized that it was
immediately afterwards seen in print: and when printed, became a part of his
works. He lived much at home, and was continually writing, when alone. Not
any of his Senators presumed to approach him when he signified his pleasure
to remain in private, and without interruption. His nightgown and slippers
were not easier put on or off, than his attendants. No Prince ever met with

more flattery to his person,[g] or more devotion to his own mandates.[h] This despotic power not only blinded him, but gave a loose to passions that ought to have been kept under a proper restraint. I am sorry to say, that whole nations are sometimes sacrificed to his resentment. Reflexions[i] of that sort appear to me the least justifiable of any kind of satyr. You will read his *Acerrima*[33] with indignation, and his *Minutiae*[34] with regret. Yet I must add, that since he has descended so low as to write, and, still so much lower, as to print riddles, he is excellent even in that kind of versification.[35] The lines are smoother, the expressions are neater, and the thought is closer pursued than in any other *riddle-writer* whatever. But, SWIFT composing riddles is TITIAN[36] painting draught-boards, which must have been inexcusable, while there remained a sign-post painter in the world.

At the latter end of the volume you will find two Latin poems. The first, *An Epistle to Dr. SHERIDAN;*[37] the last, *A description of the rocks at Carbery in Ireland.*[38] The Dean was extremely solicitous, that they should be printed among his works: and what is no less true than amazing, he assumed to himself more vanity upon these two Latin poems, than upon many of his best English performances.[39] It is said, that MILTON in his own judgement preferred the *Paradise regained* to the *Paradise lost.*[40] There possibly might be found some excuse for such a preference, but in SWIFT's case there can be none. He understood the Latin language perfectly well, and he read it constantly, but he was no Latin poet. And if the *Carberiae Rupes*, and the *Epistola ad* THOMAM SHERIDAN, had been the produce of any other author, they must have undergone a severe censure from Dr. SWIFT.[41]

Here I shall dismiss this volume of his poems, which has drawn me into a greater length of letter than I intended. Adieu, my HAM, believe me ever

Your affectionate Father
ORRERY.

---

[g]his person,] his own person, FI, FIa, FIb, FII, FV, MI, MII

[h]his own mandates. MV] his mandates. MIII

[i]Reflexions] for reflections FI, FIa, FIb, FII, FV, MI; for reflexions FIII; Reflections MII

Notes

1. 1 Kings 11:1-3.

2. In his *Proposal for Correcting . . . . the English Tongue*, Swift wrote about the role of women in conversation: "since they [the women] have been left out of all Meetings, except Parties at Play, or where worse Designs are carried on, our Conversation hath very much degenerated" (*Prose Works of Swift* 4:13).

3. Swift, *To Stella, who Collected and Transcribed his Poems*, lines 9-14.

4. In particular, see *On Stella's Birth-day 1718-19* (*Poems of Swift* 2:720-22); *Stella's Birth-day 1720-21* (ibid., pp. 734-36); *Stella's Birth-day 1724-25* (ibid., pp. 756-58); and especially *A Receipt to Restore Stella's Youth*, written March-April 1725 (ibid., pp. 758-60).

5. See Williams's remarks on the subject, in ibid., 1:xv-xviii.

6. This passage is quoted by A. C. Elias, Jr., and Elias's insightful commentary is: "In real life, Swift may or may not have been a chained eagle snapping at gnats: what matters is that a favored acquaintance like Orrery should have thought him so. It is the wretched insects more than Swift for whom Orrery betrays a feeling of empathy and understanding. Ten or eleven years after Orrery had last visited the Dean, it looks as if the memory of Swift was enough to stir up feelings of vulnerability" (Elias, *Swift at Moor Park*, p. 138).

7. *Poems of Swift* 2:524-30. Published sometime before 12 June 1732 (*Correspondence of Swift* 4:31).

8. Orrery owned a copy of one of the pieces written in answer to *The Lady's Dressing Room: The Dean's Provocation for Writing the Lady's Dressing Room. A Poem* (London: T. Cooper, 1734), offered during Christie's Orrery Sale (November 1905) as part of lot 471. See *The Orrery Sale*, p. 65.

9. Cf. Ehrenpreis's words on the subject: "Swift is ridiculing literary styles–the conventions of treating women as beings who have no minds but never experience bodily discomfort, the tradition of using pastoral imagery to celebrate pastoral beauty, the *carpe diem* theme. Ordinary lyrics of the century preceding Swift's poems rarely face the problem of women's growing old or sick, and rarely suggest that they need to clean themselves, think, or read" (Ehrenpreis, *Swift* 3:693).

10. "Grant me, O Latona's son, to be content with what I have, and, sound of body and of mind, to pass an old age lacking neither honor nor the lyre!" (Horace *Odes* 1.31.17-20).

11. In Swift, *Stella's Birth-day. A great Bottle of Wine, long buried, being that Day dug up,* there are the following references to servants: Mrs. Brent, Swift's housekeeper (line 50), Alexander McGee, or "Saunders," butler (line 56), Archy, Groom (line 57), who was later dismissed by Swift (*Correspondence of Swift* 3:139), another Archy, second butler (line 73), and Robert, valet (line 77). See *Poems of Swift* 2:742-43.

12. While Oxford was waiting for his trial (1716), Swift wrote an imitation of Horace's second ode, book 3 of *Odes,* dedicated to him (ibid., 1:209-10).

13. Swift, *To the Earl of Peterborough* (ibid., 2:396-98), written in 1726 and first published by Faulkner in 1735.

14. In following Faulkner, Orrery is making a mistake in saying that Swift wrote a poem to Carteret. The two poems to Carteret that had been ascribed to Swift were shown not to be his: *The Birth of Manly Virtue* (ibid., pp. 381-88), and an imitation of Horace *Odes* 4.9 (ibid., 3:1132-33). See Ehrenpreis, *Swift* 3:635, and James Woolley, "The Canon of Swift's Poems: The Case of 'An Apology to the Lady Carteret'" in *Reading Swift,* ed. Richard Rodino and Hermann Real, assisted by Helgard Stöver-Leidig (Munich: Wilhelm Fink Verlag, 1992), pp. 245-64.

15. Swift, *On Mr. Pulteney being put out of the Council* (*Poems of Swift* 2:537-39), written in 1731 and first published by Faulkner in 1735. See *Dictionary of National Biography,* s.v. "Pulteney, William."

16. Anne Finch (1661-1720), countess of Winchelsea and poet. Swift's poem to her is *Apollo Outwitted* (*Poems of Swift* 1:119-21), written in 1709. See Barbara McGovern, *Anne Finch and Her Poetry: A Critical Biography* (Athens: University of Georgia Press, 1992).

17. *To Mrs. Biddy Floyd* (*Poems of Swift* 1:117-18), probably written in 1708. Biddy Floyd was Lady Betty Germain's friend and companion, and she is mentioned in Swift's *A Ballad on the Game of Traffick,* lines 13-16 (ibid., p. 75).

18. In Orrery's interleaved and annotated copy of the *Remarks* MS Eng 218.14, interleaf page numbered 126 (Houghton Library, Harvard), Orrery records Swift's reference to Bolingbroke in *Verses on the Death of Dr. Swift,*

lines 209-10. Actually, in *Verses on the Death of Dr. Swift*, Swift mentions Bolingbroke five times (lines 59, 196, 209, 373, and 434).

19. Orrery tries to disprove this idea in Letter XXIII.

20. Swift, *Dr. Swift to Mr. Pope, While he was writing the Dunciad* (*Poems of Swift* 2:405-6), written probably in the summer of 1727.

21. Swift, *To Mr. Gay on his being Steward to the Duke of Queensberry* (ibid., pp. 530-36), written in 1731 (cf. Swift to Gay and the duchess of Queensberry, 13 March 1731, in *Correspondence of Swift* 3:443), and first printed by Faulkner in 1735.

22. Orrery is referring to two poems on Delany included in Faulkner's edition of Swift's works, volume 2: *To Doctor Delany, on the Libels Writ against Him* (*Poems of Swift* 2:499-505), and *A Libel on Dr. Delany and a Certain Great Lord* (ibid., pp. 479-86).

23. Orrery is referring to Swift, *On Reading Dr. Young's Satires, Called the Universal Passion* (ibid., 2:390-92), included in Faulkner's edition of Swift's works, volume 2. As Williams points out, Orrery's inclusion of the name of the poet and clergyman Edward Young (1683-1765) here is inappropriate (ibid., p. 405).

24. Quoted by Williams in (ibid.).

25. Ibid., 3:902-5. First published in 1735 by Faulkner, who dated the poem in the year 1730. Daphne was the nymph whom Apollo loved and pursued. She fled from him, and as Apollo was about to catch her, Daphne prayed to her father (identified as either the river Ladon or the river Peneus) that she might be transformed. Daphne then became a laurel tree, and the very name "Daphne" means "laurel" in Greek. See Ovid *Metamorphoses* 1.452-567.

26. Anne Savage, later Acheson (d. 1 November 1737), wife of Sir Arthur Acheson (1688-1749), baronet of Market Hill, County Armagh. Sir Arthur and Lady Anne separated about 1732. Orrery's identification of Lady Acheson remained in manuscript form (Orrery's interleaved and annotated copy of the *Remarks* MS Eng 218.14, interleaf page numbered 127, Houghton Library, Harvard).

27. This might have taken place in 1732, and after Lady Acheson's separation from her husband. See Ehrenpreis, *Swift* 3:668 n. 3.

28. Cf. Mrs. Delany's words on the occasion of a dinner at Delville (Delany's estate) in April 1733: "The Dean of St. Patrick's was there, in *very good humour*. He calls himself '*my master*' and corrects me when I speak bad English, or do not pronounce my words distinctly." In Mrs. Delany, [Mary Granville], *The Autobiography and Correspondence*, ed. Lady Llanover (London: R. Bentley, 1861), 1:402.

29. The name given by Edmund Waller to Dorothy Sidney, later Dorothy Spencer (1617-84) in the approximately twenty poems he wrote about his courtship of her.

30. The story is mentioned and partially repeated by Williams and Ehrenpreis (*Poems of Swift* 3:902-3; Ehrenpreis, *Swift* 3:668).

31. Swift, *Death and Daphne*, line 95.

32. I.e., the Ottoman emperor.

33. Superlative of *acer*, indicating very violent deeds or words. Here it is turned into the neuter substantive form.

34. Things of little importance.

35. For Swift's riddles, see *Poems of Swift* 3:911-43. Orrery apparently enjoyed Swift's riddles, as may be seen in Orrery's copy of Faulkner's edition of Swift's works, now at the Mortimer Rare Book Room, Smith College. In volume 2, beside every riddle by Swift, Orrery wrote down the solution (pp. 181-96). Orrery did the same in the riddles in volume 8 (pp. 341-51).

36. Titian, or, Tiziano Vecellio (ca. 1488-1576), painter, for whom see Charles Hope, *Titian* (London: Jupiter, 1980).

37. Swift, *Ad Amicum Eruditum Thomam Sheridan* (*Poems of Swift* 1:211-14), dated October 1717, and printed by Faulkner in 1735.

38. Swift, *Carberiae Rupes in Comitatu Corgagensi apud Hybernicos* (ibid., pp. 315-19), dated June 1723 and first published by Faulkner in 1735.

39. Williams quotes these words (ibid., p. 316).

40. See Edward Phillips, *The Life of Mr. John Milton* (1694), in *The Early Lives of Milton*, ed. Helen Darbishire (London: Constable, 1932), pp. 75-76.

41. Quoted by Williams in *Poems of Swift* 1:316.

LETTER XI

My dear HAMILTON,

THE third volume of SWIFT's works contains *The travels of* LEMUEL GULLIVER *into several remote nations of the world.*[1] They are divided into four parts; the first, a voyage to *Lilliput;*[2] the second, a voyage to *Brobdingnag;*[3] the third, to *Laputa* and other islands;[4] the fourth, and most extraordinary, to the country of the *Houyhnhnms.*[5]2 These voyages are intended as a moral political romance,[6] in which SWIFT seems to have exerted the strongest efforts of a fine irregular genius. But while his imagination and his wit delight, the venomous strokes of his satir, although in some places just, are carried into so universal a severity, that not only all human actions, but human nature itself is placed in the worst light. Perfection in every attribute is not indeed allotted to particular men: but, among the whole species, we discover such an assemblage of all the great, and amiable virtues, as may convince us, that the original order of nature contains in it the greatest beauty. It is directed in a right line, but it deviates into curves and irregular motions, by various attractions, and disturbing causes. Different qualifications shine out in different men. BACON and NEWTON (not to mention BOYLE)[7] shew the divine extent of the human mind: of which power SWIFT could not be insensible; but as I have often told you, his disappointments rendered him splenetic, and angry with the whole world.

Education, habit, and constitution, give a surprizing variety of characters; and, while they produce some particular qualities, are apt to check others. Fortitude of mind seldom attends a sedentary life: nor is the man, whose ambitious views are crossed, scarce ever afterwards indued with benevolence of heart. The same mind, that is capable of exerting the greatest virtue, by some defect in the first steps of education often degenerates into the greatest vice. These effects take their source from causes almost mechanical. The soul, in our present situation, is blended and enclosed with corporeal substance, and the matter of which our body is composed, produces strange impulses upon the mind: but the instances that might illustrate, and explain

175

the different effects arising from this formation, would carry me into a digression too extensive[a] for my present plan.

To correct vice, by shewing its[b] deformity in opposition to the beauty of virtue, and to amend the false systems of philosophy, by pointing out the errors, and applying salutary means to avoid them, is a noble design. This was the general intent, I would fain flatter myself, of my hieroglyphic friend.

GULLIVER's travels are chiefly to be looked upon as an irregular essay of SWIFT's peculiar wit and humour. Let us take a view of the two first parts together. The inhabitants of *Lilliput* are represented, as if reflected from a convex[c] mirrour, by which every object is reduced to a despicable minuteness. The inhabitants of *Brobdingnag*, by a contrary mirrour, are enlarged to a shocking deformity. In *Lilliput* we behold a set of puny insects, or animalcules in human shape, ridiculously engaged in affairs of importance. In *Brobdingnag* the monsters of enormous size are employed in trifles.

LEMUEL GULLIVER has observed great exactness in the just proportion, and appearances of the several objects thus lessened and magnified: but he dwells too much upon these optical deceptions. The mind is tired with a repetition of them, especially as he points out no beauty, nor use in such amazing discoveries, which might have been so continued as to have afforded improvement, at the same time that they gave astonishment. Upon the whole, he too often shews an indelicacy that is not agreeable, and exerts his vein of humour most improperly in some places, where (I am afraid) he glances at religion.

In his description of *Lilliput*, he seems to have had *England* more immediately in view. In his description of *Blefuscu* he seems to intend the people and kingdom of *France:* yet the allegory between these nations is frequently interrupted, and scarce any where compleat. Several just strokes of satir are scattered here and there upon errors in the conduct of our government: and, in the sixth chapter of his voyage to *Brobdingnag*, he gives an account of the political state of *Europe:*[8] his observations are delivered with his usual spirit of humour and severity. He appears most particularly affected with the proceedings of the courts of judicature, and complains of being almost ruined by a Chancery suit, which was *determined in his favour with costs.*[9] It must be confessed, that instances of this kind are too frequent

---

[a]would carry me into a digression too extensive] are too digressively extensive FI, FIa, FIb, FII, FIII, FV, MI, MII

[b]its] her FI, FIa, FIb, FII, FIII, FV, MI, MII

[c]convex] concave FI; Orrery's correction in Osborn pc 231: "concave" to "convex."

in our courts of justice, and they leave us no room to boast of the execution of our present laws, however excellent the laws, in their own original foundation, may have been. *Judgement, when turned into wormwood, is bitter,* but delays, as Lord BACON observes, turn it into vinegar:[10] it becomes sharp, and corroding: and certainly it is more eligible to die immediately by the wound of an enemy, than to decay lingering by poison, administered from a seeming friend.

The seventh chapter of the voyage to[d] *Brobdingnag*[11] contains such sarcasms on the structure of the human body,[12] as too plainly shew us, that the author was unwilling to lose any opportunity of debasing and ridiculing his own species.

Here a reflexion naturally occurs, which, without any superstition, leads me tacitly to admire, and confess the ways of Providence: for this great genius, this mighty wit, who seemed to scorn and scoff[e] at all mankind, lived not only to be an example of pride punished in his own person,[f] and an example of terror to the pride of others; but lived to undergo[g] some of the greatest miseries to which human nature is liable. The particulars of this assertion will appear, by copying a letter which one of his relations sent to me, in answer to my enquiries after his situation.

Dublin, *November* 22, 1742.[13]

My LORD,

THE easy manner, in which you reproach me for not acquainting you with the poor Dean's situation, lays a fresh obligation upon me; yet mean as an excuse is for a fault, I shall attempt one to your Lordship, and only for this reason, that you may not think me capable of neglecting any thing you could command me. I told you in my last letter, the Dean's understanding was quite gone, and I feared the farther particulars would only shock the tenderness of your nature, and the melancholy scene make your heart ach, as it has often done mine. I was the last person whom he knew, and when that part of his memory failed, he was so outragious at seeing any body, that I was forced to leave him, nor could he rest

----

[d]to] of FI, FIa, FIb, FII, FIII, FV, MI, MII

[e]scorn and scoff] scoff, and scorn FI, FIa, FIb, FII, FV, MI, MII

[f]an example of pride punished in his own person,] an example to punish his own pride, FI, FIa, FIb, FII, FV, MI, MII

[g]and an example of terror to the pride of others; but lived to undergo] and to terrify ours, but underwent FI, FIa, FIb, FII, FV, MI, MII

for a night or two after seeing any person: so that all the attendance which I could pay him was calling twice a week to enquire after his health, and to observe that proper care was taken of him, and durst only look at him while his back was towards me, fearing to discompose him. He walked ten hours a day, would not eat or drink if his servant stayed in the room. His meat was served up ready cut, and sometimes it would lie an hour on the table before he would touch it, and then eat it walking. About six weeks ago, in one night's time, his left eye swelled as large as an egg, and the lid Mr. NICHOLS[14] *(his surgeon) thought would mortify, and many large boils appeared upon his arms and body. The torture he was in, is not to be described.*[15] *Five persons could scarce hold him for a week from tearing out his own eyes: and, for near a month, he did not sleep two hours in twenty four: yet a moderate appetite continued; and what is more to be wondered at, the last day of his illness, he knew me perfectly well, took me by the hand, called me by my name, and shewed the same pleasure as usual in seeing me. I asked him, if he would give me a dinner? He said, to be sure, my old friend. Thus he continued that day, and knew the Doctor and Surgeon, and all his family so well, that Mr.* NICHOLS *thought it possible he might return to a share of understanding, so as to be able to call for what he wanted, and to bear some of his old friends to amuse him. But alas! this pleasure to me was but of short duration; for the next day or two it was all over, and proved to be only pain that had rouzed him. He is now free from torture: his eye almost well; very quiet, and begins to sleep, but cannot, without great difficulty, be prevailed on to walk a turn about his room: and yet in this way the Physicians think he may hold out for some time. I am, my Lord,*

Your Lordship's most obedient
humble servant,
M. WHITEWAY.[16]

What a shocking, what a melancholy account is this; of how small estimation must the greatest genius appear in the sight of GOD!

About a year and a half afterwards, I received a letter from another of his relations, DEANE SWIFT, Esq; in answer to a report, which I had mentioned to him, of Dr. SWIFT's having viewed himself (as he was led across the room) in a glass, and crying out, "*O poor old man!*" The letter is written long after the Dean had been totally deprived of reason.[17]

Dublin, *April* 4, 1744.[18]

My LORD,

As to the story of O poor old man! I enquired into it. The Dean did say something upon his seeing himself in the glass, but neither Mrs. RIDGEWAY,[19] *nor the lower servants could tell me what it was he said. I desired them to recollect it, by the time when I should come again to the deanery. I have been there since, they cannot recollect it. A thousand stories have been invented of him within these two years, and imposed upon the world. I thought this might have been one of them: and yet I am now inclined to think, there may be some truth in it: for on Sunday the 17th of March, as he sat in his chair, upon the housekeeper's moving a knife from him as he was going to catch at it, he shrugged his shoulders, and, rocking himself, said* I am what I am, I am what I am: *and, about six minutes afterwards, repeated the same words two or three times over.*[20]

His servant shaves his cheeks, and all his face as low as the tip of his chin, once a week: but under the chin, and about the throat, when the hair grows long, it is cut with scissars.

Sometimes he will not utter a syllable: at other times he will speak incoherent words: but he never yet, as far as I could hear, talked nonsense, or said a foolish thing.[21]

About four months ago he gave me great trouble: he seemed to have a mind to talk to me. In order to try what he would say, I told him, I came to dine with him, and immediately his housekeeper, Mrs. RIDGEWAY, *said,* Won't you give Mr. SWIFT *a glass of wine, Sir? he shrugged his shoulders, just as he used to do when he had a mind that a friend should spend*[h] *the evening with him. Shrugging his shoulders, your Lordship may remember, was as much as to say,* "You'll ruin me in wine." *I own, I was scarce able to bear the sight. Soon after, he again endeavoured, with a good deal of pain, to find words to speak to me: at last, not being able, after many efforts, he gave a heavy sigh, and, I think, was afterwards silent. This puts me in mind of what he said about five days ago. He endeavoured several times to speak to his servant (now and then he calls him by his name) at last, not finding words to express what he would be at, after some uneasiness, he said,* "I am a fool."[22] *Not long ago, the servant took up his watch that lay upon the table to see what o'clock it was, he said,* "Bring it here:" *and when it was brought, he looked very attentively at it: some time ago, the servant was breaking a large stubborn coal, he said,* "That's a stone, you blockhead."

In a few days, or some very short time, after guardians had been appointed for him, I went into his dining room, where he was walking, I said something to him very insignificant, I know not what; but instead of making any kind of answer to it, he said "Go, go," *pointing with his hand to the door, and immediately afterwards, raising his hand to his head, he said,* "My best understanding," *and so broke off abruptly, and walked away. I am, my Lord,*

---

[h]spend MV] not spend MIII

> Your Lordship's most obedient,
> and most humble servant,
> DEANE SWIFT.

These two letters will not probably occasion in you very chearful speculations.   Let us return back therefore to the *Lilliputians,* and the *Brobdingnaggians*; where you will find many ridiculous adventures, even such as must have excited mirth in[i] HERACLITUS.[23] Where indelicacies do not intervene, the narrative is very entertaining and humorous.   Several just strokes of satir are scattered up and down upon political errors in government. In some parts, GULLIVER seems to have had particular incidents, if not particular persons, in his view. His observations on education are useful:[24] and so are his improvements on the institutions of LYCURGUS.[25]   Upon reading over the two first parts of these travels, I think that I can discover a very great resemblance between certain passages in GULLIVER's voyage to *Lilliput,* and the voyage of CYRANO DE BERGERAC to the sun and moon.[26]

CYRANO DE BERGERAC[27] is a French author of a singular character, who had a very peculiar turn of wit and humour, in many respects resembling that of SWIFT. He wanted the advantages of learning, and a regular education: his imagination was less guarded, and correct, but more agreeably extravagant. He has introduced into his philosophical romance, the system of DESCARTES (which was then much admired) intermixt with several fine strokes of just satir on the wild, and immechanical enquiries of the philosophers, and astronomers of that age: and in many parts he has evidently directed the plan, which the Dean of St. PATRICK's has pursued.

I am sorry, and yet, in candour, I ought to observe, that GULLIVER, in his voyage to *Lilliput,* dares even to exert his vein of humour so liberally, as to place the resurrection (one of the most encouraging principles of the Christian religion) in a ridiculous, and contemptible light.[j]   Why should that appointment be denied to man, or appear so very extraordinary in the human kind, which the Author of nature has illustrated in the vegetable species, where the seed dies and corrupts, before it can rise again to new beauty and glory? But I am writing out of my province; and that I may be tempted no farther, here let me end the criticism upon the two first parts of GULLIVER's travels, the conclusion of which, I mean GULLIVER's escape from BROBDINGNAG,[28] is humorous, satirical, and decent. I am, my dearest HAM, by duty and inclination,

---

[i]in] from FI, FIa, FIb, FII, FIII, FV, MI, MII

[j]Original footnote in the *Remarks*: "Page 55." This refers to the page number in volume 3 of Faulkner's edition of Swift's works.

Your best Friend,
and most affectionate Father
ORRERY.

Notes

1. In *Prose Works of Swift* 11. Regarding the date of composition of *Gulliver's Travels*, Harold Williams wrote: "Internal and external evidence combine, therefore, to prove that, whatever fragmentary passages of *Gulliver's Travels* may have been written before 1720, the real composition of the work began in that year, or in 1721. In 1725 Swift, as we have seen, spent the summer and autumn of a country holiday in revising and transcribing his draft for the press; and about six months later he was in London, carrying the manuscript with him." In Jonathan Swift, *Gulliver's Travels*, ed. Harold Williams (London: First Edition Club, 1926), p. xxii. Swift himself wrote that part 4 was completed in 1723, and that part 3 was written in 1724. See Jonathan Swift, *The Letters of Jonathan Swift to Charles Ford*, ed. David Nichol Smith (Oxford: Clarendon Press, 1935), p. 101. *Gulliver's Travels* was first published on 28 October 1726 in London, and the best text is the one published by Faulkner in 1735 (the third volume of Faulkner's edition of Swift's works).

2. *Prose Works of Swift* 11:19-80.

3. Ibid., pp. 83-149.

4. Ibid., pp. 153-218.

5. Ibid., pp. 221-96.

6. See J. A. Downie, "The Political Significance of *Gulliver's Travels*" in *Swift and His Contexts*, ed. John Irwin Fischer, Hermann Real, and James Woolley (New York: AMS Press, 1989), pp. 1-19.

7. Robert Boyle, author, natural philosopher, and Orrery's distant relative.

8. *Prose Works of Swift* 11:127-32. Actually, in that chapter, Gulliver gives an account of England rather than of Europe.

9. Gulliver's words are: "Upon what I said in relation to our Courts of Justice, his Majesty desired to be satisfied in several Points: And, this I was the better able to do, having been formerly almost ruined by a long Suit in Chancery, which was decreed for me with Costs" (ibid., p. 130).

10. Francis Bacon, *Of the Dignity and Advancement of Learning*, bk. 6, chap. 3. See Francis Bacon, *The Works of Francis Bacon*, ed. James Spedding, Robert Leslie Ellis, and Douglas Denon Heath, 14 vols. (London: Longmans, 1857-74), 4:489-90. Orrery owned a copy of a four-volume edition of Francis Bacon's works (London: Andrew Millar, 1740), offered during Christie's Orrery Sale (November 1905) as lot 163. See *The Orrery Sale*, p. 23.

11. *Prose Works of Swift* 11:133-138.

12. Orrery is referring to Gulliver's remarks on the contents of Glumdalclitch's "little old Treatise," which was "in little Esteem except among Women and the Vulgar": "This Writer went through all the usual Topicks of *European* Moralists; shewing how diminutive, contemptible, and helpless an Animal was Man in his own Nature; how unable to defend himself from the Inclemencies of the Air, or the Fury of wild Beasts: How much he was excelled by one Creature in Strength, by another in Speed, by a third in Foresight, by a fourth in Industry. He added, that Nature was degenerated in these latter declining Ages of the World, and could now produce only small abortive Births in Comparison of those in ancient Times" (ibid., p. 137).

13. Orrery's *Remarks* is the earliest published source of this letter's text, printed in *Correspondence of Swift* 5:207-8.

14. John Nichols, surgeon general of Ireland, d. 1767.

15. Referring to this passage, Ehrenpreis wrote: "We now know that the disease was a painful and feverish case of orbital cellulitis, purely physiological in origin" (*Swift* 3:916).

16. Orrery wrote back to Mrs. Whiteway from Marston House in Somersetshire on 4 December 1742, to acknowledge her account of Swift. The text of this letter, in MS Eng 218.2, IV, pages numbered 339-41, Houghton Library, Harvard, remains unpublished.

17. In the investigation on Swift's mental state, it was stated that Swift began to be irresponsible for his acts on 20 May 1742. A committee of guardians then protected Swift until his death. See Ehrenpreis, *Swift* 3:915.

18. As in the case of Mrs. Whiteway's letter to Orrery, Orrery's *Remarks* is the earliest published source of the text. It is printed in *Correspondence of Swift* 5:214-15.

19. Anne Ridgeway, Swift's housekeeper and daughter of Mrs. Brent, who had also been Swift's housekeeper. Mrs. Brent died in the spring of 1735, and Ehrenpreis observes that Mrs. Ridgeway must have been installed before June 1735. Ehrenpreis remarks that there is a receipt of that date witnessed by her (*Swift* 3:806 n. 2).

20. In *Correspondence of Swift* 5:214 n. 1, there is an instructive footnote to this passage: "Among the thousand invented stories is one which may be dismissed–that the servants privately took money for admitting strangers to see the Dean, a wreck of his former greatness. The appointed guardians would prevent any gross practice of the kind. Scott (*Memoirs*, 1814, p. 459 n) does relate this story on the authority of 'one of the Editor's most intimate friends' (Lord Kineddar). Even so the veracity of the tale is much in doubt."

21. See Ehrenpreis's words on Swift's aphasia, in *Swift* 3:918.

22. As Ehrenpreis points out, these are Swift's last recorded words (ibid.).

23. Heraclitus, Greek philosopher born in Ephesus who lived around 500 B.C. His writings provided the basis for Stoicism, and he was called "the mourner," from his weeping at mankind's follies.

24. Gulliver's report on the education of children in Lilliput, and his observations on it, are in pt. 1, chap. 6 (*Prose Works of Swift* 11:60-63).

25. Lycurgus, Spartan lawgiver who died around 870 B.C. He established the Spartan system of laws, which was quite severe. For Lycurgus's notions on education, as applied in Sparta, see Plutarch *Life of Lycurgus* 16-25.

26. For *Les Estats et Empires de la Lune* and *Les Estats et Empires du Soleil*, the two parts that constitute Cyrano de Bergerac's *L'Autre Monde*, see Cyrano de Bergerac, *Les Oeuvres Libertines de Cyrano de Bergerac*, ed. Frédéric Lachèvre, 2 vols. (Geneva: Slatkine Reprints, 1968), 1:1-199. The influence of those works on *Gulliver's Travels* has been discussed in William A. Eddy, *Gulliver's Travels: A Critical Study* (Gloucester, Mass.: Peter Smith, 1963), pp. 61-64.

27. For the life of Cyrano de Bergerac (1619-55), see ibid., pp. xvii-cxii.

28. In pt. 2, chap. 8 (*Prose Works of Swift* 11:139-43).

LETTER XII

My dear HAMILTON,

THE third part of GULLIVER's travels is[a] in general written against chymists, mathematicians, mechanics, and projectors of all kinds.

SWIFT was little acquainted with mathematical knowledge,[1] and was prejudiced against it, by observing the strange effects it produced in those, who applied themselves entirely to that science.[2] No part of human literature has given greater strength to the mind, or has produced greater benefits to mankind, than the several branches of learning that may pass under the general denomination of mathematics. But the abuses of this study, the idle, thin, immechanical refinements of it, are just subjects of satir. The real use of knowledge is to invigorate, not to enervate the faculties of reason. Learning degenerates into a species of madness, when it is not superior to what it possesseth. The scientific powers are most evident, when they are capable of exerting themselves in the social duties of life: when they wear no chains, but can freely disengage themselves, and like a sound constitution of body, rise chearful, and more vigorous by the food they have acquired, being neither oppressed, nor rendered stupid by the labours of digestion.

Lord BACON has justly exposed the vain pursuits of ostentatious pedants in the different parts of learning, and their unaccountable temerity in deducing general rules from arbitrary maxims, or few experiments: he has likewise fixed upon a sure and certain basis, the procedure and limits of the human understanding. SWIFT has pursued the same plan in a different manner, and has placed the imaginary schemes of all pretenders, in a more ludicrous, and therefore in a more proper light.

Ridiculum acri

---

[a]is] are FI, FIa, FIb, FII, FV, MI; Orrery's correction in Osborn pc 231: "are" to "is."

Fortius ac melius magnas plerumque secat res.[3]

He cannot be supposed to condemn useful experiments, or the right application of them: but he ridicules the vain attempts, and irregular productions of those rash men, who, like IXION, embracing a cloud instead of a goddess, plagued the world with centaurs,[4] whilst JUPITER, from the embraces of a JUNO, and an ALCMENA, blessed the earth with an HEBE, and an HERCULES.[5]

However wild the description of the *flying island*,[6] and the manners, and various projects of the philosophers of *Lagado*[7] may appear; yet it is a real picture embellished with much latent wit and humour. It is a satir upon those astronomers and mathematicians, who have so entirely dedicated their time to the planets, that they have been careless of their family and country, and have been chiefly anxious, about the oeconomy and welfare of the upper worlds. But if we consider SWIFT's romance in a serious light, we shall find him of opinion, that those determinations in philosophy, which at present seem to the most knowing men to be perfectly well founded and understood, are in reality unsettled, or uncertain, and may perhaps some ages hence be as much decried,[b] as the axioms of ARISTOTLE are at this day. Sir ISAAC NEWTON and his notions may hereafter be out of fashion.[8] There is a kind of mode in philosophy, as well as in other things: and such modes often change more from the humour and caprice of men, than either from the unreasonable, or the ill-founded conclusions of the philosophy itself. The reasonings of some philosophers have undoubtedly better foundations than those of others: but I am of opinion (and SWIFT seems to be in the same way of thinking) that the most applauded philosophy hitherto extant has not fully, clearly, and certainly explained many difficulties in the phenomena of nature.[9] I am induced to believe, that God may have absolutely denied us the perfect knowledge of many points in philosophy, so that we shall never arrive at that perfection, however certain we may suppose ourselves of having attained to it already. Upon the whole, we may say with TULLY, *Omnibus ferè in rebus, et maximè in physicis quid non sit citius, quam quid sit, dixerim.*[10]

The project for a more easy and expeditious method of writing a treatise in any science, by a wooden engine,[c] is entertainingly satirical,[11] and is aimed at those authors, who, instead of receiving materials from their own

---

[b]decried,] descried FI, FIa, FIb, FII, FV; descried, MI; ~ ^ FIII, MIV; Orrery's correction in Osborn pc 231: "descried" to "decried."

[c]Original footnote in the *Remarks*: "Page 218." This refers to the page number in volume 3 of Faulkner's edition of Swift's works.

thoughts and observations, collect from dictionaries and common place-books, an irregular variety, without order, use or design,

> *Ut nec pes nec caput uni*
> *Reddatur formae.*[12]

The project of shortning a discourse, by cutting polysyllables into one, and leaving out verbs and participles,[d] [13] is pointed at the pernicious custom of contracting the English language, the dialect of which is naturally harsh, and that harshness is still encreased by improper contractions. As SWIFT was scrupulously exact in the pronunciation[e] of his own tongue, not the least improper expression ever escaped his censure: and I remember to have seen in manuscript a dictionary of hard words, composed by him for the use of his female senate.[14]

The sixth chapter[f] is full of severity and satir. Sometimes it is exerted against the legislative power:[15] sometimes against particular politicians: sometimes against women: and sometimes it degenerates into filth. True humour ought to be kept up with decency, and dignity, or it loses every tincture of entertainment. Descriptions that shock our delicacy cannot have the least good effect upon our minds. They offend us, and we fly precipitately from the sight. We cannot stay long enough to examine, whether wit, sense, or morality, may be couched under such odious appearances. I am sorry to say, that this[g] sort of descriptions, which are too often interspersed throughout all SWIFT's works, are seldom written with any other view, or from any other motive, than a wild unbridled indulgence of his own humour and disposition.

He seems to have finished his voyage to LAPUTA in a careless hurrying manner, which makes me almost think that sometimes he was tired of[h] his work, and attempted to run through it as fast as he could; otherwise why was

---

[d]Original footnote in the *Remarks*: "Page 220." This refers to the page number in volume 3 of Faulkner's edition of Swift's works.

[e]pronunciation MV] pronounciation MIII

[f]Original footnote in the *Remarks*: "Page 223." This refers to the page number in volume 3 of Faulkner's edition of Swift's works.

[g]this MV] these MIII

[h]of] with FI, FIa, FIb, FII, FV, MI, MII

the curtain dropped so soon?[i] or why were we deprived of so noble a scene as might have been discovered in the island of *Glubdubdrib,*[j] *where the governor, by his skill in necromancy, had the power of calling whom he pleased from the dead?*[k] [16] I have not time by this post to write to you my thoughts upon a subject, which I confess awakened, but by no means satisfied my curiosity. I lamented to find so many illustrious ghosts vanish so quickly, and so abruptly from my sight, many of whom were of the brightest characters in history. In my next letter I shall endeavour to detain them a little longer in *Leicester-fields,*[17] than SWIFT suffered them to stay in the island of Sorcerers.

I am,
My dear HAMILTON,
Your affectionate Father,
ORRERY.

---

[i]Orrery's correction in Osborn pc 231: "soon," to "soon?"

[j]Original footnote in the *Remarks*: "Chap. 7. Page 252." This refers to the page number in volume 3 of Faulkner's edition of Swift's works.

[k]Orrery's correction in Osborn pc 231: "dead." to "dead?"

Notes

1. Ehrenpreis wrote that, as a student at Trinity College, Swift cut most often lectures on mathematics (*Swift* 1:68). Writing from Holyhead on 27 September 1727 to one John Wheldon, who had applied to him for help on a project to determine the longitude, Swift said: "I understand not Mathematicks" (*Correspondence of Swift* 3:240).

2. Joseph Beaumont (d. 1731), linen draper of Trim and Swift's business agent, was interested in mathematics and researched into the problem of the longitude. He began to be deranged in 1715, and in 1722, became mad. Swift himself wrote to the secretary of the governors of Bedlam to have Beaumont sent there (ibid., 2:425). See Swift, *Journal to Stella* 1:1 n. 1.

3. "Jesting often cuts hard knots more forcefully and effectively than gravity" (Horace *Satires* 1.10.14-15).

4. Ixion was a Thessalian king who had fallen in love with Hera (Zeus's sister), and tried to rape her. To prevent that, Zeus shaped a cloud that resembled Hera, and from the intercourse between Ixion and that cloud, a son named Centaurus was born. Centaurus then became the father of the Centaurs.

5. When Alcmene's husband, Amphitryon, went on an expedition against the Teleboeans, Zeus (or Jupiter) assumed the appearance of Amphitryon and seduced Alcmene. Alcmene gave birth to Heracles (or Hercules) by her relations with Zeus. Hebe was the daughter of Zeus and Hera (or Juno).

6. In pt. 3, chap. 3 (*Prose Works of Swift* 11:167-72).

7. In pt. 3, chaps. 5 and 6, ibid., pp. 179-92.

8. Indeed, Einstein's view of the universe came to replace Newton's system.

9. Cf. Swift, *Gulliver's Travels*, pt. 3, chap. 8: "He [Aristotle's ghost] said, that new Systems of Nature were but new Fashions, which would vary in every Age; and even those who pretend to demonstrate them from Mathematical Principles, would flourish but a short Period of Time, and be out of Vogue when that was determined" (ibid., p. 198).

10. "In almost all subjects, but especially in natural philosophy, I am more ready to say what is not true than what is" (Cicero *De Natura Deorum* 1.21.61-62).

11. In pt. 3, chap. 5 (*Prose Works of Swift* 11:182-85).

12. "so that neither head nor foot can be assigned to a single shape" (Horace *Ars Poetica* 8-9).

13. In pt. 3, chap. 5 (*Prose Works of Swift* 11:185-86).

14. The reference is to the so-called Stella's wordbook, formerly in the possession of Lord Harmsworth.

15. See ibid., pp. 188-90.

16. Quoted from Swift, *Gulliver's Travels*, pt. 3, chap. 7 (ibid., p. 194).

17. Orrery was writing from his London house in Leicester Fields, now Leicester Square.

LETTER XIII

My dearest HAMILTON,

I Believe it would be impossible to find out the design of Dr. SWIFT, in summoning up a parcel of apparitions, that from their behaviour, or from any thing they say, are almost of as little consequence, as the ghosts in GAY's farce of the *What d'ye call it*.[1] Perhaps, SWIFT's general design might be to arraign the conduct of eminent persons after their death, and to convey their names, and images to posterity, deprived of those false colours, in which they formerly appeared. If these were his intentions, he has missed his aim; or at least, has been so far carried away by his disposition to raillery, that the moral, which ought to arise from such a fable, is buried in obscurity.

The first airy substance introduced is ALEXANDER the Great.[a][2] After a hint from GULLIVER, that we have lost the true Greek idiom,[3] the conqueror of the universe is made to declare upon his honour, "*That he died by excessive drinking, not by poison.*"[4] A trifling and an improper observation; because the apparition is called up as he appeared at the head of his army, just after the battle of *Arbela*.[5] I own my expectations were great, when I found his appearance was to be at such a remarkable juncture: and I particularly wished to see him properly introduced after that battle, as the compassion and generosity which he shewed to the family of DARIUS, was highly worthy of imitation. There are other circumstances in the historical records of him, that redound to his honour. His tender regard to PINDAR,[b] by sparing the house

---

[a]Original footnote in the *Remarks*: "Chap. 7. Page 234." This refers to the page number in volume 3 of Faulkner's edition of Swift's works.

[b]at such a remarkable juncture:
and I particularly wished to see him
properly introduced after that battle,
as the compassion and generosity which
he shewed to the family of DARIUS, was

of that poet (when he rased the city of *Thebes*)[6] seems to demand perpetual gratitude from all succeeding bards. The manner in which he visited the tomb

---

highly worthy of imitation. There are other circumstances in the historical records of him, that redound to his honour. His tender regard to PINDAR,] at that particular juncture. Or rather I could have wished to have seen him after the battle of *Issus*, when the temperate use which he made of his victory, was highly worthy of imitation. Such a circumstance might have graced his triumph. There are others too in the historical records of him, that redound to his honour. The tender regard which he shewed to PINDAR, FI.

A. C. Elias, Jr., explained why this change in the text has been made: "Traditionally, at least, it was at Issus that Alexander captured Darius' princesses and distinguished himself by treating them courteously. After Arbela, by contrast, he burnt down the great city of Persepolis. Though well taken in one sense, Orrery's comment still seems to concede some justice to Swift's charge of drunkenness. Orrery implies that Arbela was not the best moment for picturing Alexander, since Issus showed the hero in a more 'temperate' light. The cancellans removes this implied concession. Whether arbitrarily or as a result of further research, Orrery shifts the scene of Alexander's kindnesses back to Arbela, which Swift had associated with Alexander's intemperance." In Elias, "The First Printing of Orrery's *Remarks on Swift* (1751)," p. 312.

of ACHILLES:[7] the affection and respect paid by him to[c] ARISTOTLE;[8] the undaunted confidence placed in his physician PHILIP,[9] are instances sufficient to shew, that ALEXANDER did not want some virtues of humanity; and when we consider several of his rash actions of ebriety,[d] they convince us, how far the native excellencies of the mind may be debased and changed by passions which too often attend success and luxury,

Utcunque defecere mores,
Dedecorant benè nata culpae.[10]

It is evident, my HAM, that SWIFT had conceived an absolute disgust to ALEXANDER, whose character he aims to destroy, by touching it in so slight a manner, that he puts me in mind of the visit paid by AUGUSTUS CAESAR, to ALEXANDER's sepulchre at *Alexandria*. Upon the Emperor's arrival, the body of the Macedonian hero was found in its[e] full dimensions, but so tender, notwithstanding all the former embalming, that CAESAR, by touching only the nose of it, defaced the whole figure immediately.[11]

HANNIBAL[f] [12] seems to have been summoned with no other view than to censure LIVY the historian.[13] It is not only improbable, but impossible, that HANNIBAL should have carried a sufficient quantity of vinegar for the purpose related by LIVY:[14] but as vinegar will certainly soften, and dissolve stones, the experiment might have been improved, or so contrived by HANNIBAL, as to appear to make an easy, and expeditious opening through some particular passage, already fitted for the purpose. Such a trial, practised in that age of darkness, and properly managed, might have been universally received as a kind of miracle: so that LIVY could scarce have avoided inserting the report as an acknowledged truth: especially when[g] the fact itself seems to infer that the Romans were invincible, unless from some supernatural cause. SWIFT (no friend to military men) thinks the *Carthaginian* general unworthy of any farther notice: and hastens to call up the senate of *Rome*.[15] This gives him an opportunity of being very severe upon a certain modern

---

[c]by him to] to him by FIa, FIb, FII, FV, MI, MII

[d]ebriety,] inebriety, FI, FIa, FIb, FII, FV, MI, MII

[e]its] it's FI, FIa, FIb, FII, FV, MI, MIV

[f]Original footnote in the *Remarks*: "Page 235." This refers to the page number in volume 3 of Faulkner's edition of Swift's works.

[g]when] as FI, FIa, FIb, FII, FV, MI

assembly,[16] which he treats in a manner more resembling the Cynic[17] in his cell, than the free humoured *Rabelais*[18] in his easy chair.

POMPEY[19] and CAESAR appear only[h] to grace the entry of BRUTUS,[20] who is SWIFT's favourite patriot: but as CAESAR generously confessed to GULLIVER, "*That the greatest actions of his life, were not, by many degrees, equal to the glory of taking it away,*"[21] it would have been a proper alleviation of the dictator's crimes, to have acknowledged him the greatest statesman, orator, and soldier of the age, in which he lived: an age, fertile of eminent men: an age, when ambition was scarce looked upon as a crime: and when the Roman virtue (once the support and preservation of the commonwealth) was long since lost in vice and luxury: at such a time a single master was become necessary, and POMPEY would have seized the reins of government, had not CAESAR interposed.[22]   If the conspirators had restored liberty to their country, their act[23] had been completely glorious, and would have shewed, that CAESAR, not *Rome*, was degenerated. But if we may judge from the consequences, Heaven disapproved of the deed: a particular fate attended the conspirators, not one of whom died a natural death:[24] and even BRUTUS, perhaps recollecting in his last moments the benefits, which he had received from CAESAR,[25] was staggered in his thoughts of virtue, and imagining himself deceived by a shadow broke out into a pathetical expression, signifying, "*that he had worshipped virtue as a substance, and had found it only a shadow:*"[26] so that he seems to have wanted that fortitude of mind, which constantly attends true virtue to the grave. This defect in the character of BRUTUS is not improperly expressed in the famous galery[27] of the great duke of *Tuscany,*[28] where there is a very fine head of BRUTUS begun by MICHAEL ANGELO,[29] but left unfinished:[30] under it is engraven upon a copper plate, this distich,

> *Dum* Bruti *effigiem sculptor de marmore ducit,*
> *In mentem sceleris venit, et abstinuit.*[31]

If BRUTUS erred, it was from a wrong notion of virtue. The character of CAESAR is perhaps more amiable, but less perfect: his faults were great; however, many of them were foils to his virtues. A modern eminent writer[i] [32] has represented him as a glutton: he tells us, that when CAESAR went to the public feasts, he constantly took a vomit in the morning, with a design to indulge himself with more keenness, and to increase his appetite for the

---

[h]appear only MV] only appear MIII

[i]In Osborn pc 231, Orrery identified "A modern eminent writer" as being "Dr Middleton."

ensuing feast.[33] The fact is true; but I would willingly believe the inference unjust. It is more than probable, that he practised this custom by the advice of his physicians, who might direct such a regimen, as the most certain, and immediate preservation against epileptic fits, to which the Dictator was often liable.[34] Your grandfather, my honoured father,[35] (who was excelled by few physicians in the theory of physic) has often told me, that convulsions of this kind[j] were of such a nature as generally to come on after eating, and more violently, if the stomach was overloaded. CAESAR was so careful in observing a decent dignity in his behaviour, that he dreaded the shame of exposing publickly this weakness in his constitution; and therefore guarded against it in a prudent manner, which has since been construed into a reproach. This surmise, my HAM, rests upon the stronger foundation, as all authors agree, that he was most strictly, and remarkably abstemious.

In his public character CAESAR appears a strong example, how far the greatest natural, and acquired accomplishments may lose their lustre, when made subservient to false glory, and an immoderate thirst of power; as on the other hand, the history of BRUTUS may instruct us, what unhappy effects the rigid exercise of superiour virtue, when misapplied and carried too far, may produce in the most stedfast mind, or the soundest judgement.

GULLIVER has given to BRUTUS five companions, JUN. BRUTUS, SOCRATES, EPAMINONDAS, CATO the censor, and Sir THOMAS MOORE. Such a sextumvirate is not easily to be encreased: yet, let me hope, that the reflexion is too severely critical, when he adds, "*that all the ages of the world cannot furnish out a seventh.*"[36] Every age has produced men of virtue, and abilities in the highest degree. The race of mankind, since their first creation, have been always the same. The greatest characters have been blended with the greatest faults. Poets and historians have singled out particular persons for fame and immortality: they have adorned them with accomplishments, which perhaps they never possessed, while other men equally meritorious have been silently buried in oblivion, with only the self consciousness of deserving a rank among the companions of BRUTUS in the Elysian fields.

In this illustrious sextumvirate, SOCRATES and Sir THOMAS MOORE undoubtedly deserve the pre-eminence. The extravagant virtue of JUNIUS BRUTUS is shocking to every parent, and every good-natured mind. The important services of the father might justly have claimed from the public the pardon of his sons:[37] and if[k] his paternal piety had saved their lives, his precepts and example might so effectually have reclaimed their errors, as to

---

[j]convulsions of this kind] those kind of convulsions FI, FIa, FIb, FII, FV, MI, MII

[k]if] when FI, FIa, FIb, FII, FIII, FV, MI, MII

have made them become useful members of the commonwealth. I am fully persuaded, that if Dr. SWIFT had been a father, we should not have found the name of JUNIUS BRUTUS where it is now placed.

In EPAMINONDAS[38] the Theban glory first appeared: and died. His own merit, in overcoming the greatest difficulties, entirely fixed his reputation. A happy concurrence of circumstances has often given fame to others; but EPAMINONDAS was indebted for his superior character only to himself.

I am in some doubt, whether CATO the *Censor*[39] can fairly claim a rank among so choice a groope of ghosts. He justly indeed condemned the luxury of the Romans, and he punished their vices with an impartial severity:[40] but herein he seems to have indulged his own natural temper rather than to have acted absolutely from a love of virtue: he was a declared enemy to poetry, painting, and all the politer arts: he was proud, vain, and morose: but above all, he was so extremely avaritious, that RHADAMANTHUS[41] in the Archbishop of CAMBRAY's[42] dialogues of the dead,[43] after expressing some regard to his merits, tells him, as he was an usurer he could not be admitted into the Elysian fields: and therefore orders him to keep the gate as porter: in which situation, he might gratify the censoriousness of his disposition, by examining every ghost that attempted to come into *Elysium*, and by shutting the door against all those, who were not qualified for admittance.[44] RHADAMANTHUS then gives him money to pay CHARON[45] for such passengers, who were not able to pay for themselves,[46] and at the same time declares, that he will punish him as a robber, if he offers to lend out that money upon usury.[47] How very different, you will say, are the sentiments of Archbishop FENELON, and of Dr. SWIFT in their judgement of CATO. The one, thinks him unworthy of a place among millions in *Elysium*, while the other distinguishes him among the greatest men of antiquity. From this dissension of opinions may be traced, perhaps, the particular temper both of the Archbishop and of the Dean, and from thence may be deduced the reason, why the *Censor* was esteemed by the latter, and condemned by the former.

GULLIVER, after having taken a transient view of numberless illustrious persons, whom he does not name, closes the chapter,[48] and gives me an opportunity of finishing my letter. Late, very late, may you become a ghost! And when one, may you equal any of SWIFT's sextumvirate, and may his ghost (grown less cynical and better instructed) rejoice to admit you into the company, from which he has so arbitrarily excluded all future generations. So wishes, so prays

Your affectionate Father,
ORRERY.

Notes

1. The ghosts appear in *The What D'Ye Call It*, act 1, sc. 4.

2. *Prose Works of Swift* 11:195.

3. The reference is to these words by Gulliver: "It was with great Difficulty that I understood his Greek, and had but little of my own" (ibid.)

4. Ibid. Plutarch gives two accounts of Alexander's final illness and death. In one of them, Plutarch says Alexander "had drunk all day" shortly before his death. Alexander's drinking is omitted in the other account. See Plutarch *Life of Alexander* 75.4-6 and 76.1-9.

5. It is also referred to as the Battle of Gaugamela, fought in September 331 B.C.

6. This took place in September 335 B.C. In the autumn of 336 B.C., the League of Corinth, formed by all Greek states except Sparta, gave Alexander unlimited military powers to fight Persia. Upon the occasion of a rumor that Alexander was dead, the Thebans massacred the Macedonian garrison in their city. Alexander moved to fight the rebellion and besieged Thebes. However, Alexander first offered peace terms to the Thebans, which were refused. Alexander then destroyed Thebes and spared only the city's temples and Pindar's house. Plutarch says Alexander also spared Pindar's descendants. See Plutarch *Life of Alexander* 11.7-13.

7. Plutarch reports Alexander's honors to Achilles' tomb: "Then, going up to Ilium, he [Alexander] sacrificed to Athena and poured libations to the heroes. Furthermore, the gravestone of Achilles he anointed with oil, ran a race by it with his companions, naked, as is the custom, and then crowned it with garlands, pronouncing the hero happy in having, while he lived, a faithful friend, and after death, a great herald of his fame" (ibid., 15.7-9).

8. In 343 B.C., Aristotle was invited by Philip II (Alexander's father) to be Alexander's tutor. Aristotle left Lesbos (where he was then living), and spent three years educating Alexander and a few other friends in Mieza, a rural Macedonian village.

9. Philip of Acarnania, Alexander's confidential physician whom he had known since childhood. After entering Tarsus on 3 September 333 B.C., Alexander, who was sweating and hot, plunged into the Cydnus river, and had an attack of cramps. Alexander caught pneumonia, and was with a strong

fever for days. At that time, Darius III was offering rewards to anyone who would kill Alexander, and so Alexander's physicians declined to treat him, for fear something would happen to Alexander and they might be accused of negligence or murder. However, Philip offered to treat Alexander, and in trust, Alexander drank of the medicine prescribed by Philip, which finally helped in Alexander's recovery. See Peter Green, *Alexander of Macedon, 356-323 B.C.: A Historical Biography* (Berkeley and Los Angeles: University of California Press, 1991), pp. 220-21.

10. "Whenever righteousness has failed, faults mar even what nature had made noble" (Horace *Odes* 4.4.35-36).

11. Suetonius gave an account of Augustus's visit to Alexander's sepulchre in Alexandria (*The Lives of the Caesars* 2.18.1). However, the fact that Augustus had touched the nose of Alexander's corpse and "defaced the whole figure" is not mentioned by Suetonius. I could not trace Orrery's source.

12. Hannibal Barca (247-183 B.C.), Carthaginian general, having been appointed commander-in-chief at the age of twenty six. He led Carthage against Rome during the Second Punic War (218-201 B.C.).

13. Titus Livius (ca. 64 B.C. - ca. A.D.12), Roman historian.

14. Orrery is referring to an incident reported by Livy, which occurred when Hannibal and his army crossed the Alps: "Since they had to cut through the rock, they felled some huge trees that grew near at hand, and lopping off their branches, made an enormous pile of logs. This they set on fire, as soon as the wind blew fresh enough to make it burn, and pouring vinegar over the glowing rocks, caused them to crumble. After thus heating the crag with fire, they opened a way in it with iron tools, and relieved the steepness of the slope with zigzags of an easy gradient, so that not only the baggage animals but even the elephants could be let down." In Livy *Ab Urbe Condita* (From the foundation of the city of Rome) 21.37.1-4.

15. Gulliver describes the Senate of Rome as "an Assembly of Heroes and Demi-Gods" (*Prose Works of Swift* 11:195-96).

16. Gulliver portrays the "modern Representative" as "a Knot of Pedlars, Pickpockets, Highwaymen and Bullies" (ibid., p. 196). This "modern assembly" might be the English or the Irish Parliament.

17. Diogenes (ca. 400-ca. 325 B.C.), Greek philosopher and chief exponent of Cynicism. His main ideas included the search for happiness through disregard of worldly matters and even denial of life's basic needs.

18. François Rabelais (ca. 1490-ca. 1553), French writer and satirist.

19. Cnaeus Pompeius Magnus, Roman general and statesman, born on 29 September 106 B.C. He was one of the members of the First Triumvirate, with Julius Caesar and Crassus.

20. Marcus Junius Brutus (ca. 85-42 B.C.), Roman statesman and one of the conspirators who murdered Caesar.

21. *Prose Works of Swift* 11:196.

22. After Crassus died while fighting the Parthians in 53 B.C., there developed a power struggle between Pompey and Caesar that culminated in war. Pompey was defeated by Caesar on the field of Pharsalus, Greece, on 9 August 48 B.C. Pompey fled to Egypt, where he was killed by order of Ptolemy, Egypt's ruler. See Plutarch *Life of Pompey*.

23. For accounts of the murder of Caesar, see Plutarch *Life of Marcus Brutus* 16-18; and Suetonius *The Lives of the Caesars* 1.81-82. See also Shakespeare, *Julius Caesar*, 3.1.1-82.

24. On 17 March 44 B.C., Brutus was granted amnesty for the murder of Caesar, but left Rome in April. When Octavian became consul, in August 43 B.C., the amnesty was revoked. When the Second Triumvirate (Lepidus, Octavian, and Mark Antony) was formed, Brutus joined forces with Cassius (the chief organizer of the conspiracy against Caesar) against Octavian and Antony. Cassius was defeated by Antony at Philippi in October 42 B.C., and in a second battle, Brutus was defeated and committed suicide. For an account of the Battle of Philippi, see Dio *Roman History* 47.35-49.

25. When the war between Caesar and Pompey began, Brutus sided with Pompey. After Pompey's defeat at Pharsalus, Brutus fled, and was not only pardoned by Caesar, but also became Caesar's "highly honoured companion." In 43 B.C., Caesar gave Brutus the province of Macedonia, and also a praetorship. Plutarch says Brutus "had as large a share in Caesar's power as he wished." See Plutarch *Life of Brutus* 6-7.

26. "Now Brutus, who had made his escape up to a well-fortified stronghold, undertook to break through in some way to his camp; but when he was unsuccessful, and furthermore learned that some of his soldiers had made terms with the victors, he no longer had any hope, but despairing of safety and disdaining capture, he also took refuge in death. He first uttered aloud this sentence of Heracles:

> 'O wretched Valour, thou wert but a name,
> And yet I worshipped thee as real indeed;
> But now, it seems, thou wert but Fortune's slave.'"

(Dio *Roman History* 47.49.1-2).

27. The gallery at the Palace of the Uffizi. The palace was erected by order of Cosimo de Medici, first grand duke of Tuscany, to house the government offices (*uffizi*).

28. Cosimo de Medici (1519-74) who belonged to a junior branch of the Florentine ruling family of the Medicis. When he was seventeen years old, he became head of the Florentine republic, ruling with absolute power for thirty-two years. Cosimo expanded his political unit from Florence to all of Tuscany, and in 1569, he became the first grand duke of Tuscany.

29. A small bust, of Brutus, by Michelangelo, dated around 1539-40. Orrery may have known about this bust from some written account of it.

30. The reason why Michelangelo never finished the bust of Brutus is not known. Robert Liebert speculated about the reason: "We might speculate that to have finished carving the few remaining details of the work would have been experienced by Michelangelo as giving closure to the acceptance of murderous impulses toward Duke Cosimo, the ruler of his homeland and the current head of the Medici–the family that had been such a controlling influence in his life for half a century." In Robert Liebert, *Michelangelo: A Psychoanalytic Study of His Life and Images* (New Haven and London: Yale University Press, 1983), p. 389.

31. Cf. Robert Liebert's words on the epigram: "An enigmatic problem is presented by an epigram inscribed on a bronze plaque at the base of the bust. It states that, in the course of his work on the bust, Michelangelo was reminded of the crime of tyrannicide and therefore abandoned the work:

M. Dum. Bruti. Effigiem A.
Sculptor de Marmore Ducit
In Mentem Sceleris Venit

B. Et Abstinuit. F.

        (M.A.B.F.: Michel Angelus Buonarotus Fecit)

This inscription, however, was probably added later by order of the grand duke Francesco de Medici, who acquired the bust between 1574 and 1584, to discredit republicanism and present Michelangelo as a supporter of the Medici. It is highly doubtful that it reflects any specifically acknowledged position of Michelangelo with respect to the *Brutus*." In Liebert, *Michelangelo,* pp. 389-90 n. 2.

32. Conyers Middleton (1683-1750), doctor of divinity and university librarian at Cambridge.

33. Writing to Atticus from Puteoli on 21 December 45 B.C., Cicero mentions how Caesar had eaten and drunk on the nineteenth: "He [Caesar] was undergoing a course of emetics, so he ate and drank at his pleasure without fear" (Cicero *Letters to Atticus* 13.52). Middleton's translation of the passage is: "Having taken a vomit just before, he [Caesar] eat and drank freely, and was very chearfull." Middleton adds a footnote to these words: "The custom of *taking a vomit* both immediately before and after meals, which Cicero mentions Caesar to have done on different occasions [pro.Deiot.7], was very common with the Romans, and used by them as an instrument both of their luxury, and of their health: *they vomit,* says Seneca, *that they may eat, and eat that they may vomit* [Consol.ad Helo.9]. By this evacuation before eating, they were prepared to eat more plentifully; and by emptying themselves presently after it, prevented any hurt from repletion. Thus Vittelius, who was a famous glutton, *is said to have preserved his life by constant vomits*, while he destroyed all his companions, who did not use the same cautions: [Sueton.12. Dio 65.734]. And the practice was thought so effectual for strengthening the constitution, that it was the constant regimen of all the Athletae, or the professed Wrestler's, trained for the public shews, in order to make them more robust. So that Caesar's vomiting before dinner was a sort of compliment to Cicero, as it intimated a resolution to pass the day chearfully, and to eat and drink freely with him." See Middleton, *Life of Cicero,* 5th ed. (1755), 2:408-11. For the gluttony of Vitellius (A.D. 15-69, Roman emperor from January to 22 December 69), see Suetonius *The Lives of the Caesars* 7.13.

34. For Caesar's epilepsy, see ibid., 1.45. Suetonius says Caesar was attacked "by the falling sickness" twice during his campaigns. Suetonius also adds that toward the end of his life, Caesar was "subject to sudden fainting fits and to nightmare as well."

35. Charles Boyle, fourth earl of Orrery.

36. Gulliver's words are: "I had the Honour to have much Conversation with Brutus; and was told that his Ancestor Junius, Socrates, Epaminondas, Cato the Younger, Sir Thomas More and himself, were perpetually together: A Sextumvirate to which all the Ages of the World cannot add a Seventh" (*Prose Works of Swift* 11:196).

37. After the rape of Lucretia by Sextus (Tarquinius Superbus's son), Junius Brutus led the movement that culminated in the overthrow of the Tarquins and the establishment of the republican government. See Dio *Roman History* 2.11.13-20. Junius Brutus and Lucius Collatinus (Lucretia's husband) became consuls in 509 B.C. Junius Brutus put his two sons to death, after they were detected in a conspiracy to restore the Tarquins to power.

38. Epaminondas (ca. 425-362 B.C.), Theban general and statesman educated in the Pythagorean philosophy by Lysis of Tarentum. He had an important part in the creation of the League of Boeotian States, following the liberation of Thebes from Sparta (379 B.C.). Between 370 and 368 B.C., Epaminondas led the campaign that liberated cities from Sparta's control. He also led two further expeditions: in 363 B.C. to Byzantium, and in 362 B.C. to the Peloponnesus. At Mantinea, Epaminondas's army fought the combined forces of Sparta, Athens, Elis, Achaea, and Mantinea, when he was killed. See Cornelius Nepos *Lives* 15 ("Epaminondas"). For a detailed account of Epaminondas's heroic last campaign, see Xenophon *Hellenica* 7.5.4-27.

39. Gulliver does not include Marcus Porcius Cato (234-149 B.C.), known as Cato the Elder or the Censor in the sextumvirate of heroes. Rather, he includes Marcus Porcius Cato of Utica (95-46 B.C.), known as Cato the Younger, Roman statesman and great-grandson of Cato the Elder. See *Prose Works of Swift* 11:196.

40. Cato the Elder was consul in 195 B.C. and censor in 184 B.C. He had opposed the repeal of the Appian Law against "feminine luxury," and shortly before becoming censor, was vigorous in his attacks against Hellenism and foreign influences in general. As a censor, Cato the Elder introduced taxes on luxuries. See Plutarch *Life of Marcus Cato*.

41. Rhadamanthys, a Cretan hero. According to legend, Rhadamanthys organized the Cretan code with great skill, so that, after his death, he became one of the judges of the dead in the Underworld.

42. François de Salignac de la Mothe Fénelon (1651-1715), French prelate, theologian, and preacher. Fénelon became archbishop of Cambrai in February 1695.

43. Fénelon, *Dialogues des Morts, Composés pour l'Éducation de Mgr le Duc de Bourgogne*. The work is addressed to the duke of Bourgogne, Louis XIV's eldest grandson, to whom Fénelon was appointed tutor.

44. Ibid., p. 37.

45. Guardian of the Underworld, whose duty was to take the spirits from the marsh of the Acheron (the river of the dead) to the other side.

46. According to legend, every spirit had to pay Charon an obolus. This legend gave origin to the custom of putting a coin in the mouth of corpses when they were buried.

47. In Fénelon, *Dialogues des Morts* 37.

48. *Prose Works of Swift* 11:196.

LETTER XIV

GULLIVER, tired of heroes, changes the scene in the eighth chapter of his voyage to *Laputa*,[1] and becomes curious to know the situation of poets and philosophers,[2] who, in their turn, have as eagerly contended for fame, as CAESAR for[a] power, or BRUTUS for liberty. He desires, that HOMER and ARISTOTLE may make their appearance at the head of their commentators.[3] HOMER, says our traveller, "*was the taller, and comelier person of the two: walked very erect for one of his age, and his eyes were the most quick and piercing I ever beheld.*"[4] It is certain, that HOMER has rather gained, than lost vigour by his years. Twenty six centuries have not unbraced his nerves, or given one wrinkle to his brow: and although GULLIVER has bestowed upon him the additional ornament of fine eyes, yet I am apt to think they made the figure of this divine old man less awful: at least I am glad that he wanted his eye sight while he lived,[5] since it is impossible, not to conclude from the productions of HOMER and MILTON, that the *Mind's Eye* becomes more intensely discerning, when it is not interrupted by external objects. It is an old observation, that HOMER has nourished more persons than SYLLA,[6] CAESAR, and AUGUSTUS; and while their pictures have decayed, not a letter of the Iliad has been lost. The Grecian poet not only preserves his original form, but breathes freely, and looks beautiful[b] in other languages: a happier metempsychosis than PYTHAGORAS ever dreamt of.[7] However if HOMER was absolutely obliged to wear the different dresses, which have been given to him, he would sometimes, I believe, find the motion of his limbs uneasy and confined: and would prefer his own simple attire even to the birth day suit, which our English bard has given him.[8] The commentators have done

---

[a]CAESAR for] CAESAR did for FI, FIa, FIb, FII, FV, MI
Orrery's correction in Osborn pc 231: "CAESAR did for" to "CAESAR for."

[b]beautiful] beautifully FI, FIa, FIb, FII, FV

less honour to HOMER than the translators.[9]   Some of those[c] learned
pedants have entirely wasted their observations upon particles and words:
others have run into a minute exactness, in comparing the propriety of his
images: while others again, have endeavoured to trace out from the Iliad and
Odyssey all the rudiments of arts and sciences. Some there are, who dwell on
such narrow circumstances, as were neglected by HOMER, and can be suitable
only[d] to their own confined genius. They are not able to pursue him in his
sublime flights, and attempt therefore, to bring him upon a level with
themselves.[e] Their low mechanical notions remind me of an absurd problem
proposed by the famous Monsieur HUET,[10] whether the Iliad might not be
written upon vellum in so small a hand, that the whole might be contained
within a nutshell?[11]   This important question is said to have engaged the
thoughts and attention of the French court, and gives us a true picture of a
laborious, tasteless critic upon HOMER. The Dauphin, and his train, are for
putting the Iliad into a nutshell, when ALEXANDER, and his courtiers, chose
the richest, and[f] most curious cabinet of DARIUS, as the only proper
repository for HOMER's works.[12]

HOMER and ARISTOTLE were as opposite as possible in their characters:
but Dr. SWIFT has placed them together, chiefly with a view of shewing their
commentators, in that just and ridiculous light, in which those scholiasts ought
to appear.[13] When an age is blessed with the productions of an uncommon
genius, such as resembles HOMER, it must, in some measure, be punished by
bad imitations and comments; in the same manner that you may have
observed the sun by its heat and influence raising vapours, and animating
insects, that infect and perhaps corrupt the air, in which he shines with so
much lustre. But, when an original admired author, as ARISTOTLE, is really
erroneous, and deceives with false specious principles, what a train of errors
must arise from commentators on such subjects, who, while they endeavour
to pursue and extend a pleasing enchanted prospect, that has no real
foundation, deviate into a dark, disagreeable road of briers and thorns?

It is on this account that the Dean has introduced ARISTOTLE in company
with HOMER. The description of that philosopher is fine, and in a few words

---

represents the true nature of his works. *"He stooped much, and made use of a staff. His visage was meagre, his hair lank and thin, and his voice hollow."*[14] By not having the immortal spirit of HOMER, he was unable to keep his body erect: and the staff which weakly supported him, like his commentators, made this defect more conspicuous. He wanted not some useful qualities, but these real ornaments, like his hair, were thin and ungraceful. His style was harsh, and, like his voice, had neither force nor harmony. He was without doubt a man of great genius and penetration, but he did infinitely more prejudice than service to real literature. He studied words more than facts, and delivered his philosophy perplexed with such intricate logical terms,[15] as have laid a foundation for the endless scholastic disputations, which have corrupted and retarded the progress of learning. He waged war with all his predecessors. He never quotes an author, except[g] with a view to refute his opinion. Like the Ottoman Emperor, he could not reign in safety, till he had first destroyed his brethren.[16] He was as ambitious in science, as his pupil ALEXANDER was in arms. He aimed to be a despotic original; and not only to be the Prince, but the Tyrant of philosophy. What then can be expected from the commentators on[h] his works, who were devoid of his ingenuity, and possessed all[i] his intricate follies? RAMUS[17] with his covert ignorance, and SCOTUS[18] and AQUINAS[19] with their subdivisions, and imaginary nothings, must make a contemptible figure in the Elysian fields, which are the supposed mansions of chearfulness, truth, and candour, and consequently must be a very improper situation for that tribe of philosophers.

"I then desired, says GULLIVER, *that* DESCARTES *and* GASSENDI *might be called up: with whom I prevailed to explain their systems to* ARISTOTLE. *This great philosopher freely acknowledged his own mistakes in natural philosophy, because he proceeded in many things upon conjecture, as all men must do; and he found that* GASSENDI, *who had made the doctrine of* EPICURUS *as palatable as he could, and the vortices of* DESCARTES *were equally to be exploded.*[20] I believe you will find, my dear HAMILTON, that ARISTOTLE is still to be preferred to EPICURUS.[21] The former made some useful experiments and discoveries, and was engaged in a real pursuit of knowledge, although his manner is much perplexed. The latter was full of vanity and ambition. He was an impostor, and only aimed at deceiving.[22] He seemed not to believe the principles which he has asserted. He committed the government of all

---

[g]except] but FI, FIa, FIb, FII, FV, MI; Orrery's correction in Osborn pc 231: "but" to "except."

[h]on] of FI, FIa, FIb, FII, FV, MI, MII

[i]possessed all MV] possessed of all MIII

things to chance.[23]   His natural philosophy is absurd.[24]   His moral philosophy wants its proper basis, the fear of God.[25] Monsieur BAYLE,[26] one of his warmest advocates, is of this last opinion, where he says, "*On ne scauroit pas dire assez de bien de l'honneteté de ses moeurs, ni assez de mal de ses opinions sur la religion.*"[27] His general maxim, that happiness consisted in pleasure was too much unguarded, and must lay a foundation of a most destructive practice:[28] although from his temper and constitution, he made his actions sufficiently pleasurable to himself, and agreeable to the rules of true philosophy. His fortune exempted him from care and sollicitude. His valetudinarian habit of body from intemperance. He passed the greatest part of his time in his garden, where he enjoyed all the elegant amusements of life. There he studied. There he taught his philosophy. This particular happy situation greatly contributed to that tranquillity of mind, and indolence of body which he made his chief ends.[29] He had not however resolution sufficient to meet the gradual approaches of death, and wanted that constancy which Sir WILLIAM TEMPLE ascribes to him: for in his last moments, when he[j] found that his condition was desperate, he took such large draughts of wine, that he was absolutely intoxicated, and deprived of his senses;[30] so that he died more like a bacchanal, than a philosopher: to which the epigram alludes,

Hinc Stygias ebrius hausit aquas.[31]

I should not have ventured into this criticism and censure upon these antient philosophers, not even to you, my dearest HAM,[k] if my opinion was not in a great measure supported by Lord BACON, who, as he was certainly the most accurate judge of this subject, might be perhaps, from that pre-eminence, too severe a critic. It must be owned, that EPICURUS in particular has many followers and admirers among the antients, and among the moderns. CICERO commends him for cultivating his friendships in the most exquisite manner. The book lyes open before me, and I will transcribe the words, *De quâ [amicitiâ]* EPICURUS *quidem ita dicit omnium rerum quas ad beatè vivendum sapientia comparaverit, nihil esse majus amicitiâ, nihil uberius, nihil jucundius, neque verò hoc oratione solùm, sed multo magis vita & factis, et moribus comprobavit.*[32] DIOGENES LAERTIUS[33] praises his virtue and learning.[34] In the Augustan age the greatest names are inserted among his followers.   CAESAR, ATTICUS,[35] MÆCENAS, LUCRETIUS,[36] VIRGIL, and HORACE embraced his philosophy, and gave a lustre to his sect, and doctrines.[37] Sir WILLIAM TEMPLE says, "*that he wonders, why such sharp*

---

[j]moments, when he] moments, he FI

[k]HAM,] HAMILTON, MIV

invectives were so generally made against EPICURUS, *by the ages that followed him: especially as his admirable wit, felicity of expression, excellence of nature, sweetness of conversation, temperance of life, and constancy of death, made him so much beloved by his friends, admired by his scholars, and honoured by the Athenians."*[38] Sir WILLIAM TEMPLE imputes this injustice *"to the envy, and malignity of the Stoics, and to some gross pretenders, who assumed the denomination of that sect: who mistook his favourite principle"* (THAT ALL HAPPINESS CONSISTED IN PLEASURE) *"by confining it to sensual pleasure only. To these succeeded the Christians, who esteemed his principles of natural philosophy more opposite to those of our religion than either the Platonists, the Peripatetics, or even the Stoics themselves."*[39] This is the opinion, and these are almost the exact words of the great Sir WILLIAM TEMPLE.

SWIFT equally explodes[1] EPICURUS, and the more modern philosophers DESCARTES and GASSENDI.

DESCARTES was a knight errant in philosophy, perpetually mistaking windmills for giants;[40] yet by the strength of a warm imagination he started some opinions, which probably put Sir ISAAC NEWTON, and others, on making many experiments that produced most useful discoveries.

GASSENDI[41] was esteemed one of the greatest ornaments of FRANCE. He was a doctor of divinity, and royal professor of mathematics. He was born in *Provence* in 1592, and died in 1655. With great industry he collected whatever related to the person, and to the philosophy of EPICURUS, the latter of which he has reduced into a compleat system.[42]

I have now, my HAMILTON, cursorily gone thorough the characters of such ghosts, as are nominally specified by GULLIVER. I may be wrong either in my account, or in my observations: and I shall rejoice to be confuted by you in any point of learning whatever.

The description of the STRULDBRUGGS, in the tenth chapter,[43] is an instructive piece of morality: for, if we consider it in a serious light, it tends to reconcile us to our final dissolution. Death, when set in contrast to the immortality of the STRULDBRUGGS, is no longer the King of Terrors: he loses his sting: he appears to us as a friend: and we chearfully obey his summons, because it brings certain relief to the greatest miseries. It is in this description, that SWIFT shines in a particular manner. He probably felt in himself the effects of approaching age, and tacitly dreaded that period of life, in which he might become a representative of those *miserable immortals.*[44] His apprehensions were unfortunately fulfilled. He lived to be the most melancholy sight that was ever beheld: yet, even in that condition, he continued to instruct, by appearing a providential instance to mortify the vanity, which is too apt to arise in the human breast. Our life cannot be

---

[1]explodes] explores FIa, FIb, FII, FIII, FV, MI

pronounced happy, till the last scene is closed with ease and resignation; the mind still continuing to preserve its usual dignity, and falling into the arms of death, as a wearied traveller sinks into rest. This is that *Euthanasia* which AUGUSTUS often desired,[45] which ANTONINUS PIUS enjoyed,[46] and for which every wise man will pray.[47] GOD Almighty's providence protect and guide you, my HAM, whatever fate of life, or fortune attends

Your affectionate Father,
ORRERY.

Notes

1. *Prose Works of Swift* 11:197-202.

2. Gulliver's words, which open pt. 3, chap. 8, are: "Having a Desire to see those Antients, who were most renowned for Wit and Learning, I set apart one Day on purpose" (ibid., p. 197).

3. Gulliver says: "I proposed that Homer and Aristotle might appear at the Head of all their Commentators; but these were so numerous, that some Hundreds were forced to attend in the Court and outward Rooms of the Palace. I knew and could distinguish those two Heroes at first Sight, not only from the Croud, but from each other" (ibid.).

4. Ibid.

5. Although nothing certain is known about Homer, there had been a traditional belief that he was blind.

6. Lucius Cornelius Sulla (138-78 B.C.), Roman general and dictator. After a number of military successes, Sulla was elected consul in 88 B.C. and defeated the army of Mithridates (king of Pontus), also sacking Athens. In Rome, Gaius Marius assumed power and killed Sulla's followers. Sulla came back, defeated Marius and his supporters, and by 82 B.C., was in control of Rome, reviving the Roman office of dictator.

7. Pythagoras (ca. 575-ca. 495 B.C.), philosopher and religious teacher born on the island of Samos. He taught the doctrine of metempsychosis, or, the passage of the soul from one body to another; cf. Ovid *Metamorphoses* 15.158-59. Orrery's source may have been book 15 of the *Metamorphoses*, where Ovid wrote about Pythagoras's teachings.

8. Orrery refers to Pope's translation of the *Iliad* and the *Odyssey*.

9. Orrery may be alluding to the two commentators of Homer referred to by Gulliver: Didymus of Alexandria who lived in the first century B.C., and Eustathius, bishop of Salonica (d. ca. 1194), whose commentary on Homer was printed in 1542-50. See *Prose Works of Swift* 11:197.

10. Pierre Daniel Huet (1630-1721), French scholar and tutor to the dauphin, Louis XIV's son.

11. This was part of Huet's project for the dauphin, which consisted of volumes of the classics known as the Delphin series.

12. In Plutarch *Life of Alexander* 26.1-2: "When a small coffer was brought to him [Alexander], which those in charge of the baggage and wealth of Darius thought the most precious thing there, he asked his friends what valuable object they thought would most fittingly be deposited in it. And when many answered and there were many opinions, Alexander himself said he was going to deposit the Iliad there for safe keeping. This is attested by many trustworthy authorities."

13. See *Prose Works of Swift* 11:197.

14. Ibid.

15. Cf. Francis Bacon's definition of Aristotle as an author: *pessimus sophista, inutili subtilitate attonitus, verborum vile ludibrium* (a very bad sophist, perplexed with useless subtlety, vile word-play). In Bacon, *Temporis Partus Masculus*, chap. 2, *The Works of Francis Bacon*, ed. James Spedding, Robert Leslie Ellis, and Douglas Denon Heath, 14 vols. (London: Longman's, 1857-74), 3:529 (cited hereafter as *Works of Bacon*).

16. Orrery is alluding to these words by Francis Bacon on Aristotle: *Atque illum scilicet Ottomanorum more in fratribus trucidandis occupatum fuisse* (He [Aristotle], after the manner of the Ottomans, was busy killing his brethren), in Bacon, *Cogitata et Visa: de Interpretatione Naturae, Sive de Scientia Operativa*, *Works of Bacon* 3:602. The practice of killing the sultan's brothers was established as a fundamental state law by Mahomet II (1430-81). Mahomet III, on becoming sultan in 1595, killed nineteen of his brothers, and about twelve women supposed to be with child by his father. See Joseph *freiherr* von Hammer-Purgstall, *Geschichte des Osmanischen Reiches*, 10 vols. (Pesth: C. A. Hartleben, 1827-35).

17. Pierre Ramus (1515-72), French humanist logician and mathematician. In 1543, he issued his *Aristotelicae Animadversiones*, a criticism of Aristotelian logic.

18. John Duns Scotus (1265/66 - 1308), philosopher and theologian born in southeastern Scotland. Scotus wrote commentaries on a number of works by Aristotle, including the *Metaphysics* and *On the Soul*.

19. St. Thomas Aquinas (ca. 1224-74), Italian philosopher, theologian, Dominican friar, and doctor of the church. Toward the end of his life, Aquinas wrote a series of commentaries on works of Aristotle, including the *Metaphysics*, the *Physics*, *On the Soul*, and the *Nicomachean Ethics*.

20. *Prose Works of Swift* 11:197.

21. Epicurus (ca. 342-270 B.C.), Greek philosopher. For a list of the most important tenets of Epicureanism, see Diogenes Laertius *Lives of Eminent Philosophers* 10.139-54.

22. Even in his lifetime, Epicurus was already accused of gluttony and womanizing, among other things. See ibid., 10.10-12.

23. According to Epicureanism, the deity had no role in the creation of or activities in the universe. Any change in the universe would be due to the alteration of the position of atoms, eternally moving at an equal speed.

24. Epicurus adopted the atomistic theory of matter, which states that only atoms, the primary units of matter, possess primary qualities (size and shape). These primary qualities lie beneath the level of our senses, which thus can only perceive objects in terms of their secondary qualities, determined by the particular configuration of atoms of a given object. Since, according to Epicurus, we have no knowledge apart from our senses, it follows that we only know things as they appear to be, and not as they really are.

25. Epicureanism taught the mortality of the human soul.

26. Pierre Bayle (1647-1706), French philosopher. In 1697, Bayle issued his *Dictionnaire Historique et Critique*, in two volumes, which became a primary source of information on history and philosophy in the eighteenth century. Orrery owned a copy of Bayle's *Dictionnaire* (1730), and an English translation (1734-41), offered during Christie's Orrery Sale (November 1905), as lots 167 and 168, respectively. See *The Orrery Sale*, pp. 23-24.

27. In "Epicurus," Bayle, *Dictionnaire Historique et Critique*, cinquiéme édition (Amsterdam: Compagnie des Librairies, 1734), 2:743: "One could not say enough good things about the honesty of his habits, nor enough bad things about his opinions on religion".

28. Cf. Epicurus's words on his theory about pleasure: "When we say, then, that pleasure is the end and aim, we do not mean the pleasures of the prodigal or the pleasures of sensuality, as we are understood to do by some through ignorance, prejudice, or wilful misrepresentation. By pleasure we mean the absence of pain in the body and of trouble in the soul. It is not an unbroken succession of drinking-bouts and of revelry, not sexual love, not the enjoyment of the fish and other delicacies of a luxurious table, which produce a pleasant life; it is sober reasoning, searching out the grounds of every choice and avoidance, and banishing those beliefs through which the greatest tumults take possession of the soul" (Diogenes Laertius *Lives of Eminent Philosophers* 10.131-32).

29. Orrery is echoing this passage in Sir William Temple, "Upon the Gardens of Epicurus": "For this reason Epicurus passed his life wholly in his garden; there he studied, there he exercised, there he taught his philosophy; and, indeed, no other sort of abode seems to contribute so much to both the tranquillity of mind and indolence of body which he made his chief ends." In Sir William Temple, *Five Miscellaneous Essays by Sir William Temple*, ed. Samuel Holt Monk (Ann Arbor: University of Michigan Press, 1963), p. 10.

30. Diogenes Laertius's account of Epicurus's death is: "Epicurus died of renal calculus after an illness which lasted a fortnight: so Hermarchus tells us in his letters. Hermippus relates that he entered a bronze bath of lukewarm water and asked for unmixed wine, which he swallowed, and then, having bidden his friends remember his doctrines, breathed his last.
Here is something of my own about him:
Thus Epicurus spake, and breathed his last.
He sat in a warm bath and neat wine quaff'd,
And straightway found chill death in that same draught.
Such was the life of the sage and such his end."

(Diogenes Laertius *Lives of Eminent Philosophers* 10.15-16)

31. Orrery is echoing Francis Bacon, *Of the Dignity and Advancement of Learning*, bk. 4, chap. 2: *Scribitur etiam de Epicuro, quod hoc ipsum sibi procuraverit; cum enim morbus ejus haberetur pro desperato, ventriculum et sensus meri largiore haustu et ingurgitatione obruit; unde illud in epigrammate,*

> *–hinc Stygias ebrius hausit aquas.*
> *Vino scilicet Stygii laticis amaritudinem sustulit.*

(And it is written of Epicurus, that he procured the same [a painless and quick death] for himself; for after his disease was judged desperate, he drowned his stomach and senses with a large draught and ingurgitation of wine; whereupon the epigram was made,

> *–hinc Stygias ebrius hausit aquas.*

He drowned in wine the bitterness of the Stygian water.)
In *Works of Bacon* 4:387. The "Stygian water" refers to the Styx, a river of the Underworld.

32. "Now Epicurus's pronouncement about friendship is that of all the means to happiness that wisdom has devised, none is greater, none more fruitful, none more delightful than this. Nor did he only commend this doctrine by his eloquence, but far more by the example of his life and conduct." In Cicero *De Finibus Bonorum et Malorum* 20.65.

33. Diogenes Laertius, Greek writer born in Cilicia, who lived in the third century A.D. He is the author of *Lives and Opinions of Eminent Philosophers*, in ten books. Book 10 is entirely about Epicurus.

34. See ibid., 10.9-12.

35. Titus Pomponius Atticus (109-32 B.C.), Roman philosopher. Atticus's philosophy was entirely Epicurean, and he also owned a large library, being involved in the publishing and bookselling trade. See Cornelius Nepos *Life of Atticus*.

36. Titus Lucretius Carus (ca. 94-ca. 55 B.C.), Latin poet and philosopher. His one work is a six-book didactic poem in hexameters called *De Rerum Natura* (On the nature of the universe), which is a statement and defense of Epicurus's philosophy and ideas. Epicurus's atomistic theory is set forth in book 1. Book 2 treats of Epicurus's moral theory. Book 3 refers to the mortality of the soul and its dissolution into atoms at the moment of death. Book 4 treats of Epicurus's ideas on the senses and perception of objects. Books 5 and 6 constitute an appendix featuring both eulogies to Epicurus and applications of the atomistic theory.

37. See Sir William Temple, "Upon the Gardens of Epicurus" in Temple, *Five Miscellaneous Essays*, p. 8.

38. Ibid., pp. 7-8.

39. Ibid., p. 8.

40. Cf. Cervantes, *Don Quixote*, 1.8.

41. Pierre Gassendi (1592-1655), French philosopher and Descartes's almost exact contemporary.

42. In 1626, Gassendi began his researches on Epicurus, and in 1628, he said he had composed an apology for Epicurus to be added as an appendix to one of the future volumes of his *Exercitationes Paradoxicae adversus Aristoteleos* (published in 1624). In 1628 and 1629, during his travels in Holland for eight months, Gassendi decided to expand his apology for Epicurus into a comprehensive study of Epicurus's philosophy. This was to be entitled *De Vita et Doctrina Epicuri*, which underwent two revisions over a period of sixteen years. See Bernard Rochot, *Les Travaux de Gassendi sur Épicure et sur l'atomisme, 1619-1658* (Paris: J. Vrin, 1944); and Pierre Gassendi, *Pierre Gassendi's Institutio Logica (1658)*, ed. Howard Jones (Assen, the Netherlands: Van Gorcum, 1981), pp. xxvii-xl.

43. *Prose Works of Swift* 11:207-14.

44. Cf. Swift's words to Bolingbroke on 31 October 1729: "I was 47 Years old when I began to think of death; and the reflections upon it now begin when I wake in the Morning, and end when I am going to Sleep" (*Correspondence of Swift* 3:354). On 21 March 1730, also writing to Bolingbroke, Swift mentioned this subject again: "When I was of your age I often thought of death, but now after a dozen years more, it is never out of my mind, and terrifies me less" (ibid., p. 382).

45. Cf. Suetonius *The Lives of the Caesars* 2.99.2: "For almost always on hearing that anyone had died swiftly and painlessly, he [Augustus] prayed that he and his might have a like *euthanasia*, for that was the term he was wont to use."

46. Antoninus Pius (A.D. 86-161), Roman emperor from A.D. 138 to 161. He died sometime between 25 February and 23 March A.D. 161 at Lorium (twelve miles from Rome), to where he retired shortly before his death. On a certain day at Lorium, Antoninus Pius ate some Alpine cheese at supper, and the next day, he was feverish. After three days, he made the final arrangements of his private and public affairs, and died "as calmly as though he were falling asleep." See Ernest Edward Bryant, *The Reign of Antoninus Pius*, Cambridge

Historical Essays, no. 8 (Cambridge: Cambridge University Press, 1895), pp. 89-91.

47. Orrery is echoing Francis Bacon, *Of the Dignity and Advancement of Learning*, bk. 4, chap. 2: "For it is no small felicity which Augustus Caesar was wont to wish to himself, that same *Euthanasia*; and which was specially noted in the death of Antoninus Pius, whose death was after the fashion and semblance of a kindly and pleasant sleep."   In *Works of Bacon* 3:375.

LETTER XV

IT is with great reluctance, I shall make some remarks on GULLIVER's voyage to the *Houyhnhnms*. In this last part of his imaginary travels, SWIFT has indulged a misanthropy that is intolerable. The representation which he has given us of human nature, must terrify, and even debase the mind of the reader who views it. His sallies of wit and humour lose all their force, nothing remaining but a melancholy, and disagreeable impression: and, as I have said to you, on other parts of his works, we are disgusted, not entertained; we are shocked, not instructed by the fable. I should therefore chuse to take no notice of his YAHOOS, did I not think it necessary to assert the dignity[a] of human nature, and thereby, in some measure, to pay my duty to the great author of our species, who has created us in a very fearful, and a very wonderful manner.

We are composed of a mind, and of a body, intimately united, and mutually affecting each other. Their operations indeed are entirely different. Whether the immortal spirit, that enlivens this fine machine, is originally of a superior nature in various bodies (which, I own, seems most consistent and agreeable to the scale and order of beings) or, whether the difference depends on a symmetry, or peculiar structure of the organs combined with it, is beyond my reach to determine. It is evidently certain, that the body is curiously formed with proper organs to delight, and such as are adapted to all the necessary uses of life. The spirit animates the whole; it guides the natural appetites, and confines them within just limits. But, the natural force of this spirit is often immersed in matter; and the mind becomes subservient to passions, which it ought to govern and direct. Your friend HORACE, although of the Epicurean doctrine, acknowledges this truth, where he says,

Atque affigit humo divinae particulam aurae.[1]

---

[a]dignity] vindication FI, FIa, FIb, FII, FV, MI, MII

It is no less evident, that this immortal spirit has an independent power of acting, and, when cultivated in a proper manner, seemingly quits the corporeal frame within which it is imprisoned, and soars into higher, and more spacious regions; where, with an energy, which I had almost said was divine, it ranges among those heavenly bodies, that, in this lower world, are scarce visible to our eyes; and we can at once explain the distance, magnitude, and velocity of the planets, and can foretel, even to a degree of minuteness, the particular time when a comet will return, and when the sun will be eclipsed in the next century. These powers certainly evince the dignity of human nature, and the surprising effects of the immaterial spirit within us, which, in so confined a state, can thus disengage itself from the fetters of matter. It is from this pre-eminence of the soul over the body, that we are enabled to view the exact order, and curious variety of different beings; to consider, and cultivate the natural productions of the earth; and to admire, and imitate the wise benevolence which reigns throughout the whole system of the universe. It is from hence, that we form moral laws for our conduct. From hence, we delight in copying that great original, who, in his essence, is utterly incomprehensible, but, in his influence, is powerfully apparent to every degree of his creation. From hence too, we perceive a real beauty in virtue, and a distinction between good and evil. Virtue acts with the utmost generosity, and with no view to her own advantage: while vice, like a glutton, feeds herself enormously, and then is willing to disgorge the nauseous offals of her feast. But I shall wander too far, especially as I flatter myself, that your mind is so good, and so unprejudiced, that you will more easily feel, than I can illustrate, the truth of these assertions.

SWIFT deduces his observations from wrong principles; for, in his land of *Houyhnhnms*, he considers the soul and body in their most degenerate, and uncultivated state: the former as a slave to the appetites of the latter. He seems insensible of the surprising mechanism, and beauty of every part of the human composition. He forgets the fine description which OVID gives of mankind.

> *Os homini sublime dedit, caelumque tueri*
> *Jussit, et erectos ad sidera tollere vultus.*[2]

In painting YAHOOS he becomes one himself. Nor is the picture which he draws of the *Houyhnhnms*, inviting or amusing. It wants both light and shade to adorn it. It is cold and insipid. We there view the pure instincts of brutes, unassisted by any knowledge of letters, acting within their own narrow sphere, merely for their immediate preservation. They are incapable of doing wrong, therefore they act right. It is surely a very low character given to creatures, in whom the author would insinuate some degree of reason, that they act inoffensively, when they have neither the motive nor the power to act otherwise. Their virtuous qualities are only negative.[b] SWIFT himself, amidst all his irony, must have confessed, that to moderate our passions, to extend our munificence to others, to enlarge our understanding, and to raise our idea of the Almighty by contemplating his works, is not only the business, but often the practice, and the study of the human mind. It is too certain, that no one individual has ever possessed every qualification and excellence: however such an assemblage of different virtues, may still be collected from different persons, as are sufficient to place the dignity of human nature in an amiable, and exalted station. We must lament indeed the many instances of those who degenerate, or go astray from the end and intention of their being. The true source of this depravity is often owing to the want of education, to the false indulgence of parents, or to some other bad causes, which are constantly prevalent in every nation. Many of these errors are finely ridiculed in the foregoing parts of this romance: but the voyage to the *Houyhnhnms* is a real insult upon mankind.

I am heartily tired of this last part of GULLIVER's travels, and am glad, that, having exhausted all my observations on this disagreeable subject, I may finish my letter; especially as the conclusion of it naturally turns my thoughts from YAHOOS, to one of the dearest pledges I have upon earth, yourself: to whom I am a most

Affectionate Father,
ORRERY.

---

[b]negative.] negatives. FI, FIa, FIb, FII, FIII, FV

Notes

1. "and fastens to earth a fragment of the divine spirit" (Horace *Satires* 2.2.79). In the verso of the page featuring the map of Houyhnhnmland, in his copy of Faulkner's edition of Swift's works, Orrery wrote:

"Horace, although of the epicurean doctrine, acknowledges this truth, where he says,

> [quin] Corpus onustum
> Hesternis vitiis animum quoque pr[a]egravat una,
> Atque affigit humo divinae particulam aura[e]."

["Nay more, clogged with yesterday's excess, the body drags down with itself the mind as well, and fastens to earth a fragment of the divine spirit." Horace *Satires* 2.2.77-79.]

2. "He gave to man an uplifted face and bade him stand erect and turn his eyes to heaven" (Ovid *Metamorphoses* 1.85-86).

LETTER XVI

WHAT is to be done, my HAMILTON, with the fourth volume of SWIFT's works? How can I amuse you with any remarks from a collection of tracts, not only upon exceeding grave subjects, but entirely relative to the kingdom of *Ireland?* not only local, but temporary? In the beginning of the volume is a pamphlet entitled *A Letter from a Member of the House of Commons in Ireland, to a Member of the House of Commons in England, concerning the Sacramental Test, written in the year* 1708:[1] and it is preceded by an explanatory advertisement,[2] that was either dictated, or strictly revised by the Dean himself.[3] He held the dissenters in the utmost degree of ridicule and detestation. He had an openness in his disposition, and a frankness in his conduct, that bore an abhorrence to all kind of reserve: even to discretion. Solemnities and outward forms were despised by him. His humorous disposition tempted him to actions inconsistent with the dignity of a clergyman:[4] and such flights drew upon him the general character of an irreligious man. I remember to have heard a story of him that fully shews how little he regarded certain ceremonies, which ought always to be observed with respect. Soon after he had been made Dean of St. PATRICK's,[5] he was loitering one Sunday in the afternoon at the house of Dr. RAYMOND[6] (with whom he had dined) at *Trim,* a little town near *Dublin,*[7] of which the Doctor was vicar. The bell had rung: the parishioners were assembled, for evening prayers: and Dr. RAYMOND was preparing to go to the church, which was scarce two hundred yards from his house. "RAYMOND, said the Dean, I'll lay you a crown I will begin prayers before you this afternoon." "I accept the wager," replied Dr. RAYMOND; and immediately they both ran as fast as they could towards the church. RAYMOND, who was much the nimbler man of the two, arrived first at the door: and when he entered the church, walked decently towards the reading desk. SWIFT never slackened his pace, but, running up the isle, left Dr. RAYMOND behind him in the middle of it, and stepping into the reading desk, without putting on a surplice, or opening the prayer-book, began the liturgy in an audible voice, and continued to repeat the service sufficiently long to win his wager. To such a disposition it is impossible that the gravity of nonconformists could be agreeable. The dislike was mutual on both sides. Dr. SWIFT hated all fanatics: all fanatics hated Dr. SWIFT. The pamphlet, which now lies before me, is particularly written against *repealing the test act*:[8] and whoever considers himself related to the kingdom of *Ireland*, will find in it some arguments of weight and consideration, in case any such repeal should ever be attempted there.

I cannot help pointing out to you, one particular piece of satir, that is entirely in SWIFT's own style and manner. In the fourth page,[9] he expresses himself thus. *"One of these authors (the fellow that was pilloried, I have forgot his name) is indeed so grave, sententious, dogmatical a rogue, that there is no enduring him."*[10] The *fellow that was pilloried* was DANIEL DEFOE, whose name SWIFT well knew and remembered, but the circumstance of the pillory was to be introduced; and the manner of introducing it shews great art in the nicest touches of satir, and carries all the marks of ridicule, indignation, and contempt. The scoffs and sarcasms of SWIFT, like the bite of the rattle-snake, distinguish themselves more venomously dangerous, than the wounds of a common serpent.

The next tract is, *A Proposal for the universal use of Irish Manufacture in clothes, and furniture of houses, &c.* utterly rejecting and renouncing every thing wearable that comes from *England*. Written in the year 1720.[11] In a former letter,[a] I believe I have told you, that, upon looking over the dates of Dr. SWIFT's works, he does not appear as a political writer from the year 1714 to the year 1720. You will probably be curious to know, in what manner he employed his time from the death of the Queen till the South-sea year.[12] Not in poetry, for his poetical pieces, during that period, are in a manner domestic; being scarce any more than trifles to SHERIDAN, or *poematia* to STELLA. How then is the chasm to be filled up? I imagine, by GULLIVER's travels. Such a work must, in all likelihood, have engrossed his leisure, during five or six years. When that was finished, he found an opening to indulge his love of politics, and to commence a patriot for *Ireland*: and he made use of the opportunity, by encreasing the natural jealousy which the lesser island constantly entertains of the greater. His *treatise*,[b] or *proposal*,[c] immediately raised a very violent flame. The printer was prosecuted: and the

---

[a]Original footnote in the *Remarks*: "Letter VI." Footnote in FI, FIa, FIb, FII, FIII, FV reads "See Letter VI."

[b]*treatise*,] treatise, FI, FIa, FIb, FII, FIII, FV, MI

[c]*proposal*,] proposal, FI, FIa, FIb, FII, FIII, FV, MI
Orrery's correction in Osborn pc 231: "His treatise, or proposal," to "His *treatise*, or *proposal*,"

prosecution had the same effect, which generally attends measures of that kind:[d] it added fuel to the flame. But his greatest enemies must confess, that the pamphlet is written in the stile of a man, who had the good of his country nearest his heart, who saw her errors, and wished to correct them; who felt her oppressions, and wished to relieve her;[e] and who had a desire to rouze, and awaken an indolent nation from a lethargic disposition, that might prove fatal to her constitution.

To the proposal, in favour of the Irish manufactures, succeed, *Some Arguments against enlarging the Power of Bishops in letting of Leases*.[13] This is too serious a pamphlet for your perusal,[14] nor shall I detain you with any farther account of it, than to say, that it is intermixt with those masterly strokes of irony, which so often appear[f] in SWIFT's works.

But the general subject of the pamphlet leads me to recollect a circumstance much to the Dean's honour. He could never be induced to take fines for any of the chapter lands. He always chose to raise the rents, as the method least oppressive to the present tenant, and most advantageous to all future tenants and landlords. He constantly refused to give charity out of the chapter funds, which he alledged were scarce sufficient to maintain the necessary repairs of the cathedral. I have already told you,[g] that, among his prebendaries, the *vox Decani* was the *vox Dei*.[15]

We are now come to THE DRAPIER's *Letters*, those brazen monuments of his fame. They were written in the year 1725.[h] I have said so much in one of my former letters[i] of the cause which gave rise to them, and of the effect which they had upon the nation, that I need say no more in this place, than to recommend them to your perusal, for the stile and conduct of their

---

[d]measures of that kind:] those kind of measures: FI, FIa, FIb, FII, FV, MI, MII; such measures: FIII, MIII; ~ ~ ~ ~; MIV

[e]her;] them, FI, FIa, FIb, FII, FIII, FV, MI; them; MII, MIII

[f]so often appear] are so often intermixt FI, FIa, FIb, FII, FIII, FV, MI; Orrery's correction in Osborn pc 231: "are so often intermixt" to "so often appear."

[g]Original footnote in the *Remarks*: "See Letter V."

[h]All editions of the *Remarks*, except MV, read "1724." Orrery made this correction in MV, although the correct date is 1724.

[i]Original footnote in the *Remarks*: "Letter VI." In FI, FIa, FIb, FII, FIII, FV footnote reads "See Letter VI."

manner: but, lest they may appear too grave to so young a man, and one who is so little interested in the present, and much less in the past affairs of *Ireland*, you will find a paper at the end of them that will excite your risibility, or I am mistaken.   It is entitled, *A full and true account of the solemn procession to the Gallows at the execution of* WILLIAM WOOD, *Esq; and hard-ware-man.*[j] [16]   The author makes the several artificers attend WILLIAM WOOD (represented by a log of timber) to the gallows, and each tradesman expresses his resentment in the terms of his proper calling. "*The* COOK *will* BASTE *him.   The* BOOKSELLER *will* TURN OVER A NEW LEAF *with him.   The* TAYLOR *will sit* IN HIS SKIRTS;"[17] and so on, through a number of people of different conditions.   Then follows the procession, most humorously described.[18]   The whole is a piece of ridicule too powerful for the strongest gravity to withstand.

The next tract is, *A short view of the state of Ireland, written in the year* 1727.[k] [19] Of this I need take little notice, since the present state of *Ireland* is, in general, as flourishing as possible.[20] Agriculture is cultivated: arts and sciences are encouraged: and in the space of eighteen years, which is almost the full time that I have known it, no kingdom can be more improved. *Ireland*, in relation of *England*, may be compared to a younger sister lately come of age, after having suffered all the miseries of an injured minor;[21] such as law suits, encroachments upon her property, violation of her rights, destruction of her tenants, and every evil that can be named. At length, time, and her own noble spirit of industry, have entirely relieved her; and, some little heart-burnings excepted, she enjoys the quiet possession of a very ample fortune, subject, by way of acknowledgement, to certain quit rents payable to the elder branch of her house: and let me add by experience, that *take her all in all*, she cannot have a greater fortune than she deserves.

I shall not make any comments upon *An Answer to a Paper called A Memorial of the poor Inhabitants, Tradesmen, and Labourers of the Kingdom of Ireland, written in the year* 1728.[l] [22] The pamphlet which comes next in order of succession, is written with[m] SWIFT's usual peculiarity of humour.

---

[j]Original footnote in the *Remarks*: "Page 233." This refers to the page number in volume 4 of Faulkner's edition of Swift's works.

[k]Original footnote in the *Remarks*: "Page 240." This refers to the page number in volume 4 of Faulkner's edition of Swift's works.

[l]Original footnote in the *Remarks*: "Page 251." This refers to the page number in volume 4 of Faulkner's edition of Swift's works.

[m]with] in FI

The title of it is, *A Modest Proposal for preventing the Children of Poor People in Ireland, from being a burden to their Parents or Country; and for making them beneficial to the Public,*[n] *written in the year* 1729.[23] The proposal[o] is to fatten beggars children, and sell them for food to rich landlords, and persons of quality.

The vindication of his Excellency JOHN *Lord* CARTERET *from the charge of favouring none but Tories, High-Churchmen, and Jacobites,*[p] [24] is entirely humorous, and so I think are all the remaining pamphlets in this volume. But the last piece, entitled, *The Speech and dying Words of* EBENEZOR ELLISTON, *who was executed the second of May* 1722, *written and published at his desire for the common good,*[25] had a most excellent effect.[q] [26] The thieves, vagabonds, and all the lower class of people thought it the real work of EBENEZOR ELLISTON, who had received the grounds of a good education; and the stile of this paper is so natural for a person in such circumstances, that it would almost deceive the nicest judgement.

I have now completed my animadversions upon the four first volumes of SWIFT's works; the last of which contains abundance of ironical wit founded upon the basis of reason and good sense. But, I had almost forgot, that, at the latter end of the volume, there are three copies of verses, two of which are addressed to the Dean, and the third is his answer: the first being my property[27] may serve to conclude this letter.[28] It was occasioned by an annual custom, which I found pursued among his friends, of making him a present on his birth-day. As he had admitted me of that number, I sent him a paper-book, finely bound,[29] in the first leaf of which I wrote the following lines.[30]

Dublin, November 30, 1732.

TO thee, dear SWIFT, these spotless leaves I send;
Small is the present, but sincere the friend,

---

[n]In Osborn pc 231, Orrery underlined "*public,*"

[o]In Osborn pc 231, Orrery underlined "proposal"

[p]Original footnote in the *Remarks*: "Page 275. Written in the year 1730." "Page 275" refers to the page number in volume 4 of Faulkner's edition of Swift's works.

[q]Original footnote in the *Remarks*: "Page 363." This refers to the page number in volume 4 of Faulkner's edition of Swift's works. Orrery's correction in Osborn pc 231: "Page 36." to "Page 363."

Think not so poor a book below thy care,
Who knows the price that thou canst make it bear?
Tho' tawdry now, and like TYRILLA's face,
The specious front shines out with borrow'd grace:
Tho' paste-boards glittering like a tinsel'd coat,
A *rasa tabula* within denote;
Yet if a venal and corrupted age,
And modern vices should provoke thy rage;
If warn'd once more by their impending fate
A sinking country and an injur'd state,
Thy great assistance should again demand,
And call forth reason to defend the land;
Then shall we view these sheets, with glad surprize,
Inspir'd with thought, and speaking to our eyes:
Each vacant space shall then, enrich'd, dispense
True force of eloquence, and nervous sense;
Inform the judgement, animate the heart,
And sacred rules of policy impart,
The spangled covering, bright with splendid ore,
Shall cheat the sight with empty shew no more;
But lead us inward to those golden mines,
Where all thy soul in native lustre shines.
So when the eye surveys some lovely fair,
With bloom of beauty, grac'd with shape and air,
How is the rapture heighten'd, when we find
Her form excell'd by her celestial mind!

ORRERY.

Notes

1. *Prose Works of Swift* 2:109-25. The Sacramental Test, which had been in effect in England since 1673 and in Ireland since 1704, excluded from public offices all who were not Anglican communicants. In *A Letter concerning the Sacramental Test*, Swift expressed his opposition to the repeal of the test.

2. "The Publisher's Advertisement to the Reader" (ibid., p. 110) was first added to the tract in Faulkner's edition (1735).

3. See ibid., p. xxiii.

4. Cf. Swift's own words on his writings in *The Author upon Himself*:

> Humour, and Mirth, had Place in all he writ:
> He reconcil'd Divinity and Wit.

(lines 11-12; *Poems of Swift* 1:194)

5. This incident might have taken place sometime between late June and early August 1713. This is the period when Swift stayed in Laracor, and also visited Raymond at Trim. Swift's account books indicate his presence at Trim a number of times in July and in the first week of August. See Swift, *Account Books*, p. 159. There are also letters by Swift from Trim on 29 June, 16 July, and 7 August (*Correspondence of Swift* 1:370, 376, 383).

6. Dr. Anthony Raymond (ca. 1675-ca. 1726), rector of Trim.

7. In County Meath.

8. I.e., Swift's *A Letter concerning the Sacramental Test*.

9. That is, p. 4 of vol. 4 of Faulkner's edition of Swift's works.

10. In Swift, *A Letter concerning the Sacramental Test* (*Prose Works of Swift* 2:113). Swift added a footnote to the passage identifying "the Fellow that was *pilloryed*" as Daniel Defoe.

11. Ibid., 9:13-22. It was first published shortly before George I's sixtieth birthday (28 May 1720).

12. For a full account of the South Sea Company scandal, see Viscount Erleigh, *The South Sea Bubble* (New York: G. P. Putnam's Sons, 1933).

13. *Prose Works of Swift* 11:43-60. The text is dated 21 October 1723, and it was first published on 26 October (Dublin: John Hyde, 1723, octavo); cf. Ehrenpreis, *Swift* 3:181. The tract's next appearance was in Faulkner's edition in 1735.

14. Orrery once wrote that Hamilton had "the most true humour of any youth" he knew (Add MS 4303, manuscript pages 139-140, British Library). We may suppose Orrery thought Swift's *Some Arguments* would not please someone like Hamilton, who enjoyed humorous writings.

15. "The voice of the Dean was the voice of God."

16. *Prose Works of Swift* 10:145-49.

17. Ibid., pp. 145-46.

18. Ibid., pp. 147-48.

19. Ibid., 12:1-12.

20. For the flourishing condition of early-eighteenth-century Dublin, see Patrick Fagan, *The Second City* (Dublin: Branar, 1986), pp. 1-2, and 14-19. See also A. C. Elias, Jr., "Dublin at Mid-Century: The Tricks of *The Tricks of the Town* Laid Open," *Eighteenth-Century Ireland* 10 (1995): 110.

21. Cf. the title of Swift's earliest tract specifically addressing Ireland's problems, *The Story of the Injured Lady*.

22. *Prose Works of Swift* 12:13-25.

23. Ibid., pp. 107-18.

24. Ibid., pp. 149-69.

25. Ibid., 9:35-41.

26. Orrery is echoing Faulkner's note to his reprint of Swift's parody of Elliston's last words in 1735: "It is remarkable, that this Speech had so good an Effect, that there have been very few Robberies of that kind committed since" (ibid., p. 37).

27. Here, it sounds as if Orrery is claiming copyright.

28. The companion to Orrery's poem to Swift is *Verses left with a Silver Standish, on the Dean of St. Patrick's Desk, on his Birth-Day,* by Delany (*Poems of Swift* 2:610-11). Swift's answer to both poems is *Verses written by Dr. Swift* (ibid., p. 611).

29. For information on this notebook given to Swift by Orrery, see the introduction to the present edition, n. 53.

30. For information on this poem by Orrery, see the introduction to the present edition, p. 20.

LETTER XVII

I Have already told you, my dear HAM, that the four first volumes of SWIFT's works were published together, and passed immediately under his own inspection. Not long afterwards came out two additional volumes, both which were supervised and corrected by the author.

The Conduct of the Allies[1] begins the fifth volume. I imagine that *the Publisher's Preface*[2] was composed by the Dean himself, but affectedly written in a bad style. The last paragraph makes me suspect his hand. *"It is plainly seen,* says the Publisher, *that a spirit of liberty is diffused through all these writings, and that the author is an enemy to tyranny and oppression in any shape whatever."*[3] This is the character at which SWIFT aimed, and this is the character which indeed he deserved.

Throughout the course of these letters I have freely pointed out to you all his faults, but I beg you to remember, that with all those faults, he was above corruption. A virtue in itself sufficient to cover a multitude of human failings, since from that virtue alone can flow prosperity to the commonwealth.

The Conduct of the Allies was written in the year 1712, and it is preparatory to the peace, which the ministers were then concerting, and which was afterwards perfected at *Utrecht*.[4] It begins by reflexions on war in general, and then particularly mentions the several civil wars in our kingdom. When I am reading treatises of this sort, I cannot help pitying my unhappy country, torn to pieces by her own sons. A wretched mother of vultures, for whom, like TITYUS, she produces new entrails only to be devoured.[5]

The papers called *the Examiners*,[6] at least those of which Dr. SWIFT is the author, fill up the rest of the volume. They begin in *November* 1710, and they are carried down to the end of *July* 1711.[7] They are written in defence of the new administration,[8] and the particular revolutions at court which had introduced the Earl of OXFORD, and had displaced the earl of GODOLPHIN and his friends.[9]

Many of SWIFT's *Examiners* are personally aimed at the General.[a] [10] In a free country, the power of a general is always to be feared. The greater his military capacity, or the more successful his arms, in the greater danger are the liberties of the people. On this maxim SWIFT proceeded; and while he was writing in defence of the commonwealth, he had an opportunity of giving a loose to his own severity, of which *the house of Pride*,[11] and several other allegorical essays are very spirited examples.

But I am fettered in my animadversions on these papers. The present times, and the honour which I bear to many noble families descended from persons mentioned in *the Examiners*, make me willing to take as slight notice as possible even of the wittiest passages in those papers; because many of those passages arise from personal reflections, or party sarcasms. In general, the several points relating to the national debt[12] (alas! how encreased since the year seventeen hundred and ten)[13] the too long continuance of the war,[14] and other public topics of complaint are melancholy truths, justly becoming the pen of a man who loves his country.

Within these last forty years, the political treatises have been so numerous, so various, so local, and so temporary, that each new pamphlet has succeeded its predecessor,[15] like a youthful son to an antient father amidst a multiplicity of followers, admirers, and dependants, whilst the antiquated Sire having *strutted and foamed his hour upon the stage, is heard no more*,[16] but lies silent, and almost entirely forgotten, except by a few friends and cotemporaries, who accidentally remember some of his just observations, or prophetical aphorisms, which they have lived to see accomplished. Thus has it fared, even in my time, with the EXAMINERS, the FREEHOLDERS,[17] and the CRAFTSMAN:[18] and the same fate will attend most writings of that sort, which being framed to serve particular views, fulfill the purport of their creation, and then perish: while works of a more liberal and diffusive kind are acceptable to all persons, and all times; and may assume to themselves a certain prospect of surviving to the latest posterity.

But my dearest HAMILTON, when you enter into the commerce of life, you will be obliged, in your own defence, to look into every thing that has been written upon political subjects. In *England*, a man cannot keep up a conversation without being well versed in politics. In whatever other point of learning he may be deficient, he certainly must not appear superficial in state affairs. He must chuse his party; and he must stick to the choice. *Non revocare gradum*[19] must be his motto; and Heaven forgive you, my dear son, if the *gradus*[20] now and then enforces you to act against self conviction.

If party, and the consequences of it had arisen to that heighth among the Romans and Grecians, as it has arisen of late years among the English, their

---

[a]Original footnote in the *Remarks*: "The Duke of MARLBOROUGH."

poets would probably have added *her* to the three furies, and would have placed her in hell, as a fit companion for TISIPHONE, MEGAERA, and ALECTO,[21] from whence, according to their description, she might have made excursions upon earth, only with an intention to destroy, confound, mislead, and disunite mankind.

It is true, that all countries have their parties and their factions. But there is a certain contagious distemper of this sort, so peculiar to the British islands, that, I believe, it is unknown to every other part of the world. It encreases our natural gloom, and it makes us so averse to each other, that it keeps men of the best morals, and most social inclinations, in one continued state of warfare and opposition. Must not the source of this malady arise rather from the heart, than from the head? from the different operations of our passions, than[b] of our reason?

> *Furorne caecus, an rapit vis acrior,*
> *An culpa?*[22]

SWIFT, a man of violent passions, was, in consequence of those passions, violent in his party: but as his capacity and genius were so extraordinary and extensive, even his party writings carry with them dignity and instruction: and in that light I wish you to read *the Examiners*, where you will find a nervous style, a clear diction, and great knowledge of the true landed interest of *England.*[23]

> *I am,*
> *My dear* HAMILTON,
> *Your ever[c] affectionate Father,*
> ORRERY.

---

[b]passions, than MV] passions, rather than MIII

[c]ever] most FI

Notes

1. *Prose Works of Swift* 6:1-65.

2. Volume 5 of Faulkner's edition of Swift's works, 1741-48, sig. A2. It is dated Dublin, 18 April 1738.

3. Ibid. The words "all these writings" refer to *The Conduct of the Allies* and the *Examiners*.

4. The Treaty or Peace of Utrecht, which ended the War of the Spanish Succession. The main participants were Britain, the United Provinces, Austria, France, and Spain.

5. Tityus, a giant, was the son of Zeus and Elara. Hera, Zeus's sister, became jealous when Leto gave birth to Artemis and Apollo (Zeus's children), and unleashed Tityus against Leto. Zeus struck Tityus with his thunderbolt, and Tityus fell into the Underworld, where two snakes or two eagles devoured his liver, which grew again in accordance with the phases of the moon.

6. In Frank Ellis's words, "Swift's *Examiners* are thirty-three essays of about 2,000 words a piece, published every Thursday from 2 November 1710 to 14 June 1711" (Swift, *The Examiner*, p. xxi).

7. The numbering of Swift's *Examiners* was 14-45 (2 November 1710-7 June 1711), but, in the first collected edition of the *Examiners* (London: Printed for John Morphew and A. Dodd, 1712, duodecimo), the original number 13 (for 26 October 1710) was dropped. It was written by Atterbury, in defense of the doctrine of hereditary right, or Non-Resistance, and apparently for safety reasons, John Barber, the printer, decided not to include it. The result was that the numbers of the subsequent papers were changed (the numbers of Swift's contributions then became 13-44). Faulkner followed the wrong numbering of the first collected edition, and the original correct numbering was restored by Frank Ellis. See *Prose Works of Swift* 3:xxvii-xxviii; and Swift, *The Examiner*, p. lxx. The *Examiner* continued to appear until 26 July 1711, and was revived by John Oldisworth in December 1711. It was then issued until 1714.

8. According to Swift, shortly before he began to write the *Examiners*, Harley had told him that the administration's great difficulty "lay in the want of some good pen, to keep up the spirit raised in the people, to assert the principles, and justify the proceedings of the new ministers" (*Prose Works of Swift* 8:123).

9. Three factors helped to speed up the Whig downfall. First, the increasing demands for peace with France after the English victory of Malplaquet (summer 1709), and the Barrier Treaty for the benefit of the Dutch. Second, Marlborough's request to be made captain general for life. And lastly, the Sacheverell impeachment and trial.

10. See Swift, the *Examiner* no. 17, 23 November 1710 (*The Examiner*, pp. 49-57); no. 21, 21 December 1710 (ibid., pp. 111-18); and no. 28, 8 February 1711 (ibid., pp. 227-32).

11. The *Examiner* no. 49, for Thursday, 19 July 1711 (volume 5 of Faulkner's edition of Swift's works, 1741-1748, p. 328). This number of the *Examiner* is by Mary de la Rivière Manley (1663-1724), not by Swift. I am indebted to Dr. Frank Ellis for this information.

12. See the *Examiner* no. 14, 2 November 1710 (Swift, *The Examiner*, pp. 4-9); no. 26, 25 January 1711 (ibid., pp. 196-97); no. 35, 29 March 1711 (ibid., pp. 328-30); no. 38, 19 April 1711 (ibid., p. 379); no. 43, 24 May 1711 (ibid., pp. 439-40); and no. 45, 7 June 1711 (ibid., pp. 467-68).

13. Two measures carried in 1749 and 1750 effected an increase of the interest to 3 percent. From 1748 to 1756, £6,013,640 of the funded debt had been discharged, and still, by the time of the accession of William Pitt the younger to the office of prime minister (19 December 1783), the debt had increased to about £250,000,000. See William Lecky, *A History of England in the Eighteenth Century* (London: Longmans, Green, 1892), 5:319-30.

14. The War of the Spanish Succession.

15. See *British Pamphleteers*, ed. George Orwell et al., 2 vols. (London: A. Wingate, 1948-51). See also George Marr, *The Periodical Essayists of the Eighteenth Century* (London: James Clarke, 1923).

16. *Macbeth*, 5.5.24-25.

17. The *Freeholder* ran for 55 numbers, from 23 December 1715 to 29 June 1716. See *British Union-Catalogue of Periodicals*, 4 vols. (London: Buttersworth Scientific Publications, 1955-58), 2:233.

18. The *Craftsman* ran for 44 numbers (from 5 December 1726 to 8 May 1727). Then it changed its title to the *Country Journal, or the Craftsman* (nos. 45 to 159, from 13 May 1727 to 15 September 1750). See *British Union-*

Catalogue of Periodicals 1:671. The *Craftsman* was launched by William Pulteney and Bolingbroke as an organ of opposition to Walpole.

19. "Not to step back."

20. "Step" or "Move."

21. Tisiphone, Megaera, and Alecto were the three Erinyes, or violent goddesses whom the Romans identified with their Furies. They lived in Erebus, Hell's darkest pit, and came to be considered as divinities of infernal punishment, who tortured their victims and sent them mad. They were depicted as winged spirits, with their hair entwined with snakes, and holding whips or torches in their hands.

22. "Does some blind frenzy drive us on, or some stronger power, or guilt?" (Horace *Epodes* 7.13-14).

23. For Swift's remarks on the landed interest in the *Examiner*, see: no. 14, 2 November 1710 (*The Examiner*, pp. 4-9); no. 15, 9 November 1710 (ibid., pp. 24-26); no. 25, 18 January 1711 (ibid., pp. 181-83); no. 34, 22 March 1711 (ibid., p. 314); no. 35, 29 March 1711 (ibid., pp. 331-32); no. 36, 5 April 1711 (ibid., pp. 346-47); no. 44, 31 May 1711 (ibid., pp. 452-54); and no. 45, 7 June 1711 (ibid., p. 467).

LETTER XVIII

SUCH a confusion, such a mixture of verse, prose, politics, letters, similes, wit, trifles, and *polite conversation*, are thrown into the sixth volume,[1] that I know not in what manner to treat it, or what particular part to recommend to your perusal. The poetry, the similes, and the trifles are not worth your attention. Of the letters, the two from the earl of PETERBOROUGH to Mr. POPE are short, but excellent in their kind.[2] The others, I mean those of the Dean,[3] and of Mr. POPE,[4] have much less merit, or at least are much less agreeable. Lord PETERBOROUGH's[5] wit is easy and unaffected. At the time when he wrote those two letters, he had hung up his helmet, and his buckler, and was retired to his plough, and his wheelbarrow, wearied of courts, and disgusted with statesmen.[6] He had made a most considerable figure in his day.[7] His character was amiable and uncommon. His life was a continued series of variety. In his public and private conduct he differed from most men. He had visited all climates, but had staid in none. He was a citizen of the world. He conquered and maintained armies without money.[8] His actions and expressions were peculiar to himself. He was of a vivacity superiour to all fatigue, and his courage was beyond any conception of danger. He verified, in many instances, whatever has been said of romantic heroes. He seems to have been fixed only in his friendships and moral principles. He had a true[a] regard and affection for SWIFT and POPE. The Dean, in a short copy of verses,[b] [9] has described him in a very particular manner, but so justly, that the four last stanzas will give a most perfect, and compleat idea of Lord PETERBOROUGH's person and military virtues,

> A *skeleton* in outward figure,

---

[a]a true] a most true FI, FIa, FIb, FII, FIII, FV, MI

[b]Original footnote in the *Remarks*: "Vol. II. Page 222." "Page 222" refers to the page number in volume 2 of Faulkner's edition of Swift's works.

His meagre corps, though full of vigour,
Would halt behind him were it bigger.

So wonderful his expedition,
When you have not the least suspicion,
He's with you like an apparition.

Shines in all climates like a star,
In senates bold, and fierce in war,
A land commander, and a tar.

Heroic actions early bred in,
Ne'er to be match'd in modern reading,
But by his name-sake CHARLES of *Sweden*.[10]

The *Publick Spirit of the Whigs*[11] is a pamphlet in answer to the Crisis written by Sir RICHARD STEELE,[12] but it contains such acute satir against the nobility of *Scotland*,[13] that in an advertisement printed before it,[14] we are told, "*All the Scotch lords then in London went in a body to complain against the author; and the consequence of that complaint was a proclamation offering a reward of three hundred pounds to discover him.*"[15] It was written in the year 1712,[16] by the consent, if not the encouragement of the ministers of that aera.[17] In the style and conduct, it is one of the boldest, as well as one of the most masterly tracts that SWIFT ever wrote. And I cannot help again observing, that on whatever topic he employs his pen, the subject which he treats of, is always so excellently managed, as to seem to have been the whole study, and application of his life: so that he appears, the greatest master through a greater variety of materials, than perhaps have been discussed by any other author.

The *Bishop of Salisbury* [Dr. BURNET][18] is the next antagonist whom SWIFT attacks in single combat. I can give you no better idea of this work, than by a quotation from the tract itself, which is called, *A Preface to the Bishop of Salisbury's introduction to the third volume of the History of the Reformation of the Church of England.*[19] Towards the latter end of the Pamphlet[c] SWIFT says,

"*However he* [THE BISHOP] *thanks* GOD, *there are many among us who stand in the breach: I believe there may:*[20] *it is a* BREACH *of their own making, and they design to come forward, and storm and plunder, if they are not driven back.* THEY MAKE THEMSELVES A WALL FOR THEIR CHURCH AND COUNTRY. A

---

[c]Original footnote in the *Remarks*: "Page 89." This refers to the page number in volume 6 of Faulkner's edition of Swift's works.

SOUTH *wall, I suppose, for all the best fruit of the church and country to be nailed on. Let us examine this metaphor.* THE WALL OF OUR CHURCH AND COUNTRY *is built of those who love the constitution in both. Our domestic enemies undermine some parts of the* WALL, *and place themselves in the* BREACH; *and then they cry,* WE ARE THE WALL. *We do not like such patchwork; they build with untempered mortar; nor can they ever cement with us, till they get better materials; and better workmen:* GOD *keep us from having our* BREACHES *made up with such rubbish:* THEY STAND UPON THE WATCHTOWER! *They are indeed pragmatical enough to do so; but who assigned them that post, to give us false intelligence, to alarm us with false dangers, and send us to defend one gate, while their accomplices are breaking in at another?* THEY CRY TO GOD DAY AND NIGHT TO AVERT THE JUDGEMENT OF POPERY, WHICH SEEMS TO HASTEN TOWARDS US. *Then I affirm, they are hypocrites by day, and filthy dreamers by night. When they cry unto Him, He will not hear them: for they cry out against the plainest dictates of their own conscience, reason and belief.*

But lastly, THEY LIE IN THE DUST, MOURNING BEFORE HIM. *Hang me if I believe that, unless it be figuratively spoken. But, suppose it to be true, why do* THEY LIE IN THE DUST? *because they love to raise it; for what do they mourn? why for power, wealth, and places. There let the enemies of the Queen, Monarchy, and the Church lie, and mourn, and lick the* DUST *like* SERPENTS, *till they are truly sensible of their ingratitude, falshood, disobedience, slander, blasphemy, sedition, and every evil work."*[21]

I must follow the same method in forming your idea of the next pamphlet, by a quotation out of it, which happens to be the first paragraph. The title is, *The Presbyterians Plea of Merit in order to take off the Test, impartially examined:*[22] and the author begins in the true vein of wit and spirit, by saying, *"We have been told in the common news papers, that all attempts are to be made this sessions by the presbyterians and their abettors, for taking off the test; as a kind of preparatory step to make it go down smoother in England. For, if once* THEIR LIGHT WOULD SO SHINE, *the papists, delighted with the blaze, would all come in, and dance about it. This I take to be a prudent method, like that of a discreet physician, who first gives a new medicine to a dog, before he prescribes it to* A HUMAN CREATURE."[23] I have quoted this short passage for the style, as well as the matter; and I dare say, even from hence, you will be confirmed in one general observation, that SWIFT maintains and conducts his metaphors and allusions, with a justness particularly delicate and exact, and without the least stiffness, or affectation. In some of my former letters, I have mentioned in what degree of contempt and hatred he held the dissenters, especially the presbyterians: and I need only add, that as this pamphlet was written for the meridian of *Ireland*, it ought to have been placed with the other tracts on the same subject.[24]

The subsequent pamphlet is, *Advice offered to the Members of the October Club*.[25]   It was written in the year 1711, and is so applicable to that particular time, that I shall not make any animadversions upon it.[26]   From political tracts, the true history of *England* is to be deduced: and if foreigners were to enter into that branch of reading, they might frame a more distinct notion of our legislature, and of our manners, than from more laboured, and connected accounts of our constitution. In such a view, I am apt to think, that, at first sight, they must behold us a disunited, discontented, and seemingly an unsteady people: but I am certain, that, upon a more minute disquisition, they must find in us a fixed, and, I may say, an innate love of liberty, variegated, and perhaps sometimes erroneous in its progress, but constant, and unwearied in the pursuit of that glorious end. What people upon earth can desire a more exalted, or a more distinguished character? To speak in the dialect of the heathen world, our errors are the errors of men, our principles are the principles of gods.

The other pieces in this volume, except *The Remarks on the Barrier Treaty*,[27] are not, in my mind, sufficiently striking to deserve much notice. Some of them are the *minutissimae* of SWIFT's writings, which, I believe, he would scarce have published, fond as he was of seeing his works in print, if he had been in the full vigour of his understanding, or had considered, that trifles of that kind,[d] which are weak as feathers, in supporting a reputation, are heavy as lead, in depressing it.

> *I am, my dearest* HAM,
> *Your most affectionate Father,*
> ORRERY.

---

[d]trifles of that kind, MV] those kind of trifles, MIII

Notes

1. Faulkner's volume 6 (1746) includes *Polite Conversation*, five prose tracts, two poems, and seven letters.

2. Orrery is referring to these two letters from Peterborough to Pope, included by Faulkner in volume 6 of his edition of Swift's works: a letter probably dated April 1732, and a letter probably dated early May 1732. For the text of these letters, see Alexander Pope, *The Correspondence of Alexander Pope*, ed. George Sherburn, 5 vols. (Oxford: Clarendon Press, 1956), 3:281-83. It will be cited hereafter as Sherburn, *Pope*.

3. Faulkner's volume 6 contains only two letters from Swift: to Pope, 20 September 1723 (*Correspondence of Swift* 2:464-66), and to Peterborough, undated by Faulkner but probably written in 1733 (ibid., 4:167-68).

4. Faulkner's volume 6 includes two letters from Pope: to Swift, August 1723 (ibid., 2:457-60); and to Swift, wrongly dated by Faulkner 10 December 1725, and actually written on 14 December by Pope and Bolingbroke to Swift (ibid., pp. 119-22).

5. Charles Mordaunt, third earl of Peterborough and earl of Monmouth (ca. 1658-1735), admiral, general, and diplomatist, for whom see William Stebbing, *Peterborough* (London and New York: Macmillan, 1890). For important new information on Peterborough, see David Woolley, "An Alembicated Footnote to the King of Sicily's Watch, Including a New Letter from Alexander Pope," *Swift Studies* 6 (1991): 10-29.

6. Although Peterborough attended the House of Lords until 1731, his official career ended when Queen Anne died. In his later years, Peterborough mostly resided at Bevis Mount, a cottage near Southampton. See *Dictionary of National Biography*, s.v. "Mordaunt, Charles."

7. In 1689 alone, William III appointed Mordaunt as privy councillor (14 February), gentleman of the bedchamber (March 1), colonel of a regiment of foot (1 April), first lord of the treasury (8 April), earl of Monmouth (9 April), lord lieutenant of Northamptonshire (29 April), colonel of horse (15 June), and water bailiff of the Severn (9 August). Mordaunt became earl of Peterborough on the occasion of his uncle's death (19 June 1697). On 31 March 1705, Peterborough was appointed as admiral and commander in chief of the expedition to Spain in support of Archduke Charles, whom the Allies recognized as King of Spain. In September 1705, Peterborough led the heroic capture of Barcelona, where Archduke Charles was proclaimed king of Spain.

In December 1710, Peterborough was nominated ambassador extraordinary to Vienna, and spent the years 1711-13 mostly in diplomatic missions. In April 1714, it was announced that Peterborough had been appointed as governor of Minorca, but owing to Queen Anne's death, he never assumed office. See ibid.

8. Peterborough claimed that he had maintained the army in Spain at his own cost, although he never showed accounts to prove this statement. Ibid.

9. Swift, *To the Earl of Peterborough* (*Poems of Swift* 2:396-98).

10. Ibid., p. 398.

11. *Prose Works of Swift* 8:27-68.

12. In October 1713, the Whigs were searching for a propaganda chief, and they "particularly wanted a book that would expound with impassioned but dignified authority the panic they felt concerning the peace and the succession" (Ehrenpreis, *Swift* 2:697). The party chose Richard Steele, who launched a new periodical entitled the *Englishman*, which ran from 6 October 1713 to 15 February 1714 (57 numbers). Steele also began to prepare a work entitled the *Crisis*, which may be seen in Richard Steele, *Tracts and Pamphlets by Richard Steele*, ed. Rae Blanchard (New York: Octagon, 1967), pp. 125-81. The *Crisis* was widely circulated and read, which caused the ministry to wish for a reply to appear simultaneously with the opening of Parliament. On 30 January 1714, the first advertisements of Swift's *The Public Spirit of the Whigs* appeared in the *Post Boy* and the *Mercator*.

13. In the tract's first printing (London: by John Barber for John Morphew, 1714), the offensive passage against Scotland's nobility extended from p. 21, line 4 from foot to p. 24, line 8 from foot. The passage came to be omitted, and sheets D and E were reprinted. There are censored and uncensored versions of Morphew's first and second editions, but there are only censored copies of Morphew's third and fourth editions. More specifically, there are five states of the tract's text in Morphew's first two editions: there is an "uncensored" and a "heavily censored" first edition, and there is an "uncensored," a "lightly censored," and a "heavily censored" second edition. The offensive passage is still present in the "uncensored" state, is incompletely suppressed in the "lightly censored" state, and is awkwardly excised in the "heavily censored" state. See John Harris, "Swift's *The Publick Spirit of the Whigs*: A Partly Censored State of the Scottish Paragraphs," *Papers of the Bibliographical Society of America* 71 (1978): 92-94; and John Irwin Fischer, "The Legal Response of Swift's *The Public Spirit of the Whigs*," in *Swift and*

His Contexts, ed. John Irwin Fischer, Hermann Real, and James Woolley (New York: AMS Press, 1989), p. 30.

14. In *Prose Works of Swift* 8:30. This advertisement was included in Faulkner's volume 6 (1746).

15. Ibid. On 11 March 1714, the Lords voted to petition the queen to issue a proclamation for the discovery of the author of *The Public Spirit of the Whigs* (ibid., pp. 198-99). Queen Anne accordingly issued the proclamation on 15 March (ibid., facing p. xxii), offering a reward of £300 to anyone who would discover the author of the tract. In the end, the Crown closed the case with a *nolle prosequi* declaration. See Maurice Quinlan, "The Prosecution of Swift's *Public Spirit of the Whigs*," *Texas Studies in Literature and Language* 9 (1967): 167-84; and John Irwin Fischer, "The Legal Response of Swift's *The Public Spirit of the Whigs*," in *Swift and His Contexts*, pp. 21-38.

16. The specific publication date for the tract is unknown, but Swift certainly did not write it in 1712. See *Swift and His Contexts*, p. 34.

17. During the discussion in the House of Lords on 2 March 1714, which followed Wharton's denunciation of *The Public Spirit of the Whigs*, Oxford said "he knew nothing of the pamphlet" and he protested against the "malicious insinuations" in it (Ehrenpreis, *Swift* 2:709). However, on the next day, Oxford sent Swift a bankbill of a hundred pounds, on account of the troubles regarding the tract. On 18 May 1714, Swift wrote to the earl of Peterborough, stating: "Barber the printer was, some time ago, in great distress, upon printing a pamphlet [*The Public Spirit of the Whigs*], of which evil tongues would needs call me the author: he was brought before your House, which addressed the Queen in a body, who kindly published a proclamation, with 300*l.* to discover. The fault was, calling the Scots a fierce poor northern people. So well protected are those who scribble for the Government" (*Correspondence of Swift* 2:22).

18. Gilbert Burnet, bishop of Salisbury (1643-1715).

19. *Prose Works of Swift* 4:51-84.

20. In his copy of Faulkner's edition of Swift's works (1746), Orrery corrected "I believe they may" to "I believe there may." But the two 1713 London editions, the 1714 Dublin edition, and Faulkner's edition read "I believe they may." Accordingly, Herbert Davis and Louis Landa gave this reading.

21. *Prose Works of Swift* 4:81-82.

22. Ibid., 12:261-79.

23. Ibid., p. 263.

24. I.e., in Faulkner's volume 4.

25. *Prose Works of Swift* 6:67-80. The October Club was a gathering of about one hundred country squires who met every evening at the Bell Tavern in King Street, Westminster. The club took its name from its members' custom of drinking October beer. It consisted of extreme Tories who were dissatisfied with Harley for not having turned out all the Whigs and for having been slow in rewarding the country gentlemen and the Tories for their support to the administration.

26. In "The Publisher's Preface" to *Some Advice* (ibid., pp. 187-88), first printed in Faulkner's edition, there is a description of the circumstances that surrounded and occasioned the pamphlet. The preface closed with these words: "This Discourse having been published about the Year 1711, and many of the Facts forgotten, would have not been generally understood without some Explanation, which we have now endeavoured to give, because it seems a Point of History too material to be lost. We owe this Piece of Intelligence to an Intimate of the supposed Author" (ibid., p. 188).

27. Ibid., pp. 81-117. The Barrier Treaty, between the Netherlands and England, was signed on 29 October 1709. Charles Townshend (1674-1738), second Viscount Townshend, sent to the Hague as plenipotentiary by the Whig ministry, signed the Barrier Treaty alone, since Marlborough had refused to countenance it. It determined that the Dutch could garrison a defensive line of cities and fortresses on the French border and in the Spanish Netherlands. In return, the Dutch pledged to provide armed support to the Hanoverian succession.

LETTER XIX

THE seventh volume contains SWIFT's epistolary correspondence, from the year 1714 to the year 1737,[1] and, as it is an acknowledged observation, that no part of an author's writings give a greater insight into his natural disposition than his letters, (especially when written with freedom and sincerity) I shall endeavour to point out to you, such circumstances in SWIFT's epistles, and in the answers[a] of his friends, as may afford you materials to form your own conjectures upon the different characters not only of *the Dean*, but of his correspondents. From preceding letters, you are probably become acquainted with Dr. SWIFT, but the manners and opinions of those persons with whom he corresponded, are in every respect so blended with his own, as not to be easily separated, and in such a kind of united view, they will mutually reflect light upon each other.

To a young man just entering into the world as you are, the subject may prove of particular importance, as it may guide him not only in the choice of his correspondents, but in his manner of writing to them.

The freedom of the press is to be watched and defended with the most jealous eye. It is one of the chief articles of that great *Charter* of liberty to which the people of *England* are entitled: but as no human institution can be perfect, even this branch of liberty has its excrescences that might be pruned. I mean particularly that licence which of late has too much prevailed of publishing epistolary correspondences. Such a fashion, for I know not what else to call it, is extremely pernicious. At present, it satisfies the curiosity of the public; but for the future, it will tend to restrain that unsuspicious openness, which is the principal delight of writing to our friends. I am sorry to say by experience, that the letters which contain the most sincere, and perhaps hasty observations upon persons, times, and circumstances, are often reserved as treasures, and hoarded up, as misers hoard gold; like which, they lie concealed in cabinets and strong boxes for some time, till chancing to fall

---

[a]answers] answer FI, FIa, FIb, FII, FV, MI

into the hands of an extravagant heir, or an injudicious executor, they are not only brought into light, but dispersed and exposed, so as to become the property of the whole world. Let me advise you therefore, my HAMILTON, when you give your opinion upon any important subject, to consider it well, before you commit your thoughts to paper. Express yourself with diffidence. Preserve a prudent restraint over the sallies of wit and humour: and be cautious in all declarations of friendship; as the very common offers of civility, are too often explained into undesigned engagements.

I own, HAM, I find myself under no small difficulty in discussing this volume of SWIFT's letters. General criticisms will be attended with obscurity: and it would be tedious to consider them in their exact order. I shall endeavour therefore, to take a review only of what seems to deserve your attention. Let us begin with the letters that passed between Dr. SWIFT and Mr. POPE. The correspondence had commenced in a very early part of Mr. POPE's life,[2] and was carried on with scarce any interruption from the death of the Queen. If we may judge of Mr. POPE from his works, his chief aim was to be esteemed a man of virtue. His letters are written in that style. His last volumes are all of the moral kind.[3] He has avoided trifles, and consequently has escaped a rock which has proved very injurious to SWIFT's reputation. He has given his imagination full scope, and yet has preserved a perpetual guard upon his conduct. The constitution of his body and mind might early incline him to habits of caution and reserve. The treatment which he met afterwards from an innumerable tribe of adversaries,[4] confirmed those habits, and made him slower than the *Dean* in pronouncing his judgement upon persons and things. His prose writings are little less harmonious than his verse: and his voice in common conversation was so naturally musical, that I remember honest TOM SOUTHERNE[5] used always to call him *The little nightingale*. His manners were delicate, easy, and engaging: and he treated his friends with a politeness that charmed, and a generosity that was much to his honour. Every guest was made happy within his doors. Pleasure dwelt under his roof, and Elegance[b] presided at his table. Dr. SWIFT was of a different disposition: To his domestics he was passionate and churlish:[6] to his equals and superiors rather an entertaining than a desirable companion. He told a story in an admirable manner: his sentences were short, and perspicuous; his observations were piercing. He had seen the great world, and had profited much by his experience. He had not the least tincture of vanity in his conversation. He was perhaps, as he said himself, too proud to be vain.[7] When he was polite, it was in a manner entirely his own. In his friendships he was constant and undisguised. He was the same in his enmities. He generally spoke as he thought in all companies and at all times.[8] I remember to have heard, that

---

[b]Orrery's correction in Osborn pc 231: "elegance" to "Elegance."

he dined once at a Lord Mayor's feast in *Dublin*, and was attacked, and teized by an opulent, boisterous, half-intoxicated *'Squire*, who happened to sit next him: he bore the aukward railery for some time, and then on a sudden called out in a loud voice to the Mayor, "*My Lord, here is one of your bears at my shoulder, he has been worrying me this half hour, I desire you will order him to be taken off.*"[9]   In these last particulars he differed widely from his friend POPE, who could stifle resentment, and wait with patience till a more distant, and perhaps a more seasonable hour of revenge.   But notwithstanding the dissimilitude of minds, and manners, which was apparent between these two great men, yet the same sort of friendship seems to have subsisted between them, as between VIRGIL and HORACE.   The mutual affection of the two English poets appears throughout their works: and therefore in this place, I cannot avoid taking notice of a report very industriously spread, and not without some degree of success, "That the friendship between POPE and SWIFT was not so firm and perfect at the latter end as at the beginning of their lives."   On Dr. SWIFT's side, I am certain, it ever remained unalterable: nor did it appear less fervent on the side of Mr. POPE.[10]   Their letters are the best evidence to determine the doubt.   In one of SWIFT's latest letters to me, not long before he was lost to all human comforts, he says, "*When you see my dear friend* POPE, *tell him I will answer his letter soon; I love him above all the rest of mankind.*"[11]   In my long correspondence with Mr. POPE I scarce received the least billet from him, without the kindest mention of Dr. SWIFT: and the tenderest anxiety for his state of health.   Judge by the following paragraphs.   The first, dated July the 12th, 1737.

My Lord, The pleasure you gave me, in acquainting me of the Dean's better health, is one so truly great, as might content even your own humanity: and whatever my sincere opinion and respect of your Lordship prompts me to wish from your hands for myself, your love for him makes me as happy. Would to GOD my weight, added to your's, could turn his inclinations to this side, that I might live to enjoy him here thro' your means, and flatter myself 'twas partly thro' my own! But this, I fear, will never be the case; and I think it more probable, his attraction will draw me on the other side, which, I protest, nothing less than a probability of dying at sea, considering the weak frame of my breast, would have hindered me from, two years past. In short, whenever I think of him, 'tis with the vexation of all impotent passions that carry us out of ourselves only to spoil our quiet, and make us return to a resignation, which is the most melancholy of all virtues.[12]

And in another letter, dated April 2, 1738, he says,

I write by the same post that I received your very obliging and humane letter.[13]   *The consideration you shew towards me, in the just apprehension that any news of the Dean's condition might alarm me, is most kind and generous. The very last post I writ to him a long letter, little suspecting him in that dangerous circumstance. I was so far from fearing his health, that I was proposing schemes, and hoping possibilities for our meeting once more in this world. I am weary of it; and shall have one reason more, and one of the strongest that nature can give me (even when she is shaking my weak frame to pieces) to be willing to leave this world, when our dear friend is on the edge of the other. Yet I hope, I would fain hope, he may yet hover a while on the brink of it, to preserve to this wretched age a relique and example of the last.*[14]

One more quotation, and I have done.

TWITNAM, *November 7.*[15] *When you get to* Dublin *(whither I direct this, supposing you will see our dear friend as soon as possible) pray put the Dean in mind of me, and tell him I hope he received my last. Tell him how dearly I love, and how greatly I honour him: how greatly I reflect on every testimony of his friendship; how much I resolve to give the best I can of my esteem for him to posterity; and assure him the world has nothing in it I admire so much, nothing, the loss of which I should regret so much, as his genius and his virtues.*[16]

My excuse, for I stand in need of one, by having inserted these scraps of letters, is my real desire of convincing you, that the affection of SWIFT and POPE subsisted as entire and uninterrupted as their friends could wish, or their enemies regret. It must be owned, that we as seldom see a mutual attachment between poets, as between statesmen. "True friendship, as TULLY observes, proceeds from a reciprocal esteem, and a virtuous resemblance of manners."[17] When such is the basis, the variety in certain tenets and opinions is of no ill consequence to the union: and will scarce ever unloose the social ties of love, veneration, and esteem. Thus the friendship between ATTICUS and HORTENSIUS,[18] although they were of different sects, one a Stoic, and the other an Epicurean, subsisted like Mr. POPE's and Dr. SWIFT's, firm and constant to the last, when that of ANTONY, LEPIDUS, and AUGUSTUS,[19] continued no longer than while it was subservient to their views of interest. CATILINE says, *Idem velle, ac idem nolle, ea demum amicitia est.*[20] This often attends a vitious conspiracy; and perhaps an agreement so perfectly mutual is scarce to be met with in any other instance. Emulation generally breaks the chain of friendship between poets. They are running with the utmost eagerness to the same goal; no wonder, if, in the race, they endeavour to trip up each others heels.

As I have often reverted in my mind certain particulars relating to my two poetical friends, I have always thought, that the circumstance of their pursuing different roads in poetry, and living in different kingdoms, was probably one of the happiest incidents in their lives. Such a separation prevented all personal dissensions, and fixt them in a correspondence, that constantly tended to establish their endearments; when, perhaps, a residence near each other, might have had a very contrary effect. It is much easier to rectify any mistake, or to cool any animosity that may have arisen, in a letter, than to recal a passionate verbal answer, especially if uttered with all the actions, and vehemence of anger. The impression of such a scene remains long upon the mind of the person offended, and the old adage is transposed, *Vox audita manet, litera scripta perit*.[21] Few men can submit to contradiction. SWIFT was certainly not of the number, and therefore I am persuaded, that his distance from his English friends proved a strong incitement to their mutual affection. But, I must again repeat, that throughout the long series of letters which have been published, not the least altercations appear to have happened between SWIFT and POPE.

In all SWIFT's writings, you will find his own peculiar vein of humour. The same liberty of expression would have been improper and absurd in any other writer, but it produced the consequences which he desired. His seeming arrogance gained him more favour, than the humility and affected benevolence of others. His raillery and freedom of censure are conveyed in a manner more prevalent, and perhaps often more agreeable than flattery. He seldom praised, but where merit was conspicuous. A single stroke of his pen pleased more, and gave more honour, than a long flattering dedication from any other author. His style was masterly, correct, and strong: never diffusive, yet always clear; and, if we consider it in comparison with his predecessors, he has outdone them all, and is one, perhaps the chief, of those few select English writers, who have excelled in elegance and propriety of language.

Lord BACON is the first author, who has attempted any style that can be relishable to the present age, for I must own to you, that I think SWIFT, and his contemporaries,[c] have brought our language to the utmost degree of perfection, without the help of a LONGINUS,[22] a QUINTILIAN,[23] or even of a dictionary, or a grammar. Lord BACON has written with an infinite fund of knowledge: every science that he treats upon, is discussed by him with the greatest learning and dignity, and he shews himself at once a philosopher, an historian, a politician, and a divine: but his dialect (for, that demands our present attention) is quibbling and pedantic; and never more so than when he condescends to flatter his royal master, and the minions of that court.[24]

Consider the prosaical works of MILTON, you will find them more nervous than elegant; more distinguished by the strength of reason, than by the rules of rhetoric; his diction is harsh, his periods tedious; and when he becomes a prose-writer, the majesty, that attends his poetry, vanishes, and is entirely

---

[c]contemporaries, MV] cotemporaries, MIII

lost:[25] yet, with all his faults, and exclusive of his character as a poet, he must ever remain the only learned author of that tasteless age in which he flourished: and it is probable, that his great attention to the Latin language[26] might have rendered him less correct, than he otherwise would have been, in his native tongue.

HARRINGTON[27] has his admirers, he may possibly have his merits, but they *flow not* in his style. A later writer, of the same republican principles, has far excelled him; I mean ALGERNON SYDNEY,[28] whose discourses concerning government[29] are admirably written, and contain great historical knowledge, and a remarkable propriety of diction; so that his name, in my opinion, ought to be much higher established in the temple of literature, than I have hitherto found it placed.

Lord CLARENDON,[30] is an historian whose dignity of expression has justly given him the preference to any of our biographical authors. But his periods are the *periods of a mile*.[31] His parentheses embarass the sense of his narration,[32] and certain inaccuracies, appearing throughout his works, are delivered with a formality that renders them still more conspicuous.

Among our English writers, few men have gained a greater character for elegance and correctness, than SPRAT, Bishop of *Rochester*,[33] and few men have deserved it less. When I have read his works, I have always wondered from whence such a piece of good fortune might have arisen, and could only attribute it to Mr. COWLEY, who, in a very delicate copy of verses, has celebrated his friend Dr. SPRAT for eloquence, wit, and a certain *candid style*, which the poet compares to the river *Thames*, gliding with an even current, and displaying the most beautiful appearances of nature.[34] Poets and painters have their favourites, whom they transmit to posterity in what colours and attitudes they please: but I am mistaken, if, upon a review of SPRAT's works, his language will not sooner give you an idea of one of the insignificant tottering boats upon the *Thames*, than of the smooth noble current of the river itself.

Sir WILLIAM TEMPLE is an easy, careless, incorrect writer, elegantly negligent, politely learned, and engagingly familiar.[35]

Thus, my dear HAM, I have cursorily mentioned some of the brightest sons of fame among our English authors, only to point out to you the preference due to Dr. SWIFT: but he is not entitled alone to the olive garland: he has had his coadjutors in the victory. The triumvirate, to whom we owe an elegance and propriety unknown to our forefathers, are SWIFT, ADDISON, and BOLINGBROKE. At the sight of such names, no dispute can arise in preferring the English moderns to the English antients. The present century, and indeed all future generations may be congratulated upon the acquisition of three such men.

But to return more closely to SWIFT. He has perfectly studied the drama of human life, and particularly the tendency and irregularities of its different characters. He has chosen, (as I dare say I have mentioned in former letters) to recommend virtue, by representing vice in a disagreeable and ridiculous light. As his temper was naturally full of acrimony, a certain innate severity runs throughout all his letters. You will find him, in the advice, which he offers to his friends, and in the general account which he gives of his own conduct, too close an oeconomist. This parsimony proceeded from a desire of being independent: and since that was the cause, he will be forgiven, or, at least, excused by all honest men.

Mr. POPE had[d] different talents from his friend SWIFT: his imagination was fine and delicate: his fancy was ever on the wing. In his earlier time of life, his way of thinking was diffusive, and consequently his judgement was unconfined. As that judgement ripened with years, he shewed the full strength of it in his *Ethic Epistles*,[36] and his *Essay on Man*. There the poet has almost yielded to the philosopher; and his moral system has charmed more by the force of truth and reason, than even by the numbers with which he adorned it.

I cannot avoid thinking, that, in this particular branch of learning, Mr. POPE owed the exertion of his talents to Lord BOLINGBROKE,[37] who had studied the procedure, and limits of the human understanding, as exactly as SWIFT had considered the irregularities of the passions in different characters of the human species. Lord BOLINGBROKE had early made himself master of books and men: but, in his first career of life, being immersed at once in business and pleasure, he ran thorough a variety of scenes in a surprizing and eccentric manner. When his passions subsided by years and disappointments, and when he improved his rational faculties by more grave studies and reflection, he shone out in his retirement with a lustre peculiar to himself; though not seen by vulgar eyes. The gay statesman was changed into a philosopher equal to any of the sages of antiquity. The wisdom of SOCRATES, the dignity and ease of PLINY, and the wit of HORACE, appeared in all his writings and conversation.[38]

But my letter is growing to an intolerable length. It is time to finish it; and believe me, HAMILTON, were my letters to fill reams of paper, they would be written only with a view of repeating the dictates of my heart, which, in its last beating moments, will throb towards you, and those other dear objects, to whom I am

An affectionate Father,
ORRERY.

---

[d]had] has MIV

Notes

1. The seventh volume contains ninety letters, thus: sixty-three letters between Swift and Pope, sixteen letters between Swift and Gay, ten letters between Swift and Bolingbroke, and one letter from Orrery to Pope.

2. When the earliest recorded letter between Swift and Pope was written (8 December 1713), Pope was twenty-five years old.

3. Orrery is alluding to Pope's "Moral Essays," published between 1731 and 1735.

4. See Joseph V. Guerinot, *Pamphlet Attacks on Alexander Pope, 1711-1744: A Descriptive Bibliography* (London: Methuen, 1969).

5. Thomas Southerne (1660-1746), Irish dramatist, for whom see *Dictionary of National Biography*, s.v. "Southerne, Thomas."

6. See Delany's answer to these words (*Observations*, pp. 185-86).

7. In Swift to Pope, 10 January 1721: "I have conversed in some freedom with more Ministers of State of all Parties than usually happens to men of my level, and I confess, in their capacity as Ministers, I look upon them as a race of people whose acquaintance no man would court, otherwise than upon the score of Vanity or Ambition. The first quickly wears off (and is the Vice of low minds, for a man of spirit is too proud to be vain) and the other was not my case." (*Correspondence of Swift* 2:370). In the seventh volume of his set of Faulkner's edition of Swift's works, Orrery drew up a pointing hand against the words "too proud to be vain."

8. Cf. Swift's words on himself, in *Part of the Seventh Epistle of the First Book of Horace Imitated*, line 33:

> Went where he pleas'd, said what he thought

9. Orrery is the earliest and only source of this anecdote.

10. Maynard Mack observes: "Not that the strong bond [between Swift and Pope] was never tested by grievances. Pope was genuinely irritated when Swift in 1730 made him a compliment which was simultaneously a sneer at Walpole, with whom Pope was then still on amicable terms. Swift must have been equally annoyed by some of Pope's maneuverings to obtain the letters and by his failure to supplement the verses dedicating the *Dunciad* to him

with an epistle addressed to him formally, such as that to Arbuthnot." In Maynard Mack, *Alexander Pope: A Life* (London and New Haven: Yale University Press, 1985), p. 915.

11. In Swift to Orrery, [November 26, 1737] (*Correspondence of Swift* 5:78). However, Swift does not write "I love him above all the rest of mankind," at least not in the manuscript of the letter that has survived, and is preserved in the Pierpont Morgan Library. This is in Swift's hand, and headed by Orrery "Nov^{br} 26. 1737./N° 17." The full text was accurately printed by Williams, and the actual passage simply reads: "If you see my friend Pope say I will answer his last Lett^r soon."

12. Sherburn, *Pope* 5:18. Sherburn belatedly added it in volume 5 of his edition of Pope's correspondence. Orrery's *Remarks* is the only known source for the text.

13. This letter does not seem to have survived.

14. Sherburn, *Pope* 4:92.

15. Sherburn, probably correctly, suggests that the date of this letter is 7 November 1739. See *Pope* 5:18.

16. Ibid. As in the case of Pope's letter to Orrery of 12 July 1737, Orrery's *Remarks* is the only known source of the text, and Sherburn belatedly added it to volume 5 of his edition of Pope's correspondence.

17. See Cicero *De Amicitia* 14.48-50, 17.61, and 22.82.

18. Quintus Hortensius (114-50 B.C.), Roman orator. He supported the aristocratic party, and held a consulship in 69 B.C.

19. Members of the Second Triumvirate, formed in 42 B.C.

20. "For agreement in likes and dislikes–this, and this only, is what constitutes true friendship" (Sallust *The War with Catiline* 20.4-5).

21. The Latin words as written by Orrery read: "The voice which had been heard [i.e., verbal communication] lingers on, the written word perishes." This is an inversion of the proverb *verba volant, scripta manent*.

22. Cassius Longinus, born around A.D. 210, critic, scholar, and teacher. He was educated in Alexandria, taught rhetoric, and became the most famous scholar of his time. He is the author of the treatise *On the Sublime*, one of the most influential works of literary criticism.

23. Marcus Fabius Quintilianus, born around A.D. 35 at Calagurris, Spain. He was the first rhetorician to receive a salary from the state, having successfully taught for twenty years. He had Pliny the Younger among his pupils.

24. See Bacon's dedication of the *Novum Organum* to James I. It is supposed that Bacon wrote *The History of the Reign of King Henry VII* to flatter James I. See *The Works of Francis Bacon*, ed. James Spedding, Robert Leslie Ellis, and Douglas Denon Heath, 14 vols. (London: Longmans, 1857-74), 6:8-12.

25. See Thomas N. Corns, "Milton's Prose," in *The Cambridge Companion to Milton*, ed. Dennis Danielson (Cambridge: Cambridge University Press, 1989), pp. 183-96.

26. At Cambridge, Milton's first serious efforts at prose were oratorical exercises in Latin, and at age seventeen, he had written several elegies in Latin. Speaking of Milton's English prose by the time *Comus* had appeared, Don M. Wolfe says: "But with English prose he was still ill at ease; his sentences were often dominated by Latin rhythms. Even his personal letters he composed in Latin." In *Complete Prose Works of John Milton*, ed. Don M. Wolfe, 8 vols. (New Haven: Yale University Press, 1953-82), 1:10. Milton became, of course, Cromwell's latin secretary (1654-59).

27. James Harrington or Harington (1611-77), political theorist and author of the *Oceana* (1656).

28. Algernon Sidney, or Sydney (1622-83), republican, brother of Dorothy Spencer, countess of Sunderland and Waller's "Sacharissa."

29. Algernon Sidney's major work is entitled *Discourses concerning Government*, first printed in 1698.

30. Edward Hyde, first earl of Clarendon (1609-74).

31. This expression is in Pope, *The Fourth Satire of Dr. John Donne*, line 73. See Swift's notice of a long period in *History of the Rebellion* in his marginalia to Clarendon's work (*Prose Works of Swift* 5:304).

32. See Swift's notice of Clarendon's long parentheses in *History of the Rebellion* in his marginalia to Clarendon's work (ibid., pp. 301, 308). It is not known if Orrery knew of Swift's marginalia to Clarendon's book.

33. Thomas Sprat (1635-1713), bishop of Rochester and Dean of Westminster. Commenting on a sermon preached by Sprat ("that greate Wit"), John Evelyn observed: "Dr. Sprats talent was, a great memorie, never making use of notes, a readinesse of Expression, in a most pure and plaine style, for words & full of matter, easily delivered." In *The Diary of John Evelyn*, ed. E. S. de Beer, 6 vols. (Oxford: Clarendon Press, 1955), 4:188.

34. In Cowley's *To the Royal Society*, closing lines:

His candid Stile like a clean Stream does slide,
And his bright Fancy all the way
Does like the Sun-shine in it play;
It does like *Thames*, the best of Rivers, glide,
Where the God does not rudely overturn,
But gently pour the Crystal Urn,
And with judicious hand does the whole Current Guide.
T' has all the Beauties Nature can impart,
And all the comely Dress without the paint of Art.

See Abraham Cowley, *Poems*, ed. A. R. Waller (Cambridge: Cambridge University Press, 1905), pp. 448-53.

35. For observations on Temple's style, see *Five Miscellaneous Essays by Sir William Temple*, ed. Samuel Holt Monk, pp. vii-x, xviii-xli; *The Early Essays and Romances of Sir William Temple Bt.*, ed. G. C. Moore Smith (Oxford: Clarendon Press, 1930), pp. xvii-xxviii; and Homer Woodbridge, *Sir William Temple: The Man and His Work* (New York: Modern Language Association of America, 1940), pp. 119-53.

36. The "Moral Essays" or, as Pope always called them, "Epistles to Several Persons." They are: *To Cobham* (Epistle I), *To a Lady* (Epistle II), *To Bathurst* (Epistle III), and *To Burlington* (Epistle IV). The name "Ethic Epistles" comes from the title given in *The Works of Alexander Pope*, volume 2, published on 23 April 1735.

37. Brean Hammond demonstrated the extent of Bolingbroke's influence on the work, although Hammond also showed it has some limitations. See Brean Hammond, *Pope and Bolingbroke: A Study of Friendship and Influence*

(Columbia: University of Missouri Press, 1984), pp. 69-79, and especially pp. 84-91.

38. Writing to Orrery from Battersea on Saturday, 16 November 1751, Bolingbroke acknowledges Orrery's praise of him in the *Remarks* and thanks Orrery for it: "to me you have done much more than I can pretend to deserve." LS in Osborn Files 4.145, a sheet folded to make two leaves, [1^r], Beinecke Library, Yale. This LS is in the hand of David Mallet and is endorsed by Orrery: "Ld Bolingbroke. Saturday Nov:^{br} 16. received Sunday Nov.17.1751." Postmarks are visible. A transcript of this letter is in Houghton 16423.3.4*, manuscript page 3.

LETTER XX

I Have been reading this morning a long letter from Dr. SWIFT to Mr. POPE, dated at *Dublin, January* 10, 1721,[a] [1] and I have been confined to a greater share of attention, as it seems to furnish more materials of his life and principles, than any other of his epistolary writings. The letter breathes an air of sincerity and freedom, and is addressed to a particular friend,[2] at a time when the views of ambition were at an end. It may therefore be considered as a confession of one departing from this world, who is desirous only[b] to vindicate his own character, and is anxious that his ashes may rest in peace.

It was written immediately after the arbitrary conduct of a judge in *Ireland*,[c] who endeavoured to destroy the freedom of juries,[3] and consequently the very essence of that liberty and safety, which we have a right to possess by the constitution of our state. SWIFT very generously declares himself averse to all rigorous proceedings against persons suspected of problematical guilt.[4] *"By such strict enquiries,* says he, *a gate is left open to the whole tribe of informers, the most accursed, prostitute, and abandoned race that* GOD *ever permitted to plague mankind."*[5] Upon this subject I cannot avoid recollecting some particulars from a book, which has lately given me great delight and instruction, and which I recommend very warmly to your perusal. I mean *L'Esprit des Loix*.[6] The author of that book, MONSIEUR DE MONTESQUIEU observes, "that informers have been chiefly encouraged under the most tyrannical governments. In the reign of TIBERIUS triumphal ornaments were conferred upon them, and statues erected to their honour.[7] In the reign of NERO, upon the discovery and punishment of a pretended

---

[a]Original footnote in the *Remarks*: "Volume VII, Page 12." "Page 12" refers to the page number in volume 7 of Faulkner's edition of Swift's works.

[b]is desirous only MV] only is desirous MIII

[c]Orrery's correction in Osborn pc 231: *"Irelana,"* to *"Ireland,"*

254

conspiracy, triumphal dignities were allotted to TURPILIANUS, COCCEIUS NERVA, and TIGILLINUS."[8] In another part of his book, the BARON DE MONTESQUIEU takes notice, "that in *Turkey*, where little regard is shewn to the honour, lives, or estates of the subject, all causes are determined by the presiding Bashaw:[9] and in *Rome*, the judges had no more to do than to declare, that the person accused was guilty of a particular crime, and then the punishment was found in the laws."[10] From these and other examples of arbitrary government, this elegant author takes a particular pleasure in distinguishing, and admiring the civil constitution of *England*, where, he says, "the jury determine, whether the fact, brought under their cognizance, be proved or not; if it be proved, the judge pronounces the punishment inflicted by the law for such a particular fact: and for this, adds the BARON, he need only open his[d] eyes."[11] But if MONSIEUR DE MONTESQUIEU had read SWIFT's letter, or indeed had recollected many notorious facts of our history, he must have observed, that the judges have been often deaf to the repeated voice of the jury, and have not only shut their eyes, against our excellent laws, but have assumed "that terrible and menacing air, which COMMODUS[12] ordered to be given to his statues."[13]

The method of trials by juries is generally looked upon as one of the most excellent branches of our constitution. In theory it certainly appears in that light. According to the original establishment, the jurors are to be men of competent fortunes in the neighbourhood:[14] and are to be so avowedly indifferent between the parties concerned, that no reasonable exception can be made to them on either side. In treason the person accused has a right to challenge five and thirty, and in felony twenty, without shewing cause of challenge.[15] Nothing can be more equitable. No prisoner can desire a fairer field. But the misfortune is, that our juries are often composed of men of mean estates, and low understandings, and many[e] difficult points of law are brought before them, and submitted to their verdict, when perhaps they are not capable of determining, properly and judiciously, such nice matters of justice, although the judges of the court explain the nature of the case, and the law which arises upon it.[16] But, if they are not defective in knowledge, they are sometimes, I fear, from their station and indigence, liable to corruption. This indeed is an objection more to the privilege lodged with juries, than to the institution itself. The point, most liable to objection, is the power, which any one, or more of the twelve have to starve the rest into a compliance with

---

[d]his] their FI

[e]understandings, and many] understandings, many FI, FIa, FIb, FII, FIII, FV

their opinion; so that the verdict[f] may possibly be given by strength of constitution, not by conviction of conscience:[17] *"and wretches hang that jurymen may dine."*[18] All this by the by. Now let us return to SWIFT's letter of the tenth of *January.*

In it, is most evidently displayed his immutable attachment to *Ireland.* Such a kind of patriotism must have proceeded from a true love of liberty; for he hated individuals, and despised most of the men of property and power in that kingdom:[19] he owed them no obligations, and while by his writings he laboured to make their posterity happy, he forced from themselves an involuntary, but universal applause. His conduct was so uniform, and constant in the cause of *Ireland,* that he not only gained the praise, but the confidence of that whole nation, who are a people seldom, if ever, inclined to study and pursue their own interest, and who are always exceedingly apt to suspect any advice that is contrary, or in defiance to a ministerial direction.

SWIFT's principles of government seem to have been founded upon that excellent maxim, *Salus populi suprema est lex.*[20] He begins by clearing himself from Jacobitism.[21] He speaks of the revolution as a necessary but dangerous expedient, which has since been attended with unavoidable bad consequences.[22] He declares his mortal antipathy to standing armies in time of peace.[23] He adores the wisdom of that institution which rendered our parliaments annual.[24] He prefers the landed to the monied interest,[25] and expresses a noble abhorrence to the suspension of those laws, upon which the liberty of the subject depends.[26] When these articles of his political tenets are examined, they will leave no room for any one particular party to assume the honour of having had him in their alliance. He was neither Whig nor Tory, neither Jacobite nor Republican. He was DOCTOR SWIFT.

His judgment, in relation to the visible decay of literature and good sense, is perfectly just. He attributes this national calamity to the prevailing luxury of the times, which he instances in the encouragement of factions, and of several public diversions, all tending to the encrease of folly, ignorance, and vice.[27] His sentiments are delivered more with the air of a philosopher than of a divine: and the conclusion of the letter is so proper, and so excellent a defence of his own manner of acting and thinking, that, in regard to his memory, I must be at the trouble of transcribing it.

"*All*[g] *I can reasonably hope for,* says SWIFT, *by this letter, is to convince my friends and others, who are pleased to wish me well, that I have neither been so*

---

[f]Orrery's correction in Osborn pc 231: "he verdict" to "the verdict."

[g]Original footnote in the *Remarks*: "Vol. VII. Page 26." "Page 26" refers to the page number in volume 7 of Faulkner's edition of Swift's works.

ill a subject, nor so stupid an author, as I have been represented by the virulence of libellers, where malice hath taken the same train in both, by fathering dangerous principles in government upon me, which I never maintained, and insipid productions, which I am not capable of writing. For, however I may have been sowered by personal ill treatment, or by melancholy prospects for the public, I am too much a politician to expose my own safety by offensive words, and, if my genius and spirit be sunk by encreasing years, I have at least enough discretion left, not to mistake the measure of my own abilities, by attempting subjects where those talents are necessary, which perhaps I may have lost with my youth."[28]

I have chosen out this particular letter, as one of the most serious and best performances that he has given us in the epistolary way. But, if I am to declare my opinion of the whole collection in the seventh volume, I own to you, it has not answered my expectation. The index at the beginning will make you hope for great treasures, from the illustrious names that are there inserted: but, in your pursuit, you will scarce find any remarkable instructions of morality, or even the common reasonings and refinements that might naturally arise from so high a class of men, in the ordinary current of their thoughts. What is more surprising, you will seldom discover any keen strokes of satir, or any instantaneous sallies of vivacity. I have often heard SWIFT say, *"When I sit down to write a letter, I never lean upon my elbow, till I have finished it."*[29] By which expression he meant, that he never studied for particular phrases, or polished paragraphs: his letters therefore are the truer representations of his mind. They are written in the warmth of his affections, and when they are considered in the light of kindness and sincerity, they illustrate his character to a very high degree. Throughout his various correspondence you will discover very strong marks of an anxious, benevolent friend: and, to my great pleasure, I find the misanthrope often lost in the good-natured man. Read his letters to Mr. GAY, and you will be of my sentiment; read those to Dr. SHERIDAN, in the eighth volume,[h] and you will be farther confirmed in that opinion; we may compound therefore to lose satir and raillery, when we gain humanity and tenderness in their stead: yet, even in some of his highest scenes of benevolence, his expressions are delivered in such a manner, as to seem rather the effects of haughtiness than of good-nature: but you must never look upon him as a traveller in the common road. He must be viewed by[i] a *camera obscura* that turns all objects the

---

[h]Original footnote in the *Remarks*: "Beginning at p. 384." This refers to the page number in volume 8 of Faulkner's edition of Swift's works.

[i]by] through FI, FIa, FIb, FII, FIII, FV, MI

contrary way. When he appears most angry, he is most pleased;[j] when most humble, he is most assuming.[k] Such was the man, and in such variegated colours must he be painted.

The letters from Lord BOLINGBROKE, which are inserted in this collection, are written with an elegance and politeness that distinguish them from all the rest. We see they were not intended for the press; but how valuable are the most careless strokes of such a pen!

GAY's letters have nothing in them striking or recommendatory. His sentiments are those of an honest, indolent, good-natured man. He loved SWIFT to a degree of veneration: and the friendship was returned with great sincerity. SWIFT writes to him in the same strain as he would have written to a son; and seems to distinguish him as the correspondent to whom he has not the least grain of reserve. In the several accounts which he gives of his situation at *Dublin*, and the idle manner of his passing his time there, he writes sometimes in an ironical, and sometimes in a contrary style. But, in one of his letters, dated *August* 28, 1731,[l] [30] he tells GAY, "that the most arrant trifles of his former writings are serious philosophical lucubrations, in comparison to what he now busies himself about;" and his conclusive words are, "*As the world may one day see.*"[31] By this desire of *letting the world see* what other men of less wit, and more discretion, would carefully have concealed, he has placed himself open to the censure of his enemies, and beyond the reach of any defence from his friends. He has not only committed to the press a most despicable heap of writings, but has publicly recorded the lowest amusements of his private scenes of life, without having once suspected, that persons, whose stations, or abilities, have fixed them in a conspicuous attitude, are looked upon by the rest of mankind with a very critical, and a very envious eye. AUGUSTUS, as I remember, was a little ashamed to be discovered at a game of cobnuts;[32] and even DOMITIAN[33] was cunning enough to withdraw into his closet to catch flies.[34] Great minds, you will say, require to be often unbent. I allow it; but those relaxations might be

---

[j]Original footnote in the *Remarks*: "See his letters to GAY, and to the Duchess of *Queensborough*, in Vol. VII." The reference is to volume 7 of Faulkner's edition of Swift's works.

[k]Original footnote in the *Remarks*: "See his letter to Lord PALMERSTON, Vol. VIII, page 373." Orrery is alluding to volume 8 of Faulkner's edition of Swift's works, and the reference is to Swift's letter to Palmerston, 29 January 1726 (*Correspondence of Swift* 3:124-27).

[l]Original footnote in the *Remarks*: "Vol. VII. Letter LIII. page 185." Orrery is referring to volume 7 of Faulkner's edition of Swift's works.

chosen, so as to make idleness appear in a beautiful light: and SWIFT would have forfeited a less degree of fame by playing many years at push-pin[35] (the records of which he could not have printed), than by composing various kinds of *nonsense*, which, by his own option, have been honoured with a place in his works.

I should have been much pleased, in finding some of Dr. ARBUTHNOT's[36] letters among this collection. Although he was justly celebrated for wit and learning, there was an excellence in his character more amiable than all his other qualifications: I mean the excellence of his heart.[37] He has shewed himself equal to any of his contemporaries[m] in humour and vivacity: and he was superior to most men in acts of humanity and benevolence: his very sarcasms are the satirical strokes of good-nature; they are like slaps on[n] the face given in jest, the effects of which may raise blushes, but no blackness will appear after the blows. He laughs as jovially as an attendant upon BACCHUS, but continues as sober and considerate as a disciple of SOCRATES. He is seldom serious, except in his attacks upon vice; and then his spirit rises with a manly strength, and a noble indignation. His epitaph upon CHARTRES[o] [38] (allowing one small alteration, the word *permitted*, instead of *connived at*)[39] is a complete, and a masterly composition in its kind.[40] No man exceeded him in the moral duties of life: a merit still more to his honour, as the ambitious powers of wit and genius are seldom submissive enough to confine themselves within the limitations of morality. In his letter to Mr. POPE,[p] written, as it were, upon his death-bed,[41] he discovers such a noble fortitude of mind at the approach of his dissolution, as could be inspired only[q] by a clear conscience, and the calm retrospect of an uninterrupted series of

---

[m]contemporaries MV] cotemporaries MIII

[n]MV reads "of," but I have decided not to emend from MV, because, in his interleaved and annotated copy of the *Remarks* (MS Eng 218.14, p. 256, Houghton Library, Harvard), Orrery himself corrected the passage from "of" to "on." In the absence of evidence that, in MV, Orrery wished the passage to read "of," I decided to use the reading which could be proved Orrery wanted.

[o]Original footnote in the *Remarks*: "See POPE's Works, by WARBURTON, Vol. III. page 219."

[p]Original footnote in the *Remarks*: "See again POPE by WARBURTON, Vol. VIII. Letter XLVII."

[q]be inspired only] only be inspired FI, FIa, FIb, FII, FIII, FV, MI, MII

virtue.[42] The DEAN[r] laments the loss of him with a pathetic sincerity. *"The death of Mr. GAY and the DOCTOR[s] (says he to Mr. POPE) have been terrible wounds near my heart. Their living would have been a great comfort to me, although I should never have seen them; like a sum of money in a bank, from which I should receive at least annual interest, as I do from you, and have done from Lord BOLINGBROKE."*[43] I have chosen this last quotation, not more in honour of SWIFT's tenderness and affection to those whom he esteemed, than with a design of specifying to you as fine a groop of friends,[t] as have appeared since the Augustan age. As their letters were not intended for the public, perhaps I was unreasonable in looking for medals, and not being contented with the common current species. In our prejudices of favour or aversion we are apt to be deceived by names; nor can it be doubted, that such writers might have furnished us with familiar letters, very different from those, which have been collected in this seventh volume. They are filled indeed (especially in the correspondence between SWIFT and POPE) with the strongest expressions of mutual esteem; but those expressions are repeated too often. When friendship has subsisted so long, that time cannot encrease, nor words improve it, the commerce of affection between friends ought to be carried on in a style that neither sinks below politeness, nor rises into forced compliments. I cannot avoid observing the epistolary conciseness that was in fashion among the antients, especially their conclusive sentences, [*vale.*[44] Or again, *Si valeas, bene est, valeo*:][45] which I own seems preferable to our method of loading every letter with compliments, not only to wives and children, but to uncles, aunts, and cousins: and of consequence, every relation, that is not particularly named, is particularly affronted. It will appear too minute a criticism to affirm, that the English language is not well adapted for epistolary writeings: be that as it may, it is certainly inferior to the French, which engages, and perhaps improves us by a successive flow of phrases that are peculiar to that nation. MADAME DE SEVIGNÉ[46] has filled four volumes of letters,[47] all addressed to her daughter: they contain nothing, except different scenes of maternal fondness; yet, like a classic, the oftener they are read, the more they are relished. MONSIEUR DE PELISSON[48] has published three volumes of letters, which he calls *Lettres Historiques*,[49] and which are little else than materials for a gazette: they inform us at what time the *grand*

---

[r]Original footnote in the *Remarks*: "SWIFT's Vol. VII. Letter LXX." The reference is to volume 7 of Faulkner's edition of Swift's works.

[s]Original footnote in the *Remarks*: "ARBUTHNOT."

[t]Original footnote in the *Remarks*: "Lord BOLINGBROKE, SWIFT, POPE, ARBUTHNOT, GAY."

Monarque[50] arose; when he went to bed; at what hour he dined; and what he said while he was at supper: yet all these trifles are told in so agreeable a manner, and appear so natural and easy, that I can scarce think the skill of OVID greater, who, in his *Fasti*, has turned the Roman Calendar into elegant poetry,[51] and has versified a set of old Almanacs.[52] I need not mention VOITURE[53] or BALZAC;[54] and perhaps it was wrong to turn aside into the Roman and the French territories, when I ought to have confined myself to the British islands; but I love to wander about with you, and in writing, as in walking, to peep into every corner that may afford us matter of entertainment.

I am, my dear HAMILTON,
Your ever-affectionate Father,
ORRERY.

P.S. At the latter end of the seventh volume is a pamphlet written in the year 1714. It is entitled, *Free Thoughts upon the present State of Affairs.*[55] When you have read it, *digito compesce labellum.*[56]

Notes

1. *Correspondence of Swift* 2:365-74. Orrery could find this letter in Faulkner's volume 7, p. 12.

2. Herbert Davis mentioned that the letter was intended by Swift as a public statement, not written for Pope's private ear alone (*Prose Works of Swift* 9:xiii).

3. Orrery is referring to the prosecution of Edward Waters, the printer of Swift's *A Proposal for the Universal Use of Irish Manufactures*. On 30 May 1720, the tract was presented by the grand juries of the city and county of Dublin as "false, scandalous, and seditious." Also, Waters was ordered to be prosecuted, and finally tried at the King's Bench before Chief Justice Whitshed. Although Swift was known as the tract's author, the work's anonymity saved him from prosecution. The jury returned a verdict of innocent, but Whitshed refused to accept it, and ordered the jury to continue to consider the case. After eleven hours and nine verdicts of innocent rejected by Whitshed, the jury returned a special verdict, leaving the decision to Whitshed. Whitshed then deferred the consideration of the case to the next term. On 28 August 1721, the duke of Grafton, the new lord lieutenant, arrived in Ireland and dropped the case by an order of *noli prosequi*. See Ehrenpreis, *Swift* 3:123-30.

4.   Swift's expression is: "those diligent enquiries into remote and problematical guilt" (*Correspondence of Swift* 2:373).

5. Swift's actual words are: "so that those diligent enquiries into remote and problematical guilt, with a new power of enforcing them by chains and dungeons to every person whose face a Minister thinks fit to dislike, are not only opposite to that maxim, which declareth it better that ten guilty men should escape, than one innocent suffer, but likewise leave a gate wide open to the whole Tribe of Informers, the most accursed, and prostitute, and abandoned race, that God ever permitted to plague mankind" (ibid.).

6. On the verso of the title page in his copy of volume 7 of Faulkner's edition of Swift's works, Orrery wrote: "I have since found it and entered the place underneath. See L'esprit des Loix Chap. 3. Livre 6. P. 109. Vol. 1. In the Eng. Translation. the same Chap. Book. Vol. & Page." Apparently, Orrery had been looking for the passages in Montesquieu's *De L'Esprit des Loix* in order to include them in his remarks on Swift's "letter" to Pope. When he found them, he decided to record the exact reference as a memorandum. Orrery's copy of *De L'Esprit des Loix* was offered during Christie's Orrery Sale (November 1905) as part of lot 257. See *The Orrery Sale*, p. 36.

7. See Robin Seager, *Tiberius* (Berkeley and Los Angeles: University of California Press, 1972), pp. 151-62, 178-240. Regarding Tiberius's final years as emperor, Seager wrote (p. 239): "Delators could conjure accusations out of thin air and the outcome depended not on justice or reason but on the whim of one lonely and terrified old man." According to Dio, after the death of Germanicus (the Roman general who was Tiberius's nephew and adopted son) in A.D. 19, Tiberius "would accept accusers indiscriminately, whether it was a slave denouncing his master or a son his father" (Dio *Roman History* 57.19.1b).

8. Montesquieu, *The Spirit of the Laws*, 8.7 n. *j*. In A.D. 65 there was a plot to kill Nero, known as the "Pisonian Conspiracy." The conspiracy failed, and many innocent persons were punished. Some were falsely accused by conspirators who turned informers in the hope of helping themselves. The consular Petronius Turpilianus, the praetor-designate Cocceius Nerva, and the prefect Ofonius Tigellinus helped in the uncovering of the plot and received military honors. Cocceius Nerva and Tigellinus received triumphal decorations and their statues were erected on the palatine. See Tacitus *Annals* 15.48-74, and Miriam Griffin, *Nero: The End of a Dynasty* (New Haven and London: Yale University Press, 1985), pp. 154-55, 166-68.

9. Montesquieu, *The Spirit of the Laws* 6.2.

10. Ibid., 6.3.

11. Ibid.

12. Lucius Aelius Aurelius Commodus (A.D. 161-92), Roman emperor from 180 to 192.

13. Montesquieu, *The Spirit of the Laws*, 8.7. Cf. Dio *Roman History* 73.15.6: "Vast numbers of statues were erected representing him [Commodus] in the garb of Hercules." Dio also reports that Commodus cut off the head of the Colossus and substituted for it a likeness of his own head. Commodus then gave it a club and placed a bronze lion at its feet, "so as to cause it to look like Hercules" (ibid., 73.22.3).

14. In the fifteenth and early-sixteenth centuries, a series of statutes attempted better enforcement of property qualifications for prospective trial jurors. Examples are: Stat. 2 Hen.5, st.2, c.3 (1414): lands or tenements of an annual value of forty shillings. Stat. 23 Hen.8, c.13 (1531): in trials of murder and felony in cities and towns, jurors shall have forty pounds (suspending freehold requirement to prevent constant challenges on basis of previous statutes and substituting total worth requirement). Thomas Green wrote that the statutes "effectively reduced the pool of eligible jurors, concentrating it within a class many of whose members did not desire to serve and found means to avoid doing so." See Thomas Andrew Green, *Verdict According to Conscience: Perspectives on the English Criminal Trial Jury, 1200-1800* (Chicago and London: University of Chicago Press, 1985), pp. 114-15. Thomas Green also wrote that, in the eighteenth century (as in the past), jurors were "drawn mainly from the artisans, tradesmen, and small farmers who composed the lower-middling ranks of society" (ibid., p. 271). According to John Beattie, the jury qualification statute of 1730 (Stat.3 Geo.2, c.25) was intended to insure a steadier flow of jurors from the lower-middling groups in society. See John Beattie, *Crime and the Courts in England, 1660-1800* (Princeton: Princeton University Press, 1985), chap. 8.

15. In the early history of jury trial, recourse to challenges in criminal cases had been relatively rare. Defendants had been traditionally entitled to three dozen peremptory challenges at common law, and in the 1540s, this number was reduced to twenty. In 1555, Parliament increased the allowance in treason to the original thirty-six. For contemporary discussion of challenge in assize order books, see British Library MS Harleian 1603, f. 76^v, and British Library MS Lansdowne 596, f. 9^v. Regarding challenge rights, Thomas Green wrote: "The fact is that, by exercise of their challenge rights, defendants could have brought assizes to a standstill. Either they did not know this, or they

were discouraged from such lawful sabotage" (*Verdict According to Conscience*, p. 134). Thomas Green mentioned that Orrery's words, "without shewing cause of challenge," simply mean what we now call a "peremptory" challenge: the defendant may exclude the allotted number without assigning any cause. Exclusions for cause are also allowed, and are unlimited, but apply to very narrow classifications, such as close kin or known enemies. This last piece of information was provided in a personal letter from Thomas A. Green, John P. Dawson Professor of Law and History at the University of Michigan, to me, dated 31 May 1994.

16. Thomas Green wrote that in the eighteenth century, as in the past, "the judge's directions to the jury were brief, but pointed and leading, if not coercive" (ibid., p. 271).

17. In the eighteenth century, as now, the verdict had to be unanimous. Today, failure to achieve unanimity leads to a mistrial; in the eighteenth century (and before) practice varied, but the judge *could* keep the jury together until they reached unanimity, no matter how long it took. Thomas Green doubted that this happened very often, and wrote: "The idea was that the jurors could not eat or drink until they reached a verdict; so, if the judge refused to dismiss the jury (and empanel a new one, or dismiss the case altogether), the jurors who could hold out longest in effect 'starved' the others into agreement. So one holdout with an iron constitution (or a lot of body fat) could win over the eleven others, even just for the fun of it." However, Thomas Green observed: "Modern scholarship makes it clear that in the vast majority of cases, the system worked quickly and smoothly. The interesting question is: *why* did so many writers (like Orrery) tell those tales?" All this information was given in Thomas Green's personal letter to me, 31 May 1994.

18. Pope, *The Rape of the Lock* 3.22.

19. Cf. Swift's note introducing Charles Coote, Irish M.P. for Granard in 1723 and for County Cavan in 1737, to Pope: "Dear Pope, Though the little fellow that brings this be a justice of peace, and a member of our Irish House of Commons; yet he may not be altogether unworthy of your acquaintance" (*Correspondence of Swift* 4:167). This note was probably written in the summer of 1733 (ibid., n. 1).

20. "The welfare of the people is the supreme law." This is a principle established by the Roman laws of the Twelve Tables.

21. Swift's words in the letter are: "First, I always declared myself against a Popish Successor to the Crown, whatever Title he might have by the proximity of blood: Neither did I ever regard the right line, except upon two accounts; first, as it was established by law; and secondly, as it hath much weight in the opinions of the people. For necessity may abolish any Law, but cannot alter the sentiments of the vulgar; Right of inheritance being perhaps the most popular of all topics; and therefore in great Changes when that is broke, there will remain much heartburning and discontent among the meaner people; which (under a weak Prince and corrupt Administration) may have the worst consequences upon the peace of any state" (*Correspondence of Swift* 2:372).

22. Swift wrote in the letter: "As to what is called a Revolution-principle, my opinion was this; That, whenever those evils which usually attend and follow a violent change of government, were not in probability so pernicious as the grievances we suffer under a present power, then the public good will justify such a Revolution; and this I took to have been the Case in the Prince of Orange's expedition, although in the consequences it produced some very bad effects, which are likely to stick long enough by us" (ibid.).

23. Swift wrote in the letter: "I had likewise in those days a mortal antipathy against Standing Armies in times of Peace. Because I always took Standing Armies to be only servants hired by the master of the family, for keeping his own children in slavery: And because, I conceived, that a Prince who could not think himself secure without Mercenary Troops, must needs have a separate interest from that of his subjects. Although I am not ignorant of those artificial Necessities which a corrupted Ministry can create, for keeping up forces to support a Faction against the public Interest" (ibid.).

24. Swift wrote in the letter: "As to Parliaments, I adored the wisdom of that Gothic Institution, which made them Annual: and I was confident our Liberty could never be placed upon a firm foundation until that ancient law were restored among us. For, who sees not, that while such assemblies are permitted to have a longer duration, there grows up a commerce of corruption between the Ministry and the Deputies, wherein they both find their accounts to the manifest danger of Liberty, which traffic would neither answer the design nor expence, if Parliaments met once a year" (ibid.).

25. In the letter, Swift wrote: "I ever abominated that scheme of politics, (now about thirty years old) of setting up a monied Interest in opposition to the landed. For, I conceived, there could not be a truer maxim in our government than this, That the possessors of the soil are the best judges of what is for the advantage of the kingdom: If others had thought the same way, Funds of

Credit and South-sea Projects would neither have been felt nor heard of" (ibid., pp. 372-73).

26. In the letter, Swift wrote: "I could never discover the necessity of suspending any Law upon which the Liberty of the most innocent persons depended: neither do I think this practice hath made the taste of arbitrary power so agreeable as that we should desire to see it repeated" (ibid., p. 373). Swift is referring to the suspension of the Habeas Corpus Act in October 1722. For the probable date when Swift actually wrote this "letter" to Pope, see Ehrenpreis, *Swift* 3:136-37, 140, and 445 n.4.

27. Swift's words in the letter are: "It is true, I have been much concerned for several years past, upon account of the public as well as of myself, to see how ill a taste for wit and sense prevails in the world, which politics and South-sea, and Party, and Opera's and Masquerades have introduced" (*Correspondence of Swift* 2:368).

28. Ibid., p. 374. In his copy of volume 7 of Faulkner's edition of Swift's works, Orrery marked this passage.

29. Cf. Swift's words to Lord Bathurst in October 1730: "I swear your Lordship is the first person alive that ever made me lean upon my Elbow when I was writing to him, and by Consequence this will be the worst letter I ever writ" (ibid., 3:410).

30. Swift to Gay and the duchess of Queensberry, ibid., pp. 492-95.

31. Swift to Gay and the duchess of Queensberry, 28 August 1731: "And the meerest trifles I ever wrote are serious Philosophical lucubrations in comparison to what I now busy myself about; as (to speak in the Authors phrase) the world may one day see" (ibid., p. 495). In his copy of volume 7 of Faulkner's edition of Swift's works, Orrery underlined this passage.

32. Cf. Suetonius *Lives of the Caesars* 2.83.1: "To divert his mind he [Augustus] sometimes angled and sometimes played at dice, marbles and nuts with little boys."

33. Titus Flavius Domitianus Augustus (A.D. 51-96), Roman emperor from 81 to 96.

34. In Suetonius *Lives of the Caesars* 8.3.1: "At the beginning of his reign he [Domitian] used to spend hours in seclusion every day, doing nothing but catch flies and stab them with a keenly-sharpened stylus. Consequently when

someone once asked whether anyone was in there with Caesar, Vibius Crispus made the witty reply: 'Not even a fly.'"

35. "A child's game, in which each player pushes or fillips his pin with the object of crossing that of another player" (*OED*, 2d ed., 20 vols., 12:898). In the figurative sense, "push-pin" means "the type of trivial or insignificant occupation" (ibid.).

36. For the life, writings, and character of John Arbuthnot (1667-1735), see Lester Beattie, *John Arbuthnot: Mathematician and Satirist* (Cambridge: Harvard University Press, 1935). See also George Aitken, *The Life and Works of John Arbuthnot* (New York: Russell & Russell, 1968).

37. There is no evidence that Orrery had any personal knowledge of Arbuthnot.

38. Francis Charteris (1675-1732), colonel. While an ensign in the army, he was drummed out of his regiment for cheating at cards. On 20 May 1711, a committee of the House of Commons found Charteris guilty of having received money from tradesmen for enlisting them in his company in the first regiment of foot guards to save them from arrest. He acquired large sums of money by means of trickery in gambling, and he later lent out the money at an exorbitant interest. He ended up having £100,000 in stocks, and £7,000 a year in estates in different counties. In 1730, he was convicted for raping his maidservant and imprisoned at Newgate, but later was pardoned by George II. It is said that during Charteris's funeral, the populace "raised a great riot, almost tore the body out of the coffin, and cast dead dogs and offal into the grave along with it." See *Dictionary of National Biography*, s.v. "Charteris, Francis." See also Edwin Beresford Chancellor, *Lives of the Rakes*, 6 vols. (London: P. Allan, 1924-25), 3.

39. Orrery is suggesting that in Arbuthnot's *An Epitaph on Francis Charteris*, the words "Providence connived at his [Charteris'] execrable Designs" should be changed into "Providence permitted his execrable Designs."

40. Orrery and his readers would have found Arbuthnot's *An Epitaph on Francis Charteris* in the *Gentleman's Magazine*, April 1732 (2.718), and in the *London Magazine* for that same month (1.39).

41. Arbuthnot to Pope, 17 July 1734 (Sherburn, *Pope* 3:416-17). Arbuthnot died in his house in Cork Street, London, on 27 February 1735.

42. In the letter to Pope of 17 July 1734, Arbuthnot observes: "I have nothing to repay my Friends with at present, but prayers and good wishes. I have the satisfaction to find that I am as officiously serv'd by my Friends, as he that has thousands to leave in Legacies; besides the Assurance of their Sincerity. God Almighty has made my bodily distress as easy as a thing of that nature can be: I have found some relief, at least sometimes, from the Air of this Place. My Nights are bad, but many poor Creatures have worse" (ibid., p. 416).

43. Swift to Pope, 12 May 1735, *Correspondence of Swift* 4:334.

44. "Farewell."

45. "Hope you enjoy good health; I am fine."

46. Marie de Rabutin-Chantal, Marquise de Sévigné (1626-96), French writer.

47. *Lettres de Marie Rabutin-Chantal, marquise de Sévigné; à madame la comtesse de Grignan sa fille.* As the title indicates, Sévigné's letters were addressed to Françoise Marguerite de Sévigné, countess of Grignan, her daughter. Orrery owned a copy of Sévigné's *Lettres*, offered during Christie's Orrery Sale (November 1905) as part of lot 525. See *The Orrery Sale*, p. 73.

48. Paul Pellisson-Fontanier (1624-93), French writer.

49. *Lettres Historiques de Monsieur Pellisson,* 3 vols. (Paris: J. L. Nyon, 1729).

50. Louis XIV.

51. The *Fasti* is Ovid's most important work next to the *Metamorphoses*. It is a poetical treatise on the Roman calendar, which is depicted in chronological order. The *Fasti* begins on the first day of January and ends abruptly on the last day of June, amounting to six books corresponding to the six months.

52. Ovid himself stated that he had drawn his lore from "annals old" (*Fasti* 1.7 and 4.11).

53. Vincent de Voiture (1597-1648), French poet and letter writer.

54. Jean Louis Guez de Balzac (1594-1654), French author. He befriended many of the celebrities of his day, and the letters he wrote to them were greatly admired for their style. His *Letters* was published in 1624.

55. *Prose Works of Swift* 8:73-79.

56. "Put your finger at your lips" (Juvenal *Satires* 2.160). Orrery is telling Hamilton not to speak about the tract's contents with anybody. Orrery may have thought it would be unsafe for Hamilton to voice his opinion about the political matters referred to in Swift's tract.

LETTER XXI

My dear HAMILTON,

It is scarce possible to know in what manner to comment upon the last volume of the Dean's works.[1] A general confusion and disorder runs throughout the whole; and one of the first pieces is, what ought to have been the last, Dr. SWIFT's *Will:*[2] which, like all his other writings, is drawn up in his own peculiar manner. Even in so serious a composition he cannot help indulging himself, in leaving legacies that carry with them an air of raillery and jest. He disposes of his three hats (his best,[3] his second best,[4] and his third best beaver[5]) with an ironical solemnity, that renders the bequests ridiculous. He bequeaths "*to Mr.* JOHN GRATTAN[6] *a silver box, to keep in it the tobacco which the said* JOHN *usually chewed, called pigtail.*"[7] But his legacy to Mr. ROBERT GRATTAN[8] is still more extraordinary. "*Item, I bequeath to the Reverend Mr.* ROBERT GRATTAN, *Prebendary of St.* Audeon's, *my strong box, on condition of his giving the sole use of the said box to his brother, Dr.* JAMES GRATTAN,[9] *during the life of the said Doctor, who hath more occasion for it.*"[10] These are so many last impressions of his turn, and way of thinking: and, I dare say, the persons thus distinguished look upon these instances as affectionate memorials of his friendship, and as tokens of the jocose manner in which he had treated them during his life-time.

His monumental inscription, written by himself, and inserted at the beginning of his *Will,*[11] may confirm to you the observation which I made in a former letter, that he was not an elegant writer of Latin. An harsher epitaph has seldom been composed. It is scarce intelligible; and if intelligible, is a proof how difficult a task it is, even for the greatest genius, to draw his own character, or to represent himself and his actions in a proper manner to posterity.

I am now drawing towards the last scene of his life. The total deprivation of his senses came upon him by degrees. In the year 1736, I remember him seized with a violent fit of giddiness.[12] He was at that time writing a satirical poem, called *The Legion Club;*[13] but he found the effects of his giddiness so dreadful, that he left the poem unfinished;[14] and never afterwards attempted a composition of any length either in verse or prose. However, his conversation still remained the same; lively and severe; but his memory gradually grew worse and worse:[15] and as that decreased, and was impaired, he appeared every day more fretful and impatient. From the year *thirty-nine* to the latter end of the year *forty-one*, his friends found his passions so violent and ungovernable, his memory so decayed, and his reason so depraved, that they took the utmost precautions to keep all strangers from approaching him: for, till then, he had not appeared totally incapable of conversation: but, early in the year *forty-two*,[16] the small remains of his understanding became entirely confused, and the violence of his rage increased absolutely to a degree of madness. In this miserable state he seemed to be appointed as the first proper inhabitant for his own hospital: especially as from an outrageous lunatic, he sunk afterwards into a quiet, speechless idiot;[17] and dragged out the remainder of his life in that helpless situation. He died towards the latter end of *October* 1745.[18] The manner of his death was easy, without the least pang or convulsion. Even the rattling in his throat was scarce sufficient to give any alarm to his attendants, till within some very little time before he expired. A man in full possession[a] of his reason would have wished for such a kind of dissolution; but SWIFT was totally insensible of happiness or pain: he had not even the power or expression of a child, appearing, for some years before his death, reserved only as an example to mortify human pride, and to reverse that fine description of human nature, which is given us by *Shakespeare* in an inimitable manner: "*What a piece of work is man! how noble in reason! how infinite in faculty! in form and moving how express and admirable! in action, how like an angel! in apprehension, how like a god! the beauty of the world, the paragon of animals.*"[19] Thus poets paint; but how vain and perishable is the picture? The smallest thunderbolt from heaven blasts it in a moment, and every tinct is so effectually obliterated, that scarce the outlines of the figure remain.

SWIFT, as I have hinted in a former letter,[b] certainly foresaw his fate. His frequent attacks of giddiness, and his manifest defect of memory, gave room for such apprehensions.[20] I have often heard him lament the state of childhood, and idiotism, to which some of the greatest men of this nation were reduced before their death. He mentioned, as examples within his own time, the duke of MARLBOROUGH,[21] and Lord SOMERS:[22] and when he cited these melancholy instances, it was always with a heavy sigh, and with gestures that shewed great uneasiness, as if he felt an impulse of what was to happen to him before he died.

---

[a]in full possession MV] in possession MIII

[b]Original footnote in the *Remarks*: "See Letter VI."

Unless I am misinformed, he died worth about twelve thousand pounds, inclusive of the specific legacies mentioned in his will, and which may be computed at the sum of twelve hundred pounds;[23] so that the remainder, near eleven thousand pounds, is entirely applicable to the hospital for idiots and lunatics:[24] a charitable foundation, particularly beneficial in these kingdoms, where the epidemic distemper of lunacy is so prevalent, that it will constantly furnish the largest building with a sufficient number of inhabitants.[25]

Lunacy may in general be considered as arising from a depraved imagination; and must therefore be originally owing to a fault in the body, or the mind. We see instances every day, where, as in[c] fevers, all the powers of sense and reason are utterly overturned by a raging madness: this frenzy conquers, or is conquered, soon: but, from more slow and chronical causes, such obstructions may be formed, as gradually to produce various degrees of this disorder, and to remain invincible to the very last moments of life. Nothing more strongly disposes the mind to this depraved state, than too fixed an attention to any particular object. Mr. LOCKE, if my memory does not deceive me, defines madness as arising from some particular idea, or set of ideas, that makes[d] so strong an impression upon the mind, as to banish all others:[26] and the persons affected are chearful or melancholy, well-tempered or fierce, according as the objects and ideas of their minds are different. From hence it is evident, that we ought to consider the strength of the mind even in the pursuit of knowledge, and often to vary our ideas by exercise and amusements; constantly fixing a strict guard against any passion, that may be prevalent in too high a degree, or may acquire an habitual strength and dominion over us. Passions are the gales of life; and it is our part to take care, that they do not rise into a tempest.

Love, with all its charms, must be restrained within proper bounds, otherwise it will torture that breast which it was formed to delight. Love contains within itself a variety of other passions, and lays such a foundation of madness in the mind, that the frenzy, in this particular case, never fails to appear in its full force, and to display itself in all its strength of horror.

Religion, which alone can make[e] the mind happy, and is our surest and best defence against the passions, if considered in a wrong and melancholy view, has often perverted the seat of reason, and given more inhabitants to

---

[c]where, as in MV] where, in MIII

[d]makes MV] make MIII

[e]alone can make MV] can only make MIII

Bedlam[27] than any other cause. A religious lunatic is miserable, even to the deepest tortures of despair.

The miser, whom I must always rank among madmen, heaps up gold with an anxiety that affects his looks, his appetite, and his sleep. The wretch dreads poverty in the center of plenty; and starves, only because he dares not taste those fruits which appear most agreeable to his desires.

In some other species of madness, the persons affected are really more happy than in their senses; and it is almost a crime to banish the agreeable delusion. You remember the case of the citizen of *Argos*,[28] who, after a salutiferous dose of hellebore,[29] cried out,

> *Pol me occidistis, amici,*
> *Non servâstis (ait) cui sic extorta voluptas,*
> *Et demptus per vim menits gratissimus error.*[30]

Such again would be the case of the beau of *Bedlam*, who, amidst darkness and confinement, still retains his pride and self-admiration; dresses himself up in straw instead of embroidery; and, when suffered to go to the window, imagines that he captivates every female, who chances to pass thro' *Moor-fields*.[31] Is not such a man happier in his madness, than in his senses?

To specify the many different classes of madmen would be endless. They are innumerable: so that it is almost a rare felicity to enjoy *mens sana in corpore sano*.[32] Some men have owed their reputation and success in the world to a tincture of madness, while others, merely from a superior understanding, have been ranked among lunatics: of the latter sort HIPPOCRATES[33] (whom I wish you to look upon as a classic author, as well as a physician)[34] gives a remarkable instance in one of his letters.[35] He says, he was sent for by the people of *Abdera*[36] to cure DEMOCRITUS[37] of madness; but, to his surprize, he found him the wisest man of the age; and, by his laughing manner of talking and reasoning,[38] he almost convinced HIPPOCRATES, that all the rest of the world, except DEMOCRITUS, were mad.[39] It is not improbable, that madness has been coaeval with mankind. There have certainly been many instances of it among the Greeks and Romans: among the Jews, the enthusiastic fury of SAUL[40] is equally remarkable with the ecstatic rage of NEBUCHADNEZZAR:[41] nor have any parts of the world, I believe, entirely escaped this raging evil. It was frequently mistaken for inspiration, and the prophetic Sibyls[42] were obliged to put on the airs and looks of madness, to obtain an implicit belief to their prophecies. From these sacerdotal impositions, mad people reaped some remarkable advantages. They were often looked upon as messengers sent by heaven, to declare the will of the gods, and the prophetical decrees of fate: they were revered as persons sacred and divine; and, instead of scourges, they received tokens of adoration. In how great a degree must the subtilty of priests have prevailed, when they could make one of the greatest curses that attends human life, appear one of the greatest blessings?

Lunatics are so called from the influence which the moon has over bodies, when its attractive power is greatest;[43] by which means the pressure of the atmosphere being lessened, the humours of the body are more rarefied, and produce a greater plenitude in the vessels of the brain. This has been illustrated by our good and learned friend Dr. MEAD,[44] in his treatise *De imperio lunae et solis*;[45] and I have particularly observed, that in the last book,[f] which he published,[46] he takes notice in his chapter *de Insania*,[47] "that the blood of such persons, who have been most liable to this malady, was thick and sizy, and, upon dissection, their brain always appeared dry, and their vessels filled with black sluggish blood:"[48] from whence, perhaps, we may, in some measure, account for the principal source of SWIFT's lunacy: his countenance being dark, bilious, and gloomy, and his eyes sometimes fixed, and immoveable for a long time. HORACE, I remember, attributes the madness of ORESTES[49] to a physical cause, where he says,

vocando

Hanc furiam, hunc aliud, jussit quod splendida bilis.[50]

So that diseases, formed originally in the mind, often bring on this disorder, and by degrees affect the body; especially in such constitutions as have any tendency to this distemper. But what can be the reason, that it is so remarkably epidemical in these kingdoms? I am inclined to believe, that it must be owing to the grossness of our food, and to our immoderate use of spirituous[g] liquors: the one frequently causing the deepest melancholy, the other the most unlimited rage. Our climate is so variable and uncertain, and our atmosphere is so perpetually filled with clouds and sulphureous vapours, that these causes must necessarily have a great effect upon the natural impatience and inconstancy of the inhabitants. We are apt to revel in a free indulgence of our passions; and they are as apt to agitate and enervate the fibres of the brain, and to imprint by degrees many fatal impressions, that can never be eradicated from the mind. Even the greatest blessing we enjoy, the freedom of our laws, may, I am afraid, in some measure, contribute to those rash actions, that often end in dreadful murders of the worst kind, parricide, and suicide.[h] Men must be reckon'd in the highest class of lunatics, who are capable of offending the great Author of nature, by depriving themselves of

---

[f]Original footnote in the *Remarks*: "Entitled, *Monita & praecepta medica*."

[g]A misprint in MIII and MV.

[h]suicide.] suicism. FI, FIa, FIb, FII, FIII, FV, MI, MII

that life, which he only has a right of taking away, because he only had the power of giving it. No person in his senses can voluntarily prefer death to life. Our desires of existence are strong and prevalent. They are born with us; and our ideas of a future state are not sufficiently clear, to make us fond of hurrying into eternity; especially as eternity itself must ever remain incomprehensible to finite beings. Human nature has an abhorrence, and a terror, of its own dissolution. The philosopher submits to death; because he looks upon it as a necessary event: in the mean time, he uses every method of prudence, and every art of caution, to lengthen out life as far as he possibly can extend it, and to prevent the least accident that may bring on death one hour sooner than the laws of the human structure require. The military hero meets the king of terrors more from the dictates of reason, than the impulses of nature. His fame, his fortune, every object that can be dear to him, depend upon his resolution to die. He exposes himself to the danger of being destroyed; because an effort of securing his life must be attended with contempt and infamy. But, on the other hand, who would wantonly chuse death, unless he were agitated to such a choice by the fumes and vapours of a distempered brain?

The subjects, where arbitrary power is established, live in a continual state of dread and apprehension, and all their other passions are subdued by fear: so that fewer instances of suicide have appeared in despotic governments, than in kingdoms, where liberty is more prevalent, and where the passions are less restrained.

The diet, the air, and the political constitution of a country, give the peculiar and distinguishing character of the people: and as the characteristics change, the inhabitants undergo the same metamorphoses. How different are the modern Italians from the antient Romans! If BRUTUS were now living, he would probably acquiesce in the depending state of a cardinal, and the papal crown would be unanimously presented to CAESAR.

The melancholy case of Dr. SWIFT has, I find, seduced me into a long digression: when I am writing to you, my HAM, I give a full scope to my thoughts, and wander licentiously out of my sphere. I aim at placing all observations in your way, which I think can be of any use in your future road of life. But, why talk to you on the melancholy effects of madness? only, my dear son, to observe in general, that temperance, exercise, philosophy, and true religion, are the surest means to make men happy, and to preserve them from a contagious malady, to which the inhabitants of these kingdoms are unfortunately liable.

A state of idiotism is less deplorable, not less shocking, than that of madness. Idiots are afflicted with no turbulent passions: they are innocent and harmless, and often excite pity, but never occasion fear. The proverb tells[i] us, *They are the favourites of fortune*: but I suppose it alludes only to those *fools, who can number twenty rightly, and can tell the days of the week*; and alas! those are no idiots in the eye of the law. The absolute naturals owe their wretchedness to a wrong formation in their brain, or to accidents in their birth, or the dregs of fevers, and other violent distempers. The last was the case of the Dean of St. PATRICK's,[51] according to the account sent me by his two relations Mrs. WHITEWAY,[52] and Mr. SWIFT:[j] [53] neither of whom, I think, makes[k] the least mention of a deafness, that from time to time attacked the Dean, and rendered him extremely miserable.[54] You will find him complaining of this misfortune in several parts of his writings, especially in his letters (of the eighth volume) to Dr. SHERIDAN.[l] [55] Possibly some internal pressure upon his brain might first have affected the auditory nerves,[56] and then, by degrees, might have encreased, so as entirely to stop up that fountain of ideas, which had before spread itself in the most diffusive, and surprising manner.

Having just now hinted to you the advantages that have accrued to madmen, I ought not to omit the honours that have been paid to fools. In former ages the courts of France and England were not thought completely embellished without a favourite idiot, who bore the title of the King's Jester, and was[m] as remarkably distinguished by a cap and bells, as his royal master was distinguished by a diadem and robes. This animal, like JUNIUS BRUTUS, frequently assumed the face and behaviour of folly, to answer his own particular views and advantages.[57]   His bluntness and simplicity

---

[i]tells] tell FIa, FIb, FII, FIII, FV

[j]FI adds footnote: "See page 83, and page 85." FIa, FIb, FII, FIII, FV add footnote: "See page 138, and page 141." MI adds footnote: "See page 139, and page 142." MII, MIII add footnote: "See page 89, and page 91." MIV adds footnote: "See page 136, and page 140." MV adds footnote: "See page 94, and page 96." The page numbers refer to the location of Mrs. Whiteway's and Deane Swift's letters to Orrery in the different editions of the *Remarks*.

[k]makes] make FI, FIa, FIb, FII, FIII, FV, MI, MII

[l]FI, FIa, FIb, FII, FIII, FV add footnote: "See Vol. VIII. Page 419." MI, MII, MIII, MIV add footnote: "See Vol. VIII. page 419." MV adds footnote: "See Vol. VIII. p. 419." "Page 419" refers to the page number in volume 8 of Faulkner's edition of Swift's works.

[m]and was] and who was FI, FIa, FIb, FII, FIII, FV, MI, MII

recommended him in those places, where truths, if spoken by a man of sense, were disagreeable and dangerous. If he had not the honour, like BRUTUS, to save his country, at least he had the happiness to secure himself: and his expressions were often so full of humour and sarcasm, that, to this day, they are recorded as pieces of wit. Such was the famous reply of ARCHY[58] to *King* JAMES *the first*, when his Majesty, amidst all his wisdom, was sufficiently inspired with folly, to send his only son into *Spain.*[59] But, fools at present are no longer admired in courts, or, if they are, they appear there without their cap and bells.

And now, my dear HAMILTON, to quit reflexions, that tend in general rather to terrify, than to improve your understanding, let me observe, in honour of my friend SWIFT, that his establishment of an hospital for idiots and lunatics is remarkably generous: as the unhappy persons, who receive the benefit, must, for ever, remain insensible of their benefactor.

> *I am your affectionate Father,*
> ORRERY.

Notes

1. Faulkner's volume 8, published in 1746.

2. *Prose Works of Swift* 13:145-58. The text of the will was first printed in Faulkner's volume 8 in 1746. At first, Faulkner printed it only partially, but subsequently included the full text, featuring the private bequests. Faulkner did not include the codicil, which appeared in two separate editions of the will: an eight-page edition with no imprint, and a sixteen-page edition with the imprint "Printed in the Year, 1746."

3. "Item: I leave to the Reverend Mr. John Worral my best Beaver Hat" (ibid., p. 156). In his copy of Faulkner's edition of Swift's works, Orrery circled this passage.

4. Swift left Robert Grattan "the second best Beaver Hat I shall die possessed of" (ibid., p. 155). In the margin of this passage in his copy of Faulkner's edition of Swift's works, Orrery wrote: "2^d best beaver."

5. Swift left John Jackson, vicar of Santry, his "third best Beaver Hat" (ibid.). In the margin of this bequest by Swift, in his copy of Faulkner's edition of Swift's works, Orrery wrote "the 3^d best beaver."

6. Prebendary of St. Patrick's (d. 1754).

7. *Prose Works of Swift* 13:155. Orrery is, probably deliberately, omitting the fact that this silver box was the one in which the Freedom of the City of Cork had been presented to Swift in 1737. Orrery had been probably responsible for encouraging the aldermen of the city of Cork to send Swift the city's Freedom. The aldermen decided to send Swift a silver box instead of a gold one, and Swift was notified of this fact by Orrery himself (*Correspondence of Swift* 5:9). On 31 March 1737, Swift told Orrery: "When I get my Cork box I will certainly sell it, for not being Gold" (ibid., p. 22). Swift was annoyed by the fact that no citation accompanied the Freedom and that his name or the donor's was not engraved on the box (ibid., pp. 67-68). Swift's actual bequest reads: "Item: I bequeath to Mr. John Grattan, Prebendary of Clonmethan, my Silver Box in which the Freedom of the City of Cork was presented to me; in which I desire the said John to keep the Tobacco he usually cheweth, called Pigtail" (*Prose Works of Swift* 13:155).

8. Prebendary of St. Patrick's (ca. 1678-ca. 1741).

9. Physician (1673-1747).

10. *Prose Works of Swift* 13:155. Swift also left Robert Grattan his "Gold Bottle Screw," which the same Robert Grattan had given him.

11. Orrery is referring to Swift's epitaph (ibid., p. 149).

12. On 24 April 1736, Swift told Sheridan: "I have been very ill for these two Months past with Giddiness and Deafness, which lash'd me till about ten Days ago, when I gradually recover'd, but still am Weak and Indolent, not thinking any Thing worth my Thoughts" (*Correspondence of Swift* 4:478). In February 1737, Orrery told Pope that Swift's health was then excellent, but "his giddiness returns so often and so suddenly" that he dreaded the consequence (Sherburn, *Pope* 4:55).

13. *Poems of Swift* 3:827-39.

14. Ehrenpreis doubted the truthfulness of this statement (*Swift* 3:829 n. 2), and Williams had expressed the same doubt (*Poems of Swift* 3:828).

15. In February 1737, Orrery told Pope: "Your apprehensions of the Dean's memory are too well grounded: I think it decays apace: and I own I am shocked when I see any new instance of its failure" (Sherburn, *Pope* 4:54).

16. Swift kept cathedral accounts until April 1742, and Ehrenpreis observes: "It was in 1742 that his [Swift's] decline suddenly speeded up, perhaps with a push from some otherwise unnoticed brain lesions" (*Swift* 3:908). After the incident between Swift and Francis Wilson (ca. 1695-1743), prebendary of St. Patrick's, on 14 June 1742, a preliminary inquiry was ordered as a step toward overseeing Swift's person and his affairs. This inquiry was carried out in July 1742, and in the next month, a general investigation reached this conclusion: "[Swift] hath for these nine months past, been gradually failing in his memory and understanding, and [is] of such unsound mind and memory that he is incapable of transacting any business, or managing, conducting, or taking care either of his estate or person." It was determined that Swift had been irresponsible for his acts since 20 May 1742. For the rest of his life, Swift was protected by a committee of guardians (ibid., p. 915).

17. In this passage, one may note Orrery's responsibility for the common idea that Swift was mad in his last years. In reality, the suffering and pain undergone by Swift were normal symptoms of Ménière's disease when not properly treated. See Walter Russell Brain, "The Illness of Dean Swift," *Irish Journal of Medical Science* (August-September 1952): 337-46. See also A. S. McNalty, "The Ill-Health of Dean Swift," *Nursing Mirror* (4 March 1966): 6; and S. L. Shapiro, "The Medical History of Jonathan Swift," *Eye, Ear, Nose and Throat Monthly* 48 (1969): 486-89. Ehrenpreis mentioned that Swift was never insane by modern definitions (*Swift* 3:915), and he also wrote: "The tradition of his [Swift's] madness has been rejected for forty years by every qualified scholar who has bothered to look into the question. For a hundred years the medical experts have cleared him." In Irvin Ehrenpreis, *The Personality of Jonathan Swift* (London: Methuen, 1958), p. 125.

18. Swift died on Saturday, 19 October 1745.

19. *Hamlet*, 2.2.304-8.

20. In his letter to Sheridan from Twickenham on 12 August 1727, Swift commented on his recent attack of deafness and giddiness, and stated: "I believe this Giddiness is the Disorder that will at last get the better of me; but I had rather it should not be now; and I hope and believe it will not, for I am now better than Yesterday" (*Correspondence of Swift* 3:229).

21. On 28 May 1716, Marlborough had a paralytic stroke, and another one on 10 November. Although he recovered the use of his faculties, his health continued to decline. He had another stroke of paralysis in June 1722, and died on the sixteenth of the month.

22. Somers died of paralysis on 26 April 1716. Since October 1714, he had retired to Brookmans, his villa in Hertfordshire, due to his failing health.

23. An advertisement in the *Dublin Journal* for Tuesday, 1 January 1751, stated that Swift's whole "worldly Substance" mentioned in the will amounted to "about the Value of 10,000*l*."

24. In his will, Swift determined that land should be purchased "near Dr. Stevens's Hospital, or if it cannot be there had, somewhere in or near the City of Dublin" to build a large hospital for the reception of "Idiots and Lunaticks." See *Prose Works of Swift* 13:150.

25. Cf. Swift's own words in *Verses on the Death of Dr. Swift*:
        He gave the little Wealth he had,
        To build a House for Fools and Mad:
        And shew'd by one satyric Touch,
        No Nation wanted it so much:

                                  (lines 479-82)

26. Locke, *An Essay concerning Human Understanding*, 2.11.13.

27. The name applied to the Hospital of St. Mary of Bethlehem in London. It is mentioned as "an hospital" in 1330, and as a hospital for lunatics in 1402. In 1547, it was incorporated as a royal foundation for the reception of mentally deranged persons.

28. Greek city in Arcadia, near Mycenae.

29. "A name given by the ancients to certain plants having poisonous and medicinal properties, and esp. reputed as specifics for mental disease" (*OED*, 2d ed., 20 vols., 7:120).

30. "Egad! you have killed me, my friends, not saved me; for thus you have robbed me of a pleasure and taken away perforce the dearest illusion of my heart" (Horace *Epistles* 2.2.138-40). Horace reports how a man in Argos used to sit in the empty local theater, imagining that he was "listening to wonderful tragic actors" and applauding. The man's kinsmen gave him "strong hellebore" which drove out "the malady and its bile." But, on recovering his senses, the man said the words quoted above. See ibid., 2.2.128-40.

31. The first public park in London. Moorfields was within sight of Bedlam in Orrery's time, as it stretched from Bishopsgate to Cripplegate, and from London Wall to Finsbury Square.

32. "A sound mind in a sound body."

33. Hippocrates (ca. 460-ca. 377 B.C.), Greek physician considered to be the father of medicine.

34. Orrery owned a copy of Hippocrates, *Oeuvres*, 2 vols. (Paris: 1697). It was offered during Christie's Orrery Sale (November 1905) as part of lot 350. See *The Orrery Sale*, p. 50.

35. *De Insania Democriti Philosophi Facetum Epistolium Hipocratis Medici* (Augsburg: Hans Froschauer, 1503). This piece is a forgery.

36. Leading Greek city in Thrace, on the northern coast of the Aegean sea.

37. Democritus (ca. 494-ca. 404 B.C.), Greek natural philosopher born in Abdera.

38. Democritus was known for his optimistic temperament, which earned him the title of "laughing philosopher."

39. In *De Insania Democriti*.

40. See 1 Sam. 16:14-23, 18:10-11.

41. See Dan. 2:1-13, chap. 3, and especially chap. 4, which describes Nebuchadnezzar's loss of reason as the punishment from God for his pride.

42. Priestesses whose responsibility was to make known the oracles of Apollo.

43. The English word *lunatic* comes from the Latin *lunatic-us*, from the Latin word for *moon* (*luna*) and a particular case of the Latin suffix *-ic-us* meaning "of, of the kind of." See *OED*, 2d ed., 20 vols., 1:748 and 9:105.

44. Richard Mead (1673-1754), physician to George II, and Orrery's close friend and correspondent. See *Orrery Papers* 2:45-48, 50-51, 55, and 61-62. There are also three unpublished manuscript letters from Mead to Orrery (all in Mead's hand) in the William Andrews Clark Memorial Library, UCLA, and all are endorsed by Orrery.

45. *De imperio Solis ac Lunæ in Corpora Humana et Morbis inde oriundis*, first published in 1704 (London: Raphael Smith). In it, Mead wrote about the influence of the sun and moon upon human bodies, trying to show that heavenly bodies affect the human frame as they affect one another.

46. *Monita et Praecepta Medica (Medical precepts and cautions)* was Mead's last book, first published in 1751 (London: J. Brindley). It is a summary of Mead's practical experiences.

47. *De insania* (Of madness) is chap. 3 in Mead's *Monita et Praecepta Medica*, in Latin, pp. 67-91. It is also chap. 3 in the English translation by Thomas Stack, M.D., F.R.S., published by Brindley in London in 1751, pp. 74-102.

48. In Richard Mead, *Medical Precepts and Cautions*, translated from the Latin "under the Author's Inspection" by Thomas Stack, M.D., F.R.S. (London: J. Brindley, 1751), p. 96.

49. For the complete story involving Orestes, see Aeschylus, *Agamemnon*, *The Libation-Bearers*, and *Eumenides*.

50. "He [Orestes] merely threw ill words at both [his sister Electra and his friend Pylades], calling her a Fury, and him by some other name which his gleaming choler [black bile] prompted" (Horace *Satires* 2.3.140-41). In antiquity, the black bile was supposed to be a cause of madness and to have a glittering appearance. See ibid., 2.3.132-41.

51. Delany reported that Swift's head was opened after his death, and that his brain "was found remarkably loaded with water." Delany also wrote that one Mr. Stevens, "an ingenious clergyman of the diocese of Dublin," made this request to Swift's physicians while Swift was ill: "that his [Swift's] head might be trepanned, and the water taken away, which he was sure would remove his distemper, and recover his reason: but his physicians paid no regard to this judgment." See *Observations*, pp. 149-50.

52. Mrs. Whiteway to Orrery, 22 November 1742, in Letter XI. In the present edition, pp. 177-78.

53. Deane Swift to Orrery, 4 April 1744, in Letter XI. In the present edition, pp. 178-80.

54. On 7 October 1734, Swift told Mrs. Pendarves that, once a year, he was seized with attacks of giddiness and deafness that usually lasted a month. Swift also wrote that he had been "acquainted" with those two disorders from his youth and that his attacks of deafness made him "incapable of conversing." Swift further told Mrs. Pendarves that "of late years," his deafness and giddiness began "to come together" (*Correspondence of Swift* 5:257).

55. Cf. Swift's letter to Sheridan from Twickenham, 12 August 1727: "ten Days ago, my old Deafness seized me, and hath continued ever since with great Encrease; so that I am now Deafer than ever you knew me, and yet a little less, I think, than I was Yesterday" (ibid., 3:228-29). Swift further told Sheridan: "one thing I know, that these deaf Fits use to continue five or six Weeks, and I am resolved if it continues, or my Giddiness, some Days longer, I will leave this Place, and remove to Greenwich, or somewhere near London" (ibid., p. 229). Swift mentioned he was embarrassed because, due to his deafness, he could not see the acquaintance who went to visit him at Twickenham.

56. Cf. Ehrenpreis's words on Ménière's disease, Swift's illness: "The disease attacks the inner ear, causing either deafness or vertigo or both. Its origin is unknown; it can start at various ages, with no warning, and comes in recurrent spells which may grow more unpleasant and more extended as the victim ages. Today one finds sufferers reporting it as coming on suddenly. They may have violent fits of vomiting; often they feel too dizzy to stand up; and they sometimes lose their hearing. As a palliative, they take daily the pills prescribed against seasickness; and then they usually have no trouble. There isn't any cure. Cutting the aural nerve ends the symptoms but of course makes the patient permanently deaf." In Ehrenpreis, *The Personality of Jonathan Swift*, pp. 119-20.

57. For Lucius Junius Brutus's feigned stupidity, see Dio *Roman History* 2.11.10-13.

58. Archibald Armstrong, jester in the courts of James I and Charles I. See *Dictionary of National Biography*, s.v. "Armstrong, Archibald."

59. "When the prince [Charles] was gone [to Spain], it is said that Archy, the king's fool, clapped his cap upon the king's head. The king asking him the reason, he answered, because he had sent the prince into Spain. But, says his majesty, What if he should come back safe? Why, then, says Archy, I will take my cap off from your head, and put it on the King of Spain's." In Daniel Neal, *History of the Puritans, or Protestant Nonconformists*, 2 vols. (New York: Harper & Brothers, 1844), 1:274.

LETTER XXII

THE *Directions*[a] *to Servants,*[1] which is the tract immediately following SWIFT's *Will,*[2] is imperfect and unfinished. The editor tells us, that a preface and a dedication[b] were to have been added to it.[3] I think it was not published till after the Dean's death;[4] but I remember the manuscript handed about, and much applauded, in his life-time.[5] To say the most that can be offered in its favour, the tract is written in so facetious a kind of low humour, that it must please many readers:[6] nor is it without some degree of merit, by pointing out with an amazing exactness (and what in a less trivial case must have been called judgment) the faults, blunders, tricks, lyes, and various knaveries of domestic servants. How much time must have been employed in putting together such a work![7] What an intenseness of thought must have been bestowed upon the lowest, and most slavish scenes of life! It is one of those compositions, that the utmost strength of wit can scarce sustain from sinking. A man of SWIFT's exalted genius ought constantly to have soared into higher regions. He ought to have looked upon persons of inferior abilities, as children, whom nature had appointed him to instruct, encourage, and improve. Superior talents seem to have been intended by Providence as public benefits; and the person, who possesses such blessings, is certainly answerable to Heaven for those endowments, which he enjoys above the rest of mankind. Let him jest with dignity, and let him be ironical upon useful subjects; leaving poor slaves to *heat their porridge,* or *drink their small beer,*[8] in such vessels as they shall find proper.[c] The Dean, it seems, had not this way of thinking: and having long indulged his passions at last, perhaps mistook them for his duty.

---

[a]*Directions*] *Direction* FI

[b]and a dedication] and dedication FI

[c]Original footnote in the *Remarks*: "See Vol. VIII. page 8." "page 8" refers to the page number in volume 8 of Faulkner's edition of Swift's works.

The mistake, my dear HAMILTON, is neither extraordinary nor surprising. In points of religion it has carried men into great extravagancies; in those of morality, into no less; but in politics, into the greatest of all. Our inclinations are so apt to hurry us into inconsiderate actions, that we are afterwards inclined to flatter ourselves they are right, only because they have proceeded from our own thoughts and directions. Thus SWIFT, when he had once established the rule of *Vive la bagatelle*,[9] was resolved to pursue it at all hazards. I wish his thoughts had taken another turn. The lower classes of mankind pass on unnoticed; the great only are censured. They ought to be particularly attentive to every step they take. The Dean of St. PATRICK's should have known himself, as *Rex idem hominum, Phoebique sacerdos*,[10] and should have remembered, that kings and priests are extremely liable to be censured. Poor SWIFT! why did he sink below himself, before he was deprived of reason? Forgive him that error, my HAMILTON, and draw a veil of oblivion over certain excrescencies of wit and humour; you will then admire him, as an honour to the public, and a scourge to all the knaves and fools of his time.

Three pamphlets, relating to *Ireland*, successively follow the *Directions*[d] to *Servants*. The first is entitled, *Reasons humbly offered to the Parliament of Ireland, for repealing the Sacramental Test in favour of the Catholics*:[11] The second, *Some Reasons against the Bill for settling the Tythe of Hemp, Flax, &c. by a Modus*:[12] The third, *Some farther Reasons against the Bill for settling the Tythe of Hemp, Flax, &c.*[13] The subject-matter of these pamphlets may perhaps be little worth your consideration; but their style will always command your attention. They are very much misplaced, and, in any more methodical edition of the Dean's works, ought to appear with such other pieces, as have been composed by him against the dissenters. The first tract is written under the assumed character of a Roman catholic, by which means the author attacks his adversaries with a great advantage. He freely acknowledges the several atrocious crimes of the papists; but at the same time palliates them so skilfully, that, from that very acknowledgment, he enables himself to aim the heavier blows at the presbyterians. A paragraph extracted from the pamphlet will exemplify my meaning. *"We allow*, says he, *the* CATHOLICS *to be* BRETHREN *of the Dissenters; some people, indeed (which we cannot allow), would have them to be our children; because we both dissent from the church established, and both agree in abolishing this persecuting sacramental test; by which* NEGATIVE DISCOURAGEMENT *we are both rendered incapable of civil and military employments. However, we cannot but wonder at the bold familiarity of these schismatics, in calling the members of the national church their* BRETHREN *and* FELLOW-PROTESTANTS. *It is true, that all these sects*

---

[d]*Directions*] *Direction* FI, FIa, FIb, FII, FIII, FV, MI

(except the CATHOLICS) *are* BRETHREN *to each other in faction, ignorance, iniquity, perverseness, pride, and (if we except the* QUAKERS) *in rebellion. But, how the churchmen can be styled their* FELLOW-PROTESTANTS, *we cannot comprehend. Because, when the whole* BABEL *of sectaries joined against the Church, the King, and the Nobility, for twenty years, in a* MATCH AT FOOT-BALL; *where the proverb expresly tells us, that* ALL ARE FELLOWS; *while the three kingdoms were tossed to and fro, the churches and cities, and royal palaces, shattered to pieces by their* BALLS, *their* BUFFETS, *and their* KICKS; *the victors would allow no more* FELLOWS AT FOOT-BALL: *but murdered, sequestered, plundered, deprived, banished to the plantations, or enslaved, all their opposers who had* LOST THE GAME."[14] The greatest art, and the keenest strokes of irony, display themselves throughout the whole composition: and the conclusion of it is drawn up with a mixture of serious and ironical arguments that seem to defy all kinds of refutation.[15]

The two next pamphlets *for settling the Tythe of Hemp, &c. by a Modus,* are entirely adapted to the clergy of *Ireland*; but I cannot avoid observing in those papers a greater fund of calmness, nor[e] a less degree of spirit, than in many other of SWIFT's political writings.

The remainder of this volume is like a garden over-run with docks and thistles, among which some rose-trees accidentally make their appearance. The scythe of time, or the weeding-knife of a judicious editor, will cut down the docks and thistles, but the beauty of the roses will particularly appear in some sermons[16] that are curious; and curious for such reasons, as would make other works despicable. They were written in a careless, hurrying manner, and were the offspring of necessity, not of choice: so that you will see the original force of his genius more in these compositions, that were the legitimate sons of duty, than in other pieces, that were the natural sons of love. They were held in such low esteem in his own thoughts, that some years before he died, he gave away the whole collection to Dr. SHERIDAN,[17] with the utmost indifference: *"Here,* says he, *are a bundle of my old sermons; you may have them if you please: they may be of use to you; they have never been of any to me."* The parcel given to Dr. SHERIDAN consisted, as I have heard, of about five-and-thirty sermons.[18] Three or four only are published;[19] and those I have read over with attention. The first is upon *Mutual Subjection,*[20] and that duty which is owing from one man to another. A clearer style, or a discourse more properly adapted to a public audience, can scarce be framed. Every paragraph is simple, nervous, and intelligible. The threads of each argument are closely connected, and logically pursued: but in places where the Dean has the least opportunity to introduce political maxims, or to dart an arrow at the conduct of princes, he never fails to indulge himself

---

[e]nor] not FI, FIa, FIb, FII, FIII, FV, MI, MII

in his usual manner of thinking, as you will judge from the following quotations: "*A wise man*, says Dr. SWIFT, *who doth not assist with his counsels; a great man with his protection; a rich man with his bounty and charity; and a poor man with his labour, are perfect nuisances in a commonwealth. Neither is any condition of life more honourable in the sight of* GOD *than another; otherwise he would be a respecter of persons, which he assureth us he is not: for he hath proposed the same salvation to all men, and hath only placed them in different ways or stations to work it out. Princes are born with no more advantages of strength or wisdom than other men; and, by an unhappy education, are usually more defective in both than thousands of their subjects.*"[f] [21] Again, in the same strain, "*The best prince is, in the opinion of wise men, only the greatest servant of the nation; not only a servant to the public in general, but in some sort to every man in it.*"[g] [22] But the most extraordinary passage is a covert stroke at the highest order of his brethren the clergy. It runs thus: "*The miseries of life are not properly owing to the unequal distribution of things; but* GOD *Almighty, the great King of heaven, is treated like the kings of the earth; who (although perhaps intending well themselves) have often most abominable ministers and stewards, and those generally the vilest, to whom they entrust the most talents.*"[h] [23] Dark as it is, this paragraph requires no explanation. The author's natural turn of mind breaks forth upon all occasions, and the politician frequently outweighs the divine. If the dictates of such a spirit were capable of forcing their way from the pulpit, what a glorious, what a consistent figure, must SWIFT have made in the rostrum[24] at *Rome*, or in one of the porticos at *Athens*!

The next moral essay, for I can scarce call it a sermon, is upon the *Testimony of Conscience*:[25] in which the author inserts some very striking observations upon such false notions of honour as are too prevalent in the world. I am so far from thinking it a trouble, that I think it a pleasure, to transcribe the particular passage: "*The false principle, which some men set up in the place of conscience to be their director in life, is what those who pretend to it, call* HONOUR. *This word is often made the sanction of an oath; it is*

---

[f]Original footnote in the *Remarks*: "Page 211." This refers to the page number in volume 8 of Faulkner's edition of Swift's works.

[g]Original footnote in the *Remarks*: "Page 215." This refers to the page number in volume 8 of Faulkner's edition of Swift's works.

[h]Original footnote in the *Remarks*: "Page 218." This refers to the page number in volume 8 of Faulkner's edition of Swift's works.

reckoned a great commendation[i] to be a man of strict honour; and it is commonly understood, that a man of honour can never be guilty of a base action. This is usually the style of military men; of persons with titles; and of others who pretend to birth and quality. It is true indeed, that in antient times it was universally understood, that honour was the reward of virtue; but if such honour as is now-a-days going will not permit a man to do a base action, it must be allowed, there are very few such things as base actions in nature. No man of honour, as that word is usually understood, did ever pretend, that his honour obliged him to be chaste or temperate; to pay his creditors; to be useful to his country; to do good to mankind; to endeavour to be wise or learned; to regard his word, his promise, or his oath; or if he hath any of these virtues, they were never learned in the catechism of honour; which contains but two precepts, the punctual payment of debts contracted at play, and the right understanding the several degrees of an affront, in order to revenge it by the death of an adversary."[j] [26]

The third discourse upon *The Trinity*[27] is indeed a sermon, and one of the best in its kind. Dr. SWIFT seems not to have made such a plan his voluntary choice, nor to have built, *suo ex motu*,[28] upon such a basis;[k] but he has completed the superstructure in a most masterly manner: the materials answer the dignity of the edifice; and the artificer may assume great honour, upon the completion of so noble, so simple, and so useful[l] a pile. The mysterious parts of our religion are apt to have dreadful effects upon weak minds. The general comments upon the sacred writings, and the several sermons upon the most abstruse points of scripture, are too often composed in the gloomy style. Damnation, eternal damnation, is placed with all its horror before our eyes; and we are so terrified at the prospect, that fear makes us imagine, we can comprehend mysteries, which, on this side of the grave, must be for ever denied to our limited understandings. SWIFT has taken the safest, and the properest method of expounding these *arcana*.[29] He advances every position that can be established upon so incomprehensible a subject. He sustains the belief, avows the doctrine, and adapts the matter of faith, as well as possible,

---

[i]*commendation] condemnation* FI

[j]Original footnote in the *Remarks*: "Page 228." This refers to the page number in volume 8 of Faulkner's edition of Swift's works.

[k]Original footnote in the *Remarks*: "In the beginning of his sermon, he lets us know, that he preached it on Trinity Sunday, a day on which all the clergy think themselves confined to this theme."

[l]A misprint in MV.

to the human capacity. His manner of reasoning is masterly, and his arguments are nervous; particularly where he says, "*It is highly probable, that if* GOD *should please to reveal unto us this great mystery of the Trinity, or some other mysteries in our holy religion, we should not be able to understand them, unless he would at the same time think fit to bestow on us some new powers or faculties of the mind, which we want at present, and are reserved to*[m] *the day of resurrection to life eternal.*"[n] [30] But, my HAM, you must be weary of quotations. I will make no more: and, in excuse of those already made, I can only offer, that in comments upon original authors quotations are often the best, and perhaps the only explanations that can fully answer the end proposed. I mean, that the original spirit is so volatile, as not to admit of the least transfusion. In ordinary compositions, the essence may be extracted, and the subtilest parts distilled: but SWIFT's sermons appeared a chymical preparation of so extraordinary, and penetrating a nature, that I was resolved to send you as much of the aethereal spirit, as might be safely conveyed by the post.

I shall take no notice of a fourth sermon, as it is evidently not composed by the Dean:[o] [31] but I find, that I have omitted to mention two poems of great wit and humour. They are previous to the sermons. The first[p] [32] was artfully published by Dr. SWIFT in a manner so different from those rules of poetry to which he confined himself,[33] that he hoped the public might mistake it for a spurious, or incorrect[q] copy stolen by memory from his original poem.[34] He took great pleasure in this supposition: and I believe it answered his expectation. One of his strictest rules in poetry was to avoid *triplets*.[35] What can have given rise to so nice a peculiarity, is difficult to determine. It might be owing only to a singular turn of thinking; but the reason which he publicly assigned seemed not so much against the

---

[m]*to*] *till* FI, FIa, FIb, FII, FIII, FV, MI

[n]Original footnote in the *Remarks*: "Page 246." This refers to the page number in volume 8 of Faulkner's edition of Swift's works.

[o]Original footnote in the *Remarks*: "*The difficulty of knowing one's self*, p. 255." "p. 255" refers to the page number in volume 8 of Faulkner's edition of Swift's works.

[p]Original footnote in the *Remarks*: "*The Life and Genuine Character of the Reverend Dr.* SWIFT."

[q]incorrect] uncorrect FI, FIa, FIb, FII, FIII, FV, MI;
Orrery's correction in Osborn pc 231: "uncorrect" to "incorrect."

practice itself, as against the poets who indulged themselves in that manner of writing. "A custom (according to the Dean's opinion) introduced by laziness, continued by ignorance, and established by false taste." With deference to so great a critic, it is a custom, that has frequently been pursued with remarkable success. Mr. DRYDEN abounds in triplets;[36] and in some of his most elegant poems, the third concluding verse forms the finest climax in the whole piece.[37] Mr. WALLER, the father of all flowing poetry,[38] has generally reserved the nicest point of wit to his triplicate line: and upon an impartial enquiry, it is almost to be questioned, whether, in many instances, this despicable triplet may not add a greater beauty to a poetical composition, than any other circumstance. To be confined, on any terms, by the links of rhyme, is of great disadvantage to our English poetry. The finest poem that we can boast, and which we equalize, and perhaps would willingly prefer, to the Iliad, is void of those fetters.[39] But, when it is our destiny to wear chains, surely we may be allowed to make them as light and easy as we can.

The second poem,[r] entitled, *Verses on the Death of Dr.* SWIFT, *occasioned by reading a Maxim in* ROCHEFOUCAULT,[40] is a most pointed piece of sarcasm. Not any of the Dean's poems have more wit; nor are any of them more severe. In it he has summoned together his whole powers of satir and poetry. It is a parting blow; the legacy of anger and disappointment; but as the two last lines[s] [41] are grammatically incorrect, and as they were not inserted in the first edition published at *London*,[42] I cannot tell how they have crept into a poem, that is otherwise as exactly polished as any of SWIFT's nicest compositions.[43]

The remaining pieces in this volume are neither worthy of SWIFT's pen, nor of your perusal.[44] Many of them are spurious, and many more are trifling, and in every respect improper for the public view: so that what was once ludicrously said upon a different occasion, may be applied not only to the last volume, but indeed to some of the former, as "they put us in mind of the famous machine in WINSTANLEY's[45] water-works,[46] where, out of the same vessel, the spectators were presented with tea, coffee, chocolate, champaigne, and sour small beer."

> *I am, my dear Son,*
> *Your truly affectionate Father,*
> ORRERY.

---

[r]Original footnote in the *Remarks*: "Page 151." "Page 151" refers to the page number in volume 8 of Faulkner's edition of Swift's works.

[s]Original footnote in the *Remarks*:
> *That kingdom he hath left his debtor,*
> *I wish it soon may have a better.*

Notes

1. *Prose Works of Swift* 13:1-65.

2. Swift's will precedes *Directions to Servants*, which begins on p. 1 of Faulkner's edition of 1746, which Orrery owned.

3. See "The Preface by the Dublin Bookseller," preceding *Directions to Servants*, in the 1746 volume 8 of Faulkner's edition of Swift's works.

4. It was first published by Faulkner in November 1745.

5. See Herbert Davis, "The Manuscripts of Swift's 'Directions to Servants'" in *Studies in Art and Literature for Belle da Costa Greene*, ed. Dorothy Miner (Princeton: Princeton University Press, 1954), pp. 433-44.

6. In his letter to Herbert Davis, dated 12 March 1948, commenting on Mildred Prince's dissertation on Orrery, James Clifford wrote: "It is interesting that Orrery was evidently not much interested in some works which we today think the very best of Swift's works. His judgment on *Directions to Servants* would seem to be a black mark against his critical ability" (copy attached at the end of Prince, "The Literary Life and Position of Orrery," p. 3).

7. On 12 June 1732, Swift told Pope he had begun writing *Directions to Servants* "about twenty-eight years ago" and that it would "require a long time to perfect" *(Correspondence of Swift* 4:31-32).

8. In Swift, *Directions to Servants*, "Rules that Concern All Servants in General": "When you have broken all your earthen Drinking Vessels below Stairs (which is usually done in a Week) the Copper Pot will do as well; it can boil Milk, heat Porridge, hold Small-Beer, or in Case of Necessity serve for a Jordan; therefore apply it indifferently to all these Uses; but never wash or scour it, for Fear of taking off the Tin" *(Prose Works of Swift* 13:10).

9. On 10 July 1732, Swift mentioned *Vive la Bagatelle* as being "my rule" *(Correspondence of Swift* 4:40).

10. "At once king of the people and priest of Phoebus [i.e., a poet]" (Virgil *Aeneid* 3.80).

11. *Prose Works of Swift* 12:281-95.

12. Ibid., 13:93-105.

13. Ibid., pp. 105-8. It was included with *Some Reasons*, and it was apparently drawn up by other persons with Swift's aid (Ehrenpreis, *Swift* 3:768).

14. *Prose Works of Swift* 12:288-89.

15. See ibid., pp. 294-95.

16. In Faulkner's volume 8, the following sermons by Swift are included: *On Mutual Subjection, On the Testimony of Conscience,* and *On the Trinity.* Faulkner also included *The Difficulty of Knowing One's Self,* of doubtful authorship.

17. The first sermons by Swift to be published, *On Mutual Subjection, On the Testimony of Conscience,* and *On the Trinity,* appeared in 1744 in London, published by Robert Dodsley. Dodsley received the manuscripts from Thomas, Sheridan's son (*Prose Works of Swift* 9:375), who went to London on 19 March 1744, and offered to Dodsley the Swift manuscripts he had bought from his father's executors. Sheridan had the manuscripts (which included Swift's sermons) ready for Dodsley on either 15 August or 22 August 1744, and on 23 August, Sheridan acknowledged Dodsley's payment (£50) for the Swift manuscripts. See *The Correspondence of Robert Dodsley, 1733-1764,* ed. James E. Tierney (Cambridge: Cambridge University Press, 1988 [1989]), pp. 80-81, and 524.

18. In John Nichols's 1779 *Supplement* (p. 415), there is an account by Faulkner to the earl of Chesterfield about eleven sermons by Swift. Faulkner mentioned that Sheridan rescued thirty of Swift's sermons from the fire, of which three were published later.

19. *On Mutual Subjection, On the Testimony of Conscience, On the Trinity,* and *The Difficulty of Knowing One's Self,* not certain to be Swift's.

20. *Prose Works of Swift* 9:139-49.

21. Ibid., pp. 142-43.

22. Ibid., p. 144.

23. Ibid., p. 147.

24. "The platform or stand for public speakers in the Forum of ancient Rome, adorned with the beaks of ships taken from the Antiates in 338 B.C.; also, that part of the Forum in which this was situated" (*OED*, 2d ed., 20 vols., 14:119).

25. *Prose Works of Swift* 9:150-58.

26. Ibid., p. 153.

27. Ibid., pp. 159-68.

28. "By his own initiative."

29. "Mysteries."

30. *Prose Works of Swift* 9:165.

31. *The Difficulty of Knowing One's Self* (ibid., pp. 347-62). Robert Dodsley, who first printed the sermon in 1745, added an "Advertisement" to it: "The Manuscript Title Page of the following Sermon being lost, and no Memorandums writ upon it, as there were upon the others, when and where it was preached, made the editor doubtful whether he should Print it as the Dean's, or not. But it's being found amongst the same Papers; and the Hand, tho' writ somewhat better, bearing a great Similitude to the Dean's, made him willing to lay it before the Publick, that they might judge whether the Stile and Manner also do not render it still more probable to be his." Faulkner reprinted Dodsley's advertisement in his volume 8 in 1746. Louis Landa wrote: "Since Orrery was using Volume 8 of Faulkner's edition, we may reasonably assume that his doubts were raised by the 'Advertisement' and then possibly confirmed by a reading of the sermon. If he had other and more definite grounds for rejecting Swift's authorship, unfortunately he did not disclose them" (ibid., p. 104).

32. *The Life and Genuine Character of Doctor Swift* (*Poems of Swift* 2:541-50).

33. In his judgment that Swift wanted people to think the poem was spurious, Orrery is probably drawing on a note printed along with the poem in volume 8 of Faulkner's edition of Swift's works, 1746 (the edition which Orrery used). The note stated that the poem "was published with Breaks, Dashes and Triplets, (which the Author never made Use of) to disguise his Manner of Writing; by which, however, they were deceived."

34. Cf. the words by "L. M." in the address to Pope in the *Life and Character*: "He [Swift] shewed some Parts of it to *several Friends*, and when it was compleated, he seldom refused the sight of it to any *Visitor*: So that, probably, it has been perused by *fifty Persons*; which, being against his *usual Practice*, many People judged, likely enough, that he had a desire to make the People of *Dublin* impatient to see it *published*, and at the same time resolved to *disappoint* them; For, he never would be prevailed on to grant a *Copy*, and yet several Lines were retained by *Memory*, and are often repeated in *Dublin*." (*Poems of Swift* 2:544).

35. These words by Orrery are quoted in the *OED* under the entry "triplets" (*OED*, 2d ed., 20 vols., 18:553). Swift had once defined *triplets* as "a vicious way of rhyming, wherewith Dryden abounded, and was imitated by all the bad versifiers in Charles the Second's reign" (*Correspondence of Swift* 4:321).

36. Cf. Dryden's words in the "Dedication of the Aeneis": "When I mention'd the Pindarick Line, I should have added, that I take another License in my Verses: For I frequently made use of Triplet Rhymes, and for the same Reason: Because they bound the Sense. And therefore I generally join these two Licenses together: And make the last Verse of the Triplet a Pindarique: For besides, the Majesty which it gives, it confines the sense within the barriers of three Lines, which wou'd languish if it were lengthen'd into four." In *The Works of John Dryden*, ed. Edward Niles and H. T. Swedenberg, Jr., 19 vols. (Berkeley: University of California Press, 1956-), 5:331.

37. Mark Van Doren pointed to a function of Dryden's triplets: to supply a colloquial, firsthand note. Van Doren wrote: "The third line of a triplet in Dryden frequently represents a lowering of the voice to the level of parenthesis or innuendo." In Mark Van Doren, *The Poetry of John Dryden* (New York: Haskell House, 1969), p. 101.

38. Cf. John Aubrey's words on Waller: "One of the first refiners of our English language and poetry. When he was a brisk young spark, and first studied Poetry; me thought, said he, I never saw a good copy of English verses; they want smoothness; then I began to essay." In *Aubrey's Brief Lives*, ed. Oliver Lawson Dick (London: Secker and Warburg, 1950), p. 308.

39. *Paradise Lost*.

40. *Poems of Swift* 2:551-72. In his copy of volume 8 of Faulkner's edition of Swift's works, Orrery completed the blanks in these lines: 180, 181, 184, 186, 187, 189, 272, 345, 386, 387, 438, 440, 445, 446, 447, 448, 452, and 453. In two instances, Orrery gives readings that are different from those adopted by

Williams. Orrery has completed line 447 as "The Parliament go joyful back," whereas Williams prints "The Nation stript go joyful back." And, Orrery has completed line 452 as "A Jayl or Turnpike to repair," while Williams prints "A Jayl or Barrack to repair." Unfortunately, Orrery did not mention the source from which he had drawn his readings.

41. Lines 483-84 of the poem.

42. By Charles Bathurst, 1739. Orrery owned a copy of Bathurst's first edition (Rothschild 1497, in *The Rothschild Library*, 2 vols., 1:399).

43. Quoted by James Woolley in *Swift's Later Poems: Studies in Circumstances and Text* (New York and London: Garland, 1988), pp. 55-56. Woolley commented on Orrery's words: "He [Orrery] seems to think that the London edition was copy-text for the Dublin edition; it is strange that he mentions only the one difference between the texts" (ibid., p. 56). Mentioning the fact that Orrery owned both a copy of Bathurst's first edition (Rothschild 1497, in *The Rothschild Library*, 2 vols., 1:399) and Faulkner's 1746 volume 8 including the poem (used in preparation for the *Remarks*), Woolley explained Orrery's words on the last two lines of *Verses*: "Volume 8 (1746) collects 'Verses' for the first time; prefixed to the poem is a 'Publisher's Advertisement' much like that in the first (1739) edition, which in haste and forgetfulness might have misled Orrery as to the relationship of the London and Dublin texts: 'The following Poem was printed and published in *London*, with great Success. Many Lines and Notes were omitted in the *English* Edition; which we have inserted, to make this Work as compleat as possible' (VIII, 152). Orrery, though using Faulkner's text, assumes–as the note implies–that the text comes from the London edition, and that that edition was authoritative" (*Swift's Later Poems*, p. 56 n.1). James Woolley also wrote about the last two lines of *Verses*: "As the *OED* states, 'better,' when used to mean 'one's superior,' occurs with a possessive pronoun. It makes no sense to hope for 'a better,' in the sense of a superior, for Ireland–whose better was clearly England (if personification be indulged to this extent). Surely Swift intended some such meaning as 'I hope Ireland, heavily indebted to Swift, may soon find another, even better "creditor."' But the need to rhyme overrode the need to make sense" (ibid., p. 3 n. 1).

44. Besides the works discussed by Orrery, Faulkner's volume 8 (1746) features: *The Beasts Confession to the Priest; Advertisement for the Honour of Ireland; Part of the 9th Ode of the 4th Book of Horace, addressed to Dr. King, Archbishop of Dublin; A modest Defence of a Poem called the Lady's Dressing Room; A French Epigram, and the Translation; Verses made for Women, who cry Apples, &c.; Verses to Love; Lines upon a Glass of Sir Arthur Acheson's,*

with the Answer; The Elephant, a Poem; Advice to the Freemen of Dublin, in the Choice of a Member to represent them in Parliament; The Duty of Servants at Inns; Bons Mots de Stella; Thoughts on various Subjects; The Story of the Injured Lady; An Answer to the Injured Lady; Considerations offered to the Right Hon. the Lord Mayor, &c. of the City of Dublin, in the Choice of a Recorder; An Epitaph on Frederick Duke of Schomberg; A Ballad on the Game of Traffick; Verses said to be written on the Union; Will Wood's Petition to the People of Ireland; An Epigram on Wood's Brass Money; An Epigram on the D--e of C-s; An Epigram on Scolding; Catullus de Lesbia; Motto on Mr. Jason Hassard's Sign; The Author's Manner of Living; Verses cut on a Pane of Glass; On another Window; To a Lady who desired the Author to write Verses on her in the Heroic Style; A Love Poem from a Physician to his Mistress; On a Printer's being sent to Newgate; Upon stealing a Crown while the Dean was asleep; The Dean's Answer; On the little House by the Church of Castleknock, near Dublin; Riddles; To Doctor Sheridan; A Rebus written by a Lady; The Answer; A Letter from Dr. Swift to Archbishop King; The Archbishop to Dr. Swift; The Lord Primate and Archbishop of Dublin to Dr. Swift, about the Tax on First-Fruits; The Archbishop of Dublin to Dr. Swift; The same to the same; Dr. Swift to the Archbishop of Dublin; Swift to Lord Carteret; Swift's Answer to Lord Palmerston's Letter; Swift to Mrs. Moore; From Mr. Pope to Dr. Sheridan; Pope to Dr. Sheridan; Letters from Dr. Swift to Dr. Sheridan; Prayers for a sick Person, during her Illness; Letters to Dr. Sheridan; To Dr. Helsham; To Dr. Sheridan; A Love Song; An Epigram; A whimsical Consultation of four Physicians upon a Lord that was dying; A humorous Letter to Dr. Sheridan on a Literalia Scheme of Writing; A Letter to your Mistress; Another Letter in the Literalia Style; Verses on Dr. Swift's Deafness; and *A Cantata set to Musick.*

45.   Henry Winstanley (1644-1703), engineer and engraver, for whom see *Dictionary of National Biography*, s.v. "Winstanley, Henry."

46. Cf. these remarks by John Evelyn on 20 June 1696: "I saw those ingenious Water works invented by Mr. Winstanley wherein were some things very surprising & extraordinary." In *The Diary of John Evelyn*, ed. E. S. de Beer, 6 vols. (Oxford: Clarendon Press, 1955), 5:247. Winstanley's water works were fanciful devices kept by him in a place of entertainment that he owned, known as the "Water Theatre" in Piccadilly near Hyde Park Corner.

LETTER XXIII

WE have now gone through FAULKNER's edition of SWIFT's works; but there are still remaining three of his pieces, *The Tale of a Tub*,[1] *the Battle of the Books in St. James's Library*,[2] and *The Fragment*,[3] which, although not absolutely owned by the Dean, *aut Erasmi sunt aut Diaboli*.[4]

The first of these, *The Tale of a Tub*, has made much noise in the world. It was one of SWIFT's earliest performances,[5] and has never been excelled in wit and spirit by his own, or any other pen.[6] The censures that are[a] passed upon it, are various. The most material of which were such as reflected upon Dr. SWIFT, in the character of a clergyman, and a Christian. It has been one of the misfortunes attending Christianity, that many of her sons, from a mistaken filial piety, have indulged themselves in too restrained, and too melancholy a way of thinking. Can we wonder then, if a book, composed with all the force of wit and humour in derision of sacerdotal tyranny, in ridicule of grave hypocrisy, and in contempt of phlegmatic stiffness, should be wilfully misconstrued by some persons, and ignorantly mistaken by others, as a sarcasm and reflexion upon the whole Christian Church? SWIFT's ungovernable spirit of irony has sometimes carried him into very unwarrantable flights of wit. I have remarked such passages with a most unwilling eye. But, let my affections of friendship have been ever so great, my paternal affection is still greater: and I will pursue candour, even with an aching heart, when the pursuit of it may tend to your advantage or instruction. In the style of truth therefore, I must still look upon *The Tale of a Tub*, as no *intended* insult against Christianity;[7] but as a satir against the wild errors of the church of *Rome*, the slow and incomplete reformation of the Lutherans, and the absurd and affected zeal of the Presbyterians. In the character of PETER, we see the pope seated on his pontifical throne, and adorned with his triple crown. In the picture of MARTIN, we view LUTHER, and the first

---

[a]are] have FI, FIa, FIb, FII, FIII, FV, MI, MIV

reformers: and in the representation of JACK, we see[b] JOHN CALVIN and his disciples.[8] The author's arrows are chiefly directed against PETER and JACK. To MARTIN he shews all the indulgence that the laws of allegory will permit.

The actions of PETER are the actions of a man intoxicated with pride, power, rage, tyranny, and self-conceit. These passions are placed in the most ridiculous light: and the effects of them produce to us the tenets and doctrines of papal *Rome*, such as purgatory, penance, images, indulgences, auricular confession, transubstantiation,[9] and those dreadful monsters, the pontifical bulls,[10] which, according to this ludicrous author, derived their origin[c] from the famous bulls of COLCHIS,[11] described by OVID.[12]

> *Terribiles vultus, praefixaque cornua ferro;*
> *Pulvereumque solum pede pulsavere bisulco;*
> *Fumificisque locum mugitibus implevere.*[d] [13]

"But LORD PETER'S BULLS, says *The Tale of a Tub*, *were extremely vitiated by time in the metal of their feet, which, from* BRASS, *was now degenerated into common* LEAD.[14] *However, the terrible roaring peculiar to their lineage was preserved, as likewise that faculty of* BREATHING *out fire at their nostrils.*"[15] These passages, and many others, no doubt, must be construed as antichristian by the church of *Rome*. When the chief minister, and his minions, are exposed, the keener the satir, the more liable is it to be interpreted into high treason against the king.

In the character of JACK, a set of people were alarmed, who are easily offended, and who can scarce bear the chearfulness of a smile. In their dictionary, wit is only another name for wickedness: and the purer or more excellent the wit, the greater and more impious the *abomination*. However wide therefore the difference of PETER and JACK might have been in fashioning their coats, the two brothers most sincerely agreed in their hatred of an adversary so powerful as this anonymous author. They spared no unmannerly reflexions upon his character. They had recourse to every kind of abuse that could reach him. And sometimes it was the work of SWIFT, and his companions: sometimes not a syllable of it was his work; it was the work of one of his uncle's sons, a clergyman:[16] and sometimes it was the work of a person, who was to be nameless. Each of these malicious conjectures reigned in its turn; and you will find, my HAMILTON, that bold assertions,

---

[b]see] behold FI, FIa, FIb, FII, FIII, FV, MI

[c]origin] original FI, FIa, FIb, FII, FIII, FV, MI

[d]Original footnote in the *Remarks*: "OVID Metam. Lib. VII. ver. 112."

however false, almost constantly meet with success; a kind of triumph, that would appear one of the severest institutes of fate, if time, and truth, did not soon obliterate all marks of the victory.

The criticisms[e] of the Martinists (whom we may suppose the members of the church of *England*) were, it is to be hoped, more candid: for MARTIN, as I have just now hinted, is treated with a much less degree of sarcasm than the other two brothers. What relates to him is so short, that I will venture to transcribe it. "*They both* [LUTHER and CALVIN] *unanimously entered upon this great work* [THE REFORMATION], *looking sometimes on their coats, and sometimes on the* WILL. MARTIN *laid the first hand; at one twitch brought off a large handful of* POINTS; *and, with a second pull, stript away ten dozen yards of* FRINGE. *But, when he had gone thus far, he demurred a while: he knew very well, there yet remained a great deal more to be done: however, the first heat being over, his violence began to cool, and he resolved to proceed more moderately in the rest of the work; having already very narrowly escaped a swinging rent in pulling off the* POINTS, *which, being* TAGGED WITH SILVER *(as we have observed before), the judicious workman had, with much sagacity, doublesown to preserve them from* FALLING. *Resolving therefore to rid his coat of a huge quantity of* GOLD LACE, *he picked up the stitches with much caution, and diligently gleaned out all the loose threads as he went; which proved to be a work of time. Then he fell about the embroidered* INDIAN *figures of men, women, and children; against which, as you have heard in its due place, their father's testament was extremely exact and severe. These, with much dexterity and application, were, after a while, quite eradicated, or utterly defaced. For the rest, where he observed the embroidery to be worked so close, as not to be got away without damaging the cloth, or where it served to hide or strengthen any flaw in the body of the coat, contracted by the perpetual tampering of workmen upon it; he concluded, the wisest course was to let it remain, resolving in no case whatsoever, that the substance of the stuff should suffer injury, which he thought the best method for serving the true intent and meaning of his father's* WILL. *And this is the nearest account I have been able to collect of* MARTIN's *proceedings upon this great revolution.*"[17]

The church of England can scarce be angry at such a favourable account of LUTHER: especially as we have since reformed from LUTHER himself, and, so far as our judgments can teach us, have restored our *habits* still nearer to the original fashion, which they bore at the perfection of the *Testament*. The best, and, what is more extraordinary, the most serious apology, that can be made for the author, was written by himself, and is dated *June* 3, 1709; from which time, it has been constantly printed in a prefatory manner to the work

---

[e]Orrery's correction in Osborn pc 231: "critisms" to "criticisms."

itself.[18] In this apology, Dr. SWIFT candidly acknowledges, that *"There[f] are several youthful sallies, which, from the grave and the wise, may deserve a rebuke."*[19] And further adds, that *"He will forfeit his life, if any one opinion can fairly be deduced from the book, which is contrary to religion or morality."*[20]

The dedication to *Prince Posterity*[21] will please you: nor will you be less entertained by the several *digressions* which are written in ridicule of bad critics, dull commentators, and the whole fraternity of Grub-street philosophers.[22] *The Introduction*[23] abounds with wit and humour: but the author never loses the least opportunity of venting his keenest satir against Mr. DRYDEN, and consequently loads with insults the greatest, although the least prosperous, of our English poets.[24] Yet who can avoid smiling, when he finds the *Hind and Panther*[25] mentioned as *a complete abstract of sixteen thousand schoolmen,*[26] and when TOMMY POTTS is supposed written by *the same hand, as a supplement to the former work?*[27] I am willing to imagine, that DRYDEN, in some manner or other, had offended my friend Dr. SWIFT,[28] who, otherwise, I hope, would have been more indulgent to the errors of a man oppressed by poverty, driven on by party, and bewildered by religion.

But although our satirical author, now-and-then, may have indulged himself in some personal animosities, or may have taken freedoms not so perfectly consistent with that solemn decency, which is required from a clergyman; yet, throughout the whole piece, there is a vein of ridicule and good humour, that laughs pedantry and affectation into the lowest degree of contempt, and exposes the character of PETER and JACK in such a manner, as never will be forgiven, and never can be answered.

The *Battle of the Books* took its rise from the controversy between Sir WILLIAM TEMPLE and Mr. WOTTON:[29] a controversy which made much noise, and employed many pens, towards the latter end of the last century. This humorous treatise is drawn up in an heroic comic style, in which SWIFT, with great wit and spirit, gives the victory to the former. The general plan is excellent; but particular parts are defective. The frequent chasms puzzle and interrupt the narrative: they neither convey any latent ideas, nor point out any distant or occult sarcasms. Some characters are barely touched upon, which might have been extended; others are enlarged, which might have been contracted. The name of HORACE is scarce inserted,[30] and VIRGIL is introduced[31] only for an opportunity of comparing his translator DRYDEN, to *the Lady in a Lobster: to a Mouse under a Canopy of State: and to a shrivelled Beau within the Penthouse of a full-bottomed Perriwig.*[32] These similies carry the true stamp of ridicule: but rancour must be very prevalent

---

[f]that *"There*] that *"That there* FI, FIa, FIb, FII, FIII, FV

in the heart of an author, who could overlook the merits of DRYDEN; many of whose dedications and prefaces are as fine compositions, and as just pieces of criticism, as any in our language. The translation of VIRGIL[33] was a work of haste and indigence:[34] DRYDEN was equal to the undertaking, but unfortunate during the conduct of it.

And now, as I have mentioned VIRGIL, and as I indulge myself in an unlimited manner of expressing to you my thoughts, I must plead that kind of habit for[g] inserting a conjecture, which, perhaps, is purely chimerical, but which, in the pursuit of it, has given me no small degree of pleasure, as the motive tends to vindicate one of your favourite poets from the censure of ingratitude.

The critics have been justly surprised, that VIRGIL seems entirely to have neglected HORACE,[35] when it is evident, that HORACE takes frequent occasions of expressing the greatest tenderness, esteem, and gratitude, for VIRGIL.[36] They have endeavoured to account for this neglect, by supposing, that some of VIRGIL's poems have been lost; otherwise, who could imagine, that the author of the Aeneid should have passed over in silence the name of so excellent, and so estimable a friend? In the Greek and Roman writers it is not to be doubted, that there are many expressions, which, at the time when written, were evident marks to distinguish particular characters. These, by the course of years, are now rendered doubtful and obscure. HORACE's *Glycon*[37] was always taken for a gladiator,[38] till at the bottom of the statue of the HERCULES FARNESE[39] an old inscription was discovered, that shews it was so called from the name of the famous sculptor who made it. Many passages in Mr. POPE's poems, which are now easily explained, may, in a few centuries, become entirely unintelligible, and (excuse the improbability of the circumstance) when it is no longer remembered that he lived at *Twitnam*, he will no longer be known for *the Swan of Thames*.

VIRGIL, in his Eclogues,[40] celebrates POLLIO,[41] VARUS,[42] and GALLUS,[43] and he dedicates his Georgics[44] to MAECENAS:[45] but in the Aeneid, he could not introduce any of his contemporaries,[h] except by feigned names: and even then, the connexion of the fable must be preserved, and some poetical differences must be allowed. Such a conduct has induced some of the commentators to affix various names to particular characters in the Aeneid. They have mentioned MARIUS,[46] POMPEY, CURIO,[47] and others; but their hints and sketches have been imperfect, and written at random.

---

[g]I must plead that kind of habit for] let me pursue that kind of freedom by FI, FIa, FIb, FII, FIII, FV, MI

[h]contemporaries, MV] cotemporaries, MIII

Bishop ATTERBURY[48] is more explicit. That learned prelate, in all the elegance and delicacy of criticism, illustrates the passage relating to IAPIS,[49] and fixes to it the name and character of ANTONIUS MUSA,[50] an eminent physician, and polite scholar, at *Rome*.[51] The BARRY[i] [52] of his day.

From these attempts, I have been encouraged to search for the character of HORACE; and instead of an imperfect picture, I hope, I shall be able to point out a very remarkable likeness in the following lines.

> *Et amicum Cretea musis,*
> *Cretea musarum comitem, cui carmina semper*
> *Et citharae cordi, numerosque intendere nervis;*
> *Semper equos, atque arma virûm, pugnasque canebat.*[53]

An ode in HORACE, which appears, by the mention of TIRIDATES,[54] to have been written at the same time with the seventh book of VIRGIL,[55] bears a very striking resemblance to some part of this quotation. You remember

> *Musis amicus tristitiam et metus*
> *Tradam protervis in mare Creticum*
> *Portare ventis.*[56]

The *Musis amicus* was, in all probability, a synonymous name of HORACE, by which he was then distinguished, and perfectly well known at *Rome*. Such an appellation might be given to him from this gay and spirited ode. He begins it by delivering at once all his cares and fears to be buried in the Cretan sea. TIBULLUS[57] and ANACREON[58] have the same general sentiment; but HORACE chooses this particular part of the ocean for the eternal grave of all his cares. A circumstance which might occasion VIRGIL to give him the name of CRETEUS: and I dare say, HAM, you will agree with me in observing, that VIRGIL repeats that name with a certain tenderness and esteem, as if he was unwilling to quit the subject, and as if he could wish to dwell longer in the description of so excellent a genius, and so remarkable a poet.

But the line,

> *Et citharae cordi, numerosque intendere nervis,*[59]

seems directly to point out HORACE, and to celebrate him for his lyric performances. MONSIEUR DACIER,[60] in the preface to his HORACE,[61]

---

[i]Original footnote in the *Remarks*: "Dr. EDWARD BARRY of *Dublin*."

gives an history of the progress and decay of lyric poetry. He observes, that from the foundation of *Rome* to the reign of AUGUSTUS CAESAR (a space of above seven hundred years) not one lyric poet had appeared.[62] HORACE was the first Roman, who, with a surprising natural genius, having studied and acquired the beauty and strength of numbers, formed himself upon the Grecian plan, and became the best Latin lyric poet of the Augustan age.[63] From whence, it almost evidently appears, that this passage can be adapted only[j] to him.

Thus far, without straining the explanation of these lines, I would willingly hope, that the features of HORACE are discernible. The last verse indeed does not seem to answer so exactly his poetical character.

> *Semper equos, atque arma virûm, pugnasque canebat.*[64]

Let us try, if we cannot banish the objection, and establish a perfect confirmation of the resemblance.

Several of the odes of HORACE are remarkably fine in the warlike strain, particularly the ode to AUGUSTUS after the battle of *Actium*,[65] when the senate had agreed to address solemn hymns to the Emperor in the same manner as to the celestial deities.[66] The ode beginning *Caelo tonantem*,[67] and occasioned by the conquest over the Britons and Persians,[68] is full of fire. But the address to ASINIUS POLLIO[69] breathes war and slaughter still in a more exalted strain.

> *Jam nunc minaci murmure cornuum*
> *Perstringis aures: jam litui strepunt:*
> *Jam fulgor armorum fugaces*
> *Terret equos, equitumque vultus.*[70]

MONSIEUR SANADON[71] observes, that this stanza, and the four which follow it, are written with the greatest spirit of lyric poetry.[72] His expression is *La force de Poesie lyrique ne va point au delà.*[73]

It is very certain, that HORACE was a perfect master of the poetical array of battle, the din of war, and the sound of clarions: or, in the words of VIRGIL, *equos, atque arma virûm, pugnasque canebat.*[74] But, notwithstanding his powers in that style, he seems constantly desirous of declining any long poem, or laboured performance, upon those subjects. In his ode beginning *Motum ex Metello*,[75] he advises ASINIUS POLLIO to lay aside all intentions of writing tragedy; and he further urges him to complete a poem upon the

---

[j]be adapted only] only be adapted FI, FIa, FIb, FII, FIII, FV, MI, MII

civil wars, between ANTONY and OCTAVIUS:[76] but he damps this advice, by pointing out the danger of the theme. He tells POLLIO,[k]

> Periculosae plenum opus aleae
> Tractas; et incedis per ignes
> Suppositos cineri doloso.[77]

Thus,[l] while he expatiates upon the difficulty of the undertaking, he shews himself superior to the labours that deter him.[78]   As a Poet, we may be assured he was equal to the task: as a politician, we may presume, he avoided it. He was unwilling to remind his imperial master of a war, in which he had appeared in arms against his prince:[79] and in which the character of AUGUSTUS had not been distinguished with the most perfect degree of lustre. Yet, that such a kind of work was expected from him, may undoubtedly be deduced from what he says in one of his odes to MAECENAS.[80]

> Tuque pedestribus
> Dices historiis proelia Caesaris,
> Maecenas, MELIUS.[81]

---

[k]to lay aside all intentions of writing tragedy; and he further urges him to complete a poem upon the civil wars, between ANTONY and OCTAVIUS: but he damps this advice, by pointing out the danger of the theme. He tells POLLIO,] to lay aside his tragic muse, in which he had so eminently excelled, till he had executed his great design in describing the civil wars between ANTONY, and OCTAVIUS: and yet he seems to deter him from the undertaking, by pointing out the difficulties which must attend it. FI, FIa, FIb, FII, FIII, FV; to lay aside all intentions of writing a tragedy upon the civil wars, between ANTONY and OCTAVIUS and he fortifies this advice, by pointing out the danger of the theme. He tells POLLIO MI; to lay aside all intentions of writing tragedy, and he farther urges him to complete a poem upon the civil wars, between ANTONY and OCTAVIUS: but he damps this advice, by pointing out the danger of the theme. He tells POLLIO, MII, MIII; to lay aside all intentions of writing tragedy; and he further urges him to complete a poem upon the civil wars, between ANTONY and OCTAVIUS: but he damps this advice, by pointing out the danger of the theme. He tells POLLIO MIV; In Osborn pc 231, Orrery corrected this passage.

[l]Thus,] But, FI, FIa, FIb, FII, FIII, FV, MI; ~ ˄ MIV, MV

Here you see, HORACE assigns to his patron MAECENAS all the laurels that might accrue from a complete poem upon the wars of AUGUSTUS: and in another place, the poet, with more modesty than justice, says,

> *Cupidum, pater optime, vires*
> *Deficiunt: neque enim quivis horrentia pilis*
> *Agmina, nec fracta pereuntes cuspide Gallos,*
> *Aut labentis equo describat vulnera Parthi.*[82]

These lines are in such a strain, as to demonstrate the powers of the muse much less deficient than the will. It is very probable therefore, that, during the time, while the public expectations were raised in hopes of seeing HORACE undertake some poem entirely formed upon the military plan, VIRGIL might have composed that part of the Aeneid from whence I have drawn my quotation, and might very justly have given HORACE the character of CRETEUS, not only in consequence of the odes already written, but under a kind of certainty, of seeing future and more perfect poems in the same strain.

I submit to your judgment, whether these surmises are just. I really think they bear a great resemblance to truth. Positive assertions on such doubtful points I leave to more established critics: and return from the civil wars in *Italy* to the civil wars in St. JAMES's library.

The two chief heroes among the modern generals are WOTTON and BENTLEY.[83] Their figures are displayed in the most disadvantageous attitudes. The former is described, *full of spleen, dulness, and ill manners.*[84] The latter is represented, *tall, without shape or comeliness: large, without strength or proportion.*[85] But, I will not anticipate your future pleasure in reading a performance that you will probably wish longer, and more complete.

The *Battle*, which is maintained by the antients with great superiority of strength, though not of numbers,[86] ends with the demolition of BENTLEY and his friend WOTTON by the lance of your grandfather.[m] [87] And here, my son, it is not possible for me to avoid taking notice of one particular passage relating to my father. "BOYLE, says the author, *clad in a suit of*

---

[m]FI, FIa, FIb, FII, FIII, FV add footnote: "CHARLES BOYLE, youngest son of ROGER the second Earl of *Orrery*. By the death of his elder brother, he became Earl of *Orrery* and Baron *Broghill* in *Ireland*; and was afterwards created by Queen ANN, Baron BOYLE of *Marston* in *Somersetshire*. He was appointed by that Queen Envoy Extraordinary to the states of *Flanders* and *Brabant*. He received the Order of the Thistle for his gallant behaviour as an officer. He was a fellow of the royal society, and invented the astronomical machine, called, THE ORRERY."

armour, WHICH HAD BEEN GIVEN HIM BY ALL THE GODS, *advanced towards the trembling foe, who now fled before him.*"[88]

I shall not dispute about the gift of the armour: but thus far I will venture to observe, that the gods never bestowed celestial armour, except upon heroes, whose courage, and superior strength, distinguished them from the rest of mankind; whose merits and abilities were already conspicuous; and who could wield, though young, the sword of MARS,[89] and adorn it with all the virtues of MINERVA:[90] and let me assure you, my dearest HAMILTON, that your grandfather sustained the character, which he had so early acquired, to the last moment of his life, and, on many occasions, exerted his abilities in such a manner, as evidently shewed, that he wanted neither armour, nor extraordinary assistance, to add to his first victory such superior ornaments, as will for ever be reposited among the brightest trophies, in the temple of fame.

But before I quit this subject, give me leave to own how sensibly I felt the force of an arrow directed from his hand. The wound, I believe, was not designed to be lasting. It was given in a passion, and upon an extraordinary occasion: but afterwards he was so desirous to heal it, by a return of the greatest degree of friendship and affection, that he had directed the remaining scar to be entirely erased, when his unexpected and too sudden death prevented the completion of his kind intentions, and the perfection of my cure. With difficulty I survived the shock. As it was not in my power to avoid the severe decree, I obeyed: and, by my obedience, have flattered myself, that I submitted to the will of heaven. However, I have since thought, that I could not offer a more grateful sacrifice to his manes, than by exerting those faculties, which he had, at first, cultivated with so much care; and had depressed, at last, perhaps only to raise them higher. Oh my son! how often have I reflected upon the happiness of AENEAS, in hearing the ghost of ANCHISES[91] say,

> *Sic equidem ducebam animo rebarque futurum,*
> *Tempora dinumerans: nec me mea cura fefellit!*[92]

The name of my honoured father has insensibly drawn me into this digression, which, to speak the truth, I look upon as due to his memory, to my own sentiments, and to your filial tenderness.

The Fragment, or *a Discourse concerning the mechanical operation of the Spirit*, is a satir against enthusiasm,[93] and those affected inspirations, which constantly begin in folly, and very often end in vice. In this treatise, the author has revelled in too licentious a vein of sarcasm: many of his ideas are nauseous, some are indecent, and others have an irreligious tendency: nor is the piece itself equal in wit and humour either to *The Tale of a Tub*, or *The Battle of the Books*. I should constantly choose rather to praise, than to arraign, any part of my friend SWIFT's writings: but in those tracts, where he tries to make us uneasy with ourselves, and unhappy in our present existence, *there*, I must yield him up entirely to censure.

> *I am, dear* HAMILTON,
> *Your most affectionate Father,*
> ORRERY.

Notes

1. *Prose Works of Swift* 1:1-135.

2. Ibid., pp. 137-65.

3. Ibid., pp. 171-90.

4. A proverbial sentence: "They are either Erasmus's, or the devil's."

5. In the *Apology* for the work, written anonymously for the work's fifth edition in 1710, Swift stated: "The greatest part of that book [*A Tale of a Tub*] was finished above thirteen years since, 1696, which is eight years before it was published" (ibid., p. 1). In the work's preface, Swift mentioned "this present month of August 1697" (ibid., p. 26). Deane Swift told Orrery that Swift had shown *A Tale of a Tub*, "in his own hand writing," to "Mr. Waring," Swift's chamber fellow at Trinity College Dublin (cf. notes in Orrery's interleaved and annotated copy of the *Remarks*, MS Eng 218.14, interleaf page number 301, Houghton Library, Harvard). Herbert Davis believed that Swift began to write the work while he was at Kilroot (Swift had been installed on 15 March 1695, and left Kilroot in mid-May 1696). See *Prose Works of Swift* 1:xvi. Guthkelch and Smith wrote that "it is not impossible that the first rough sketch of it [*A Tale of a Tub*] was made while he [Swift] was still an undergraduate at Trinity College, Dublin." In Jonathan Swift, *A Tale of a Tub*, ed. A. C. Guthkelch and David Nichol Smith, 2d ed. (Oxford: Clarendon Press, 1958), p. xlvii.

6. See Swift's words on the "imagination" he had when he wrote *A Tale of a Tub*, according to Deane Swift's account to Orrery, in MS Eng 218.14, interleaf page number 300, Houghton Library, Harvard.

7. Jean-Paul Forster challenged the idea that Swift's parable of the father, the will, the three brothers, and their coats represents a satirical history of

Christianity. See Jean-Paul Forster, "Swift and Wotton: The Unintended Mousetrap," *Swift Studies* 7 (1992): 23-35.

8. The parable of the father, his will, his three sons and their coats is in sections 2, 4, 6, 8, and 9, which are headed "A Tale of a Tub." It is possible that a section on Martin had been lost, as suggested by the heading of *The History of Martin* and by the fact that section 10, a digression, is headed "A Tale of a Tub." See Jonathan Swift, *A Tale of a Tub and Other Works*, ed. Angus Ross and David Woolley (Oxford and New York: Oxford University Press, 1986), pp. xii and xvii.

9. Defined as the change of the whole substance of bread and wine into the Body, Blood, Soul, and Divinity of Christ during the Consecration at Mass, even though the physical appearance of bread and wine remains unchanged.

10. The *bullae majores* or *privilegia*, which contained the signatures of the pope and cardinals and bestowed rights without time limitation, has not been in use since the fourteenth century. The *bullae minores* or *litterae* dealt with matters of lesser importance, and were classified as either rescripts or executive documents. Since 1878, the leaden seals for bulls have been discontinued, except for solemn ones. The papal documents, letters, and bulls now bear a red ink stamp with the pope's name encircling the heads of St. Peter and St. Paul. See *New Catholic Encyclopedia*, s.v. "Bulla."

11. Colchis was a country lying at the foot of the Caucasus, on the coast of the Black Sea.

12. When Jason and his Argonauts landed in Colchis to bring the Golden Fleece to Iolcos, Aeetes, the local king, told them they could have the Golden Fleece on one condition: that, unaided, Jason should yoke two bulls with brazen hoofs that breathed fire from their nostrils. See Ovid *Metamorphoses* 7.1-120.

13. "Terrible faces and sharp horns tipped with iron, pawed the dusty earth with their cloven feet, and filled the place with their fiery bellowings" (ibid., 7.112-14).

14. A reference to the papal lead seal or "bull."

15. *Prose Works of Swift* 1:68.

16. Thomas Swift (1665-1752), Swift's cousin. See Deane Swift's words to Orrery on Thomas Swift's supposed authorship of *A Tale of a Tub*, in MS Eng 218.14, interleaf pages numbered 304-6, Houghton Library, Harvard. Woolley and Ross wrote thus on the subject: "Enough is known now about this contentious matter to make possible some firm conclusions. Thomas Swift's claim cannot be dismissed out of hand. That the Swift cousins conferred, even over an *ur*-text of *A Tale*, seems likely. Ideas or 'hints' Thomas may well have contributed. In the seven years before publication it appears that he did not even see the work. Considering Jonathan Swift's extreme sensitivity to any charge of plagiarism, it is at least a fair supposition that the 1704 volume is entirely Jonathan's, while some broad and some specific influences may be seen at work in the final text, and Section I of *The Mechanical Operation* may preserve segments by Thomas turned to the satirist's own use. There is, moreover, personal testimony in Thomas Swift's lifetime that *he* was not capable of writing *A Tale of a Tub*" (*Tale of a Tub*, ed. Ross and Woolley, p. 198).

17. *Prose Works of Swift* 1:85.

18. The *Apology* appeared separately in 1711, as *An Apology For The Tale of a Tub. With Explanatory Notes By W. W-tt-n, B. D. And others* (London: John Morphew, 1711). After the London fifth edition of *A Tale of a Tub*, the *Apology* is traditionally printed as a prefatory matter to the work, immediately before the *Dedication to Somers*, even though it is a later commentary. The small duodecimo editions of 1711 do not include the *Apology*. See *A Tale of a Tub*, ed. Guthkelch and Smith, p. lxx.

19. *Prose Works of Swift* 1:2.

20. Ibid.

21. *The Epistle Dedicatory to His Royal Highness Prince Posterity* (*Prose Works of Swift* 1:18-23).

22. *Section III. A Digression concerning Critics* (ibid., pp. 56-64); *Section V. A Digression in the Modern Kind* (ibid., pp. 77-82); *Section VII. A Digression in Praise of Digressions* (ibid., pp. 90-94); *Section IX. A Digression concerning Madness* (ibid., pp. 102-14); and, *Section X. [A Further Digression]* (ibid., pp. 115-19).

23. *Section I. The Introduction* (ibid., pp. 33-43).

24. Cf. Swift's words on Dryden's dedications, prefaces, and introductions in *Section V. A Digression in the Modern Kind*: "This expedient was admirable at first. Our great Dryden has long carried it as far as it would go, and with incredible success. He has often said to me in confidence that the world would have never suspected him to be so great a poet, if he had not assured them so frequently in his Prefaces that it was impossible they could either doubt or forget it." (Ibid., pp. 81-82).

25. Dryden's *The Hind and the Panther: A Poem, in Three Parts* (London: Jacob Tonson, 1687).

26. "*The Hind and Panther.* This is the masterpiece of a famous writer now living, intended for a complete abstract of sixteen thousand schoolmen from Scotus to Bellarmin" (In *Section I. The Introduction, Prose Works of Swift* 1:41).

27. "*Tommy Potts.* Another piece supposed by the same hand, by way of supplement to the former [*The Hind and the Panther*]" (ibid.).

28. For accounts of a reported incident involving Swift and Dryden, see Theophilus Cibber, *Lives of the Poets of Great Britain and Ireland to the time of Dean Swift*, 5 vols. (London: R. Griffiths, 1753), 5:97-98. See also Deane Swift, *Essay*, p. 117. In his *Essay on the Genius and Writings of Pope*, 3d ed., 2 vols. (London: J. Dodsley, 1772-82), 2:312-13 n, Joseph Warton gave his account of the incident while naming Elijah Fenton (who had been Orrery's tutor) as his source.

29. In 1689, Temple wrote *An Essay upon Ancient and Modern Learning*, printed in Temple's *Miscellanea, The Second Part* (1690), in which he argues that the moderns were not superior to the ancients. See Clara Marburg, *Sir William Temple: A Seventeenth-Century "Libertin"* (New Haven: Yale University Press, 1932), p. 26. In 1694, the scholar William Wotton (1666-1727) published a rejoinder to Temple's essay, entitled *Reflections upon Ancient and Modern Learning*. Temple at first refused to answer Wotton's *Reflections*, but ended up writing "Hints: written at the Desire of D^r F and of His Friend" (manuscript at Trinity College Library, Cambridge; Rothschild 2253). See Elias, *Swift at Moor Park*, pp. 115, 120-21, 191, 269-70, 272, and 325. Temple's expansion of the "Hints" resulted in *Some Thoughts Upon Reviewing the Essay on Antient and Modern Learning*, first published after Temple's death, in Temple's *Miscellanea, The Third Part* (London: Benjamin Tooke, 1701).

30. Horace is mentioned only once in *The Battle of the Books* (*Prose Works of Swift* 1:158).

31. Ibid., p. 157.

32. Ibid.

33. *The Works of Virgil: Containing His Pastorals, Georgics, Aeneis. Translated into English Verse; By Mr. Dryden* (London: Jacob Tonson, 1697).

34. Dryden was "in financial and political decline" when he signed the contract with Jacob Tonson (1694) to translate Virgil's works. See *The Works of John Dryden*, ed. Edward Niles Hooker and H. T. Swedenberg, 19 vols. (Berkeley: University of California Press, 1956-), 6:847.

35. Horace is not mentioned in any of Virgil's writings.

36. For Horace's references to Virgil, see: *Satires* 1.5.40, 48; 1.4.55; 1.10.45, 81; *Epistles* 2.1.247; *Ars Poetica* 55; *Odes* 1.3.6; 1.24.10.

37. Horace *Epistles* 1.1.30-31.

38. The index to the Loeb Edition of Horace's *Satires, Epistles and Ars Poetica* identifies Glycon as "a famous athlete" (p. 497).

39. The Farnese Hercules was made by an Athenian named Glykon, and it was found in the baths erected in Rome by the Emperor Caracalla (reigned 211-17 A.D.). See Martin Robertson, *A History of Greek Art*, 2 vols. (Cambridge: Cambridge University Press, 1975), 1:467. Orrery saw "a model" of the Farnese Hercules in Dr. Richard Mead's library. See MS Eng 218.14, interleaf page 312, Houghton Library, Harvard.

40. The collection of ten short poems known as the *Eclogues* or *Bucolics* is Virgil's earliest extant work.

41. Caius Asinius Pollio, Roman statesman, orator, historian and tragic poet who flourished in the first century B.C. He became Virgil's friend and patron, and it was through Pollio that Virgil was introduced to Octavian. Virgil dedicated *Eclogues* 4 and 8 to Pollio, and there are references to Pollio in *Eclogues* 3.84, 86, and 88.

42. L. Alfenus Varus, who, in 41 B.C., succeeded Asinius Pollio as governor of Cisalpine Gaul. The references to him are in *Eclogues* 6.7, 10, 12; 9.26-27.

43. C. Cornelius Gallus, poet and first prefect of Egypt. He committed suicide in 26 B.C. The references to him are in *Eclogues* 6.64; 10.2-3, 6, 10, 22, 72-73. After the defeat of Brutus and Cassius at Philippi (42 B.C.), the members of the Second Triumvirate confiscated lands and allotted them to the victorious veterans. Cremona and Mantua (where Virgil was living) greatly suffered from the confiscation, and Virgil was dispossessed of his farm. Virgil befriended Asinius Pollio, then governor of Cisalpine Gaul, and also Alfenus Varus, Pollio's successor, who had been in charge of the confiscation of lands in Virgil's district. Likewise, Virgil befriended Cornelius Gallus, who was then a member of the land commission, and helped Virgil to recover his farm. Virgil's indebtedness to Pollio, Varus, and Gallus is mentioned in Suetonius *De Poetis*, "The Life of Virgil," 19-20.

44. The *Georgics*, a four-book poem on agriculture, was written about 37 or 36-30 or 29 B.C.

45. The *Georgics* is dedicated to and was written at the request of Maecenas. Regarding Virgil's dedication of the work to Maecenas, Suetonius wrote: "Then he [Virgil] wrote the 'Georgics' in honour of Maecenas, because he had rendered him aid, when the poet was still but little known, against the violence of one of the veterans, from whom Vergil narrowly escaped death in a quarrel about his farm" (Suetonius *De Poetis*, "The Life of Virgil," 20-21).

46. Caius Marius (157-86 B.C.), Roman general and statesman.

47. Caius Scribonius Curio (d. 49 B.C.), son of another Caius Scribonius who had been Cicero's friend and opponent of Caesar.

48. Francis Atterbury (1662-1732), bishop of Rochester.

49. Iäpix, physician to Aeneas. He was son of Iasus, as well as Apollo's pupil. The passage about him is in Virgil *Aeneid* 12.391-440.

50. Physician to Augustus. A statue of Antonius Musa was raised after Augustus had recovered from "a dangerous illness" under Musa's care. See Suetonius *The Lives of the Caesars* 2.59 and 81.

51. *Antonius Musa's Character, represented by Virgil, in the person of Iapis: a dissertation: by F. Atterbury, late bishop of Rochester* (London: C. Corbett, 1740).

52. Dr. Edward Barry, physician from Dublin and Orrery's close friend.

53. "And Cretheus, delight of the Muses–Cretheus, the Muses' comrade, whose joy was ever in song and lyre and in stringing of notes upon the chords; ever he sang of steeds and weapons, of men and battles" (Virgil *Aeneid* 9.774-77).

54. Tiridates II, king of Parthia and Armenia. He became king in 32 B.C., after having driven out Phraates IV who, in turn, evicted Tiridates II. Tiridates II regained the kingdom but was again expelled and took refuge with Augustus in Spain. See Dio *Roman History* 51.18.3, 53.33.1-2. Tiridates II is mentioned in Horace *Odes* 1.26.5.

55. It is not known exactly when book 7 of the *Aeneid* was written. However, Brooks Otis believed it was one of the books of the *Aeneid* that first engaged Virgil's attention. See Brooks Otis, *Virgil: A Study in Civilized Poetry* (Oxford: Clarendon Press, 1964), pp. 319-29, and 419-20. As for Horace's *Odes*, book 1 was published in 23 B.C., and many of the odes in it had been written several years before, possibly as early as 32 B.C.

56. "Dear to the Muses, I will banish gloom and fear to the wild winds to carry over the Cretan Sea" (Horace *Odes* 1.26.1-3).

57. Albius Tibullus (ca. 53 - 18 B.C.), Roman poet. There are four books of elegies attributed to Tibullus, but he was probably responsible for two of them only.

58. Anacreon (563-478 B.C.), Greek poet born at Teos in Ionia. Only fragments of his poetry survive.

59. "And lyre and in stringing of notes upon the chords."

60. André Dacier (1651-1722), French classical scholar.

61. André Dacier, *Oeuvres d'Horace en latin et en français, avec des remarques critiques et historiques,* troisième edition (Paris: Chez J.-B. Christophe Ballard, 1709).

62. Ibid., p. 44.

63. Ibid.

64. "Ever he sang of steeds and weapons, of men and battles."

65. Horace *Odes* 1.37. The Battle of Actium was the naval battle of 2 September 31 B.C., in which the joint fleet of Antony and Cleopatra was defeated.

66. In 29 B.C., by a decree of the Roman Senate, Augustus's name was included in the hymn of the Salii, an ancient priesthood. This hymn was an incantation accompanied by a dance, originally designed to ensure the safety of Rome in war. The inclusion of Augustus's name in the hymn meant that he was on a par with the gods. See Dio *Roman History* 51.20.1-2.

67. Horace *Odes* 3.5.

68. See ibid., 3.5.2-4. In 54 B.C., the princes of southeast Britain became nominally vassals of Rome, but soon defaulted in payment of tribute. Augustus was often adjured to resume the conquest of Britain, but in the end, he deferred it indefinitely. See Tacitus *Agricola* 13. In 20 B.C., Phraates IV, king of the Parthians, fearing that Augustus would lead an expedition against him, sent the Emperor the standards and captives taken during the defeat of a Roman army under Crassus by the Parthians at Carrhae (northern Mesopotamia) in 53 B.C. According to Dio, Augustus took pride on the return of the standards and the captives, for he "had recovered without a struggle what had formerly been lost in battle" (Dio *Roman History* 54.8.1-3).

69. Horace *Odes* 2.1.

70. "Even now with threatening blare of horns you strike our ears; even now the clarions sound; even now the gleam of weapons strikes terror into timid horses and into the horsemen's faces" (ibid., 2.1.17-20).

71. Noel Etienne Sanadon (1676-1733), Jesuit professor born in Rouen. He is the author of some orations, poems, and a translation of Horace's poems.

72. In Horace, *Les Poésies traduites en Français par Sanadon,* 2 vols. (Paris; 1728), 1:226. Orrery owned a copy of this work, offered on Wednesday, 22 November 1905 in the Orrery Sale at Christie's, London, as part of lot 356 (*The Orrery Sale,* p. 50).

73. Horace, *Les Poésies traduites en Français Par Sanadon,* 1:226. The sentence reads: "The force of lyric poetry does not get any better than it was back then."

74. "he sang of steeds and weapons, of men and battles."

75. Horace *Odes* 2.1. The ode's opening line is *Motum ex Metello consule civicum* (You are treating of the civil strife that with Metellus's consulship began). Horace is addressing Caius Asinius Pollio on the writing of his history of the Civil Wars.

76. Pollio undertook a history of the Civil Wars, which covered the period from the first consulship of Metellus in 60 B.C. (the year when the First Triumvirate of Caesar, Pompey, and Crassus was formed) down to 42 B.C., the year of the Battle of Philippi, where Brutus and Cassius were defeated. Neither this nor any other of Pollio's works survive. We know that Pollio used the iambic trimeter in his tragedies.

77. "A task full of dangerous hazard–and [you] are walking, as it were, over fires hidden beneath treacherous ashes" (Horace *Odes* 2.1.6-8).

78. For Orrery's work of revision of this passage, beginning on "In his ode beginning *Motum ex Metello*, . . ." see MS Eng 218.14, interleaf pages numbered 318-24, Houghton Library, Harvard (in the present edition pp. 358-59).

79. Around 46 B.C., Horace went to Athens to study philosophy. In March 44 B.C., Caesar was murdered, and in September of that year, Brutus arrived in Athens. Attracted by Brutus's republican ideals, Horace joined the cause of Brutus and Cassius, and was appointed *tribunus militum* in Brutus's army. Following Brutus's defeat at the Battle of Philippi (November 42 B.C.), Octavian confiscated the scanty patrimony that Horace would have inherited from his father, as a consequence of Horace's support to Brutus and Cassius. With the general amnesty granted by Octavian, Horace could return to Rome in 41 B.C.

80. Horace *Odes* 2.12.

81. "So you yourself, Maecenas, would better treat, and treat in storied prose, of Caesar's battles" (ibid., 2.12.9-11).

82. "Would that I could, good father, but my strength fails me. Not everyone can paint ranks bristling with lances, or Gauls falling with spear-heads shattered, or wounded Parthian slipping from his horse" (Horace *Satires* 2.1.12-15).

83. Richard Bentley (1662-1742), scholar and critic, for whom see James Henry Monk, *The Life of Richard Bentley*, 2d ed. (London: J. G. & F.

Rivington, 1883). For William Wotton, see *Dictionary of National Biography*, s.v. "Wotton, William."

84. "Having spoke thus, she [the goddess Criticism] took the ugliest of her monsters, full glutted from her spleen, and flung it invisibly into his [Wotton's] mouth, which flying straight up into his head squeezed out his eyeballs, gave him a distorted look, and half overturned his brain. Then she privately ordered two of her beloved children, Dullness and Ill-Manners, closely to attend his person in all encounters" (*Prose Works of Swift* 1:155).

85. "Bentley, in person the most deformed of the Moderns; tall, but without shape or comeliness; large, but without strength or proportion" (ibid., pp. 159-60).

86. Cf. this sentence in *The Battle of the Books*: "The army of the Ancients was much fewer in number" (ibid., p. 152).

87. See Bentley, *Dissertations upon the Epistles of Phalaris*, ed. Wilhelm Wagner (London: G. Bell & sons, 1883), pp. 582-85. See especially Joseph M. Levine, *The Battle of the Books: History and Literature in the Augustan Age* (Ithaca and London: Cornell University Press, 1991) pp. 50-68, and 80-81.

88. *Prose Works of Swift* 1:163.

89. In the classical period of Rome, Mars was regarded as the god of war, and also as the god who presided over agriculture. The festivals of Mars, which took place during the month dedicated to him (March), had markedly agrarian characteristics. Mars was also regarded as the father of Romulus and Remus, and was the one who sent the she-wolf to nurse the two boys when they were abandoned on a mountain.

90. Roman goddess identified with the Greek goddess Athena. Minerva presided over intellectual and academic activities.

91. Father of Aeneas and husband of the goddess Aphrodite. Aphrodite saw him tending his flocks on Mount Ida, near Troy, and claiming to be the daughter of Otreus, king of Phrygia, she married him. Later, Aphrodite told Anchises who she was, and predicted that she would bear him a son, Aeneas. When Troy was captured, Aeneas saved his father, who then became the companion of his wanderings. According to Virgil, after Anchises' death, Aeneas established the funeral games in his father's honor. These games gave origin to the Trojan Games held in Rome until the beginning of the empire.

92. "Even so I mused and deemed the hour would come, counting the days thereto, nor has my yearning failed me" (Virgil *Aeneid* 6.690-91). In book 6 of the *Aeneid*, Aeneas goes to the Underworld, where he meets the spirit of Anchises, his father. The above-mentioned words are uttered by the spirit of Anchises as he sees Aeneas. Father and son try to embrace each other, but Anchises' spirit flees away. See Virgil *Aeneid* 6.679-702.

93. Woolley and Ross observe that one of the main functions of *Mechanical Operation of the Spirit* is to attack "one of the abuses of religion, the cultivation of Enthusiasm (Greek *enthousiasmis*, from *entheos*: possessed by the god)" (*Tale of a Tub*, ed. Ross and Woolley, p. xvi).

LETTER XXIV

DR. SWIFT left behind him few manuscripts.[1]   Not one of any consequence, except an account of the peace of *Utrecht*, which he called *an History of the four last Years of Queen* ANNE.[2] The title of an history is too pompous for such a performance. In the historical style, it wants dignity, and candour: but as a pamphlet, it will appear the best defence of Lord OXFORD's administration, and the clearest account of the treaty of *Utrecht*, that has hitherto been written.[3]

In some of his leisure hours, he had begun an history of *England*, and had pursued it through two or three reigns, from WILLIAM the Conqueror.[4] The contempt which he[a] conceived of our antient monarchs, made him soon lay the design aside.[5] His aversion to kings was invincible. You will say perhaps, this aversion was rooted in pride: possibly it might: but, in your course of reading, you will find so very few princes whose merits and abilities entitle them even to a crown of rushes, that you will probably think no small degree of prudence necessary to reconcile us to a monarchical state. What has not this nation suffered from our former princes? Even from the best of them? If we speak candidly of our boasted Queen ELIZABETH, she was, in many instances, a tyrant:[6] but she was a tyrant with sense and dignity. She knew the true interest of the nation, and she pursued it;[7] but she pursued it in an arbitrary manner. She was fortunate in the time of reigning: for her character has been exalted by the want of merit in her successor,[8] from whose misconduct gushed forth that torrent of misery, which not only bore down his son,[9] but overwhelmed the three kingdoms.[10] If you ask what were the precious fruits of the restoration? the answer will be, An exchange only from one confusion to another: from jealousies between general MONK[11] and LAMBERT,[12] to jealousies between the dukes of *York*[13] and *Monmouth*:[14]

---

[a]contempt which he] contempt he FI, FIa, FIb, FII, FIII, FV, MI

a perpetual rotation of false politics: a king[b] with the best-natured disposition imaginable,[15] suffering innocent blood to be shed without remorse. Or, if you enquire, what was the effect of a lawful sovereign? A shameful submission to a neighbouring kingdom, which, not long before, had trembled at the frowns of an usurper.[c] Such was the fate of poor *England*! To these wretched times, succeeded the religious fooleries, and the weak attempts, of JAMES the second. Then followed the revolution. But, I must descend no lower. Let us therefore turn our eyes from home, and take a momentary view of other nations. If we look towards antient *Rome*, and consider her first seven monarchs,[16] how wicked, or how insignificant, were their characters? And, when the name of *Monarch* was changed into that of *Emperor*, what a tyrannical pack of CAESARS pass before our eyes! Many of them, the greatest monsters that human nature ever produced: yet these were lords, emperors, and kings of the world. If you read the Old Testament, and consult the Chronicles of the kings of *Judah*, you will find them a set of the proudest, and the most obstinate princes upon earth.[17] Tell me then, my HAMILTON, is not such a retrospect enough to disgust us against kings? Bad as it is, it must not disgust an Englishman. We ought ever to regard, honour, and preserve, our original constitution, which of all regal states is the best framed in the universe. The balance of our government is hung indeed in the nicest manner imaginable: a single hair will turn it; but when it is held exactly even, there cannot be a finer system under heaven: and I must freely own to you, that I think our kings have been often less blameable than their people. You remember the exclamation of the Scotchman, upon seeing the flatteries paid to JAMES the first at his accession, "*By my saul, mon, yon feulish folk will spoil a geud king.*"[18] The Scotchman was in the right: but we continued in our foolish ways to JAMES and his successors. Our courtly adulations are always outrageous, we know no bounds. The person flattered, must be more than human, not to be sometimes blinded by such perpetual incense. Perhaps we borrow this kind of servility from the *French*, who, in the last century bestowed the title of JUST upon LEWIS the thirteenth, during whose reign, such repeated acts of cruelty, oppression, and injustice, were perpetrated, as scarce any other annals can produce.[19]

An additional excuse, that may be made for the errors of our *English* kings, is the different treatment which they find at the beginning, from what they receive at the latter end of their reigns. At the beginning, all is smoothness, all is joy and felicity: but the sun-shine is seldom of a very long duration.

---

[b]In Osborn pc 231, Orrery identified the king as being "K. C. ye 2^d."

[c]In Osborn pc 231, Orrery identified the "usurper" as being "Usurper Cromwell."

Clouds of jealousy arise, and the whole atmosphere of the court is[d] soon filled with noxious vapours, with heart-burnings,[e] animosities, and personal altercations between ministers: which often ascend[f] to such a height, as even to molest the king in his chair of state. *Delirant Achivi, plectuntur reges.*[20] These are the unhappy effects that proceed,[g] as I have before observed, from the very noblest cause, the thirst of liberty. A free people are constantly jealous of their rights. A wise king will preserve to them those rights, and by such a maxim will establish his own. But, the great misfortune of our former *English* princes has been their indolent submission to the name, without the least attempt of discharging the duties of a sovereign. The life of such a prince must have proved inglorious to his people, and unhappy to himself. He must have found himself only the second person in his kingdom, nay perhaps the third or fourth; the leviathans of power being seldom, if ever, without their coadjutors: and in that case, it is a point of condescension, to permit their royal master to be one of the group. Our *English* commentaries, which are in truth a very melancholy, and a very reproachful history, gives[h] us many mortifying instances of this kind. I live so detached from the great world, and I keep myself at such a distance from the high commerce of politics, that I know little or nothing of the present times; and therefore can only instruct you from my reading, and not from my experience. Your fate perhaps may lead you to have admittance to the sacred closet, or to approach the exalted steps of the throne. If that honour is in reserve for you, use it in such a manner, as shall shew, that you think yourself accountable to GOD, and your country, for every action of your life. Begin by conquering your own prejudices, and then endeavour to conquer those of your master. Make him in love with parliaments, but let those parliaments be free. Bring him thoroughly acquainted, even with the minutest branch of the constitution. Study his honour. Prevent his passions. Correct his errors. Keep *England* ever

---

[d]atmosphere of the court is] atmosphere is FI, FIa, FIb, FII, FIII, FV, MI

[e]vapours, with heart-burnings,] vapours; so that the remaining chasm is filled up with heart-burnings, FI, FIa, FIb, FII, FIII, FV, MI

[f]which often ascend] and they often arise FI, FIa, FIb, FII, FIII, FV, MI

[g]proceed,] arise, FI, FIa, FIb, FII, FIII, FV, MI;
Orrery's correction in Osborn pc 231: "arise," to "proceed,"

[h]gives MV] give MIII

uppermost in your thoughts: and consider the king of *England* as born only[i] for the good of his people. Shield him, if possible, from flattery: it is a rock more fatal to princes, than *Charybdis* ever was to mariners.[21] Guide his leisure to manly employments, such as may preserve him from the enervating delicacies of a court. In your public capacity forget your relations, and your private friends. Know none but the friends of your country. Despise all dignities that you have not more than thoroughly deserved. Fear nothing but your own conscience. Aim at nothing but the prosperity of the state. Remember, that *Great Britain* is an island; and that nature, by detaching it from the continent, has rendered our situation particularly fortunate: and has pointed out to us, in what element our chief strength is destined.[j] Cherish upon all occasions our naval armament: and fail not to oppose your voice, against any greater number of land-forces than are absolutely necessary: I had almost said, necessary for reviews in *Hyde Park.*[22] A king, who enjoys the true affection of his people, will never stand in need of soldiers to defend him. He will dread no competitor: he will apprehend no domestic danger. He will distinguish which of the powers abroad are his natural and political enemies, and which are so situated, as to require[k] his friendship and alliance. He will attend to the improvement of the colonies in the *West Indies,* and to the different branches of trade that may safely and wisely be encouraged in the three different kingdoms.

You find, my HAMILTON, that I suppose your imaginary sovereign capable of receiving instruction, and *you* of giving it. But far be it from me to wish you his only counsellor, or (to express myself more properly) his sole minister: one, who draws every thing within the vortex of his own power; who is at once admiral, general, treasurer, archbishop, judge, and perpetual legislator. Such a kind of magistrate is odious to the *English* constitution.

If from the two houses of parliament you separate or withdraw the king, the government will remain in the form of a republic, where every man has his part allotted to him, and is to co-operate with the rest, for the benefit of the collective body of the people. What then is the king? Only the first and chief magistrate, who acts in a superior degree to the rest. All dignities, all honours, flow from the crown. Such a power alone, exclusive of every other, will give a prince sufficient authority throughout all his dominions: but he has many more prerogatives. He has the glorious privilege of pardoning offences,

---

[i]born only] only born FI, FIa, FIb, FII, FIII, FV, MI, MII

[j]destined.] appointed. FI, FIa, FIb, FII, FIII, FV, MI; Orrery's correction in Osborn pc 231: "appointed." to "destined."

[k]require] acquire MIV

and rewarding great actions: while the odious, or at least the reluctant parts of jurisdiction, such as punishment, and condemnation, are allotted to his officers; to himself alone is left the godlike power of mercy and forgiveness. From hence perhaps, kings have thought themselves representatives of GOD. Would to GOD, they thought themselves representatives of the people! The law, indeed, generously looks upon the king as incapable of doing wrong. Of what pernicious consequence therefore must be the interposition of a single man between the king and the people? How much must he eclipse his master's glory, and the prosperity of the state? His situation will necessarily make him act in an arbitrary manner. He is answerable to the laws; and, if his orders are disputed, he is unhinged; if they are disobeyed, he is undone, unless he has artfully brought his adversaries to a greater degree of corruption than himself; and, in that case,—But having already finished my most material observations upon the life and writings of the Dean of St. PATRICK's, I must remember the boundaries of a letter, and consider, that it is time to draw towards an end.[1] I originally chose the topic, my dearest HAMILTON, because few characters could have afforded so great a variety of faults and beauties. Few men have been more known and admired, or more envied and censured, than Dr. SWIFT. From the gifts of nature he had great powers, and, from the imperfection of humanity, he had many failings. I always considered him as an *Abstract and brief chronicle of the times*;[23] no man being better acquainted with human nature, both in the highest, and in the lowest scenes of life. His friends, and correspondents, were the greatest and most eminent men of the age.[24] The sages of antiquity were often the companions of his closet: and although he industriously avoided an ostentation of learning, and generally chose to draw his materials from his own store; yet his knowledge in the antient authors evidently appears from the strength of his sentiments, and the classic correctness of his style.

---

[1]But having already finished my most material observations upon the life and writings of the Dean of St. PATRICK's, I must remember the boundaries of a letter, and consider, that it is time to draw towards an end.] But I must remember the boundaries of a letter, and must consider that, having already finished my most material observations upon the life and writings of the Dean of St. PATRICK's, it is time to draw towards an end. FI; But I must remember the boundaries of a letter, and must consider, that, having already finished my most material observations upon the life and writings of the Dean of St. PATRICK's, it is time to draw towards an end. FIa, FIb, FII, FIII, FV, MI, MII, MIII; But having already finished my most material observations upon the life and writings of the Dean of St. PATRICK's, I must remember the boundaries of a letter, and consider that it is time to draw towards an end. MIV

You must have observed, my dear son, that I could not submit to be confined within the narrow limits of biographical memoirs. I have gone into a more extensive field; and, in my progress, I wish I may have thrown out such hints, as shall tend to form your mind to virtue and learning: the ultimate end of all my wishes, and all my cares. Heaven grant, my HAMILTON, that I may deserve from you, the honour which HORACE pays to his father (*Insuevit pater hoc me, ut fugerem exemplis vitiorum, &c.*),[25] when you drop a filial tear over the grave of

> *Your most affectionate Father,*
> *your sincerest Friend, and*
> *your happy Companion,*
> ORRERY.

Leicester Fields,
August 28, 1751.

The END.

Notes

1. For lists of Swift manuscripts, see: *Poems of Swift* 1:xlviii-lii; *The Rothschild Library*, 2 vols., 2:609-23; *The Orrery Sale*, pp. 103-9; and *A Catalogue of Printed Books and Manuscripts, by Jonathan Swift, D. D. Exhibited in the Old Schools in the University of Cambridge* (Cambridge: Cambridge University Press, 1945), pp. 38-44. See also *Correspondence of Swift* 1:xi.

2. *Prose Works of Swift* 7:xxix-167.

3. On 3 January 1713, Swift told Archbishop King: "Some Accidents and Occasions have put it in my Way to know every step of this Treaty [of Utrecht] better, I think, than any Man in England" (*Correspondence of Swift* 1:328).

4. Swift, *Reigns* of William Rufus, Henry I, and Stephen, with fragments on Henry II (*Prose Works of Swift* 5:9-78). It was first published in Deane Swift's edition of Swift's works, London, 1768, volume 13 (or volume 4 of the *Correspondence*). Orrery may have learned about the *Reigns* from some manuscript copy of it. Also, Orrery's source may have been Swift himself or Deane Swift.

5. Cf. Herbert Davis's words on this point: "He [Swift] abandoned the work partly because of the extreme difficulty he found in carrying it out, and partly because he found himself 'engaged in thoughts and business of another kind'. Perhaps he had some intention in 1719 of preparing it for publication, but was again diverted by becoming involved in public affairs in Ireland. Clearly he never became interested in the writing of this sort of history" (*Prose Works of Swift* 5:x). Actually, Swift began the work as an exercise under Temple and adapted it for publication in 1700-1703. See Elias, *Swift at Moor Park*, pp. 321-24.

6. In the forty-four years of Elizabeth I's reign, Parliament was called together only thirteen times. In the last thirteen years of her reign, Parliament assembled only in 1592, 1597, and 1601. See *Dictionary of National Biography*, s.v. "Elizabeth."

7. For England's prosperity under Elizabeth I, see A. L. Rowse, *The England of Elizabeth: The Structure of Society* (New York: Macmillan, 1950), pp. 107-57.

8. Comparing himself to Elizabeth I in his opening speech to Parliament in 1621, James I said: "I will not say I have governed as well as she did, but I may say we have had as much peace in our time as in hers." See William McElwee, *The Wisest Fool in Christendom: The Reign of King James I and VI* (New York: Harcourt, Brace, 1958), p. 277. Orrery's source of information about Elizabeth I was the following works that he owned: William Camden, *History of the Most Renowned and Victorious Princess Elizabeth*, 4th ed. (1688); Sir S. D'Ewes, *Journals of the Parliaments of Queen Elizabeth* (1693). See *The Orrery Sale*, pp. 27, and 62.

9. I.e., Charles I.

10. Orrery's source of information about James I was his copy of W. Lilly, *History of Kings James I and Charles I* (1715). See ibid., p. 4.

11. George Monck or Monk, first duke of Albemarle (1608-70).

12. John Lambert (1619-83), military commander.

13. James II (1633-1701), king of England, second son of Charles I and Henrietta Maria, was created duke of York and Albany soon after his christening.

14. James Scott, duke of Monmouth and Buccleuch (1649-85), natural son of Charles II and Lucy Walters.

15. Evelyn wrote that Charles II was "Debonaire, Easy of access, not bloody or Cruel." In *The Diary of John Evelyn*, ed. E. S. de Beer, 6 vols. (Oxford: Clarendon Press, 1955), 4:409-11.

16. Romulus was the first king of Rome, and the traditional date ascribed to his reign is 753-717 B.C. The traditional dates of Romulus's successors as kings of Rome are: Numa Pompilius (715-673 B.C.), Tullus Hostilius (673-642 B.C.), Ancus Marcius (642-617 B.C.), Tarquinius Priscus (616-579 B.C.), Servius Tullius (578-535 B.C.), and Tarquinius Superbus, Rome's last king (535-510 B.C.). See W. W. How and H. D. Leigh, *A History of Rome to the Death of Caesar* (London: Longmans, Green, 1896), pp. 20-31.

17. See 1 Kings 12-22, 2 Kings, and 2 Chron. 10-36.

18. In Arthur Wilson, *The History of Great Britain, Being the Life and Reign of King James the First* (London: Printed for Richard Lownds, 1653): "But our King coming through the North, (Banquetting and Feasting by the way) the applause of the people in so obsequious and submissive a manner (still admiring Change) was checkt by an honest plain Scotsman (unused to hear such humble Acclamations) with a Prophetical expression: 'This people will spoil a gud King.' The King as unused, so tired with Multitudes, especially in his Hunting (which he did as he went) caused an inhibition to be published, to restrain the people from hunting him" (p. 3).

19. See A. D. Lublinskaya, *French Absolutism: The Crucial Phase, 1620-1629* (Cambridge: Cambridge University Press, 1968), pp. 154-56. See also Elizabeth Wirth Marvick, *Louis XIII: The Making of a King* (New Haven and London: Yale University Press, 1986), pp. 96-100 and 164-67.

20. "Whatever folly the Achaeans commit, the kings pay the penalty." This is an inversion of Horace *Epistles* 1.2.14: *quidquid delirant reges, plectuntur Achivi* (whatever folly the kings commit, the Achaeans pay the penalty).

21. Charybdis, daughter of Earth and Poseidon, lived on the rock near Messina, beside the straits between Italy and Sicily. As a punishment for stealing some beasts from Heracles, Zeus struck her with a thunderbolt and cast her into the sea, where she became a monster. Three times every day, Charybdis drank great quantities of sea water, swallowing everything that was floating in the vicinity, including ships. See Homer *Odyssey* 12.104, 113, 235, 260, 428, 430, 436, 441; 23.327.

22. One of the five great London parks, consisting of 360 acres contiguous to Kensington Gardens.

23. *Hamlet*, 2.2.526-27.

24. See the index of Swift's correspondents, in *Correspondence of Swift* 5:279-87.

25. Horace *Satires* 1.4.105-6. The full sentence is: *insuevit pater optimus hoc me, ut fugerem exemplis vitiorum quaeque notando* (It is a habit the best of fathers taught me, for, to enable me to steer clear of follies, he would brand them, one by one, by his examples). For the reason why Orrery did not quote the sentence in full, see MS Eng 218.14, interleaf page numbered 339, Houghton Library, Harvard (in the present edition, pp. 360-61).

ORRERY'S MANUSCRIPT NOTES IN HIS ANNOTATED COPIES OF *REMARKS ON SWIFT*

Manuscript Notes in Houghton MS Eng 218.14

[inner front cover:]

Orrery. September
14th:1751. Leicester-Fields.

[page numbered A:]

In the Spectator N° 422. Vol. 6th is this Motto from Tully's Epistles,
Haec Scripsi non otii abundantia, sed amoris erga te.

This might have been a proper motto for this book.

[page numbered B:]

			Mem.
Page	6th		Swift born in the year 1667.
	10th	–	At six years old sent to Kilkenny School}
			1673.
	10th	–	Eight years afterwards sent to Trin. Coll. Dub.} 1681.
	11th	–	Batchelor's degree. 1685.

13th & 14th –Master of Arts . . . 1688.
Eighty eight being the year of the revolution [and particular confusion] in
Ireland, It is to be supposed that <u>Swift</u> could not take his Master's
degree till [near the year] 1692. the date of his letter to his uncle <u>William</u>.
Page 17th.

[page numbered C:]

Whatever appears in the Interleaves of this book, not written in my own
hand, was entered from my papers, and by my direction.

J. E. of O.

[portrait of Orrery]   Aetatis
44.

B. Wilson fecit.
1751.

This first Edition, was published on Thursday Nov:[br] 7th. and on Saturday
November 9th M[r] Millar told me, that he had disposed of the whole edition,
fifteen hundred, at 4 shillings a volume bound.

[Editorial note: The words in italics represent the printed text of the *Remarks*.
The words in Roman type beneath them indicate Orrery's notes in the copy's

interleaves referring to the respective passage in italics. The hand is Orrery's unless otherwise noted.]

[Letter I]

than possibly might have attended me, . . .

[interleaf p. 3:]

The word <u>possibly</u>, follows too closely I think upon the word <u>possible</u>, page 2^d. L 20th. therefore I have altered it to <u>probably.</u>

His friendship was an honour to me, . . .

[interleaf pp. 4-5:]

MEM. The Light in which Doctor Swift's character generally stands, makes him rather appear in the manner of a drol buffoon wit, than of a distinguished eminent writer. His trifling manner in writing and conversing have put him into this disadvantagious situation. Name him, and some ridiculous jest is expected to follow. His Puns and Rebusses are still hoarded up in Cabinets. I mean the few which have escaped Print.

All dignity of character seems lost, partly owing to the low stuff which he has printed, and partly to the want of distinction in the generality of readers. They mistake ^{and confound} the pictures for the painters; and think it impossible that a man can laugh at folly, without being dresst up in a fool's coat.

If a man writes the life of a Pickpocket, or a Highwayman, must he therefore be a Highwayman, or a Pickpocket?

<u>Swift</u> wants dignity more in the choice of his subjects, than in the manner of treating them. Yet I own, Dignity is far from being his characteristic. A more correct writer, I have never seen.

He was born in Dublin, . . .

[interleaf p. 6:]

In Hoey's Alley. I have seen him often point at the House where he was born, but it was always when he was in perfect good humour, which he generally was, when walking the Streets: probably because he never went many steps, without meeting some instance of respect, admiration, or applause.

The greatest part of Mr. Jonathan Swift's income . . .

[interleaf p. 9:]

I have since heard, that <u>Swift</u> was born seven months after his father's death, and that he used to say, "He came just time enough to save his mother's reputation." The note may be altered in any future edition.

Leicester, the place of her nativity.

[interleaf p. 10:]

<u>Swift</u> affected to have such a respect, and regard for the birth place of his mother, that I remember a Map of Leicester, constantly hung up in his bed chamber: a wretched ordinary map, but he said, "He honoured it, and took a melancholy pleasure in viewing the Scene of that place, where his mother first drew breath."

Swift was full of indignation at the treatment . . .

[interleaf p. 12:]

No man was more susceptible of indignation, and all violent passions (except Love) than Dr Swift.

Mr. Swift exhibited his Testimonial

[interleaf p. 12:]

See Page 17$^{th.}$

[Letter II]

your care in my Testimonium, . . .

[interleaf p. 17:]

This seems to have been the <u>Testimonium</u> already spoken of Page 12th which <u>Swift</u> perhaps had purpose[d]ly left behind him at Dublin: His Uncle probably sent it after him, and the effect it had at Oxford, might naturally lead him to say, It was to very good purpose.

few weeks to strangers, than ever I was in seven years to Dublin College.

[interleaf pp. 17-19:]

A Friend of mine observed to me, that the expression Seven Years, made the degree of Master of Arts seem more probable to be granted, <u>Speciali gratia</u>, than that of Batchelor of Arts, but Although <u>Swift</u> was not a resident in Trin. Coll. Dub. He had belonged to that College seven years: and probably looked upon himself as a member of it, and expected (for he had pride enough to expect any favour) that his former disgrace should have been, in some measure, recalled, or obliterated. However my friend, who has one of the most quicksighted minds I have ever known, and who is one of the best critics of this or any age, has hit upon a particular, which did not Strike me before he mentioned it. The particulars I received, in the manner which I have inserted (tho' not in the words) from <u>Deane Swift</u> Esq: and ^{lately} <u>George Faulkner</u> confirmed them to me again. <u>George</u> had begun a life of the Dean.

Upon the whole, I shall endeavour to make farther enquiries into the time and manner of Swift's taking his degree at Oxford, and at Dublin.

Nov:^{br} 9. 1751.

As during my friend Swift's residence . . .

[interleaf pp. 21-28:]

My Accounts of <u>Stella</u>, are drawn in general, from anecdotes sent to me by M^{rs} <u>Whiteway</u> or Mr Swift, but as there are among those anecdotes, Some particulars, which ought to be remembered, not printed, I shall here cause them to be transcribed, word for word, from the original Letters.
[scribe's hand:]

<u>Stella</u> was the daughter of <u>Sir William Temple's</u> Steward. She was allowed by the Dean's sister (a bitter enemy of hers) to be the very picture of her mother's husband: and this M^{rs} <u>Fenton</u> would insist on whenever she heard the aspersion of her being Sir William Temple's daughter mentioned, because as she expressed herself, "<u>she ought to give the Devil his due</u>" [Orrery's hand:] In another letter, Mrs Whiteway says, [scribe's hand:] Stella was a most amiable woman both in mind and person. <u>Doctor Sheridan</u> who attended <u>Stella</u> in her long and last sickness said, that before he gave her the Sacrament for the last time, she talked largely to him on her intimacy with the Dean. She said, she well knew, how much her Character had suffered: that what the world said, had no effect upon her because she knew herself his wife: but his being unwilling to acknowledge her as such, had torn her mind, untill her body was unable to support life. That about three months before her death, he had offered, and prest her to let him acknowledge the marriage, which was all the satisfaction that was then in his power. She answered, that it was then too late for her to enjoy the only honour she had ever wished: that her own conduct freed her from any fears of hereafter, and as she was now past the world's farther censures, it would do her no service. Thus died a Woman

whose merit deserved a better fate. The Dean's grief was violent and lasting. He shut himself up for a week even from the sight of his Servant, who was not permitted to make his bed; and took so little nourishment, that his friends feared for his life: for many years after, he never named her, and to the last of his understanding, never without a sigh. He kept two public days in every week from the time he was made Dean untill her death: but then dropt it, and never cared after to see more in his house than a few select friends.

[Orrery's hand:] I much question whether the Dean ever offered to own the marriage. I have many reasons to think that he did not. If he had, I cannot see the least cause, why his wife should refuse the offer.

In another Letter Mrs Whiteway says,

[scribe's hand:] Stella certainly lived in Ireland from the year 1704, but how long before I cannot tell. When she came over first, her wit and politeness recommended her to a large acquaintance in the best families there. Her own fortune was a thousand pounds. She lived in handsome lodgings. She was always intimate with Doctor Swift. She was not married to him till two or three years after he was Dean. Yet after marriage she lived just in the same manner she had done before: for it was an established resolution between them never to live in the same house together, nor in the same neighbourhood. From the time she first came over, she always lodged on the north side of the river in Stafford Street, Caple Street and upon Ormond Quay, where she lodged in 1723. Indeed after her marriage, she was scarce acquainted with any woman. Her companions and his were the same: during her life he kept two public days a week, Sunday and Thursday, and then she always dined with him, as I believe she did with him, or he with her, at all other times, when they were not engaged abroad. In private houses wherever he dined she was generally, if not always one of the Party. When he was out of Town, as he frequently would be for a Month, six weeks, and sometimes a whole Summer: she then resided in his house, and entertained his Company, in the same manner as if he was at home. In the year 1724, her health began to be impa[i]red, and her illness was encreased and confirmed about a year after. she died at Harbourhill near the Deer-park where she had lived about eight months; for the benefit of the air. She left her fortune after the decease of some two or three relations in England to support a Chaplain at Stephen's Hospital in Dublin, provided the Clergyman were of episcopal ordination: She signed her Will by her Maiden name.

[Orrery's hand:] In another Letter Mrs Whiteway says,

[scribe's hand:] These are moral reasons sufficient to convince us, that Stella was the Dean's wife. Yet, if she was not, it is impossible for the most inveterate enemy that the Dean or Stella ever had, to fix a dishonour upon either of them: for it was never known, that they had been in private together, nay all the precautions imaginable were used, to hinder even the colour of suspecting it, and in all companies nothing was ever observed between them, but the highest friendship affection, and decorum.

[Letter III]

satyrical copy of verses entitled The Discovery.

[interleaf p. 31:]

In the London edition of Swift's works This Poem is printed, but, I believe, imperfectly.

Laracor and Rathbeggan, were bestowed upon Dr. Swift.

[interleaf pp. 31-32:]

These Livings were given to Dr Swift, by the Earl of <u>Drogheda</u> (C.M.'s Father) with a kind of tacit agreement that the livings should be given back to Lord Drogheda when Dr Swift was farther and more advantagiously preferred in the Church. L^d <u>Drogheda</u>, as soon as <u>Swift</u> was made Dean of St. Patrick's, sent to put him in mind of the agreement, and desired him to give up the livings. <u>Swift</u> returned in answer, "That till he saw <u>Lord Drogheda</u>, give up any one thing of which he was in possession, He was resolved to follow his Lordship's example, and retain his two Livings: because he possessed them."

He generally chose to dine with waggoners, hostlers, and persons of that rank

[interleaf p. 34:]

He has often told me, that he did this, in search of humour, and vulgar witticisms: but, in general, was disappointed in the search. The vulgar, (as he expressed it) being much more of the brute, than of the human, Species.

Swift was accordingly set aside on account of youth,

[interleaf p. 36:]

This Story is told, I think, by some other author. I cannot recollect by whom. I hope, and believe, It is an Author of no great note.

[Letter IV]

By reflexions of this sort, we may account for his disappointment in an English bishoprick.

[interleaf pp. 48-49:]

In Volume the 2^d. Page 129th. Is a very severe poem, that evidently proves the violence of <u>Swift's</u> resentment, The two first Lines may be read thus,

By an old red hair'd, murd'ring Hag pursued,
A crazy Prelate, and a royal Prude.

And again in Page 131st, Line[s] [53-54] of the same Poem, The Asterisks are to be thus filled up,

Now ^{Madam Coningsmark} her vengeance vows,
On <u>Swift's</u> reproaches for her murdered Spouse.

This alludes to the murder of Mr Thynne (<u>Tom</u> of ten thousand) who some time before his death, had been privately married to Lady <u>Ogle</u> (widow of Lord <u>Ogle</u>) afterwards Dutchess of <u>Somerset</u>. M^r <u>Thynne</u> was killed in Pall-Mall: Shot in his coach: by Count <u>Coningsmark</u>. His Lady was, entirely innocent of his death: but <u>Swift's</u> revenge knew no limits: his motto was,
<u>Hectore Si nequed Supros Acheronta movebo.</u>

[Letter V]

Binfield, December 8, 1713.

    Sir,
[interleaf p. 53:]

I am of opinion, that this letter has more wit in it, than any one letter of M^r <u>Pope's</u> that has been hitherto printed. Certain I am, that it is more entertaining than, in general, <u>Pope's</u> letters are. No fears for his mother. No complaints of the age, of booksellers, of Philips, Lord Harvey, or Lady Mary, are to be found here. Yet here is bitterness in abundance.

He saw the Queen declining in her health, . . .

[interleaf p. 59:]

Dr Arbuthnot, in January 1714, told the chief Ministers, "If you have any great design in hand, you must do it soon, for, I am very certain the Queen cannot live a year."

[Letter VI]

If we consider his prose works, we shall find a certain masterly conciseness in their style, . . .

[interleaf pp. 62-64:]

I am afraid that in this ^{Instance,} I am vulnerable. correctness would be a better word, in this place, although the conciseness of Swift's Style, is very remarkable. But ^{from} what follows, I fear, a seeming impropriety. Do I not seem to prove the conciseness, by the majestic, nervous, grave, style of Tillotson? Yet on the other hand I may boldly answer, that Swift is, in many places as easy, and delicate, as Addison, as grave & majestic as Tillotson. but neither Tillotson nor Addison, are in any part of their works as concise as Swift.

In these interleaves, I write down my thoughts, just as they occurr to me: and I have entered this memorandum, by way of shield, in my storehouse of arms against snarling, nibbling Critics.

[Letter VII]

I should hope that all the minutiae of his idle hours might be entirely excluded

[interleaf p. 83:]

See Letter the 20th, and Page the 255th of the manuscript Leaves.

Dr. Sheridan was a schoolmaster, . . .

[interleaf pp. 84-87:]

Many years ago, A Copy of Verses were given to me, by Dean Ward, upon Doctor Sheridan. These, I had intended to introduce into Sheridan's Character, but upon reviewing them, I altered my design, as finding the Satyr too severe: and more especially as they might be thought indecent, and filthy in the Close. They are witty, and run thus,
                    [scribe's hand:]
Tom was a little merry grig,
Fiddled and danc'd to his own jigg:

Good-natur'd, but a little silly,
Irresolute and shally shilly.
What he cou'd do he cou'd not guess
They mov'd him like a man at chess.
Swift told him once that he had wit,
Swift was in jest, poor Tom was bit.
Thought himself Son of a second Phoebus,
For ballad, pun, lampoon, and rebus.
He took a draught of Helicon,
And swallow'd so much water down
He got a dropsy. Now they say 'tis
Turn'd to poetic diabetis:
And all the liquor he has past,
Is without spirit, salt, or taste.
But since it past, Tom thought it wit,
And therefore writ, and writ, and writ.
He writ the wonder of all wonders:
He writ the blunder of all blunders.
He writ a merry farce for poppet,
Taught Actors how to squeak and hop it:
A treatise on the wooden man[a],
A ballad on the nose of Dan[b],
The art of making April fools,
And four and thirty punning rules.
The learned say that Tom went snacks,
With philomaths for almanacs.
Though they divided are, and some say,
He writ for Whaley[c], some for Compsay[c]
Hundreds there are who will make oath
Nay who will swear, he writ for both.
And tho' they made the calculations,
Tom writ the monthly observations.
Such were his writings. But his chatter
Was one continued clitter clatter.
Swift slit his tongue, and made him Talk,
Cry, Cup of sack, and walk, knaves, walk.
And fitted little prating Poll,
For wiry cage in common hall.
Made him expert at quibble jargon,
And quaint at selling of a bargain.
Poll he cou'd talk in diff'rent linguos,
But, he could never learn distinguos.
Swift tried in vain, and angry thereat,

Into a Spaniel turn'd his parrot.
Made him to walk on the hind legs,
And now he dances, fawns, and begs.
Then cuts a caper o'er a stick,
Lies close, will whine, and creep, and lick,
Swift puts a bit upon his snout,
Poor Tom he dares not look about:
But, soon as Swift once gives the word,
He snaps it up, tho' it were a ****.

a. The sign of a wooden man in Essex Street. Dublin.
b. A person remarkable for a nose of an enormous size.
cc. Two almanac makers in Dublin.

Candour and truth are the chief points that I have had in view,

[interleaf p. 89:]

Hanc veniam petimusq damusq vicissim.
Horat. De Arte poetica. V.11.

I had once inserted this line from Horace, but upon second thoughts, I imagined it too trite, and quotations ought if possible to be new. at least very uncommon. Of all Authors, we may find the most apt quotations in Horace. But he has been so thoroughly gleaned both by good and bad Writers, that it is a little difficult sometimes, to chuse out and extract such passages as shall be equally good, both in propriety, and novelty.

[Letter VIII]

Phocion is the Earl of Portland . . .

[interleaf pp. 94-97:] [scribe's hand:]

1. Phocion who had been guilty of no other crime, but negotiating a Treaty for the Peace and Security of his Country. Page 39.
2. Aristides, besides the mighty service he had done his Country in the Wars, he was a person of the strictest justice, and best acquainted with the Laws, as well as forms of their Government; so that he was in a manner Chancellor of Athens. Page 16.
3. Themistocles was at first a Commoner himself. It was he who raised the Athenians to their Greatness at Sea, which he thought to be the true and constant interest of that Commonwealth; and the famous Naval Victory over the Persians[a] at Salamis,[b] was owing to his Conduct. Page 16.

4. The People of Athens impeached Pericles for misapplying the public ^{Revenues} to his own private use. He had been a person of great Deservings from the Republic, was an admirable Speaker, and very popular; his accounts were confused; and he wanted time to adjust them.

[Orrery's hand:] So far seems perfectly applicable to the Character of <u>Lord Hallifax</u>, but what follows, is not so perfectly intelligible: he continues the paragraph and says, [scribe's hand:] "therefore merely to divert that difficulty, and the consequences of it, he was forced to engage his Country in the Peloponnesian War, the longest that ever was known in Greece; and which ended in the utter ruin of <u>Athens</u>." Page 17.

[Orrery's hand:] This last part does not tally, with the account given to us by <u>Tindal</u>, in his continuation of Rapin. Vol. XIX Book 25. Page 279. 8vo edition. <u>Tindal</u> tells us, that, [scribe's hand:] The Commons charged him, ^[Lord Hallifax] for a grant that he had in Ireland, for another grant out of the forest of Dean, for holding places that were incompatible, and for advising the two Partition treaties.

[Orrery's hand:] <u>Swift</u>, in the same Pamphlet, again draws up the four characters in a clearer manner, his words are [scribe's hand:] <u>Aristides</u> was the most renowned by the People themselves for his exact Justice and knowledge in the law. <u>Themistocles</u> was a most fortunate Admiral, and had got a mighty victory over the great King of Persia's fleet. <u>Pericles</u> was an able Minister of State, an excellent Orator, and a Man of Letters: and lastly <u>Phocion</u>, besides the success of his Arms, was also renowned for his negotiations abroad; having in an embassy brought the greatest Monarch of the World, at that time to the Forms of an honourable Peace, by which his Country was preserved. Page 21.

[Orrery's hand:] Here the characters seem to answer each other exactly enough, and <u>Phocion's</u> success in arms (Lord Portland was no military man) being printed in different characters, shows the author obliged to introduce that sentence, to keep up the Grecian story.

    a. The French.   b. La Hogue.

The tritical essay on the faculties of the mind, will make you smile.

[interleaf p. 99:]

Here the word Smile comes too close upon the same word used in Page 98th in the last line but one.

he would be startled for to find himself guilty in a few sentences,

[interleaf pp. 99-100:]

For to and A few are introduced as instances of bad english. The word <u>For</u> immediately before <u>To</u>, is unnecessary, improper and absurd: and <u>A Few</u> is ungrammatical. <u>A</u> must always belong to the singular number. <u>Few</u> must always have a plural Signification.

[Letter IX]

A bad rhyme appeared to him one of the capital sins in poetry

[interleaf pp. 104-5:]

Swift, notwithstanding his care and correctness has fallen into an error, which he always censured in others. I mean, <u>Irish rhymes</u>, for so he called them: for example,
[scribe's hand:]

> Or harness'd to a Nag at Ease,
> Take Journeys in it like a Chaise;
> > Vol. 2^d. Page 28th. V. 111.
> My Lord, who, if a Man may say't
> Loves Mischief better than his Meat.
> > Vol. 2^d. Page 80th. V. 13th.
> Soon grows domestick; seldom fails
> Either at Morning, or at Meals.
> > Vol. 2^d. Page 83^d. V. 77th.
> Despis'd luxurious wines and costly meat;
> Yet still was at the Tables of the Great.
> > Vol. 2^d. Page 130th. V. 15th.

Her mother, whose name I forget,

[interleaf p. 105:]

I have since learnt, that her name was Esther Stone.

"Nature," said Vanessa, "abhors a vacuum, . . .

[interleaf p. 112:]

The Cartesian Doctrine, taught by <u>Cartesius</u>, or <u>Descartes</u>.

nor to conceive the distinctio rationis

[interleaf p. 112:]

"Distinctio rationis, is that between several things which are really one and the same and whereof one cannot exist without the other: such as, the rational distinction between a thing, and it's essence: between the Essence and properties &c."
See Chambers. Word Distinction & Seq.

He answered her in the non-essential modes.

[interleaf p. 112:]

"Non essential modes, (or Separable Modes) are attributes affecting created substances, and remaining affixed thereto, so long as it is necessary. Such as coldness of water. &c."–Peevishness and ill humour of D[r] Swift.–See Chambers. Word, Mode.

[Letter X]

But, still I cannot recollect one poem, nay, scarce a couplet, to his noble patron Lord Bolingbroke.

[interleaf p. 126:]

In the 8th Volume of Swift's works, Page 163[d]. in the Poem entitled Verses on the death of D[r] Swift, are these Lines,

> St. John himself will scarce forbear
> To bite his Pen, or drop a Tear.

But these only commend L[d] Bol[ke's] humanity & friends[p]. not a word of his genius.

In that instance, he has been as silent, as Virgil has been to Horace,

[interleaf pp. 126-27:]

I am a little doubtfull whether this assertion be perfectly reconcileable with an attempt afterwards in these letters, Letter 23, Page 314, to prove that Virgil has mentioned Horace. The truth [is] that attempt was begun, late in the series of these letters. I had finished, and I believe had printed twenty one of my letters, before I was resolved, or indeed had settled that criticism. As it stands in this collection, many passages, and quotations are omitted: and possibly I may think it worth my leisure, to form that essay into a more perfect and enlarged commentary. However, I hope what is said in Page

311th, makes my application, concerning Lord <u>Bolingbroke</u>, perfectly reconcileable with all that is said hereafter in favour of <u>Virgil</u>, for I do not pretend to prove, but I would willingly flatter myself, that <u>Virgil</u> has mentioned Horace.

that the portrait of Daphne was drawn for herself:

[interleaf p. 127:]

Lady Atchison. wife of Sir Arthur Atchison. Separated from her husband.

[Letter XI]

as if reflected from a concave mirrour,

[interleaf pp. 135-38:] [scribe's hand:]

Copy of M^r. Benjamin Wilson's letter to the Earl of Orrery.
Saturday. 2^d. Novr. 1751.
My Lord,

On my return home last night I sat down to read the Remarks on Swift, and in page 135, I met with the following lines. The Inhabitants of Lilliput are represented as if reflected from a concave mirrour, by which every object is reduced to &c.

The Printer, I believe, has made a mistake in the word concave as your Lordship will readily perceive. In a Work so truly great and elegant as this, it would be pity any thing should be inserted that May hurt the Reader. Errors of the like kind I have experienced in my own little trifling performance, where, instead of <u>elastic</u> the printer has put <u>electric</u>, and <u>restitution</u> for <u>restitutive</u>. I beg your Lordship's pardon for taking this liberty. I was induced to it from two Reasons. The one, that so little a circumstance might very easily escape your Lordship's observation, and the other, that as the Book is not yet published the mistake may be corrected time enough.

I would have waited upon your Lordship on this occasion, but could not with convenience.

> I am, My Lord,
> your Lordship's
> most obliged & most obedient
> humble Servant
> Benjamin Wilson.

[Orrery's hand:]

What Chambers, in his dictionary says, of concave & convex mirrours, confirms Mr Wilson's Observation, his words are, [scribe's hand:] Objects placed between the focus and mirrour must appear of enormous magnitudes in concave mirrours; the image being so much the greater in the concave mirrour, as it is less in the convex.
[Orrery's hand:]
The Error, was the error of the Press, for, I think it is impossible that even in the manuscript, such a mistake could have escaped my eye, but it has ^{so} unscientific an appearance, that I recalled as many of the copies as I had given to particular friends, (except some few, about three which were gone beyond Sea) and reprinted the leaf, so that the public edition stands now corrected in that instance, which gives me no small Satisfaction.

> *humble servant,*
> *M. Whiteway.*

[interleaf p. 141:]

Dr Swift, used to call Mrs Whiteway, M^{rs}

as to place the resurrection . . . in a ridiculous, and contemptible light.

[interleaf pp. 146-47:]

The Passage is this, They bury their dead with their heads directly downwards, because they hold an opinion, that in eleven thousand moons, they are all to rise again: in which period, the Earth (which they conceive to be flat) will turn upside down, and by this means they shall at the resurrection, be found ready standing on their feet. The Learned among them confess the absurdity of this doctrine: but the practice still continues in compliance to the vulgar.

[Letter XII]

in general written against chymists, mathematicians,....

[interleaf pp. 147-48:] [scribe's hand:]

Mem. Mathematicians have been so fond of shewing the extensive uses of their art, that they would have it considered as a master key of all knowledge human and divine. Craig a Scotchman in a Treatise dedicated to the Bishop of Salisbury has from these principles demonstrated the duration of the Christian religion. he lays it down as an axiom that all human Testimony whether given by a person inspired or otherwise, amounts only to a probability, which must ^{want} its original force in a certain proportion to the distance of time from the origine of it, and become at last an evanescent Quantity. And from thence attempts Algebraically to demonstrate, that the christian religion can last only 1454 years longer, but as he firmly believed Revelation, he from thence concludes, that Jesus Christ will come to judge the World before that time, and prevent the total eclipse of the true religion.

However wild the description of the flying island,

[interleaf pp. 150-53:]

Roger Bacon who is said to have been a good mathematician, a knowing mechanic, a rare chymist, and a most accomplished experimental philosopher, (but in that dark age, accounted a Magician) affirms that he knew how to make an engine in which a man sitting, might be able to carry himself through the air like a bird, and that there was a person who had tried it with Success. Later instances have not been wanting in England of several ingenious men, who have employed their wits and time about the design, and particularly one Mr Gascoigne, about 40 years since with good success, but soon dying, the art also died with him.

Another flying Philosopher, was the Sieur Besnier: his manner is described in the Philosophical Transactions. From this, Projector Swift seems to have borrowed his description of his flying island, and the order of it's motion.

The Figure of a flying Man is described in Lowthorpe: and his demonstration is this, [scribe's hand:] When the right hand strikes down the right wing before A, the left leg by means of the string E pulls downwards the left wing before B, then immediately after the left hand moves, or strikes downwards the left wing before C; and at the same time the right foot by the string F moves or pulls down the right wing behind D, and so successively or alternately, the diagonally opposite wings always moving downwards. Swift's scheme is more simple: for by only changing the situation of the load stone, the island performs its alternate motions in an oblique direction.^a it's motion is likewise more uniform, one degree in a day agreeable to the System of Copernicus, tho' it must be allowed, that Swift's manner of demonstrating his project is more perplexed than Besnier's as he employs one letter more of the Alphabet.

[Orrery's hand:] Bishop Wilkins

[scribe's hand:] See Lowthorp's abridgement of the Philosophical transactions Vol. 1. Page 499. See Philosophical transactions Vol. 1. Page 500, Fig. 182, between the pages 538 & 539.

[Orrery's hand:] a. Swift. Volume 3^d Chap. 4th P. 205.

[Letter XIII]

The first airy substance introduced is Alexander the Great . . .

[interleaf p. 157:]

Plutarch tells us (in his Life of Alexander) that Darius spoke of Alexander, in the last moments of his life, in these words, But Alexander, whose kindness to my mother, my wife, and my children, I hope the Gods will recompense, will doubtless thank thee.

The famous picture of Lebrun, is a representation of Alexander's compassion to the Family of Darius. The royal tent is there represented, and the conqueror sees the mother wife and children of Darius at his feet. Tenderness, pity, and generosity are visible in Alexander's countenance.

his rash actions of inebriety,

[interleaf pp. 158-59:]

Inebriety. This word, in an anonymous letter, is thought new, and affected. I own that it is new, and I believe it is not to be found either in Bailey, Dyche, or Defoe. I have ventured to coin it from the verb inebriate, [To make drunk] and I think it is justifiable, not only from such a derivation, but as it avoids a very impolite word, [drunkenness] and is neither shocking to the ear, nor difficult to be understood.

Perhaps the Author of the letters, loves his friend drunkenness so well, that he is sorry to see any word substituted in it's room. I leave him therefore to enjoy his drunkenness at leisure, wishing him as much drunkenness, as he can possibly desire.

with no other view than to censure Livy the historian.

[interleaf pp. 159-62:]

See Livy Lib: 21. Cap: 37. The words are, [scribe's hand:] Quum caedendum esset saxum, arboribus circa immanibus dejectis detruncatisque struem ingentem lignorum faciunt: eamque (quum et vis venti apta faciendo igni coorta esset) succendunt, ardentiaque saxa infuso aceto putrefaciunt. Ita torridam incendio rupem ferro pandunt, molliuntque anfractibus modicis clivos, ut non jumenta solum, sed elephanti etiam deduci possent. [Orrery's hand:] The english translation of which, runs thus, [scribe's hand:] "Then the Soldiers were set to level the rock, by which alone they could find a passage. In order to split it, huge trees were felled and laid round it. Thus they raised a great pile of Wood, and when the wind blew favourably for it, set it on fire. When the rock was red hot they poured vinegar on it to calcine and dissolve it. Being thus heated by the fire, they dug into it with pickaxes, and made the descent easy by moderate windings, so that not only the cattle, but even the elephants could be brought down it."

[Orrery's hand:] In the tenth Satire of Juvenal, This fact is mentioned, in a very strong manner: beginning at V. 146. Quandoquidem data sunt ipsis quoque fata Sepulcris. Expende Hannibalem: quot libras in duce summo invenies? Hic est. Quem non capit Africa Mauro Percussa Oceano Niloque admota tepenti. Rursus ad Aethiopum populos, aliosque Elephantos additur imperiis Hispania: Pyrenaeum Transilit Opposuit Natura Alpemque nivemque: Diducit Scopulos et montem rumpit aceto. These lines are translated by Mr Dryden, and The four last being most to the present purpose, need only be inserted. V 242. Spain first he won, the Pyrenaeans past, And Steepy Alps, the mounds that Nature cast; And with corroding Juices, as he went, A Passage through the living Rocks he rent. This seems to confirm my observation that the Romans lookt upon the story of the Vinegar to be true. otherwise Juvenal would scarce have inserted this circumstance, which the poet here signalizes as one of the great actions of Hannibal's life.

Pliny the elder, speaks of the passage over the Alps, as a miracle. his words are, Quos transcendisse quoque mirum fuit. In perbento prope majores hebure Alpes ab Hannibale exsuperatis, et postem a cimbris.

Cap.1. Vol. 2 Pag. 723.

A modern eminent writer,

[interleaf pp. 163-65:]

This eminent writer is Doctor Middleton: who thus translates, a part of one of Tully's Letters,

[scribe's hand:] Caesar, having taken a vomit just before, he eat and drank freely, and was very chearfull.

[Orrery's hand:] Upon which the Doctor makes the following remark. [scribe's hand:] The custom of taking a vomit both immediately before and after meals, which Cicero mentions Caesar to have done on different occasions [pro Deiot 7] was very common with the Romans, and used by them as an instrument both of their luxury, and of their health: they vomit, says Seneca, that they may eat, and eat that they may vomit [Consol. ad Helo. 9] by this evacuation before dinner, they were prepared to eat more plentifully; and by emptying themselves presently after it, prevented any hurt from repletion. Thus Vittelius, who was a famous glutton, is said to have preserved his life by constant vomits, while he destroyed all his companions who did not use the same caution: [Sueton: 12. Dio 67.734.] and the practice was thought so effectual for strengthening the Constitution, that it was the constant regimen of all the <u>Athletae;</u> or the professed Wrestlers, trained for the public shews, in order to make them more robust. So that <u>Caesar's</u> vomiting before dinner was a sort of compliment to <u>Cicero,</u> as it intimated a resolution to pass the day chearfully, and to eat and drink freely with him. See Doctor Middleton's life of Cicero Vol. 2. Pages 245 & 246.

[Orrery's hand:] I am a little apprehensive, that I may have Stretched D[r] <u>Middleton's</u> meaning rather too far. yet the words seem to bear very strongly against Caesar, especially in instancing <u>Vitellius.</u>

The extravagant virtue of Junius Brutus . . .

[interleaf p. 166:]

Plutarch, in his Life of <u>Marcus Brutus,</u> speaks thus of <u>Junius Brutus,</u> [scribe's hand:] "But that ancient Brutus was of a severe and inflexible Nature, (like Steel of too hard a temper) and not at all softened by Study or Education; nay, he suffered himself to be so far transported with his Rage and Hatred against Tyrants, that for conspiring with them, he proceeded to the execution even of his own Sons."

In Epaminondas the Theban glory . . .

[interleaf pp. 166-67:]

<u>Cornelius Nepos,</u> has written the life of <u>Epaminondas:</u> and concludes it by saying, Thebas & ante Epaminondam natum et post ejusdem interitum perpetuo alieno paruisse imperio: contra ea quam diu ille praefuerit reipublicae caput fuisse totius Graeciae, ex quo intelligi potest unum hominem pluris quam civitatem fuisse. See Plutarch, Zenophon, <u>Diodorus,</u> and <u>Polybius.</u>

I am in some doubt, whether Cato the Censor . . .

[interleaf p. 167:]

<u>Marcus Portius Cato,</u> Native of Tusculum, Great Grandfather of <u>Cato</u> of <u>Utica.</u> See Plutarch. Cicero. Corn. Nepos.

Rhadamanthus in the Archbishop of Cambray's dialogues of the dead, . . .

[interleaf pp. 167-68:]

The words are (I have not the original at present, and by way of memorandum must have recourse to the english translation) in Dialogue 34.th ~ [scribe's hand:] 'Twould be scandalous to place an Usurer in the Elysian Fields; you shall therefore remain at the Gate.

[Orrery's hand:] The Conclusion of the Dialogue terminates thus, [scribe's hand:] "Here's Money for you, lend it the Dead, who shall not have wherewith to pay <u>Charon's</u> Fare; but if you lend Money in Usury, <u>Scipio</u> will give me notice of it, and I'll punish you as the most infamous of Villains."

Late, very late, may you become a ghost!

[interleaf p. 169:]

The expression, Late very late may you become a ghost, has been criticised. Take it singly, perhaps it may sound affectedly, but surely it is natural enough in consequence of the preceeding Subject of the Letter.

[Letter XIV]

a happier metempsychosis

[interleaf p. 171:]

<u>Translatio Anima</u>, A passing of the Soul from one body to another. This doctrine of Pythagoras, is particularly mentioned by <u>Ovid</u>. Metam. Lib XV. V 158.

> Morte carent anima: semperque priore relicta
> Sede, novis domibus habitant, vivuntque receptae.

Homer and Aristotle were as opposite as possible in their characters:

[interleaf p. 173:]

[scribe's hand:] They speak variously of <u>Aristotle's</u> conduct towards his Master Plato.
                    Vide Bayle's Dictionary. Arts: Aristotle.

It is on this account that the Dean has introduced Aristotle. . . .

[interleaf p. 174:]

Lord <u>Bacon</u> speaking of <u>Aristotle</u> says, <u>Pessimus Sophista, inutili Subtilitate attonitus, verborum vile Ludibrium</u>. See Bacon. De Interpretatione Naturae. Cap. 2. Vol. 2. P. 259. In the same Chapter, he mentions, <u>Scotus</u>, <u>Petrus Ramus</u>, and <u>Aquinas</u>. He says, Nullum mihi ^{commercium} cum hoc ignorantiae latibulo [Petro Ramo] &c. and again Atque <u>Aquinas</u> quidem cum <u>Scoto</u> et sociis etiam in non rebus rerum varietatem effinxit hic vero &c.

He never quotes an author but with a view

[interleaf p. 175:]

but] This word has escaped me. It ought to be [except] as the word <u>But</u>, in my opinion is always improper in the middle of a sentence. It may be altered in future Editions.

Like the Ottoman Emperor, he could not reign in safety, till he had destroyed his brethren.

[interleaf p. 175:]

Lord Bacon's expression is, Reliquos vere physicos certe fuisse, atque ex iis non nullos, qui <u>Aristotele</u> longe et altius acutius in naturam penetraverint; Atque Illum Scilicet Ottomanorum more in fratribus trucidandis occupatum fuisse. Page 273. Vol. 2.

He passed the greatest part. . . . he taught his philosophy.

[interleaf p. 177:]

Taken from Sir Wm Temple, almost word for word. See Vol. 1. P. 175. folio edition.

for in his last moments . . . hausit aquas.

[interleaf p. 178:]

I took this from <u>Lord Bacon</u>, whose words are, [scribe's hand:] <u>Scribitur etiam de Epicuro, quod hoc ipsum sibi procuraverit; cum enim morbus ejus haberetur pro desperato, ventriculum et sensus meri largiore haustu et ingurgitatione obruit. Unde illud in Epigrammate:</u>
  <u>Hinc Stygias ebrius hausit aquas</u>
<u>vino scilicet stygii laticis amaritudinem sustulit.</u>

[scribe's hand:] See Lord Bacon de Augmentis Scientiarum Lib. 4. Vol. 1. Pag. 126.

De qua [amicitia] Epicurus . . . et moribus comprobavit.

[interleaf p. 179:]

Cicero De Fin. Bon. et Mal.

> Lib 1. S 20.
> Verbuggii. Edit. Folio.
> Vol. 2. P. 601.
> Lib: 10. Vide Segm. 10.

Sir William Temple says, . . .

[interleaf p. 179:]

[scribe's hand:] See Sir William Temple upon the Gardens of Epicurus; or of Gardening, in the year 1685. Volume the first, Page 174. folio.

Gassendi was esteemed one of the greatest ornaments of France.

[interleaf p. 181:]

His works are printed in six volumes in folio. (curante Nicolas Averanio Advocato Florentino) 1737. In the first of which is a kind of dedicatory preface, Samuelis Lorberii, in which is continued the life of Peter Gassendi.
Gassendi has written the life of Peiresscius (Monsieur Peiresc). See the Article in Bayle. Peiresc.

[Letter XV]

Atque affigit humo divinae particulam aurae.

[interleaf p. 186:]

. . . Vides ut pallidus omnis Cena desurgat dubia? quin corpus onustum Hesternis vitiis animum quoque praegravat una atque affigit humo &c.
Horat. Satir. 2. Lib. 2 V.76.

[Letter XVI]

His treatise, or proposal,

[interleaf p. 196:]

The words Treatise, and Proposal ought to have been in Italics.

which are so often intermixt in Swift's works.

[interleaf p. 197:]

Here the word <u>intermixt,</u> is twice repeated, too close to each other. In the next edition, this fault shall be amended, but it is impossible to avoid errors of this Kind.

[Letter XVII]

If party, and the consequences of it . . .

[interleaf p. 209:]

Mr Addison has written an excellent Spectator upon Party. N°. 125. Vol.2. Page 169.

[Letter XIX]

Thus the friendship between Atticus and Hortensius, . . .

[interleaf pp. 231-32:]

<u>Doctor Middleton,</u> speaking of the Death of <u>Hortensius,</u> (in his life of Cicero, Sect. 7. P. 61. Vol. 2. 8vo) says, [scribe's hand:] Cicero, in the case of his exile, discovered the plain marks of a lurking envy and infidelity in <u>Hortensius:</u> yet his resentment carried him no farther than to some free complaints of it to their common friend Atticus.

[Orrery's hand:] <u>Atticus,</u> was an Epicurean, see Middleton. Sect. 1. P. 42. Vol. 1. 8vo.

Cornelius Nepos, in his life of Atticus, Cap. 16 has this expression, [scribe's hand:] <u>cum aequalibus autem suis Q. Hortensio & M. Cicerone sic vixerit, ut judicare difficile sit, cui aetati fuerit aptissimus: quanquam eum praecipue dilexit Cicero, ut ne frater quidem ei Quinctus carior fuerit, aut familiarior.</u>

Harrington has his admirers, . . .

[interleaf p. 236:]

His chief ^{and I believe only} work is his Oceana, An account of it, may be found in the notes upon his name, in Bayle's dictionary. He was appointed Groom of the Bedchamber to K Charles the 1st in his troubles. was esteemed by him, but his principle of republicanism, the King much detested. He behaved himself to the King with fidelity & honour. His life is written by Toland. He is mentioned by Sr Thomas Herbert in the memoirs of Charles the 1st. Page 89 & 90.

and could only attribute it to Mr. Cowley, . . .

[interleaf p. 237:]

In <u>Bayle's</u> Dictionary, under the article <u>Sprat</u>, in the notes Letter C are inserted these Verses, from an Ode of Cowley's to the royal Society.

> His candid Stile like a clear Stream <u>does</u> Glide,
> And his bright Fancy all the way,
> <u>Does</u> like the Sun-Shine in it play,
> It <u>does</u> like Thames, the best of rivers glide,
> Where the God <u>does</u> not rudely overturn
> But gently pour the chrystal Urn,
> And with judicious head <u>does</u> the whole current guide.
> T'has all ye beauties nature can impart,
> And all the comely dress, without the paint of art.

Cowley's poetical style <u>does</u> not <u>do</u> him much honour.

See Mr Addison's account of Cowley,
Great Cowley then, a mighty genius, wrote &c.

the dignity and ease of Pliny, . . .

[interleaf p. 241:]

<u>Pliny</u>, in the character of politeness, must certainly have been very remarkable. His conversation was easy, and although there is a peculiar stiffness and affectation, in his letters, yet his private life, and manners, appear from those letters to have been amiable and engaging. He lived in Courts, unenvied & unblameable. (Else the parallel [with Bolingbroke] will not hold) In private retirement, with greatness of Soul, and superiority of manners.

[Letter XX]

He must be viewed through a camera obscura. . . .

[interleaf p. 252:]

Quaere. Is the expression Through perfectly proper? Might it not rather be expressed From? or By?

than by composing various kinds of nonsense, . . .

[interleaf p. 255:]

When I ^have^ mentioned and regretted the great quantity of Nonsense, I would not be understood false English or ungrammatical paragraphs, of which there are few or no instances   when I complained to Lord C—d of the Nonsense, in Faulkner's Edition, Aye, says he, But It is Swift's nonsense. Many I suppose may be of L^d C—d's opinion, and therefore we must despair of ever seeing an elegant edition of Swift's Works.

(allowing one small alteration, the word permitted, instead of connived at)

[interleaf pp. 256-59:]

The word connived, generally, if not always carries with it a bad sense. It implies a disposition not to be named, or thought of with the Deity, whose justice, and decrees are right in whatever manner they may appear to our limited sight. I have somewhere read a remarkable story, applicable and in support of my Assertion.

"It is recorded," says my anonymous Author, "among the records of the jewish rabbis, that God called to <u>Moses</u>, as he stood on <u>Mount Sinai</u>, and ordered him to look on the plain below. <u>Moses</u> in obedience to God's Command, looked down, and saw a soldier come from the Camp of the Israelites, to an exceeding fine spring, (in a wood) where he quenched his thirst, but in drinking dropt his purse. After he was gone, a little boy came to drink at the Spring, and seeing the purse took it up, and went away with it. Soon afterwards, an old venerable man came much fatigued, to drink and refresh himself at the same fountain, but before he would taste of the water, he knelt down, and worshipped God in the devoutest manner: and then sat down by the side of the Spring. The Soldier, who had mist his purse, returned to the Fountain, and finding the old man there, taxed him with having stolen the purse. The other protested his innocence, and called heaven to witness to his truth and asseverations. The Soldier, still more and more enraged, at not finding his money, killed the old Man, and fled into the wood, in security. <u>Moses</u> was astonished at the sight of so much injustice. but God called to

Moses, and said, Wonder not Moses, at the ways of my providence. The Boy's Father was murdered and robbed by the old man, and the Soldier who lost the purse had stolen it."

I cannot recollect the story so particularly as it is related, and I have only written down the heads of it here, that I may search for the book in which I read it. But the Story, tho' a Fable carries with it an excellent moral.

digito compesce labellum.

[interleaf p. 261:]

Juvenal. Satir.1. V.160.
Be Silent, and Beware if Such you See.

Dryden. V 243.

[Letter XXI]

Lunacy may in general be considered

[interleaf p. 267:]

In the last Spectator on the Pleasures of the Imagination. Vol. 6. N° 421. Mr Addison treats of a distempered Brain, & says, "that Babylon in Ruins is not so melancholy a Spectacle."

Pol me occidistis, . . . gratissimus error.

[interleaf p. 270:]

Horat. Epis. 2. Lib.2. V.138. The Story begins, Fuit haud ignobilis Argis. The Epistle has been translated, or rather imitated by Mr Pope: and the particular passage relating to the madman (whom Mr P. turns into a Lord) is thought by Mr Warburton, to exceed the original.

Warburton's Pope. Vol. 4. Page 228 & 229.

and suicism.

[interleaf pp. 275-76:]

Suicism. In an anonymous letter, without a name, This word is criticised, as new, and created by me. a power, which the author thinks, I ought not to assume. I dare assume such a power, in defiance to all critics whatever, when I make no wanton or improper use of this literary license. Such, I hope, is the instance of the word <u>Suicism,</u> which distinguishes the fact, from the person who commits it. It is equally ^{as} proper, as <u>deism</u> and <u>deist</u>: and therefore I cannot allow the criticism to be just.

Critics in the dark, are the Sons of envy, pride, and malice. I despise their envy, I detest their pride, and I scorn to revenge their malice.

[Letter XXII]

to heat their porridge, or drink their small beer . . .

[interleaf p. 284:]

This alludes to this particular paragraph, [scribe's hand:] "When you have broken all your earthen Drinking Vessels below stairs (which is usually done in a Week) the Copper Pot will do as well; it can boil Milk, heat Porridge, hold Small Beer, or in Case of Necessity serve for a Jordan; therefore apply it indifferently to all these uses; but never wash or scour it, for fear of taking off the Tin."

and many more are trifling,

[interleaf p. 299:]

Among his Trifles, There are some so low and ridiculous, that they are astonishing; for example, In a letter to Dr Sheridan, Vol. 8. P. 465. He invents a letter to a Mistress, consisting only of the Alphabet without forming it into Syllables. Thus.
[scribe's hand:]
Dear Ellin, you are a beauty. I esteem you a Deety. Your Empire endures. O! be your beauty endless. A tear effaces your beauty. You are a gem. A jewel. A ruby. I see a bee pick your eye. I beseech you take care O'your eye. I seek a remedy. You are eaten. Your excellencies are seen. You are too wise. You are a peeress. I see a Peer be for you. I obey you. I desire your pity. O! happy you are. You are experience. You are generosity. You are perspicuity. You are eloquence. Your decency, and sincerity, affability appear. You are a curiosity. Right honourable your elogy. Your beauty defies Apelles a painter. You see I entertain you well. You see Katty's jealousy.

[Letter XXIII]

The first of these, The Tale of a Tub,

[interleaf pp. 300-301:]

An Extract of a Letter from Deane Swift Esq; to me, in answer to one wherein I had exprest the general surmizes, that Swift was not Author of the Tale of a Tub.

[scribe's hand:] "There is no doubt, but that he was Author of the Tale of a Tub. He never owned it: but as he one day made his Relation Mrs Whiteway read it to him, he made use of this expression. Good God! what a flow of imagination had I, when I wrote this. And another time in the Battle of the Books Well I think I was revenged on those pinioned Woodcocks Wooton and Bently, for attacking my two favourites Boyle and Temple.

He shewed it to M^{r} <u>Waring</u> his Chamberfellow at the College in his own handwriting."

one of his uncle's sons, a clergyman:

[interleaf pp. 304-6:]

[scribe's hand:]   The Character of the Revd Mr Thomas Swift, Cousin German of the Dean of St Patrick's In a Letter from Dean[e] Swift Esqr.

The Son of <u>Thomas Swift</u> by a daughter of <u>Sir William Davenant</u>. He and Doctor <u>Swift</u> are much of the same age: both were educated at Kilkenny School. It is certain that Thomas Swift is a man of abilities, but Wit and Humour are not his talent, as may be judged from his Sermon occasioned by the peace, and dedicated to my Lord Oxford, in which, without the least genius for Wit and Humour, he seemed in his dedication, and sermon to be eternally aiming at both.   He was led into that mistake by the great encouragem^{t} which was given by that ministry to all sorts of genius. I have several letters by me from <u>Thomas Swift</u> written from the year 1690 to 1708. They are honest, plain, good sense, yet I confess they sometimes squint a little at Wit and Humour. The style of them is neither Ease nor elegant. The phrases are not ill chosen, but then they have a cast of rusticity. In short, let <u>Thomas Swift</u> be what he will, he never was capable of writing three lines in the Tale of the Tub.

NB. This last paragraph was in answer to a letter from the Earl of Orrery, wherein he had told him, of a report that had reached him, that a Cousin of Doctor Swift's had been the real Author of the Tale of a Tub: A performance which although never owned by the Dean of St Patrick's was certainly his own, as Mrs Whiteway has assured Lord Orrery.

Horace's Glycon

[interleaf p. 312:]

<u>Invicti membra Glyconis</u>. Lib.1. Ep.1. V.30.

at the bottom of the statue of the Hercules Farnese

[interleaf p. 312:]

A. Γ λ υ ϰ ω ` γ   A θ ε , ν α ι̃ ο ς   E ϰ ο ι̃ ε ι   A model of this statue, [The Hercules] is in Doctor Mead's Library: with the greek inscription.

Tibullus

[interleaf p. 315:]

  A. Et Quodcunque mali est, et quicquid triste timemus
     In Pelagus rapidis devebat omnis aquis
Tibull. Lib.1. Carm.4.

Anacreon

[interleaf p. 315:]

B. ' Α ϰ ο ϰ ρ ι ϰ ⸴ τ ο ν τ α I   μ ε ρ ι μ ν α̃ I
    Π ο λ υ Τ ρ ο ν τ ι δ ε ς   τ ὲ β α̃ λ α I
    E ς ά λ ι ϰ τ ύ ϰ α ς   ά η ΄ τ α ς.
Ode λ θ.39.

Monsieur Dacier,

[interleaf p. 316:]

  <u>Monsieur Dacier</u>, expresses himself thus. [scribe's hand:] On ne trouve ancun Poete Lyrique dans tout le temps que s'ecoula, depuis la premiere guerre Punique, jusqu'au siecle d'Auguste. Ainsi depuis la foundation de Rome, jusqu'a cet empereur, c'est a dire dans l'espace de plus de 700 ans, les Romains n'avoient connu d'autre Poesie Lyrique que sa premiere ebauche, c'est a dire Les Hymnes Saliens, et ces cantiques informes que l'on chantoit a table en l'honneur des Heros. Mais alors, on vit tout d'un coup, paroitre Horace qui né avec un heureux naturel et aidé par la lecture des Lyriques Grecs, imita, la premier, la poesie <u>d'Alcée</u>, de <u>Stesichore</u>, <u>d'Anacreon</u>, de <u>Sapho</u>.
[Orrery's hand:] Dacier. Preface P.44.
Semper equos atque arma virûm pugnasque canebat.

[interleaf p. 317:]

The word Semper, seems to be the greatest objection to this conjecture.

Monsieur Sanadon observes, that . . .

[interleaf p. 317:]

Quarto Edition. In his remarks upon Ode 17 (Ode 1) of the 2^d Book. Tom 1. Page 226.

to lay aside all intentions of writing a tragedy . . . the danger of the theme.

[interleaf pp. 318-24:]

This, upon a more carefull review of the Ode, is, I am afraid a mistake. Horace at the same time that he advises Pollio, to pursue his design of writing an account of the civil wars in verse, seems to dissuade him from it by representing the difficulty of the undertaking, and shews his own Skill on that Subject, which, in all probability he had a mind to reserve to himself.

The mistake therefore lies in saying that Asinius Pollio intended to form a tragedy on that Plan. He had been eminent for his performances in theatrical poetry before. Monsieur Sanadon's words are, "On vit sortir de sa plume plusieurs tragedies, qui, au jugement de Virgile et d'Horace, egaloient le teatre de Rome a celui d'Atene." Horace now encourages Pollio to pursue a different way of shewing his talents, and recommends to him, to reassume, (after a poem on the civil wars) the subjects in which he had formerly acquired such a reputation. The words are

> −Mox ubi publicas
> Res ordinaris, grande munus
> Cecropio repetes cothurno.

You may reassume the Task in hereafter. &c. The sentence, in the next edition, must be altered, perhaps something in this manner.

In his ode, beginning Motum ex Metello, He advises Asinius Pollio, to lay aside his tragic muse in which he had so eminently excelled, till he had executed his great design in describing the civil wars between Anthony & Octavius: and yet the poet points out such dangers as might alarm and terrifye him from the attempt. Then pursue the present form from the words He tells Pollio. page 318.

These are only hints, and memoranda, to be executed, or laid aside as I shall see proper, but as I have discovered the mistake it is proper that it should be altered and amended.

NB. I have now hit upon an amendment which, I think, will answer the purpose, and the paragraph runs thus.

P. 318, & 319.

–he advises Asinius Pollio to lay aside all intentions of writing tragedy and he farther urges him to compleat a poem upon the civil wars between Anthony and Octavius, but he damps this advice, by pointing out the danger of the theme. He tells Pollio,

> Periculosae plenum opus aleae
> Tractas: et incedis per ignes
> Suppositos cineri doloso.

Thus, while he expatiates &c. In a full and correct Essay upon Creteas, (wch I intend to undertake and perfect, one day or other) This quotation from Horace, and the observations upon it, may be more minutely expatiated, and the design of the Ode, more amply ascertained. Sanadon's ^account (Translated by Mr Dunkin) is this, [scribe's hand:] "Pollio since the Year 715 [from the foundation of Rome] lived in a private manner at Rome, and in his retirement had written several Tragedies, which in the judgement of <u>Horace</u> and <u>Virgil</u>, had equalled the Stage of Rome to that of Athens. But a Work better meritting his whole strength and attention was a History of the Civil Wars. <u>It was already far advanced, when the Poet wrote this Ode</u>, and being apprehensive lest that applause which Pollio received from the Stage, might interrupt an History so interesting to the Republic, he urges him in the strongest manner to continue it, yet tells him at the same time, how delicate and dangerous a work he had undertaken."

[Orrery's hand:] The Title to the Ode, <u>Motum ex Metello Consule</u>, in the Edition <u>Delphini</u> is, this, [scribe's hand:] Lib.2. Ode 1.

C. Asinium Pollionem monet ut bella civilia describere intermittat: tum laudat ejus scripta.

[Orrery's hand:] The Title in Sanadon, stands thus,

[scribe's hand:] Carmen XVII. Lib.II. Ad Asinium Pollionem. Hortator ut, intermissis tragaediis, det se totum scribendiae bellorum civilium historiae.

[Letter XXIV]

His aversion to kings was invincible.

[interleaf pp. 326-27:]

In the 8th Volume of <u>Swift's</u> Works, in a Poem, To a Lady, who desired the Author to write some verses upon her in the heroic Style, are some asterisms, Page 329, which the Dean filled up in this manner,
[scribe's hand:]

> Where a Monkey wore a Crown,
> Must I tremble at his frown.
> Cou'd I not, through all his Ermin,
> Spy the strutting chatt'ring Vermin.
> Safely write a smart lampoon,
> To expose the brisk Baboon.

> *and the whole atmosphere*

[interleaf p. 331:]

Atmosphere. [scribe's hand:] [Atmospherae, L. of ʾΑτμὸς a Vapour, and ΣΤαῖρα a Sphere, Gr.] is the lower Part of the Region of the Air or Aether, with which our Earth is encompassed all round; and up into which the Vapours are carried, either by reflection from the Sun's heat, or by being forced up by the subterraneous fire. F.

and has pointed to us, in what element our chief strength is appointed.

[interleaf p. 334:]

Notwithstanding all the pains I have taken, I found two words of a similar sound (although of a different sense) have slipt in here too close to each other.
The word pointed . . . . Line 8.
And the word disappointed . . . . Line 9.
Mem. This must be altered in all future editions. commencing with Mr Faulkner's.

(Insuevit pater hoc me, ut fugerem exemplis vitiorum &c.)

[interleaf p. 339:]

The whole Passage in Horace runs thus

> Insuevit pater Optimus hoc me
> ut fugerem exemplis vitiorum quoque notando.

Horat. Sat 4: Lib.1. V.106.

The <u>Pater Optimus</u>, was not an expression which I could decently use. I have therefore thrown the quotation into a Parenthesis, in a careless manner. I am far from thinking that I deserve the title of <u>Optimus</u>, in any point whatever, but were I capable of such an acquisition, I own I could wish for it particularly in the character of a Father.

[Index follows]

[first unnumbered page:] [scribe's hand:]

A List of the Persons to whom the Earl of Orrery gave his Life of Swift.
1. The Countess of Orrery.
2. Lord Boyle.
3. The Honble. Hamilton Boyle.
4. The Honble. Edmund Boyle.
5. Lady Lucy Boyle.
6. Lord Chesterfield.
7. Countess Dowager of Sandwich.
8. Countess Dowager of Peterborow.
9. Mr Dawkins.
10. The Rev^d. D^r. Nicholls.
11. The Rev^d. Mr Birch.
12. Dr Mead.
13. John Lowes Esqr.
14. Wm Melmoth Esqr.
15. Moses Mendez Esq.
16. Dr Hill.

[second unnumbered page:]

17. Dr Tibal.
18. Mr Johnson.
19. Doctor King.
20. David Garrick Esq.
21. Mr Mossop.
22. Mr Saldkeld.
23. Mr Marsh.
24. Dr Haye.
25. Mr Wilson.
26. Mr Bale.
27. M^r. Coniers.
28. M^r. James Scott.
29. M^r. Jempson.

30. M^r. Bickle.
31. M^r. James Harris.
32. Daniel Hughes.
33. The Rev^d. D^r. Pickering.
34. The Rev^d. M^r. Dickings.
35. D^r. Matty.

[third unnumbered page:]

36. William Cowper of Chester Esq.
37. M^r. Carbridge.
38. The Honble Mr Hamilton Boyle.
39. Mr Herbert Bowen.
40. Lady Eliz:th Worsley.
41. The Honble. Caple Moore.
42. Doctor Armstrong.
43. M^{rs}. Long.
44. M^r. Deards.
45. M^r. Carte.

[all the names in the list have a mark drawn by Orrery next to them, except Lord Boyle, Countess Dowager of Sandwich, Countess Dowager of Peterborough, Mr. Dawkins, William Melmoth, and Dr. Pickering]

[fourth unnumbered page blank]

[fifth unnumbered page:] [scribe's hand:]

In the London Evening Post, of Tuesday November 5th. 1751 was printed the following Advertisement,
[pasted:]
In a few Days will be published,
Beautifully printed on a fine Paper in one Volume, Octavo,
Price bound Five Shillings,
(*With a Head of the* DEAN, *etch'd by Mr.* WILSON)
REMARKS on the LIFE and WRITINGS of
Dr. JONATHAN SWIFT,
Dean of St. Patrick's, Dublin.
In a Series of LETTERS from JOHN Earl of ORRERY, to
his Son, the Hon. HAMILTON BOYLE.
"Haec sunt quae nostra liceat te voce moneri.
"Vade, age.

Virg. Aeneid III. p. 461.
Printed for A. Millar, opposite Catherine-street in the Strand.

[scribe's hand:]
and on Thursday the 7th of Nov[r]. 1751, was printed, in the same paper, the following Advertisement

[pasted:]
This Day are publish'd,
Beautifully printed on a fine Paper, in one Volume, Octavo, Price bound 4s.
(With a Head of the Dean, *etched by Mr.* Wilson)
REMARKS on the Life and Writings of Dr. JONATHAN SWIFT, Dean of St. Patrick Dublin. In a Series of Letters from JOHN Earl of ORRERY to his Son the Hon. *Hamilton Boyle.*
Printed for A. Millar, opposite Katherine-Street in the Strand.

[scribe's hand:]
Mem: The whole impression of 1500, being published according the above Advertisement, were all disposed of by the Editor M[r]. Andrew Millar, on Saturday November the 9th.
The quickest sale that has ever been known of any book.

[sixth unnumbered page:] [scribe's hand:]

In the London Daily Advertiser of Wednesday November the 13th. 1751, was printed the following Advertisement
[pasted:]
To-morrow will be Published,
A NEW EDITION of
Mrs. PILKINGTON'S MEMOIRS.
In which is inserted,
Her celebrated Account of the Immortal Dean SWIFT.
Very proper to be read and compared with that just
published by the Earl of ORRERY.

[scribe's hand:]
In the London Daily Advertiser of Thursday November 14th. 1751 came out this Advertisement thus

[pasted:]
This Day at Noon will be Published,
Complete, in Two Volumes, TWELVES,
(Price Six Shillings bound in Calf)
A NEW EDITION of
Mrs. PILKINGTON'S MEMOIRS.
In which is inserted,

Her celebrated Account of the Immortal Dean SWIFT.
Very proper to be read and compared with that just
published by the Earl of ORRERY.
ALSO,
Her Anecdotes of the late Mr. POPE, and several other
eminent Persons, living and dead.
Printed for R. Griffiths, at the Dunciad in Paul's Church-yard.

[inner back cover:] [Orrery's hand:]
Errors. to be amended in future Editions.
Letter 14. P. 175.
Letter 16. P. 201. the Note at the bottom 363.
Letter 24. P. 331.
Letter 11. P. 135. For <u>Concave</u>, read <u>convex</u>.
Letter 23. P. 305. For <u>Critisms</u> read <u>Criticisms</u>.

Manuscript Notes in Houghton 16423.3.4*

[inner front cover:] [Orrery's hand:]

Orrery. Leicester Fields, November 21ˢᵗ 1751.

[page numbered 1:] [scribe's hand:]

In the London Evening Post of Saturday November 23ᵈ 1751, was printed this Advertisement

[pasted:]

Next Week will be publish'd,
A NEW EDITION,

Beautifully printed on a fine Paper in a small Octavo Size,
With a Head of the DEAN *finely engrav'd by* Ravenet,
Price 2*s*.6*d*. sew'd in blue Paper,
REMARKS ON THE LIFE AND WRITINGS OF
DR. JONATHAN SWIFT,
Dean of St. Patrick's, Dublin.
In a Series of LETTERS from JOHN Earl of ORRERY, to
his Son, the Hon. HAMILTON BOYLE.
"Haec sunt quae nostra liceat te voce moneri.
"Vade, age.   Virg. Aeneid III. v.461.

Printed for A. Millar, opposite Catherine-street in the Strand. ***As there is a very great Demand for the above Book, it will be only sew'd in blue Paper, both on Account of the Sheets not being dry enough to bear binding, and that the Publick may be supplied with it as soon as it's possible.

[page numbered 2:]

[Orrery's hand:] From the London Magazine.
[The Monthly Catalogue for November 1751, section headed "Divinity and Controversy," is pasted, and Orrery marked the entries referring to the *Remarks*:]

18. Remarks on the Life and Writings of Dr. Jonathan Swift, in a Series of Letters from John Earl of Orrery, to his Son Hamilton Boyle, pr. 4s. Millar. (See p. 483.)

19. The same in a small Size, pr. 2s.6d. sew'd. Millar.

[page numbered 3:]

[Orrery's hand:] From the Gentleman's Magazine.

[Heading "New Books, &c. published Nov. 1751," section "History, Geography," is pasted, and Orrery marked the entry referring to the *Remarks*:]

2. Remarks on the life and writings of Dr. Jonathan Swift; in a series of letters from John E. of Orrery, to his son the hon. Hamilton Boyle. 8vo. 4s. *Millar*. See p. 483.

[frontispiece, title page, text, and index of MI follow. Then, pages with manuscript notes follow. The hand is the scribe's throughout, except where otherwise noted.]

[page numbered 1:]

Particular papers, and Memorandums relating to this Edition of Doctor Swift's Life.
Mem.

This first edition was published on Thursday November 7th, and on Saturday November the 9th Mr Millar, the Editor, had disposed of the whole Edition, fifteen hundred, at 4^s a Volume bound.

[page numbered 2:]

N° 1.

An Epigram published in the London Daily Advertiser and Litterary Gazette of Saturday November the 16th 1751.

On reading Lord Orrery's Remarks on Dean Swift.

If common Mortals common Failings share
(And who's exempt that is frail Adam's Heir?)
What wonder, Pride should swell the enlighten'd Mind
That shone superior to half Human Kind;
Yet from Swift's faults does this advantage flow,
It is to Him another Boyle we owe.
C. Marsh.

[page numbered 3:]

N° 2.

Copy of a Letter from Lord Bolingbroke, on having received from Lord Orrery a present of Swift's Life.

Battersea. Saturday night.

My Lord,

I make my humble acknowledgements to your Lordship for the Remarks on the Life and Writings of Doctor Swift, which you have been so good as to send me.

You have done great honour to his memory, without making to it the sacrifice of any truth. To me you have done much more than I can pretend to deserve, except by the sincerity and zeal with which I shall continue as long as I live, a friend to my country, and to your Lordship

> a most devoted friend and a most
> obedient humble Servant
> H S^t J V Bolingbroke.

[page numbered 4:]

N° 3.
The London Daily Advertiser. Wednesday November 20th 1751.
The Inspector N° 225.

Dic verum mihi, Marce, dic amabo,
Nil est quod magis audiam libenter.

Horace.

The Observations which accompany a late Translation of the Letters of Pliny, raised expectations in me, from a second work by the same Hand, not easily to be satisfied; nor had the friendship the noble Author has since honoured me with, a little share in that warmth with which I waited this later fruit of his pen. It is with more than joy, it is with a kind of triumph that I find the Friend and Critic equally satisfied in the perusal: that I see the Earl of Orrery expressing as happily

[page numbered 5:]

his fondness for his British Friend, as his reverence for the Roman Consul; and painting in as glowing colours the open honesty of the one, as the reserved greatness of the other.

The piece is an Essay in biographic writing, of a quite new kind: There is in it nothing of the aukward formality, nothing of the stiff harangue with which those writings are in general too much loaded, and which is the characteristic of most of them. A pleasing air of familiarity runs through the whole: We are all the way hearing from a Friend, not learning from a Writer, the several passages of the History; but the written Conversation, if I may be allowed the phrase, though it have [*sic*] none of the false pomp of these Writings, wants nothing of their genuine Dignity; and is throughout at least as

[page numbered 6:]

far removed from the mean or trifling as from the ostentatious.

His Lordship has shewn himself in it, a consummate Master of Style, and has exerted more of the happy Art of varying it in order to adapt it to the several occasions, than I can remember to have met with in any English Author. He no where forgets that he is an Epistolary, not an Historical Writer: There is not a passage that bespeaks his ever losing sight of his being a Father writing to a Son; to one whom he at once makes his Pupil and his Companion, his Disciple and his Friend; yet there is not any one of the Letters in which the Subject rises, or becomes more familiar; in which it is copious or steril; where every phrase, every Sentence, and almost every word, are not adapted to its immediate Object. When he delivers his general opinion of the writings of his Author, he preserves the

[page numbered 7:]

true, simple, unaffected Language of the Critic; but where he speaks of his, and occasionally mentions with it, that of several other of our British Writers, he follows closely the Steps of the noble Greek, and gives its precepts which are themselves Examples.

'Tis easy to discern the benignity of Heart in this noble Author, throughout the whole Course of the Work, and to discover that the raising a Trophy to the Immortal Memory of his Friend was the original motive to his writing. The bestowing applause upon the illustrious Dead, was evidently the first principle; but Applause only could not have satisfied the public Candour which accompanies the private warmth of affection that is visible in this, and all other writings of his Lordship. We see him every where the friend of Socrates; but we see him also the Inviolable friend of Truth. The failings of the great character he draws are touched, though it be lightly, as well

[page numbered 8:]

as its Excellencies: and tis in many places, easy to see the affection of the Friend struggling with the Impartiality of the Historian, and giving up the Contest with a glorious Reluctance.

It is extremely happy for us to have the Character of a Man we so much interest ourselves about, drawn by a hand as incapable of partiality, as above misrepresentation. There has, perhaps, scarce ever lived a Man so singular in his Humour and Manners as Dr Swift; nor any one whose Singularities we could be more earnest to be acquainted with: The greatness of his genius gives us an eagerness to be informed of every particular of his temper; and 'tis no common piece of good fortune, that we have the means of seeing these displayed by an intimate acquaintance who has talents equal to his opportunities of judging of them; and who, while he comprehends all the Excellencies of his genius

[page numbered 9:]

as a Critic, can tell us of the Foibles of the Man as a Friend.

There are a Multitude of little Incidents delivered in the Life of this eminent Man, which were wholly unknown to the World before, but which are so perfectly consistent with ^{the} rest of his Character, that we should not have doubted of their truth, though related on a less authority. That he was married to his Stella, is a Circumstance which but few had even suspected, and which scarce any body had ever known with Certainty, but from this Work: and his private Friendships and Animosities are not only mentioned in it, but traced to their origin; and they serve, in this light, to explain many parts of his Conduct otherwise scarce intelligible.

The Character of Dr Sheridan, in the Seventh Letter, is drawn with an uncommon Spirit and Accuracy: It is every where

[page numbered 10:]

consistent, and, tho' far from a common one, is, in all its parts, so regularly deducible from nature, actuated by the Passions which his Lordship has given as the characterising ones of the Man, that there remains no room, even for one who is a Stranger to every thing relating to the person, to doubt the reality. I may add, that tho' we were before well acquainted with the Name of Dr Sheridan, we never at all understood his real Character, and for want of that first step, could never form any true idea of the nature of Swift's friendship for, and connection with him. The Wife of the Dean is pictured in the same happy manner; and the sketches of other persons interested in the history, though less at large, are not less accurately, or less characteristically drawn.

Such are the occasional pictures exhibited by his Lordship of the friends and dependants of Dr Swift; but 'tis in his own character that

[page numbered 11:]

we see the most perfect touches of this kind. There is not a single incident in his Life that does not point out the Man, and vouch for its own Truth, without appealing to the Authority from whence it comes. His beginning the Church Service, when no body but his Clerk was present, with <u>Dearly beloved Roger the Scripture moveth You and Me in sundry places</u> and a number of others of the same kind, are not only things that could have happened to no Man in the World but himself, but they are such as he could not have missed. Such are the strokes of his private Character as an Author, it is certainly no more than Justice that Lord Orrery does him, when he declares, <u>There is a masterly conciseness in his Style, that has never been equalled by any Writer.</u>

[page numbered 12:]

I cannot finish my Observations on a Work which has given me so much pleasure without a proper notice of the generous pains the Author has occasionally taken to vindicate the Character of <u>Virgil</u> from the charge of Ingratitude, with which it has been long branded, on a supposition of his never having mentioned his friend and cotemporary <u>Horace</u>, in any of his Writings. His Lordship delivers it as his Opinion, that the <u>Creteas</u> of <u>Virgil</u> is this Poet. The thought is perfectly new, and the Lines

> – <u>Amicum Cretea Musis,</u>
> <u>Cretea Musarum comitem, cui carmina semper,</u>
> <u>Et citharae cordi, numerosque intendere nervis</u>

very strongly countenance the opinion. The succeeding line, tho' to a common Reader it may seem not quite so applicable to the Character his Lordship has very happily reconciled to his judgement of the Passage, and upon the whole, tho' the thing itself

[page numbered 13:]

be incapable of demonstrative proof, there is great appearance of Reason on its Side; and 'tis evident that we receive, as undoubted Certainties, many things supported by much weaker Testimonies, though mellowed by Time, and familiarized by Custom to our Belief.

I'm sorry that I find it necessary, after giving my own Sentiments of the Author of these Letters, to mention those of the Writer of half a dozen lines* published without my knowledge in one of these Papers: I hope I shall be excused from saying more on this subject, than that I am confident, they were meant as a Compliment.

*See the Epigram Page the 2^d.

[page numbered 14:]

N° 4.

To Doctor Hill at the Bedford Coffee House
in Covent Garden.
<blockquote>The Post Mark Oxford.
Received by Doctor Hill November 23^d, 1751.</blockquote>

Mr Inspector,

As you favoured me with some Critical Observations upon my Lord Orrery's excellent account of Dr Swift, we have been much surprized here to find, that you took no notice of the many elegant new words with which his Lordship has enriched our Language: such as are <u>inebriety, suicism, revert</u> &c. We cannot but with pleasure observe, that you yourself have profited much in this last paper, by an exact imitation of the dignity of style, so eminent in some parts of his Lordship's works. "<u>You follow closely the steps of the noble Peer, and give us pre-</u>

[page numbered 15:]

<u>-cepts which are themselves examples</u>." We very readily allow, that his Lordsp's Essay <u>in the Biographic kind is entirely new</u>; as he has copied no one, so we are apt to imagine, that no one will, or can copy him: at least the familiar part (such as, my Ham, my dear Ham, dearest Ham &c) we are confident is inimitable. We are as willing to clear his Lordship from any imputation of Pedantry; he has even given room to some dull fellows to suspect, that he has not lately been very conversant in the Greek tongue, since rather than shock our Ears with the Name of <u>Cretheus</u> (a rough old fashioned Greek) he has introduced <u>Horace</u> with the Nom de Guerre of <u>Creteas</u>, borrowed as we presume, from that polite people the Aethiopians.

[page numbered 16:]

To take leave of you in his Lordship's most affectionate phrase, <u>Late, Mr Inspector, very late may you become a Ghost</u>: long, very long may you survive your Works: May you meet with a <u>Diamond</u> as fair, and more constant than the last: and when at last you go where <u>Ridpath</u>, where <u>Roper</u>, and where <u>Osborne</u> went before, may you be one of those chosen few, whose daily labours encourage young Actors, flatter bad Authors, and put ten shillings into the Writer's pocket.

[unnumbered page:]

N° 5.
An Epigram on the foregoing Letter to the Inspector, N° 4.
By Mr Tibal.

> Manners and Learning once Oxonium apud
> Mollibant mores, polibantque Caput.
> Fate lik'd it not, the Place she sat a Curse on.
> There now each Mind's as awkward as each person.

[page numbered 18:]

N° 6.

The London Daily Advertiser
of Wednesday November 27. 1751.

The Inspector. N° 231.

Variety is so essential an Article in the plan of this Undertaking, that I shall very rarely devote two papers to the same Subject: I have not however, any where absolutely protested against this; and I am willing to believe it will be long, before I have an occasion on which the Public will more readily be reconciled to the doing it, than in my paying a proper regard to the farther Observations of a Correspondent, on a Subject which has lately, and I would hope not dissatisfactorily employed my own pen.

[page numbered 19:]

To the Inspector.

> Tum uno ore omnes
> Bona dicere, & laudare fortunas meas
> Qui Patrem haberem tali ingenio praeditum.

Ter.

Sir,

I have been sharing with thousands of <u>my Countrymen</u> the pleasure of that rational Entertainment with which the Earl of <u>Orrery</u> has presented us; and though I am sensible none but such a hand as wrote the Observations on <u>Pliny's</u> Epistles, should presume to give Remarks on the Letters of this noble Author, I cannot help giving you my thoughts on an Entertainment, which yourself have enabled me to taste with a higher relish.

I cannot content myself with say-

[page numbered 20:]

-ing in general that these Remarks on the Life and Writings of Dr Swift afford at once one of the most curious Essays in Biography, and the most delicate piece of Criticism, that have appeared in our Language, I must descend to particular Observations on the united excellencies of the Work. It is impossible to employ one's thoughts on the Subject without observing, that but very few of our English Life-writers have suc[c]eeded. Take away that of <u>Cicero</u> by Doctor <u>Middleton</u>, that of <u>Lord Bacon</u> by M^r <u>Mallet</u>, and the Enquiry into the Life and Writings of Homer by $\underline{M^r}$ <u>Blackwell</u>, and the pieces of $\underline{M^r}$ <u>Birch</u>, and a very few others, and we may reckon the rest of our Biographers on a footing with our common Journalists, News writers, Registers, and Ordinaries: The Birth, Age

[page numbered 21:]

Office, and Death of their Author is all they inform us of; unless they add to these accounts some common place Character, applicable in general to any good or any bad person, without the Singularities which characterize every one, or the private anecdotes, which as a judicious Critic observes, are the best Openings to the real Character.

These kind of Writers may, I think, be compared to the modern Sign-post Painters, who undertake to draw every thing, and draw every thing alike: One may have as adequate an idea of the Person of the <u>Duke of Cumberland</u> who conquered the Rebels in 1746, or <u>Admiral Vernon</u> who took <u>Porto Bello</u> in 1738 from these sign dawbings, as of the Characters of <u>Pope</u>, <u>Addison</u> and <u>Gay</u>, in such Histories of their Lives as have hitherto appeared. M^r <u>Cowley</u> indeed met a happier fate: but if he be immortalized by having had D^r <u>Sprat</u> for his friend and his historian, yet greater circumstances of honour will attend to latest Posterity the name of D^r <u>Swift</u>, in that he had a person of his Rank and Genius for his friend, his biographer, and his Commentator.

[page numbered 22:]

If we are pleased with the varied manner in which his Lordship relates the minute but essential parts of his Author's character, we must be charmed in almost every Letter with the several other parts of the Character of this amiable Historian. It is impossible to read them, without being in love with the tender affection, and the conscious happiness of the Father, joined with the unambitious disposition of the Philosopher, and the candid impartiality of the Friend. If we are eager to know all the Historical Circumstances in the Life of so extraordinary a person as Dr Swift, we must be happy to find we hear them from an intimate Friend, and on an indisputable Authority.

So much for the manner in which his Lordship has introduced his account of Dr Swift: I shall now give you, Mr Inspector, a few Remarks which I made in the perusal. The first five Letters

[page numbered 23:]

contain the great Occurrences of Swift's life; these gave me all that pleasure which I have felt from the just Conduct of the five Acts in a Dramatic Performance, and in all these the Character of Dr Swift rises to our knowledge with a kind of Theatric effect. In the first Letter, we have his earliest Appearance as it were on the Stage of Life; and the Act closes with a circumstance that may appear very astonishing, Dr Swift's being stopt in the taking a Degree in the University for Insufficiency. On this occasion, Sir, I would, though at an humble distance, attempt to follow this noble Author in his Observations on Pliny's epistles, and after his manner remark, that we have more than this one instance of a great genius being obscured from a Conjunction with the brightest bodies. There is a Tradition in the University of Cambridge, that Sir Isaac Newton was

[page numbered 24:]

stopt in his degree there; the reason was the not following the Philosophy of Descartes, but attending to the progress of his own Understanding, and experience in those Studies. What success Mr Locke met with at Oxford every body knows; and if he was above the reach of any Attack in matters of learning, yet he suffered the severe blow of expulsion from his College for his political principles, by Royal Mandate. That Milton also took some disgust at the usage he met with at Cambridge, is evident; for, in one of his Latin poems to a friend at College, we find these lines

> Jam me arundiserum mihi cura revisere Camum
> Nec dudum vetiti me laris angit amor

> Nec duri libet usque minas perferre magistri
> Caeteraque ingenio non subcunda meo.

But there was a time to appear in which these several Geniuses should break from this Eclipse with a more triumphant splendor.

The Character of <u>Stella</u> in the second

[page numbered 25:]

Letter, and her private History, is very affecting; and <u>Dr Swift's</u> not owning her for his Wife, though married to her may appear extremely surprizing: but, perhaps, our Astonishment may be lessened, if we reflect that very few of the Men of Wit and Genius, either in Antient or Modern Times have been married. They have thought, perhaps, that it might have seemed a reproach to them, that Men of their exalted and irregular Genius should be bound in Chains of any kind; and indeed of the very few that have been married, it is an unlucky Observation, that the greater part have been unhappy. Among the Antients, <u>Epicurus</u> lived single all his Life; and so did almost all his followers. And among the Moderns, we find <u>Pope, Gay</u>, and <u>Cowley</u>, Batchelors: <u>Milton</u> & <u>Addison</u> indeed were married, and they were unhappy. Within these last years indeed, we have been happy enough to see the Scholar and the Husband shedding mutual lustre on each other; tho' as if it was

[page numbered 26:]

decreed, that such happiness was too great for human beings, it has been, alas! but of short Continuance! And the very Muses seem to have condemned each of these their Favourites to lament the loss of his Lucy,^A and his Harriot.[&]

Lord <u>Orrery</u> has drawn a very happy parallel between the Writings of <u>Horace</u> and <u>Swift</u>; and I cannot help thinking it will equally hold in their Manners. <u>Swift's</u> way of travelling mentioned in the third letter, exactly tallies with Horace's <u>Brundusium</u> Journey; and when we hear of his associating with Waggoners and Hostlers, one cannot help recollecting what Horace says of himself,

> Nunc mihi curto
> Ire licet mulo, vel si libet usque Tarentum
> Mantica cui lumbos onere ulcerit atque eques armos.

Sat: Lib.I.6.

^ASee Monody to the Memory of Lady –

&See Verses to the Memory of Harriot in Lord Orrery's Pliny.

[page numbered 27:]

Dr Swift's innocent Seraglio is quite in the taste of Epicurus, who, we are assured by Diogenes Laertius, had always a Company of Ladies in his Garden, whom he regarded no more than as his Disciples and Scholars in philosophical Conversations.

Instead of farther pursuing the Parallel between Swift and Horace, or Epicurus, I could with pleasure digress into the Resemblance there appears between the Epistles of Lord Orrery and those of Pliny in the drawing the Characters of others, and at the same time shewing us their own. But Lord Orrery is a Father, and here we may with yet greater pleasure observe the resemblance of his epistles to those of Cicero in the tender expressions of his love for his Children, in whose engaging Conversation, the Orator assures us, he used to drop all his Cares, and relieve himself from his Struggles in the Senate and the Forum. With what fondness does the

[page numbered 28:]

Roman speak of his Marcus and his Tullicola? The Son he endearingly calls his Suavissimus et mellitus Cicero, and he preferred, as he tells us, the Company of his daughter to Life itself. The British Writer has addressed with equal tenderness, his Hamilton and his Charles; he has addressed them not only with the fondness of a Father, but with the affection of a Friend. To pursue the allusion still farther, each of the Authors have given tokens of their paternal love to their Sons, while under the course of their Studies; the one to his Marcus at Athens, the other to his Hamilton at Oxford. Cicero formed a project of building a temple to perpetuate the Memory of his daughter; Lord Orrery has actually raised a much nobler trophy to the praises of his Sons, a trophy more durable than marble, and as lasting as the names of Pliny and of Swift.

[page numbered 29:]

And having occasionally mentioned the Marriage of Men of Genius, and their Consequences, I cannot but be curious to know what could induce the Inspector to think of Matrimony, and what will be the Event of his Proposals on that head.

You see the Examples before you: and if you are disposed to be as cold a Lover as the Dean was to his Stella and Vanessa, pardon a Man who wishes your happiness, that he advises you to continue in the State of Pope and his Brother Batchelors.

I am, Sir,
your humble Servant,
Phares.

[page numbered 30:]

This Life of Dr Swift is mentioned in three of the Magazines for the Month of November 1751.

The Gentleman's Magazine.
The London Magazine.
The Monthly Review.

In the Gentleman's Magazine Page 483 is an extract of the work, and some few short passages expressing a defect of certain particulars relating to Dr Swift, as these, "Jonathan married Mrs Aibgail [sic] Erick of Leicestershire, by whom he had one daughter, born in the first year of his marriage, and one Son, afterwards Dean of St Patrick's, who was born on the 30th of November 1667, two months after his Father's death in Dublin, but what called this family thither does not appear."

[page numbered 31:]

And again, in the same page, "What was Mr Swift's profession we are not told." And again "but whether his mother, his uncle, or any other of his Relations had received information where he was, to whom he was delivered, when carried back into Ireland; or whether his Uncle Godwin, who took charge of his education, resided in Ireland or in England, are circumstances about which his Lordship is silent."

The Subject is to be continued in the next Magazine.

In the London Magazine Page 483, is also an extract of Swift's Life, not intermixt with any criticisms, and concluding Page 486, thus, "This will serve to give the Reader some idea of the Life and Writings of the famous dean Swift; but the letters from which it is extracted ought to be read by, and cannot fail

[page numbered 32:]

of being entertaining to every person in the kingdom."

The Monthly Review is not only an extract of Swift's Life, but is intermixt with various criticisms. They begin thus, "The Republic of letters is much obliged to the ingenious and worthy Lord Orrery for this curious and most entertaining performance. For never was there besides the immortal <u>Dean Swift</u>, so famous a writer with whose real birth and private life, the public have been so little acquainted; or concerning which they have been so much misinformed. And though his Lordship's account may not prove entirely satisfactory in every particular

[page numbered 33:]

to the very inquisitive Reader, yet he has given us many facts and circumstances of importance, of which the World might have for ever remained in entire ignorance had not this work appeared."

Again, Page 408. "Here we cannot help observing, that our Noble Author's charity seems to have somewhat biassed him in favour of Dr Swift, whose behaviour and conversation throughout his whole life, were never thought to be very highly tinctured with piety. His Lordship himself has related some instances which at least shew, that he did not always restrain the sallies of his humour from saying and doing things no way consistent with that due reverence for religion, without which the amiable character of

[page numbered 34:]

a good Clergyman will be but poorly sustained. Two of these instances are as follow[s], not to mention others of a more striking and decisive nature, which might be produced from his works."

And again in page 409 & page 410. "<u>Lord Orrery</u> himself introduces this second story with the following observation, 'His humorous disposition,' says his Lordship, 'tempted him to actions unbecoming the dignity of a clergyman: and such flights drew upon him the character of an irreligious man. I remember to have heard a story of him [the story we have just quoted] that fully shews how little he regarded certain ceremonies which ought always to be observed with respect.' But ought such irreverent behaviour in the more immediate presence of God, to be con-

[page numbered 35:]

-sidered only as a disregard of ceremonies? or can a palpable burlesque of the forms of service appropriated to divine worship be supposed to flow from any other than a heart, which was either indifferent to any kind of public Worship, or that really despised the forms he had solemnly assented and subscribed to? The brilliancy of wit, however it may dazzle or delight, or, however humour and drollery may please, when directed to proper object, they certainly become criminal when employed to ridicule things sacred, or that are esteemed as such by truly pious and good persons. Can it be deemed a trifle or an innocent jest, for a person whose more immediate indispensible duty it was, as a divine, to edify others by his good example as well as preaching, to run abruptly, and like a bacchanal, into the midst of an assembly of people supposed to be met together for the most serious and

[page numbered 36:]

awfull purpose, and thereby making such ludicrous impressions upon their minds, as must unfit them for any real devotion for that time – But to proceed with our Author's general character of this most extraordinary man."

Again Pages 415, 416, & 417, "We will not take upon us to affirm, whether our noble Author, or ourselves, have been misinformed in this particular; but we are credibly assured, that the dean, who certainly was excessively fond of his Stella, frequently visited her in private. An honest sober woman who lived in the same house with that unfortunate Lady, declares that the dean particularly visited her very often when she was ill, and usually devoted the time to Religion; and that she frequently, in an adjoining room, overheard him praying extempore, and with greater fervency than ever she heard any other person pray in her life.

[page numbered 37:]

Certainly the Dean must have had some other motive, and a more weighty one, than the ridiculous pride mentioned by Lord Orrery, for his never living or conversing with his Wife, as such. And we cannot yet persuade ourselves not to afford some degree of credit to the report which has been so generally believed, that Swift was really Sir William Temple's Son, and that Stella was also Sir William's natural daughter. This might be very true, and yet neither the Doctor, nor Mrs Johnson know it before they were married. It has been generally asserted, that Swift received a letter from England, the day after his marriage, the purport of which was, That the writer thereof hoped it would not come to his hands too late, to prevent the consummation of a Match which it was rumoured was intended betwixt Dr Swift and Mrs Johnson, for that they were both the natural children of one father: and gave the Doctor sufficient reason to believe that this information was true - But whether the Dean ever did receive, or credit

[page numbered 38:]

such information, or not, it may be impossible for any one now living to prove or disprove. However, certain it is, that such reports have prevailed. It is well known that Sir William Temple was a very amorous man, and much addicted to intrigue with various women; and it is not improbable that such a man as

Sir William should take uncommon precautions to provide well for his natural children, without letting the public, or even themselves, know that they were such.

Lord Orrery reasons thus upon the supposition of Stella's being the Dean's relation in any other degree beside that of matrimony.

'A conduct so extraordinary,' says he [meaning that of the Doctor's manner of living, or rather not living with Mrs Swift] 'in itself &c.'

But will not his Lordsp's supposition of Swift's pride being a probable motive for his owning the daughter of Sir William

[page numbered 39:]

Temple for his wife, appear a little premature, when we recollect, that the same public rumour that made her Sir William's daughter, made him also Sir William's Son? Therefore he could never, with decency, have acknowledged Mrs Johnson as his wife, while that rumour continued to retain any degree of credit: and if there really had been no foundation for it, surely it might have been no very hard task to have entirely obviated its force, by producing the necessary proofs and circumstances of his birth: yet we do not find that ever this was done, either by the Dean, or his Relations.

Indeed for the honour of the Dean himself, we are somewhat inclined to wish that this supposed too near consanguinity between him and Mrs Johnson may appear to have been really fact? As then his conduct towards her may be rationally accounted for, and much more to his credit, than by supposing him capable of

[page numbered 40:]

treating so amiable a Woman (and one too, whom he most tenderly loved) like a brute, merely to gratify an inhuman caprice, or a foolish and vicious pride; and of being the cause of her death, by his tyrannical usage."

Again Page 421. "Here our noble Author introduces a parallel between Horace and the Dean; which his Lordship has ingeniously drawn, but in our opinion it is in some respects rather too much forced. We cannot however but think his sentiments extremely just, in his comparison of Swift with the Archbishop and Mr Addison."

And again, P. 422. "Our Author here gives a short account of the occasion of these letters, which no one can be a stranger to, who has read the Doctor's prose works: and who is not acquainted with the story of Wood and

[page numbered 41:]

his half pence?"

The subject is to be continued in the Monthly Review for next Month.

Doctor Bernard. A letter from the Bishop of Derry to the Earl of Orrery

Dublin Novr 22^d 1751.

My Lord,

I take the earliest opportunity of returning my acknowledgement to your Lordship for the honour done me in remembering me among the List of your Friends, and giving me the additional pleasure of possessing your Works, as an instance of your favour.

[page numbered 42:]

Your own illustrious Ancestors, my Lord, had rendered your task arduous enough: and I find you are determined to give your Sons no easy one. May they follow you in the paths of Virtue and Learning, till they make good the promise they have already given of being worthy such a Parent.

These, my Lord, are the sincere wishes of your Lordship's most obliged, and most faithfull

humble Servant
W: Derry.

[page numbered 43:]

Doctor Clayton. A letter from the Bishop of Clogher to the Earl of Orrery

Dublin Novr 26th 1751.

My Lord,

It was with Pride and with Pleasure that I received your Lordship's acceptable present, by the hands of Mr Faulkner, which I have read over for the first time with greediness; but intend to give it a second reading with more deliberation; as several of your Observations and Reflexions have a solidity in them, not to be thoroughly penetrated into, with a cursory view.

[page numbered 44:]

Your style is nervous and strong. Your Observations are just: and I think you are almost the only Biographer I ever read that would allow his Hero to be a Man.

The Paragraph about your Father I admire. You there exemplify that Christian Doctrine, which you every where recommend: and I cannot help observing, that one stroke of your pen, both as a Nobleman and a Layman, in favour of Christianity, does more service to that Cause, than Volumes written by us hireling Clergy.

May the great God give you

[page numbered 45:]

health and inclinations to persist in the pursuit of those Studies, which, as I am confident, entertain yourself, contribute at the same time to the Improvement of Mankind, and in particular of

> your Lordship's
> most obliged
> and obedient
> humble Servant
> Rob:^{t} Clogher.

[page numbered 46:]

Doctor Barry to the Earl of Orrery.

Dublin Decr 3^d 1751.

My dearest Lord,

Praise from a Friend, who is raised to fame by your pen, may be thought partial, yet give me leave to assure your Lordship, that this elegant performance has far exceeded my warmest expectations, and that I had less pleasure in being made equal to <u>Antonius Musa</u>, than in seeing your Lordship vying the first in fame, and superiour to any modern Writer in the justness of your Sentiments, and purity of style.

[page numbered 47:]

But while you meet with an universal approbation in England, you must, I find, be censured by some here, who think you have treated the Dean's character with too much severity. These persons owe their little Consequence in the World by being formerly distinguished so far by the Dean, as to be admitted to his vacant idle hours, either to offer incense to him, or to receive his censure, or the Evacuations of his Spleen.   They think their whole character in Danger, when the Dean's imperfections and failings are hinted at, tho' as foils to give greater force to his good qualities.   Nat told me, that Dr Barber was very angry, as I suppose he found his Mother.   Sheridan

[page numbered 48:]

told him, he would publish something in defence of his Father; and insists on it, that he was never <u>slovenly</u>, but rather a Fop in his dress.   The Bishop of Clonfert told me, he dined two days ago, where Dr Delany was, who said, you had treated the Dean cruelly, while you called him your Friend.   I read two paragraphs afterwards to the Bishop, where the Dean's character is given.   He thought it very just, and owned, that he was surprized to find him mentioned with so much regard and praise; for that from Dr Delany's account, he imagined, that he had been placed in a very different light-Some think that Mrs Vannumrigh's character has been treated with too much severity: but

[page numbered 49:]

has Lord Orrery said more than what Cadenus has published?   However, all agree, that the performance has many Beauties.   I thought this account to your Lordship necessary; for I should not be surprized, if some Squibs & Serpents made their appearance.   I spoke to <u>Nat</u>, to endeavour to find out from his conversation with Dr Barber, if any answer to the Remarks would be published.   He thinks, they will endeavour to prevail on one Evelyn, Author of a Poem on a Country Church's Yard.   I own, I should dread his pen. - Would it be improper in your Lordship to write to Dr Delany on this subject, not suspecting his Censure, but to answer any general unreasonable objections?   Or is it better to despise it with Silence?

[in the margin, in Orrery's hand:] Evelyn was not the author of that poem.

[page numbered 50:]

The old Bishop of Corke told me, he would not publish a Ballad in Ireland. 'Tis certain, that they are here particularly fond of illnatured Criticisms. They have not been accustomed to that liberty of expressing their Sentiments, which in England they Enjoy.   I thought proper to mention what I hear, tho' it is probable, that all this resentment may subside.   Ask Faulkner, if he knows of any designed Vindication of the Dean-I think an <u>artificial</u> one would silence them, and turn the Argument against them-I am not sollicitous about the event of any [of] their schemes.   They must vanish, as they have no

[page numbered 51:]

real foundation. But, I would avoid having your name mentioned in any of their trifling pamphlets to any disadvantage, tho' there should be no necessity to vindicate it from their censures.

> I am, my dearest Lord,
> ever yours.
> Ed Barry.

Mr George Faulkner to the Earl of Orrery.

Dublin Novr 26th 1751.

My Lord,

My state of health is so indifferent that I have not been able for above a

[page numbered 52:]

for above a [*sic*] Week past to quit my Chamber; yet I cannot forbear writing to your Lordship, to let you know, that I published your Remarks on the Dean's life, last Saturday, with amazing success, having sold more of them that day, and every day since, than I ever did of any Book before. I sent all your presents as you commanded, for which your Lordship has the humble thanks of all the persons that were obliged. I am sure, that I made Dr Barry very happy by letting him have most of the Sheets, more than a Week before publication, by which I am well assured, that he obliged many of his greatest patients. I likewise obliged the Duke of Dorset, who had one bound three days before

[page numbered 53:]

publication, by which he hath been entertained in the most agreeable manner. I sent one by Post, sewed in blue paper, to my Lady Orrery, several days before any one else could see it, with which her Ladyship was very much pleased, as your Lordship will be convinced, by the following words, <u>I am</u> <u>extremely pleased with the Life &c, which you sent me, both as to my Lord's</u> <u>writing, and your performance in printing it, as the paper is good, the print</u> <u>correct, and the Type very clear</u>. The Speaker (although it is the hurry of parliament) hath read the Remarks, and is ravished with them. A Clergyman, who was in my Shop yesterday, said it was the best written book in the World, except the Bible, and that he would carry it constantly in his pocket.

[page numbered 54:]

Were I to tell your Lordship all that I hear of the Book, I must write you an History of every one that I sell. This day I was favoured with a long visit from the Bishop of Clogher, who desired me to send his Compliments and thanks to your Lordship for your most entertaining, agreeable, and generous present, which hath given him more pleasure and satisfaction than any book he ever read. The Speaker sent, this day, for your present of your Remarks to the Bishop of Cloyne, which I delivered and by this Post (blind as I am) I have wrote to his Lordship to acquaint him therewith. Dublin would at this time, were it not for your Lordship's Remarks, be the most wretched, horrid, desponding Town in the whole World, there

[page numbered 55:]

being five packets due this day, in which are the King's Speech, the Lords & Commons Addresses, and ten drawings in the State Lottery; and yet, your Lordship diverts them all, and turns the Current of Politics, and the mighty Expectations of the large prizes in the Lottery Tickets to the reading your Book. My Eyes are so weak, and am so very ill, that I am obliged to conclude with most humble respects to Lord & Mr Boyle, and am your Lordship's most obliged, most dutifull, most obed. and most humble Servant

George Faulkner.

[page numbered 56:]

Mr George Faulkner to the Earl of Orrery.

Dublin Novr 30th 1751.

My Lord,

The six mails that arrived on Thursday, honoured me with five letters from your Lordship. I told you in my last, that there was an amazing demand for the Remarks, which still continues. All the judicious and learned, as well as those that are unprejudiced, allow it to be the finest, and best written piece in the English Tongue. I think my Sale is not inferior to Mr Millar's, having sold above 300 in one Week, which is more than ever was known to be disposed of in so short a time in Dublin. I am likely to be hanged, drawn, and quartered for

[page numbered 57:]

printing and publishing this Libel against my best Friend and Benefactor, and am charged on this account, with the utmost Ingratitude to the Dean: and my ill state of health still confining me to my chamber, some ignorant people have given out, that I dare not come into my Shop, for fear of being insulted, or very ill used: but these reports do not give me the least uneasiness. I am well enough to see Company in my own Apartment, although I am not well enough to go into the air: and those persons who are gentlemen of the best taste and learning in the kingdom all agree, that your Lordship's Remarks are beyond any Work that they have seen. And here, my Lord, I must be very proud, for they all tell me, it is not only the best written, but the

[page numbered 58:]

best printed Book that ever was done in Ireland. There is a loud complaint against your Lordship from the Manager, the Musicians, the Vinters, and the Coffee Men, that this week they have all been neglected on your account: for instead of the Ladies and Gentlemen going to Play, Balls, Assemblies, Taverns and Coffee houses, they are all now taken up with reading the Earl of Orrery's Remarks on Dr Swift's Life, and what is worse, more and more people are likely to read it, and to neglect all diversions whatever. Even Cards are laid aside to read this bewitching book; and the Ladies (let their numbers be ever so great) are silent and dumb as Mutes to <u>listen and catch with greedy Ears</u>. I am told there are to be several thrusts and shots

[page numbered 59:]

made at me in different papers next Week: but as I fight under your Lordship's banner, I hope I shall be able to resist them. I thank your Lordship most heartily for the letter you wrote to Wilson & Williamson, from whom I have not heard lately, and suppose they have dropped their design.

I cannot recollect, that I ever omitted any one of your Lordship's Letters: but the Winds are sometimes very contrary this time of the year. I believe, I did once tell your Lordship, that as I could not sleep one night, I got up early in the morning, and began a Life of the Dean, upon which I never proceeded further, not having time or capacity for such a Work, and indeed your Lordship's is so well executed, and

[page numbered 60:]

in such universal reputation, it will be in vain for any one else to attempt it, as immortal fame will spread yours thro' the World, whilst any other must limp very slowly even thro' this kingdom. I never did think Mr Bettenham to blame because, I know him to be a gentleman of unblemished and universal good character; but there might be sheets stolen from his press, as well as there have been from mine, and from others in both kingdoms. I am sorry this affair has given him so much uneasiness, which I did not intend, but for his Service. I would write to him, but that I can hardly see to finish this Letter.

> I am, my Lord, &c.
> George Faulkner.

[page misnumbered 63, being 61:]

The Countess of Orrery to the Earl of Orrery.

Caledon Decr 1st 1751.

My Dear Lord,

At length I have got again into my possession, your <u>Remarks &c</u>: and am just going to give them a carefull reading. I begin on Sunday Evening, and have sent <u>Lucy</u> and all the house to play, while I examine, with great delight, this work which has charmed every person, who has read this book.

The beginning of the first Letter which we may call the Introductory occasion of your publishing this book: contains a high proof of paternal affection, you had publicly testified your tenderness and care in forming <u>Lord Boyle</u> on the plan of an illustrious antient: you point out to your no less deserving Son <u>Hamilton</u>

[page misnumbered 64, being 62:]

many things which must contribute to his improvement, even from the faults of Dr Swift: particularly one most usefull lesson, tho' you do not exactly lay a stress thereon, but leave your Son like the Bee, to collect honey from the flowers you lay before him. What I mean is this, that Swift's <u>views were checked in his younger years, and the anxiety of that disappointment had a visible effect upon all his actions</u>. What proper Observations both your Sons may draw from this, as they are both entering upon the Theatre of this World! Yourself suffered by early disappointments, both in your health & fortune. You suffered severely for the disappointments your father had undergone: and indeed there are few minds have philosophy sufficient to bear frequent disappointments, even tho' we draw them upon

[page misnumbered 65, being 63:]

ourselves by wrong placed Ambition, or any other motive, we cannot receive them, without being visibly chagreened in our tempers. Therefore, no doubt, young persons cannot be too often cautioned to get the better of this Child of Pride, and ^{to} submit to the Will of Almighty God (from whom all things immediately proceed) with chearfullness and resignation; which may be so pleasing in the Sight of God, as to send us a blessing infinitely more for our happiness, than that particular thing would have been, on which we had so strongly fixt our inclinations.

The latter part of this first letter contains an entertaining nar[r]ative of <u>Dr Swift's</u> birth & education, which is much to be commended, for the short manner in which so dry a subject is comprehended, as well as the agreeable manner in which it is told.

In the second letter, what you

[page misnumbered 66, being 64:]

have said of <u>Stella</u> is so full, that I cannot even make one observation, but only drop a Tear on the Ashes of so valuable a woman so cruel[l]y treated. Yet I must mention one reflection, which, tho' it occurs to a Mother, will not, these twenty years enter into Mr Boyle's head. That it is a dangerous thing for a young man, to converse much with a young Woman of Beauty, Sense, and Merit, if she be not a suitable and proper Wife for him in all particulars: for it generally ends in mutual love; often in a foolish marriage, and always in repentance.

The Third Letter is a lively description of <u>Dr Swift's</u> disappointments during the reign of King W^m. I dont wonder, that a Dutch Prince should not distinguish the merit

[page misnumbered 67, being 65:]

and Wit of an English Man sufficiently, as to provide for him on that account. But, that a King should break his Word, ought to surprize every body: yet <u>Swift</u> was used to breach of Royal Words, from <u>William</u> down to the Promiser of the Medals.

The fourth letter opens a new and more entertaining Scene than any of the former: yet still filled with false promises from the Great, Swift must have (with his strong passions) experienced, during the thirteen years of Queen Ann's reign all the hopes, fears, and vexations of an ambitious disappointed man: and I am confident must have concluded with Solomon, that <u>All was Vanity and Vexation of Spirit.</u>

I wish my paper was larger, that

[page misnumbered 68, being 66:]

I might not leave off with so mortifying a Sentence: but had <u>Solomon</u> lived with one Wife quietly, and had had Sons like <u>Lord</u> and <u>Mr Boyle</u>, I think he would have acknowledged <u>there</u> was happiness. And that you may long enjoy happiness with these sons is the sincere wish of, my Dear Lord,

your aff^{te} & obedient Wife
M. Orrery.

The Countess of Orrery to the Earl of Orrery.

Caledon Decem^r 7th 1751.

My Dear Lord,

The 5th Letter begins with <u>Swift's</u> return to Ireland in 1713.

[page misnumbered 69, being 67:]

The aversion of the Chapter of St Patrick's to him, and of the whole body of the People of Dublin. But here we find the exact same instance of popular aversion and applause given to <u>Swift</u> that we have since beheld given to persons, who, as your Letter ends, are too near our own times to speak of with Truth. But, I may say, that as the affection of the people of Ireland to <u>Swift</u> was founded on reason, so the aversion of England and Ireland to their former Idol has as solid a foundation.

We come in the 6th Letter to examine his Works. We have buried a good English Queen, who certainly intended the welfare of England: and had her head been blessed like her

[page misnumbered 70, being 68:]

Predecessor <u>Elizabeth</u>, with a thorough discernment of Mankind, she would have made as great a figure as ever Prince did, who filled the English Throne. The Glory and Advantage of England, and England alone, was her sole view. But favourite Ladies, Treasurers & Generals prevented the Blessings which would have flowed from so excellent an English heart on an English People. And therefore here we must leave the good Queen <u>Ann</u>, whose character will rise some ages hence, when this, and the next Generation are no more. They shall then judge as impartially of this excellent Queen, as we do of our Edwards and Henrys.

[page misnumbered 71, being 69:]

Your critical Observations on his writings, which begin in this sixth letter are most pleasing, and instructive. They have no fault but that they are too short: for here the Observations are so just, and the style so harmonious, that it is impossible not to be angry with you every Letter you end, only because you have ended. And yet I think no pen but your own could ^{add} another word to what you have said on each subject.

The great regularity of his Life, constantly measured by his Watch, plainly shewed his Mind to be uneasy: and I suppose he said with the Israelites <u>In the Evening, would God it were Morning: and in the Morning, would God it were Evening</u>. For, certainly those who are at ease will sometimes say <u>What have we to do with hours</u>?

[page misnumbered 72, being 70:]

And tho' there is a great fault in forgetting time and regularity too much: and in hurrying life away, yet an agreeable forgetfullness sometimes can be no fault: and I believe no happy person is ever without this unbending of the Soul.

The second volume of <u>Swift's</u> works, is certainly the most amusing of all his works. His compliments to <u>Stella</u> are very pleasing, and testify his affection to her: but his Poem to <u>Vanessa</u> is the most perfect in its kind, that I have ever read, and merits all you have said in its commendation. Tho' <u>Vanessa</u> was very unfortunate, she does not stir up one Sentiment of Pity for her hard fate in our breast: whereas

[page misnumbered 73, being 71:]

no eye can read the misfortunes of <u>Stella</u> without a Tear.

Your observation, that tho' he sometimes appears indecent, yet there is much Wisdom in even his dirty Dressing Room, is certainly right, and I make no doubt has been of service to many a fair Lady: and as all Women wish to be thought Goddesses, why should we take it ill to see what is disagreeable, set in so strong and striking a light as may make us avoid it. And thus will I finish my Remarks upon your eight Letters. And as nothing has happened worth your attention in, or about Caledon, I need only add, we are well, and that I am, my dearest Lord,

> your very aff^{te} & obedient Wife
> M. Orrery.

[page misnumbered 74, being 72:]

The Countess of Orrery to the Earl of Orrery.

Caledon Decr 16th 1751.

My dear Lord,

I have more leisure this day than I was allowed last Post, and therefore I will return to our friend Swift, and go thorough as many of his writings along with you, as my Sheet of paper will contain.

You have in your ninth and tenth letters done justice to the poetical performances of Doctor Swift by the commendations you bestow on those poems which are worthy the reading, and approbation of all persons of taste, nay of all <u>who have ears to</u>

[page misnumbered 75, being 73:]

<u>hear</u>: and you have made us find beauties even in the most trifling performances, by saying they have far exceeded any verses on the same kind of subjects. The account of his female Senate composed chiefly of old Ladies, must surprize many fine gentlemen who do not regard venerable Matrons, and may lead us to make a comparison between the female companions of the Dean of S^t <u>Patricks</u>, and those of <u>Anacreon</u>. <u>Swift</u> represented his Ladies as Daphnes, the Greek crowns his favourit[e]s with beauties and roses: and perhaps, after all, the Ladies of both poets had all the strong passions of other Women; and each of these assemblies of Damsels

[page misnumbered 76, being 74:]

raised their spirits to be sprightly enough to converse with these sons of <u>Apollo</u>, with the best of greek and french Wines.

The eleventh Letter is the melancholy account of <u>Dr Swift's</u> loss of his Senses. All your reflexions are so just and so religious, that they must please all persons, who reflect upon the time which is approaching to us all; when death shall disincumber us from these bodies, which can by the changes they undergoe, so entirely extinguish so superiour a Soul, and almost makes us wish to quit our Prisons, while we are only confined to the rules of the Tower, least it should please

[page misnumbered 77, being 75:]

the Almighty power to throw us, like poor Swift, into the lowest Dungeon.

Your Observations on all the Travels of <u>Gulliver</u>, are full of justice, wit and spirit: and I must return you my thanks for your justification of <u>Caesar</u>, whose fall I must lament, at the same time I acknowledge it was more fortunate for his glory than any event that could have happened to him: for I question whether even this first of Men would not have grown giddy with power. But, in death he had a greater Triumph over his murderers, than over all the Nations he had conquered.

Queen Elizabeth died also just in the most fortunate period immaginable.

[page misnumbered 78, being 76:]

Her last Speech to her Parliament testified her Mind as undecayed, as [in] her first when she declared her People were both her Husband and Children. She was just going to fall into the infirmities of old age in private life as a Woman, and she could not have guarded against these infirmities appearing soon after in public as a Queen. I will now shut my eyes, and fancy Elizabeth admitted into (not the Xtian) but the Heathen Paradise: what a contention must there have been among the illustrious Dead who shall have this Queen for his Wife? Will it be a Sin to bring <u>Solomon</u>, <u>Caesar</u>, <u>Henry</u> the 4th of <u>France</u>, Pope <u>Sextus Quintus</u>, Anthony even from

[page misnumbered 79, being 77:]

<u>Cleopatra</u>, The <u>Black Prince</u>, <u>Henry Plantagenett the 5</u>th and <u>Oliver Cromwell</u>? <u>Elizabeth</u> will not take <u>Solomon</u>, because he is wiser than herself. She would have preferred the Black Prince, as an English Hero, only she was his grandaughter. She coquets a little with the <u>Pope</u>, and the two <u>Henrys</u>, kicks <u>Oliver</u> to <u>Tartarus</u>, and accepts of the hand of <u>Caesar</u>.

I am awake, and will put an end to this letter by subscribing myself to my dearest Lord,

> an aff^{te} & obedient Wife
> M. Orrery.

[page misnumbered 80, being 78:]

The Revd Doctor Pococke to the Earl of Orrery.

Dublin December 31st 1751.

My Lord,

I am to acknowledge the honour of your Lordship's engaging favour, and to return my thanks for the news your Lordship is so good as to impart, of such a kind, as is not to be seen in the public prints, which is very acceptable to those who are so far from the scene of action.

Your Bookseller's account, my Lord, of the sale of the Memoirs, and of the approbation they meet with among unprejudiced persons, is very true: but it might as reasonably be expected, that the Memoirs of Mahomet as an Impostor

[page misnumbered 81, being 79:]

should be well received at Constantinople, as that any thing should be approved of by the lower and middling rank of people, which denies any one virtue to Dean Swift, as he was revered by them, and they have still the utmost regard for his memory. They are even angry with Faulkner for his ingratitude as they call it, and he was so strongly reproached by some persons, that 'tis said he pretended an indisposition, and did not afterwards appear for some time. Even the Poet, Divine, the Dean's friend, is not pleased: but however, he says, he wishes those confounded Travels had been burnt.

But, my Lord, all persons of Sense and Judgement highly approve, except some few who must appear for him as patriots, for they confirm the opinion they had of him, and that of the World in 1713, which appear from a most bitter copy of verses put up at St Patrick's the day he was to be installed as Dean, which I have heard Serjeant Marshall repeat, but I believe are not to be seen in writing. That Gentle-

[page misnumbered 82, being 80:]

-man also has the letters from Cadenus to Vanessa, which I have seen. I heard a person of Sense, Learning, and Judgement say, that there was not a page in the Memoirs in which he did not find something new and constructing, and every good Man is charmed with that spirit of Virtue and Religion which runs thro' the whole.

And such a candid disquisition is certainly, my Lord, of use in many respects; and one of the principal, That great Genius's may see, that it is not proper to give themselves up to humour and passion, but that they ought to apply their abilities in a usefull manner, otherwise they will loose [sic] much of their future reputation, whatever applause they may meet with by falling in with the popular stream.

If Dean Swift had been advanced according to his desires, so as to have had no need of attaching himself closely

[page misnumbered 83, being 81:]

to Ministers, and to have been above writing for them; or if they had not known his capacity, which latter would probably have been the case: I much question, whether his genius would ever have been known, the strength of which seem to have laid in description and satirick raillery which made him the best Pamphleteer against a Party that perhaps ever writ.

There are many, my Lord, who think your Lordship has been too favourable to the Dean, in allowing him to be a Patriot on Principle, or above Corruption.

Suppose his preferment to the Deanery in the time of King Charles the 2^d, and that what passed in the beginning of the reign of George the 1st, had happened in King James's reign, that then he had writ his Gulliver, and had never been popular in Ireland; but that King W^m and other Princes had preferred him in England according to his desire; refused his degree at the College at first as insufficient, every where a most unpopular

[page misnumbered 84, being 82:]

Man! would he, as opportunity offered have given some strokes at Ireland? Would not he have been for lowering the Coin? Would he have spoken a word against Woods's [sic] halfpence? Would not he, upon all occasions, have railed both against the People and Country, as we see he did as well about the time he found himself forced to be, as he looked on it, banished to it, as well as before [?]

When he went to Oxford he seemed to have a great distaste for Ireland, and when he came to pay a visit in this Country, he was soon weary of it, and was glad to return to England. He could not bear it when he had a Prebend, and resigned it, probably to fix himself more surely on England. As long as he had any hopes in that Kingdom, he seemed rather to be an enemy to Ireland, which no man ought to be, as Ireland is a part of the public weal of England, as well as Yorkshire, and

[page misnumbered 85, being 83:]

ought to be regarded by every subject.

When the Dean had expectations, he was a friend to Ministers & Kings, and would not have said that he courted their friendships only out of ambition or vanity, though it might be both; and was certainly the former. They were Men, some of them at least, for their abilities, that a Man of Sense might have been happy in, abstracted from their power. But Ministers, tho' they had not been so proper for the conversation of a Genius, are great in knowing every thing that passes, and in their influence on public affairs, to which the Dean was not privy except when they wanted materials true or false for the subject of a Pamphlet. The Dean was encouraged by them for this end, and for their amusement and diversion, and the person with ribbands and bells may despise his Master who is so weak as to take delight in him, at the same time that his abilities are esteemed by those who bear

[page misnumbered 86, being 84:]

any public character. Swift had no opportunity of appearing untill upon these accounts he became intimate with Lord Oxford, and then the part he was to bear was plain.

I believe your Lordship, when all things are considered, will judge him rather a Man of a resolute humour than above Corruption. His political pamphlets are written on inconsistent principles, and if he had no Principle moral or religious, which it is to be feared was the case, that will determine it. A man of sense who stood up for him, acknowledged to me, that he was not a Patriot on Principle. His visit to Lord Carteret shewed he was not above fear. It was an instance of his pride, which prevailed, that he left the Castle after waiting so long? If the story is true of the Couplets said to be writ by the Courtier and Governor, and it would be a curious

[page misnumbered 87, being 85:]

thing to know what passed between that Lord and the Dean, if they had ever any conversation together, as I suppose they had.

It is said, that he wrote an Intelligencer or Examiner for lowering the Coin here, and that it was printed when he so violently opposed it, in order to expose him; and if this is true it is a strong proof of his want of principle and integrity. At the time he hated the Country of Ireland, it is probable he disregarded the interests of it, and when he came to settle here he was very unpopular, for inclinations and aversions are commonly mutual. He then turned his thoughts against Mankind, and writ the Travels, a picture of himself, and in which he has described his own heart. All this time he was neglected and hated, which his pride could not bear, and he saw he could not be significant in any other way than by making himself popular, which would give him an opportunity of venting

[page misnumbered 88, being 86:]

his spleen against the government of England. He begun by throwing out some pieces in favour of our Manufactures; and in order to become popular among the lowest people he set on foot that charity of having a Fund to lend to poor house keepers on good security, which is the great proof of his extraordinary charity which they say your Lordship has not mentioned.

I do not say if Swift's passions had not been moved, he would not have chosen Virtue, for I am persuaded, in that case every Man would. But a person who gives himself up entirely to passion is only more or less abandoned in the eye of the World, according to the nature of the passions that influence him.

If the heart of the Dean had been right: if after his disappointments he had properly judged that he was not fit for a higher station of life, and had in this

[page misnumbered 89, being 87:]

light submitted to the dispensations of Providence and not have given way to those violent passions which agitated his pride, and had endeavoured to have made himself as usefull as he could in the station he was in, he would probably have never been mad, and might have lived longer. He might indeed at a greater age have fallen into that state which is very common, especially in thinking and studious Men, of loosing [*sic*] the memory of things and words which reduces to a second Childhood. How just is this reflexion? Of how small estimation must the greatest genius appear in the sight of God? Especially if their abilities are not properly applied: and what a plea will it be at one time; that he writ good English: that he made pretty verses.

I heard one particular of Swift which might not have come to your

[page misnumbered 90, being 88:]

Lordship, that is, when Mrs Johnson pressed him to own the Marriage, he told her, if he did, he should hate her from that Moment.

I imagine your Lordship's Memoirs will be printed abroad. Nothing will make it <u>Liber prohibitus</u>: if then there is nothing in it against Peter which may give offence, they might add to it the Translation of the Notes on Pliny.

I suppose your Lordship has seen the Primate's Sermon. I have read here a pretty piece of Oratory, a sort of a funeral Sermon on Lord Gainsborough.

Your Lordship is too indulgent to your friends. If I should ever trouble the World with any thing more, it will give no entertainment to your Lordship, as it can be only a work of labour.

But, it is time to free your Lordship

[page misnumbered 91, being 89:]

from the trouble of this rhapsody, with an Observation (by way of Apology) on your Lordship's advice in relation to Epistolary correspondence, which is doubtless very proper where there is not an entire confidence, and is very natural advice to those for whom I suppose, at different times, we are apt to fear, as well as hope every thing. But, I cannot but think that such writings ought to be looked on as the freest discourse, thinking aloud, between two friends, which should not be divulged, and when letters are of such a nature, they ought to be destroyed: if they are not it amounts to the same as disclosing private conversation if ever they are seen.

But, I begin to be sensible I am wrong, and ought to have followed your Lordsp's advice, which would have prevented the inconvenience of endeavouring to read

[page misnumbered 92, being 90:]

so long a letter: and your Lordship will not commit it to the flames, if you would punish my presumption in taking a liberty to which I still fear I had no right. But the reception of the Memoirs led me insensibly into this subject. Your Lordship's candour withheld me from a reserve which might have been more becoming, as it does from being the Executioner myself and sending a shorter and more discreet epistle; as there is no one can have a more real regard for your Lordship than, My Lord,

> your Lordship's
> most obedient & most
> humble Servant
> Richard Pococke.

[page misnumbered 93, being 91:]

The Earl of Orrery's answer.

> Marston house near Frome
> in Somersetshire.

Sir,

I return you thanks for every syllable of your letter, except some few of the last lines in which you make excuses for the letter itself. Give me leave to say, it is injustice, perhaps not to my understanding, but most certainly to my gratitude. My heart feels every stroke of your pen, and, I hope, my head relishes every branch of your knowledge and instruction. Let me entreat you therefore to save yourself any future trouble of making apologies to a friend, who honours and esteems you in an unconfined manner far beyond the narrow limits of ceremony and compliments.

In the book which you have favoured with your notice, one of my chief difficulties was to form Swift's character with any tolerable degree of consistency. I say this, from his works, and not from my personal

[page misnumbered 94, being 92:]

observations, although the latter afforded as many intricacies as the former. The situation of his different pieces in poetry and prose, resembled his various humours: and to enjoy his conversation or his writings, a man must necessarily change himself into a variety of dispositions.

Many of your remarks relating to Swift are more just than perhaps I care to own. I think I have said enough against him, to shew at least, that he was not absolutely above the human species in perfection, and yet many of his Survivors would make him a Deity that they might make themselves one of his Dii minores. They may as well attempt to make him a planet, in hopes of being one of his Satellites.

I have taken no notice of the five hundred pounds allotted to the benefit of poor tradesmen, because I was apprehensive, that the fact in general was not exactly represented. If it were true, it is much

[page misnumbered 95, being 93:]

to his honour: but I have heard, that most of the money was lost, and that the fund was discontinued, and even when continued was attended with some circumstances like poundage. The whole scene appeared to me so mysterious, that I was afraid to vouch for the truth of it, and therefore left the fame of it to Mrs Pilkington.

I am not surprized that the book, so soon published after Dean Swift's death, should meet with the severity of criticism in Ireland. But as I have writ it with the candour that a parent will, and must write to his Son, I am little sollicitous about the present set of Critics, being in some flattering hopes (as you tell me that Men of judgement honour me with their approbation) that Time will be my friend, and do me that justice of which I am now deprived by pride, passion,

[page misnumbered 96, being 94:]

and prejudice.

I am once more buried in Somersetshire: in a corner, which I own I love better than any other on the Globe. I will hope that you will visit me in my vault, before I am quite mouldered into dust. A western Mummy is a curiosity worth seeing. Our hieroglyphics differ from all others, but in plain english let me ever boast myself,

    Sir,

        your obliged and obedient
        humble Servant
        Orrery.

Jan: 13th 1752.

[page misnumbered 97, being 95:]

The Countess of Orrery to the Earl of Orrery.

Caledon Jany 8th 1752.

Wednesday at least of our three weekly post days for writing to my dearest Lord, allows us the greatest leisure to chuse our Subjects, for we have no Answers to return to W. G., I. T. or Mr M.C: and if my neighbour M-ll be so kind as to keep at home, I may in quiet resume my pen, and run thro' the rest of your most agreeable Observations on Dr Swift's writings.

There is one thing which I wonder it did not strike me before, and I much more wonder it escaped your judicious eye. It is in your second Letter wherein you have the following words

[page misnumbered 98, being 96:]

"His uncle Godwin Swift had fallen into a kind of Lethargy or Dotage which deprived him by degrees of his Speech and Memory, and rendered him totally incapable of being of the least service to his family and friends." A case so similar to that of poor Doctor Swift, that we might almost imagine there was something hereditary in that dreadfull disorder, which first attacked the Uncle, then the Nephew, and reduced them both to the melancholy state you so well describe in the same letter, that of one of <u>Swift's</u> own <u>Struldbruggs</u>.

I think (for I real[l]y am not quite certain) I carried my pen thro' your letters to the end of <u>Gulliver's</u> travels, and I esteem myself to be now running thro' the 16th Letter. Swift's bitterness against the Presbyterians I am con-

[page misnumbered 99, being 97:]

-fident did a great deal of harm, in keeping up that spirit of division amongst us so unworthy in Christians, and sowing dislike in the breast of one honest man to another honest man. This I know by myself, till your superiour reasoning made me look upon all prejudice as unjust, a great folly, and indeed a great Wickedness. I held both Presbyterian and Roman Catholic in the utmost abhorrence. I never considered, that not having been educated in the same Church made difference only in point of faith: but I esteemed Presbyterians not what I know many of them are, men of Sense, Learning, and Honesty, but as cunning, designing, canting, ignorant hipocrites: and for Roman Catholics, I thought every one of them held a knife at my throat; and though amongst others of their Principals, I must ever condemn the persecuting

[page misnumbered 100, being 98:]

Spirit of the latter. Yet I have so far got the better of these strong prejudices, as to see the merit of persons in both these Sects: and to pray to God Almighty, that he will be pleased mercifully to break down the middle wall of partition between us.

The Compliment you make to Ireland is extremely elegant and polite: and you do it great justice in saying, it is much improved: and as there is room for very great improvement, I hope in eighteen years more you will see it yet vastly higher improved than it has hitherto been.

Your copy of verses which concluded this letter, I have (even before I knew and loved you) esteemed as one of the most compleat commendatory Poems that I ever read.

[page misnumbered 101, being 99:]

The 17th Letter has in it, two of the most glorious paragraphs I have ever read. The first, by <u>Swift</u>, the second by yourself: both of which I shall transcribe, that by <u>Swift</u> is as follows: "A spirit of Liberty is diffused thro' all these writings, and that the Author is an Enemy to Tyranny and Oppression in any shape whatever."

Your words are these, "Throughout the course of these letters, I have freely pointed out to you all his faults; but I beg you to remember, that with all these faults, he was above Corruption: a virtue in itself sufficient to cover a multitude of human failings, since from that virtue alone can flow prosperity to the Common wealth."

[page misnumbered 102, being 100:]

The next Observation you make is a fine, but melancholy reflection: But ever since Ambition, and the desire of more than we possess was introduced into the World, which no doubt was very early, it has, and ever will be the case in all States: but on Party matter I had certainly better stop the carreer [*sic*] of my pen. I am apt to speak Truth, and I will therefore end this Letter with the old proverb, that Truth is not to be spoken at all times. Yet, I cannot help wishing, that truth might as openly be declared, even into the Ears of Princes, and that they would be as well pleased to hear it, as you will be to hear me say, that I am with great truth, my dear Lord, your aff^{te} & obed.^t Wife

M. Orrery.

[page misnumbered 103, being 101:]

A copy of verses sent to Lord Orrery by an unknown Author.

A Prophecy.

When Garrick, turns to Farce great Shakespear's rage;
And vacant, looks, or awkward treads the Stage:
When Barry's softness in the love sick Tale
Insipid grows, and can no more prevail:
When Cibber, lifeless in the Scene appears,
And strives, in vain, to melt us into tears:

[page misnumbered 104, being 102:]

When Laura's charms, beam only from her eye,
And her good sense is pass'd unheeded by.
When learned Young, his modesty foregoes,
And turns loquacious where he nothing knows:
When Akinside writes poor, and rugged Lyric,
And the false Loon,* on Milton, panegyric:
When ** has more grace than to defame,
Cold in his urn, great Pope's immortal name

*Lauder.

[page misnumbered 105, being 103:]

When these things happen, Orrery shall find,
Tho' candor, goodness, wit, adorn his mind,
Himself no longer deem'd a friend to humankind.

[page misnumbered 106, being 104:]

In the Whitehall Evening Post of the 11th of January 1752, was inserted the following Epigram by an anonymous Author.

[pasted:]

To the AUTHOR, &c.

SIR,

*If you think the following Lines worthy a Place in your Paper pray insert
them.*

To the Earl of ORRERY.

The Chronicles of Fame cou'd Swift explore
In Search of Worthies? and collect no more?
What can no Age, past, present, or to come,
Swell the bright Circle to the Wisemen's Sum?
Mankind confess a Seventh, Swift's juster View
Beholds the six epitomis'd in you.

Canterbury, Jan 9, 1752.

Lady Orrery to the Earl of Orrery

Caledon Jany 13th 1752.

We are now, my dear Lord, at the 18th letter of your Remarks &c. The
character you give of Lord Peterborough, comprehends a great deal in a few
lines, and is written with full as much spirit as inhabited the body of the
person you describe.

[page misnumbered 107, being 105:]

The latter part of this letter contains your own sentiments, "that ^{the} People
of England love Liberty." Indeed, in that I must differ from you: they love
Corruption, and of consequence they love Slavery. But, I will not say any
more on this subject, but proceed to the nineteenth Letter wherein you
mention Swift's epistolary correspondence, the subject of the Seventh Volume
of his Works.

Every body who has received Letters from you, allow, that no person can
write, in that way, with more spirit and wit than yourself: that the Sentiments
delivered by your pen flow all from the heart, of consequence they must affect
the hearts of those to whom they are addressed, and your advice and
directions in this point must be of singular service not alone to Mr Boyle to
whom they are addressed, but to every person who has eyes to see, and ears
to hear: the latter part of advice, to be cautious, even in offering civilities, I
doubt every body

[page misnumbered 108, being 106:]

has experienced; and those who have an open, undesigning heart cannot but often suffer in their purse for dropping words of kindness. But, in this World, persons of design and cunning, must ever have the better of the honest part of mankind. Ah Gentlemen, we shall one day be even with you, tho' indeed it will not be in this World, of which you are so fond.

What you have said of <u>Pope</u> is true, and does him honour, but the rough honest manners of Swift, though less agreeable, certainly at the same time his passions terrify you, his honest sincerity must charm you.

Pope's mind and conversation was [sic] like ^{his} gardens, full of windings neatly trimmed, beautifull walks and prospects present themselves wherever you turn your eye. His Wit sparkled like his Thames. Roses and the sweetest flowers sprung all around you as you walked,

[page misnumbered 109, being 107:]

and the nettles and thorns were all hid behind the hedges.

Swift was like (for I can compare him to nothing more great and a[u]gust) the Coast of the Giant's Causeway: the rocks had a majestick horror; the Sea sometimes rageing and foaming, at other times placid, and rolls along in a thousand pleasing waves. Yet while you admire this stupendious [sic] Ocean, and were pleased at the gentle motion of the Sea, you were not entirely easy, least [sic] a storm should arise, and a Wave should wash you away, at least one of the stupendious [sic] rocks should tumble on your head, and crush you to pieces.

Swift certainly loved Pope from his soul, Pope rather feared than loved Swift: and your remark is certainly very just in regard to Pope, that their pursuing different roads in poetry, and living

[page misnumbered 110, being 108:]

in different kingdoms, prevented rivalship.

The character you give of some of our English Writers I am not much acquainted with; for, I confess, the tedious heavy manner in which the greatest number of our English Authors wrote, always set me to sleep, and I never have done more than look into them for some particular passages, and then closed the book. Yet at the same time you mention Lord Clarendon, I wish you had mentioned his strength in drawing Characters in which he can alone be equalled by your Pliny.

Your joining <u>Swift</u>, <u>Bolingbroke</u>, and <u>Addison</u> together as the best of our English Writers, both for case of style, and dignity of Sentiments shall not pass with me, for I must join to them a fourth, in whose writings there is no less Elegance and dignity, and whose sentiments of Religion, Virtue, and Honour are full

[page misnumbered 111, being 109:]

as high, and this is the person to whom I am a most affectionate and obedient Wife

M. Orrery

The Countess of Orrery to the Earl of Orrery.

Caledon Jany 15th 1752.

My dear Lord,

To morrow we shall have three packets due from England, no doubt I am extremely impatient for their arrival, because I have not received any account of your motions since the 31st of December, and tho' I address my letters to Marston, perhaps you are still in London: but I must wait with patience till Thursday or Saturday, and as I cannot write on any subjects of business, I will proceed to your twentieth letter of your Remarks on the Life and Writings of Swift.

[page misnumbered 112, being 110:]

Your observation in relation to Juries is certainly very just; and I cannot but think, that the french manner of trials is better than the English. A great number of Judges of which there must always be a majority for the person in whose favour the decree passes, we may certainly call our jurymen judges, where even life and death as well as property to be tried only by men of the largest possessions in the kingdom. Were every man's cause tried at a hundred miles from the part of the World where he lived: were his juries to consist of twenty five men: the majority to decide the cause, we might hope to see rogues hanged for murder, and honest men possesst of their just rights.

Swift's Sentiments in the letter you mention to Pope you have given in a very concise manner, and they ought to be the Sentiments of every honest man, for the uncorrected Jacobite or Republican Principles must destroy all government: yet, quaere,

[page misnumbered 113, being 111:]

whether blind submission to a corrupt parliament may not destroy it as effectually?

Had <u>Swift</u> lived till this present time in his sound state of mind, since he very justly condemns the vast encrease of luxury and public diversions, what would he now say, when every day in the Week has (even in the small city of Dublin) two or three public places for each night, besides musics [*sic*] and walking parties for the mornings and card parties for Sundays. I think it is wonderfull that the continual hurry in which our young people live, does not unsettle their uncultivated understandings so far as to render them all Inhabitants of Swift's hospital for lunatics.

No doubt all your observations on the trifling compositions of Swift are very just, but fond of publishing as

[page misnumbered 114, being 112:]

he was, his letters were to both our knowledge published by another hand; tho' I believe, at the same time; had he been so much in his senses as to have had any communication with the World, he would not have been displeased, even to have these trifling epistles given to the public.

Most men in the beginning of their lives are carefull, in letting any of their Works make their appearance in the World, till they have passed the eyes of the most juditious of their friends, afterwards they write on: heaps of papers lie by, and either their own partial fondness while they live, or the fondness, or avarice of an heir or widow after their death, exposes to the World a heap of stuff, which we may say as <u>Homer</u> does of <u>Achilles</u> dragging <u>Hector's</u>

[page misnumbered 115, being 113:]

dead body, <u>Are unworthy of themselves, and of the dead</u>. I think it would be an excellent method for any person who had obtained fame by his writings, once in a year to settle accounts between Sense and Nonsense. To read over all he has written during that period: to burn all that belonged to Nonsense, then commit his papers that he thinks Sense, every copy to the hands of half a dozen juditious friends, desiring them to meet all in the great room with a great fire before them, and while he retired into his closet, they should examine, and restore him what was worthy to live, and commit to the flames what was worthy to burn.

Your character of Dr Arbuthnot is finely drawn. The simile of the slap on the face, very beautifull. From what you have said of this man it is impossible not to love and admire him in his life, but particularly in his death, which

[page misnumbered 116, being 114:]

alone can make us say, that that Man was virtuous, for such is the frailty of human nature, that untill the last period is past we may change. It is now passed with poor Lord Bolingbroke, as well as with all those mentioned in these letters. That Heaven may place that day at a great distance from my dear Lord is the sincere prayers of his ever affectionate and obedient Wife

M: Orrery.

The Countess of Orrery to the Earl of Orrery.

Caledon Jany 18th 1752.

My dear Lord,

Your twenty first letter to your son Mr Boyle, is thro' the whole very affecting, and fills the mind with melan-

[page misnumbered 117, being 115:]

-choly reflections, as it treats of human nature deprived of the only treasure which places it above the Brute, Reason. The noble faculties of the mind lost in a man of so uncommon a genius, we naturally lament more, than in a person who possesst inferiour talents: and no doubt as these may prove of benefit to mankind, we have more reason for the former than for the latter: but, otherwise all is equal. Yet it must be a great consolation to us to think, that the same disorder which deprived poor Dr Swift, (and almost all other persons who lose their reason, either by dotage, idiotism, or lunacy) of his reason took from him all sensibility of the misery of his condition: and though he could not think for himself, every person who beheld him, or any of

[page misnumbered 118, being 116:]

these sad Spectacles, must thank God, that mortality will end their miseries, and that the clouded Soul will after death again shine out above the brightness of the Sun, without farther decay: at the same time every creature who sees, or but thinks of these sad objects should return Almighty God most sincere thanks for his goodness to them, in preserving the understanding he has given them, from being destroyed, and your advice to guard ourselves against our passions, if followed, would render this World Paradise. Yet I believe, God is sometimes pleased to permit us to fall a prey to our Passions, on purpose to let us see how weak, how defenceless we are, and that alone thro' his assistance, and putting our trust in him, we can be defended.

[page misnumbered 119, being 117:]

I think the beginning of your 22^d letter, wherein you so justly condemn Swift's <u>bagatelle</u> must add strength to what I affirmed in my last letter, that the works of all authors ought to stand a trial annually, before the bar of their friends judgements.　Had his works undergone such a scrutany, [sic] they would have appeared like refined gold, whereas, at present, every volume has so much base mettle mixt with the sterling, that till you have taken care to sort the coin, and rub off the durt [sic] from many places, few people give themselves the trouble to examine thoroughly, whether they are gold, silver, copper, or lead: but you have evinced, that there is gold mixt thro' the whole.

[page misnumbered 120, being 118:]

The Sermons I shall say nothing of till I see the Answer you are to expect, which I pray you to send me when it comes out.

The verses on the death of Dr Swift &c. I well remember you got from the Dean for me before we were married, and I believe I have still in manuscript. You remember how it was mangled by the person to whom it was trusted to publish.

In your 23^d letter, your Sentiments on the <u>Tale of a Tub</u>, are incomparable. I think this, and the two other pieces you mention, should be printed in the next edition of his works, since he never denied, or owned them; and as this was the way he always made use of, whenever he was asked, whether he was the Author of any particular poem, Surely these may be justly acknowledged to be the produce of his pen, since no other pen but

[page misnumbered 121, being 119:]

his own could have wrote them.

My Sentiments I have heretofore delivered on the honourable mention you have made of your Father, I shall not therefore repeat them here: and as the last letter treats upon poetical [a mistake: this should read "political"] matters, <u>I shall not meddle in matters that are too high for me</u>: but humbly present my prayers to to [sic] Almighty God to give us a prince worthy to receive such advice for the benefit of England alone, and next my prayers must be, that you may live to see your Sons walking in the pointed out [sic] by my dearest Lord, to whom I am a very aff^{te} & ob^t Wife

M: Orrery.

[page misnumbered 122, being 120:]

Mr Geo: Faulkner to the Earl of Orrery.

Dublin Jan 30th 1752.

My Lord,

By this post I send you Satyr and Panegyric. Your favours to me have caused the first, and your merit the latter. I should write more to you, but that my eyes grow worse. The Archbishop of Dublin is in raptures with your Pliny and Remarks, and says, your Lordship is the best Writer of the age: and that your observations are superiour to any that he hath met with. But his Grace told me, that he is afraid, you

[page misnumbered 123, being 121:]

have been imposed on, for he has often been assured from Mrs Dingley, Mrs Johnson's only friend and companion in Ireland (with both of whom he was very well acquainted) that she was never married to the Dean.

I am, My Lord,
your Lordship's most dutifull
and obedient Servant
George Faulkner.

[pages misnumbered 124 and 125, being 122 and 123, blank]

[page misnumbered 126, being 124:]

Mr Purcell to the Earl of Orrery.

Kanturke 17th Feby 1752.

My Lord,

In my letter to your Lordship of the 30th Ult^o I mentioned, that I had heard from various parts of this Province, that your Lordship's Remarks on the Life and Writings of the late Dean Swift were censured, and though I wished to learn the particular parts which were objected to, I could not hear more than in general, that your Lordship has treated the Dean's character very severely.

I never heard any body speak of Swift's character in his life time who did not deem him an irreligious malitious Man, and I am therefore amazed, that, now he is dead, the public should find fault with your Lordship's telling

[page misnumbered 127, being 125:]

Truths of him, many of which were publicly known long before his death. I believe that, on the first publication of that Work, a few, through friendship for the Dean's memory; a few others, at the head of whom I believe I may place Sheridan the Player, through malice, and others through envy at the honour which your Lordship acquired by the translation of Pliny, took pains to decry it in Dublin, and thence the Country, as they do their fashions. I have however had the pleasure of hearing many persons vindicate your Lordship, but these were all of the virtuous or moral class, and if I do not mis-

[page misnumbered 128, being 126:]

-take many who first imbibed the Prejudice against that work begin to think better of it.

I have not been yet able to learn the Bishop of Cloyne's opinion of it, but will if I can, and will let your Lordship know it.

> I am, my Lord,
> your Lordship's most obliged
> and obedient Servant
> Rich:^d Purcell.

Richard Purcell ^{Esqr} to the Earl of Orrery.

Kanturke 2 April 1752.

My Lord,

I wrote to your Lordship on the 22^d ult^o from Corke, and I give your Lordship

[page misnumbered 129, being 127:]

the trouble of this Letter, only to communicate to your Lordship, a paragraph of a letter I lately received from my son of Trinity College, of which the following is a Copy.

"I hear, that Mr Dunkin, to whom Lord Chesterfield gave the care of a School in the North, with a Salary annexed to it of four hundred pounds a year, is come to Town with an intent to write against Lord Orrery. Mr Radcliffe (a Fellow of the Colledge) told me, that Dunkin is determined on it, having no other business to Town: and that Serjeant Marshall has for that purpose given him several letters (Originals) to and from Dean Swift and Mrs Vanumery, contradicting what my Lord has advanced.

[page misnumbered 130, being 128:]

I had hopes that the great cry here against that work of his Lordship's would have before now subsided, but it is so far from it, and such is the Spirit yet kept up against it, that I have heard it said, that his Lordship will be insulted by the Mobb (who always had great veneration for Swift) whenever he ^{may} appear in Dublin."

I would not choose to write any thing to your Lordship which may be disagreeable, but I hold it my indispensible duty to let you know every thing affecting your Lordship which may come to my knowledge, and having shewed that paragraph of my Son's letter to Mr Walter Goold last Saturday, and to him only, he was opinion [*sic*] with me, that I should communicate it to your Lordship.

[page misnumbered 131, being 129:]

I have made all the enquiry I could, but cannot hear a tittle of the judgement of the Bishop of Cloyne of your Lordship's Remarks on the life and writings of Swift. If the Bishop had censured that Work I think it very probable that it must have some how or other come to my Ears, and I therefore think it not improbable, that he is silent on the score of Mrs Vanumery, as he was one of her Exe^{rs} but that he looks upon Swift in your Lordship's light of him, as a great Genius, but as a wicked immoral Man.

> I am, My Lord,
> your Lordships
> most obliged & obedient
> Servant
> Richard Purcell.

[page misnumbered 132, being 130:]

In the London Daily Advertiser, N° 364, of Thursday April 30th 1752, was inserted the following Advertisement

[pasted:]

Next Tuesday will be Published,
SOME
OBSERVATIONS

ON THE
WRITERS of the PRESENT AGE,
AND
Their Manner of Treating each other.

More particularly relative to the Treatment of Lord O-y, and the INSPECTOR, in a Pamphlet, entitled, Some Remarks on the Life and Writings of Dr. J-H-.

> Qui non defendit, alio culpante–
> –Hic niger est.
>
> HOR.

[Orrery's hand:]

On Thursday May 7th 1752 I received a Pamphlet from Ireland entitled

[scribe's hand:]

A Letter from a Gentleman in the Country to his Son in the College of Dublin, relating to the Memoirs of the Life and Writings of Doctor Swift Dean of St Patrick's: ascribed to the Right Honourable the Earl of Orrery. Dublin printed by Oli: Nelson, at Milton's-head in Skinner Row. MDCCLII.

[next page, unnumbered, which should be 131, blank]

[page now numbered correctly, 132, blank]

[page numbered 133:]

An Epistle to Dean Swift occasioned by the publication of his Works in 1735.

> This from a friend to thee and all Mankind,
> To Truth, to Virtue, and the gentle mind
> O thou, with greatest Talents greatly curst,
> In Genius, and abuse of genius, first.
> When did thy heaven-born prostituted muse
> Attempt aught great, unless 'twere great abuse?
> Which has thy ranc'rous spleen insulted most,
> Thy King, Mankind, or Him that's Lord of Hosts?
> Thy Maker's works, and the prophetic strain,
> Were the first subject of thy Jest prophane.

Each page of such prophane outrageous trash
Demands the Critic's, or the Beadle's lash.

How glares in Gulliver's unhallow'd page,
Against thy God, and human race, thy rage?
There stands the law of amity repeal'd,
Grounds of Religion, moral, and reveal'd.
Nor can we find the genuine low-sublime,
Elsewhere more just than in thy doggrel rhime.

[page numbered 134:]

So mixt thy uncommon humour, wit, and Sense,
With trash, prophaness, filth, and insolence.

Thus in bright Climes the God of Wit and Day,
Darts thro' each way his all enlivening ray;
But when on Principles corrupt it falls,
The reptile shineing filth each Sense apalls.

[page numbered 135:]

[Orrery's hand:]

Copy of a Letter received by Ld Corke at Marston. Jan^{ry} 19th 1756.
[scribe's hand:]

Dickleburgh Jan^{ry} 12 1756.

My Lord,

I had thoughts sometime ago to have inserted in ye London or Gent^s Magazine an observation, wch occurred to me on perusing a Passage in your Remarks on ye Life & Writings of Dr Swift; But upon Consideration, I was inclined to Trouble y^r L^{dsp} wth it in private, hoping that your Candour & Humanity will be an Asylum for my forwardness. – Indeed, my Lord, when I Think upon the vast distance of Station in Life between you & myself, I lay aside my Pen with Despair. But when I ruminate on y^r L$^{dsp's}$ amiable & endearing Qualities as a man & a Christian, I am inspired wth some small degree of Confidence to resume it, & approach your

[unnumbered page, which should be 136:]

Presence by Proxy. – You Great & Good Sir, are sufficiently conspicuous in the World, I mean by Learning as well as Birth, & an Honour to ye Commonwealth of Letters, Yet I Trust you will not disdain ye receipt of this Epistle from One, who is Buried (as it were) in a Country Curacy, & almost an Exile from ye Literary World; However, my Lord, in this obscure Station I endeavour to Serve God with Contentment & Chearfullness; & as I have no further Expectations of Preferment in y^e Church, (tho' only in my 30th year) yet I shall gain Mr Pope's Beatitude, & y^t "that I shall never be disappointed." – I have chuse before me a large Field, in wch I could with great pleasure expatiate (were it not for incurring a Suspicion of Flattery, to wch I am no small Enemy) on y^r L$^{dsp's}$ excellent Qualities, but shall forbear;–& rather choose to admire Them in Silence, as well on account of your Modesty as my own Inabilities. – Yet I cannot help observing, (& that wth Concern too) how rudely & dishonestly y^r L^{dsp} has been Treated by the Pen of a person who publish'd last year An Essay on Dr Swift's Life & C; wch I have lately read, & shall dismiss it wth this short (but True I believe) Reflection – "That

[unnumbered page, which should be 137:]

it will not be easy to meet with his Equal in Egotisms, Pedantry, & (I had almost said) Scurrilous Impudence." – I am firmly persuaded to think that y^r L$^{dsp's}$ Philanthropy is Universal, & therefore as it is now high time for me to be drawing near y^e Subject of my Epistle, you will forgive me I hope in applying to y^r L^{dsp} a Distich of y^r late friend, the Dean – "Hated by Fools, & Fools to hate, Be that your Motto, &c;" – To proceed now to That wth wch I heare [*sic*] beg leave to Trouble y^r Lordship. – At page 175.6. in y^r letter on Dr Swifts Life &c, you say thus; "No person in his Senses can voluntarily prefer Death to Life; Our desires of Existence are Strong & prevalent – They are born with us; & our Ideas of a future State are not Sufficiently clear to make us fond of hurrying into Eternity; especially, as Eternity must forever remain incomprehensible to Finite Beings."

I perfectly agree here wth y^r Lordship that our desires of Existence are very strong; They are Indeed inextinguishable; – Such Desires being very wisely implanted in our Nature by our great & wonderfull Creator; – But then, I Beg leave to Say, that I do not clearly understand y^r L^{dsp} why no man

[unnumbered page, which should be 138:]

in his Senses can be supposed to prefer Death to Life – By Death, I here mean, not an Extinction of Being, but a Translation of the Soul from this Vale of Sorrow into a new & happier State of Existence; Such a State, as according to ye assurance in our Holy Scriptures, the Righteous enter into thro' the Gates of Death; on which account, St Paul might truly Say "To die is Gain to all such persons" – as it introduces Them into a State, ye happiness of wch is inconceivable – A Man, I humbly think my Lord, may therefore prefer such an happy change as this, to life here, without being Supposed to have lost his Senses.

Indeed, no man, who thinks seriously & rationally, would wilfully dissolve the Union of his Soul & Body, i.e. be guilty of Self Murder, but would much rather choose to wait his Case to leave the World who Sent him into it, "All ye days therefore (as Job says) of his appointed Time Every wise & good man would wait till his Change comes." – But notwithstanding all this, Many may think it infinitely better to be in the other World, than in This, & yet not deserve ye Title of mad or Irrational in their choice. You Say again, My Lord, "Our Ideas of a Future State are not

[unnumbered page, which should be 139:]

Sufficiently clear, to make us fond of Hurrying into Eternity." – If y^r L^{dsp} means "by being fond of hurrying into Eternity," "A rash & inconsiderate Desire to leave this World, & to try an unknown, eternal State, merely thro' Impatience under the troubles of this Life, or Dissatisfaction wth what Providence is pleased to Allot a Man here." – In this Sense of y^r L$^{dsp's}$ Phrase I heartily concur, & is most certainly highly Blameable; as it argues no small want of faith in the Wisdom, Power, & Goodness of y^e Almighty; It Shows that Such a Person has not that well grounded Persuasion, wch He ought to have, that all Things are ordered for the best by Him who made us; But yet it Seems to me my Lord, to be perfectly consistent wth Sound Wisdom to prefer being wth Christ in Heaven, to ye best condition of Life here upon Earth. – Indeed, it is impossible for us to have an adequate Idea of ye Felicities, wch ye Blessed Saints Enjoy in Heaven, while we are here below; But yet we have Sufficient reason to believe, since we are infallibly told, that the Righteous will be perfectly happy after Death – So that tho' we don't at present know what Heaven is,

[unnumbered page, which should be 140:]

& ye Nature of its Felicities, Yet we can make no doubt, but it must be good for us to be there. – Hence, I don't See why a wise & good man may not be very desirous, when God's wisdom sees it fit, to be Translated into a World, where, out of ye reach of Trouble & Sorrow, It will be Fixed in Fullness of Joy for ever. – To illustrate this Point from the following Instance; The nearest I can think of here below. – "The Case of a person born Blind. Such an One can have no more Idea of the Pleasure and advantage of Sight, while He continues Blind, than we can have, while we are here, of ye Joys of ye Blessed in a Future State; Now, my Lord, please only to Suppose Such an One to be informed how He might receive his Sight, & also to be well assured by all he converses with, that the Enjoyment of Sight would greatly add to the Comfort & Happiness of his Life; Might not this Blind man very rationally desire to have his Eyes opened, tho', till then, He could not form [a] just Idea of the pleasure & Benefit of Sight? Or, would any one check his desire of being Blest wth this happy Faculty, by Telling him, that as He has

[unnumbered page, which should be 141:]

no clear Ideas of the nature of Light, therefore He would not be fond, if He were in his Senses, of hurrying into it? – I suppose No one would use this Sort of argument to disuade him from Indulging an Inclination to receive Sight; For tho' He can't, as He never Experienced what Light is, So much as Form ye Least Idea of ye pleasure wch He would receive from Sight, – Yet, as He has undoubted assurance, that Sight is a most valuable Blessing, He may therefore very rationally desire to have his Eyes open'd."

I need not enlarge to y^r L^{dsp} to make ye Application to the point in hand; I shall only add This that I wish to God, all in your high Station had ye Same Reverence for the Great God & Lord Almighty, & y^e Same Just Sense of Religion wch y^r L^{dsp} Seems to have by y^r Writings. – I Take it for granted, My Lord, that you take y^e Passages Mention'd here, in the Same Sense wth myself – If I have Mistaken your meaning thro' Inadvertency or want of Apprehension, I heartily Beg y^r L$^{dsp's}$ pardon for Troubling you wth This, & Should be glad to have y^e

[unnumbered page, which should be 142:]

Honour of a Letter from you to be better informed, wch if you will please to vouchsafe, by directing to me thus, it will come very safe, "To y^e Revd Mr Scott at Dickleburgh, to be left at Mr Walton's, Sadler in Diss, Norfolk." This Parish is about 9 little Miles from Diss, a Market & Post Town & am my Lord with my most hearty wishes to you & y^r noble Family, in y^e Roman Phrase of a Multos & Felices. –

> your Lordship's most obed^t
> Servant
> William Scott

P.S. The observations lately publish'd on y^r L$^{dsp's}$ Remarks, I have not yet had y^e opportunity of Perusing, it being very Seldom that I can catch at a new Book.

[unnumbered page, which should be 143:]

[Orrery's hand:]

Ld Corke's Answer.

[scribe's hand:]

Revd Sir,

Civilities from a Stranger, a[t] least demands a requital. I am totally ignorant to whom I am writing: however I can do no less than answer your letter which came to me late, and might not have reached me at all: I having quitted my house in Leicester fields some years ago, and about two years since by the death of a kinsman my appellation is altered. If you have any commands for me you must direct to the E. of Corke at Marston near Frome in Somersetshire.

God forbid there should be anything in my book inconsistent with the wise just & revered tenets of the Gospel. – you, Sir, explain my meaning, I cannot do it in better words than you have done it for me. only I must add that in the place you mention, I tacitly Speak of persons, who are not Christians

[unnumbered page, which should be 144:]

of whom I fear there are too many in this kingdom.

The Lashes written against me, I have Scarce Seen: and the moment I found abuse, I entirely threw them aside. My book must Stand or fall by its own merit, or defects: & cannot either be raised by panegeric, [*sic*] or depressed by malice. both which I have lived long enough in the world, equally to despise.

> I am, Sir, very thankfully
> your most obedient
> humble Servant
> Corke.

Marston
Jan^{ry} 22^d 1756

[two unnumbered pages, which should be 145 and 146, blank]

[unnumbered page, which should be 147:]

In the London Evening Post of Tuesday February the 11th 1752 was inserted the following Advertisement

[pasted:]

This Day are publish'd,
In One Volume Octavo, Price bound 4s.
(With a Head of the DEAN, *etch'd by Mr.* Wilson,)
The FOURTH EDITION of
REMARKS on the LIFE and WRITINGS of
Dr. JONATHAN SWIFT,
Dean of St. Patrick's, Dublin.
In a Series of LETTERS from JOHN Earl of ORRERY, to
his Son, the Hon. HAMILTON BOYLE.

Printed for A. Millar, opposite Catherine-street in the Strand.

Where may be had,
The same Book in a small Octavo Volume, Price sew'd in
blue Paper 2s.6d. or 3s. bound.

[last page, unnumbered:]

[pasted:]

170 SWIFT (Dean) Remarks on the Life and Writings of Dr. Jonathan Swift, Dean of St. Patrick's, Dublin, in a series of letters from John, Earl of Orrery, to his son, the Honourable Hamilton Boyle, *portrait engraved by Wilson*, FIRST EDITION, LARGE PAPER, THE AUTHOR'S OWN COPY, WITH AUTOGRAPH INSCRIPTION, "ORRERY, LEICESTER FIELDS, NOVEMBER, 21st, 1751," *inside cover*; also a few contemporary cuttings, and at the end 144 pages of manuscript, roy. 8vo, calf, £10 10s.

Printed for A. Millar, 1752

The manuscript additions are headed, "Particular Papers and Memorandums relating to this edition of Doctor Swift's Life, *Mem.* This first edition was published on Thursday, November 7th, and on Saturday, November the 9th. Mr. Millar, the Editor, had disposed of the whole edition, fifteen hundred, at 4s a volume, bound." Then follow various extracts from contemporary press notices, and copies of letters to the Earl of Orrery from Lord Bolingbroke, the Bishop of Derry, Bishop of Clogher, Doctor Barry, two most interesting letters from George Faulkner, respecting the publication of the Dublin edition of the book. Two letters from Richard Purcell to the Earl of Orrery. Several letters from the Countess of Orrery to the Earl of Orrery, &c.

Manuscript Notes in Williams.473

[The hand is Orrery's throughout, except where otherwise noted]

[inner front cover:]

Orrery.
Leicester Fields.
November 29th
1751.

[in the hand of someone from Cambridge University Library:]
Williams 473

[pasted:]

Cambridge University Library
From the bequest of
SIR HAROLD WILLIAMS
F.B.A., F.S.A., M.A., Christ's College
Sandars Reader in Bibliography, 1950
† 24 October 1964.

[page numbered 1:]

[scribe's hand:]

This Edition was published on Thursday November the 19th, according to the following Advertisem^t:

[pasted:]

This Day is publish'd,
A NEW EDITION,
Beautifully printed on a fine Paper in a small Octavo Size,
With a Head of the DEAN *finely engrav'd by* RAVENET,
Price 2*s*.6*d*. sew'd in blue Paper,
REMARKS on the LIFE and WRITINGS of
Dr. JONATHAN SWIFT,
Dean of St. Patrick's, Dublin.
In a Series of LETTERS from JOHN Earl of ORRERY, to
his Son, the Hon. HAMILTON BOYLE.
"Haec sunt quae nostra liceat te voce moneri.
"Vade, age.   Virg. Aeneid III. v.461.
Printed for A. Millar, opposite Catherine-street in the Strand.

***As there is a very great Demand for the above book, it will be only sew'd in blue Paper, both on Account of the Sheets not being dry enough to bear binding, and that the Publick may be supplied with it as soon as it's possible.

[scribe's hand:]

Mr Millar printed three thousand of these Volumes.

In less than a Week, Mr Millar had disposed of above two thousand of this Edition, and applied to Lord Orrery for leave to begin another edition in two sizes, one in a large, and the other in a lesser Octavo.
    The Demand for the book

[page numbered 2:]

continuing excessively great, Millar put four presses to work, and on Saturday Decr 7th 1751, was published in the London Evening Post the following Advertisement.

[pasted:]

Next Week will be publish'd,
The Third Edition, carefully corrected,
(*Adorn'd with a Head of the* DEAN, *engraven by* RAVENET,)
In One Volume, Small Octavo,
REMARKS on the LIFE and WRITINGS of
Dr. JONATHAN SWIFT,
Dean of St. Patrick's, Dublin.
In a Series of LETTERS from JOHN Earl of ORRERY, to
his Son, the Hon. HAMILTON BOYLE.
Printed for A. Millar, opposite Catherine-street in the Strand.

***The great Demand for these Book [*sic*] continuing, it is impossible to get them bound, without soiling the Beauty of the impression, they will therefore continue to be sold for 2s.6d. sew'd.
In the Press, and will be publish'd with all convenient Dispatch,
A new Edition of this Work in large Octavo, with a Head of the Dean, etch'd by Mr. Wilson, bound 4s.

[scribe's hand:]

And on Tuesday Decr 10th 1751, the third Edition was published: of these Mr Millar printed three thousand: so that from Novr the 11th to Decr 11th 1751, were printed of this book 7500: the largest sale that has ever been known of any book in so short a time.

[page numbered 3:]

[Orrery's hand:]

Persons to whom I have given this Edition.
Mr Boyle.
Mr Tibal.
Mr Laws.
Daniel Hughes.
Robert Bickle.
Mr Johnson.
The Revd Mr Lloyde.
Lady Allen. &c. &c. &c. &c.

[page numbered 4:]

As some Censures have been passed upon the Severity with which Swift's Character is treated, I have marked some passages that are particularly in his favour with a [pointing hand]
[page blank]

[frontispiece, title page, and text of MII follow]
[passages in the text marked out by Orrery with a pointing hand:]

[Letter IV, p. 30:]

Perhaps the deeper bottoms were too muddy for his inspection.

[Letter VIII, p. 57:]

[misprint "ruest" corrected to "truest"]

[Letter XVII, p. 131:]

"It is plainly seen, says the Publisher, *that a spirit of liberty is diffused through all these writings, and that the author is an enemy to tyranny and oppression in any shape whatever.*" This is the character at which SWIFT aimed, and this is the character which indeed he deserved.

to remember, that with all those faults, he was above corruption. A virtue in itself sufficient to cover a multitude of human failings, since from that virtue alone can flow prosperity to the commonwealth.

[Letter XIX, p. 146:]

his observations were piercing. He had seen the great world, and had profited much by his experience.

[Letter XXIII, p. 191:]

I have remarked such passages with a most unwilling eye. But, let my affections of friendship have been ever so great, my paternal affection is still greater: and I will pursue candour, even with an aching heart, when the pursuit of it may tend to your advantage or instruction.

[Letter XXIV, p. 213:]

I always considered him as an *Abstract and brief chronicle of the times*; no man being better acquainted with human nature, both in the highest, and in the lowest scenes of life.

[Index follows]

[After Index, two pages blank]

[page numbered 1:]

[scribe's hand:]

Some particular Stories of Doctor Swift, intermixt with some of his particular Sayings.

[Orrery's hand:]

The Dean's Hat.

Dr Swift, could little bear the least repartee. It knocked him down: and he remained under the greatest confusion. Not so much from bashfullness, as from pride.

He called one day upon his hatter, and said to him, "This Hat of mine lets in the rain,

[page numbered 2:]

What shall I do with it? Can't you find some method, so as to secure me against the wet weather?" One of the scholars of Trinity College who was standing in the Shop, immediately replied, "I'l[l] tell you Sir, an effectual method to secure you against the rain." "Pray what is it?" replied the Dean. "Only to buy a new One," rejoined the Scholar. The Dean, snatched up his hat from the counter where it lay,

[page numbered 3:]

and went out of the Shop in great rage and indignation.

The Dean's Influence over the Rabble.
    After <u>Serjeant Bettesworth</u> had threatened to cut off the Dean's Ears, and make his head as round as an apple, a great number of the Rabble assembled in the Dean's Court-Yard, and sent him word "They were resolved to revenge the affront he had sustained, by pulling down <u>Bettesworth's</u> house, and demolishing the

[page numbered 4:]

Serjeant himself."
    The Dean immediately drew up a writing, in the exact style of an absolute monarch, by which manifesto, He commanded them, as his subjects, not to proceed, till they received from him farther orders, or such directions, as he should think fit to give.
    They obeyed his edict, and went peaceably home. Such was his influence over the Rabble.

[page numbered 5:]

The Dissection of Princes.
    The Dean, used to say, "He should be glad to see half a dozen Kings dissected, that he might know, what it was that stamped a greater value upon one Prince, than upon eleven millions of People."

Best Lyars in Europe.
    He was outragiously angry if he discovered any of his Servants attempting to deceive him. "What impudence" (he used to say) "have those ignorant Rascals? They pretend

[page numbered 6:]

to impose their nonsensical Lies upon me who have conversed with the best Lyars in Europe."

The Dean's Boots.

It was a custom with Dr Swift, to walk to the end of the Town, and there get upon horseback; He constantly made one of his footmen carry one boot, and the other, another, and he gave as his reason, because if one man carried both boots, his fellow Servant would laugh at him.

[page numbered 7:]

Stumpanthe & her sister beggars.

Dr Swift had five beggars whom he kept in constant pay. He called them his mistresses, and carried his friends frequently to visit, and relieve them in the Streets. He named them Stumpanthe, Fritterilla, Ulcerissa, Cancerina and Fourleganda.

Stumpanthe had lost one of her hands.

Fritterilla, was lame and made Apple Fritters for Shoeboys.

[page numbered 8:]

Ulcerissa, was full of Sores.

Cancerina, had a sore breast.

Fourleganda, went upon her arms and knees.

At what age, Judgement ripens.

In the year 1737, the ^{Dean} asked me how old I was. I told him turned of one and thirty. "That's the time," says he, "when judgement, begins to ripen. Nourish It: and do not let fancy nip it in the Bud."

[page numbered 9:]

[Deane Swift's letter to Orrery, as well as the affidavits, are in the scribe's hand]

An Account of the ill treatment, which the Dean of S^t
Patrick's received from Dr Wilson.
In a Letter from Deane Swift Esqr To the Earl of Orrery,
With Affidavits annexed.
December 19th 1742.

My Lord,

In obedience to your Lordsp's commands I send you an account of that abominable usage which the Dean of St Patricks met with last Summer from one Dr Wilson, and that your Lordship may see the man who was capable of abusing so great a person, I shall close the Relation of that business with part of Wilson's Character, which I propose to sketch

[page numbered 10:]

out with all the impartiality of an indifferent Spectator. To give your Lordship some light into this proceeding, it may perhaps be requisite to say, that Wilson is one of the Dean's Prebendaries, and that ever since his Acquaintance with the Dean, he has used all the means in his power to subvert Doctor Wynne in the Office of Sub-Dean, that he himself might succeed in his place. This Fellow is besides Tenant of the Deanery Tythes, which Circumstance of his life, did all at once so fix his acquaintance and intimacy with the Dean, that for these last five or Six years, ever since he became Tenant, he has lived full half the time, in the Dean's house. What this Man's

[page numbered 11:]

intentions were the morning he invited the Dean to dine with him in the Country, are not known: but this is certain, that he took all imaginary pains to hurry the Dean out of Town in a Hackney Coach, without taking his friend Mrs Ridgeway along with him, which the Dean has always done, ever since he began to be conscious of his want of memory, and other infirmities. However, it doth not as yet appear, that any abuse was committed by Wilson before dinner, in the absence of the Dean's Servant: and it is probable, from Wilson's behaviour in the afternoon, that if he attempted to impose upon the Dean in the morning, he mis-

[page numbered 12:]

-carried in his design. This I mention, because it was the general opinion of those who are to be the Dean's Executors, and of many others, that Wilson's honesty, in regard to money matters, was not to be trusted; and therefore it was not unlikely, if for small payments he could get large Receits, it would not disturb his conscience, and indeed every body was inclined to believe the worst of the Doctor, because it was notorious that so long as the Dean's memory and judgement were tolerable, Wilson seldom or ever paid the Dean any money but in the presence of Mrs Whiteway, and after the Dean's memory failed, he always paid the Dean in private, notwithstanding he was frequently warned

[page numbered 13:]

to the contrary. There was one circumstance, which the Dean's friends thought proper to have suppressed in the Servant's examination, which was, that Wilson made the <u>Dean</u> drunk. Now the <u>Dean's</u> stint for about half a year before, was two large bumpers of Wine somewhat more than half a pint. When the <u>Dean</u> had drunk this quantity, <u>Wilson</u> pressed him to another glass, which the Dean's footman observing, told Wilson, in a low voice, that his Master never drank above two glasses, and if he forced him to a third, it would certainly affect his Head. But <u>Wilson</u> not only made light of this caution, and imposed another glass upon the <u>Dean</u>, but called afterwards for a

[page numbered 14:]

Bottle of strong White Wine, and forced the <u>Dean</u> to drink of it, which, in a short time, did so intoxicate him, that he was not able to walk to the Coach without being supported: and after all this, <u>Wilson</u> called at an Ale House in his way to Dublin, and forced the poor <u>Dean</u> to swallow a dram of Brandy. It was not long after, when <u>Wilson</u> began to grow very noisy, and to curse and swear, and to abuse the <u>Dean</u> most horribly, as it is at large set forth in the Servant's Examination. Whether he struck the <u>Dean</u> or not is uncertain, but, one of the Dean's arms was observed, next morning, to be black and blue. The noise of this

[page numbered 15:]

bustle in the Street, sudden as it was, drew a small handfull of the Common people together, who have since declared, that if they had known it was the <u>Dean</u>, whom <u>Wilson</u> had abused, they would have torn the Wretch to pieces: but he escaped the justice of a gratefull people, for the measure of his Iniquity was not then full. I had almost forgot to acquaint your Lordship with the most deplorable Circumstance of that whole day, which was, That within a quarter of an hour after the <u>Dean</u> had received this treatment, as soon as he had entered his

[page numbered 16:]

own house, he asked for this Fellow with a kind of surprize, saying, "Where is <u>Doctor Wilson</u>? Ought not the Doctor to be here this Afternoon?" So absolutely was he then lost to all Reason and memory: and indeed it was the talk of the Town, that a Statute of Lunacy ought to be taken out, in order to guard the Dean against further insults, and wrongs of all kinds. In justice to the Dean's friends here, give me leave to assure your Lordship, that if an action of law could have been grounded upon the Servant's examination, <u>Wilson</u> would have been severely handled; for, the whole Nation, to a Man, resented the affront.

[page numbered 17:]

All that was in my power to do upon this occasion was to leave orders with the Dean's servants, that I might be sent for privately whenever that fellow presumed to visit the Dean; and this I did, with a Resolution to expose the Villain, and make the Dean sensible of the usage he had received: but this I never had an Opportunity of doing: for since that time, he never once attempted to enter the Dean's house.

> I am, My Lord,
> your Lordship's
> most obedient and
> most humble Servant
> Deane Swift.

[page numbered 18:]

Copy of the Affidavit of Richard Brenan, Servant to Doctor Swift, in relation to Doctor Wilson's treatment of his Master   June 16th 1742.

Who being duly sworn on the Holy Evangelists, and examined, saith, that on Monday the fourteenth instant June, the Reverend <u>Doctor Wilson</u> came to the Deanery House in S[t] Kevin Street Dublin, and in some short time after the said <u>Wilson</u> came to the said House, there was an Hackney Coach called for by directions of said <u>Wilson</u>, and as soon as the said Coach

[page numbered 19:]

came to the entrance or door of the said house, the said Wilson, assisted by this Exam[t]: put this Defend[t]: and his said Master the Rev[d] <u>Doctor Swift</u> into said Coach, and then Wilson gave this Exam[t] some directions, and desired this Exam[t] to take his the said <u>Wilson's</u> mare, and follow them, and immediately ordered the Coach man to drive to Newland in the County of Dublin (a place where the said <u>Wilson</u> lives) and thereupon the Coachman [set] off, and this Exam[t] saith, that as soon as this Exam[t] could get ready, which was in less than an hour, he took said <u>Wilson's</u> Mare, and followed his said <u>Master</u> and said <u>Wilson</u>, and saith he overtook them on the Road. This Exam[t] saith, that his

[page numbered 20:]

said Master having dined with the said <u>Wilson</u>, his said Master and said <u>Wilson</u> set out from <u>Newland</u> aforesaid in said Coach, between the hours of five and six in the Evening in order to return to <u>Dublin</u>. And this Exam[t] further saith, that at some small distance from the <u>Black Lyon</u> Turnpike, this Exam[t] being behind said Coach, he, this Exam[t] heard the said <u>Wilson</u> (who was in the said Coach with his said Master) say to his said Master, "<u>Sir, make me Sub-Dean</u>:" and immediately said <u>Wilson</u> began to abuse Doctor <u>Winn</u>, and thereupon made use of this expression, "He is a stupid fellow, which I am not;" To which this Exam[t] heard his said Master make this answer, "<u>Psha, pay me my money</u>." To which said <u>Wilson</u> returned, "<u>Sir, I am paying</u>

[page numbered 21:]

<u>you your money, and will pay you</u>." This Exam[t] further saith, that in a few minutes after he had so heard the said Wilson express himself as aforesaid, he heard the said Wilson break out into a most violent passion, and begin to curse and swear, and heard said <u>Wilson</u> frequently repeat this expression, "<u>By God, no man shall strike me; and if King George should strike me I would cut his throat</u>." And so continued cursing and swearing, and abusing this Depon[t's] Master, till they came a little way past M[r] Bradstreet's near Hillmainham, at which place the said <u>Wilson</u> called out to the Coachman, "<u>You</u>

[page numbered 22:]

<u>Villain, you Rascall, stop the Coach</u>." Upon which this Exam[t] immediately jumpt from behind the Coach, and opened the Door thereof, to let said Wilson out. When he had stept out, he turned about to this Exam[t's] said Master, and expressed himself in these words; "<u>You are a stupid old Blockhead, and an old Rascall; and only you are too old I would beat you, and God damn me, but I will cut your throat</u>." Whereupon this Exam[t] endeavoured all in his power to get the said Coach door shut, which when this Exam[t] had done, he desired the Coachman to drive to the Deanery House. Upon

[page numbered 23:]

which the said Wilson made use of this expression, "<u>God damn him, drive away the old stupid Blockhead</u>." And further this Exam[t] saith not.

Sworn before me this 16th June 1742.
Jo: Rochfort.

Richard Brenan.

> Copy of Doctor Wilson's Affidavit
> in relation to his conduct towards
> Dr Swift July 13th 1742.

Who being sworn on the Holy Evangelists saith, that on Monday the 14th of June last, he made a visit to the Revd Doctor Swift Dean

[page numbered 24:]

of St Patrick's, who rec^d him said Wilson with his usual fondness, which was always very great. That he told the said Wilson, he would take the air that morning, and dine with him at his house in the Country: and that he did call accordingly for his Coach, and one Mrs Ann Ridgeway who usually attends him, but the Coachman and she being both abroad, an Hackney Coach was sent for, in which the said Doctor Swift and Wilson arrived at Newland the said Wilson's House, where the said Dean did dine, and as this Exam^t believes, drank half a pint of White Wine. That soon after dinner they again went into the Coach in order to return to Dublin. That for about the first

[page numbered 25:]

two miles of the road, the Dean treated the Dean [sic] with remarkable civility and love: but that of a sudden he cryed out "The said Wilson was the Devil, and bid him go to Hell:" which words he afterwards repeated in a most astonishing rage, but of which the said Wilson took no other notice than by an endeavour to appease him in repeating some passages out of such Authors as the Dean admired most: but that instead of giving any attention to what the said Wilson said, he struck him several times on the face; scratched him, and tore off his Wig. All which usage the said Wilson bore in pity for

[page numbered 26:]

the poor Dean's infirmities, and in love for his person, untill he thrust his fingers into the said Wilson's eyes; upon which the said Wilson ordered the Coach to stop, which he left with the natural expressions of Resentment and indignation, declaring he would not again tamely suffer the greatest Man on Earth to strike him. And the said Wilson further saith, that he did not once attempt to strike, or in any sort to violate the Dean's person, notwithstanding the provocation was as above set forth.

Sworn before me 13th of July 1742.

David Chaigneau.
Francis Wilson.

[unnumbered page, which should be 27:]

[Orrery's hand:]

To Shut the Door.
    One of the Dean's servants came into his Master's Bedchamber to ask leave
to visit a sick relation about ten miles out of Dublin. The Dean gave him
leave. And when he had been gone about an hour, the Dean sent another
servant, after him, on horseback, with orders to command him to return
immediately. The Fellow was near seven miles from Dublin, when he was
overtaken

[page numbered 28:]

by his fellow-servant. He immediately returned to the Deanery, and appearing
before his Master, asked what were his particular commands? "You went
out," said the Dean, "and left open my bedchamber door. I sent for you back
to shut it."

Q. Caroline's Charms.

    The Dean, in his later years, wrote, in any of his own books, which he was
reading, such Criticisms

[page numbered 29:]

as occurred to him, (a circumstance which made his library sell much better
after his death) and I remember to have seen written with a Pencil, in the
Margin of Addison's Freeholder, N° 21   March 2^d, which describes the
personal beauties of the late Queen Caroline, then Princess of Wales, a Note
in these Words, or to this purpose, "My Eyes are certainly very dim, for I
never could perceive any of these charms."

[page numbered 30:]

Dr Garth.
    The Dean's first acquaintance with Doctor Garth began in this manner.
    Swift came into Button's Coffee-house, very much covered with Dust, and
very dirty, whilst Dr Garth was writing a letter. The D^r could not help smiling

at so odd a figure, but continuing to write his letter, as soon as he had finished it, he looked in

[page numbered 31:]

Swift's face, and sneeringly said to him, "Parson, can't you help me to a little sand to sand my letter?" "No," replied Swift, "I have no sand about me, but I have some gravel, and if you please I'l[l] piss upon it."

ArchB^P of Dublin.
The Dean used to say of Dr King, ArchB^P of Dublin, "He has wit, and is a scho-

[page numbered 32:]

-lar, but I hate him, as I hate Garlick."

The reason for this aversion may be deduced from Page 22.^{d} [of the *Remarks*, MII edition, the account of King's objection to Swift's preferment]

Servant's faults.

Doctor Swift dined with me one day in Dublin. We had only two dishes of meat for dinner. One servant, a footman, waited. When the first dish was removed, and the second was brought upon the table, the Dean became for some time pensive, and very grave. I asked him the meaning. "I am thinking" says he, "how often, if your servant had been mine, I should

[page numbered 33:]

have chid him for faults, which I have seen him commit: and I find the number of times, amount to twenty two."
These faults were, not giving a plate with the right hand. Not taking off a dish with both hands. Putting the plates too near, or too far from the fire. And such kind of trifles, which gave him constant causes of fretfullness, and passion and made his servants, to whom he was in general, a very kind and indulgent master, very fearfull, and uneasy.

[page blank]

[inner back cover:]

[pasted:]

231   SWIFT (Dean) Remarks on the Life and Writings of Dr. Jonathan Swift, Dean of St. Patrick's, Dublin, in a series of letters from John, Earl of Orrery, to his son, the Honourable Hamilton Boyle, THE SECOND EDITION, corrected, *portrait engraved by Ravenet*, THE AUTHOR'S OWN COPY, WITH AUTOGRAPH INSCRIPTION, "ORRERY, LEICESTER FIELDS, *November*, 29th, 1751," *inside cover, contemporary advertisements inserted, a list in Lord Orrery's handwriting of the names of some of the persons to whom he gave copies of this edition (includes "Mr. Johnson"); and at the end 33 pages of manuscript, partly in his Lordship's hand, entitled,* "SOME PARTICULAR STORIES OF DOCTOR SWIFT, INTERMIXT WITH SOME OF HIS PARTICULAR SAYINGS," sm. 8vo., rough calf, £12 12s

Printed for A. Millar, 1752

This volume also contains some interesting memoranda relating to the sale of the book. It is stated that Millar printed three thousand copies of this edition, and that over two thousand of them were disposed of in less than a week. The demand was so great that Millar put four presses to work. "From Novr. the 11th to Decr. 11th, 1751, were printed of this book 7,500, the largest sale that has ever been known of any book in so short a time."

[written in the pasted slip's margin:]

P. J. & A. E. Dobell
London
Bruton Sl. Cat: N° 6
(Septr 1921)

INDEX

LIST OF ABBREVIATIONS USED IN THE INDEX

Bart.: baronet.

co.: county (of Ireland).

Discourse: *Discourse of the Contests and Dissensions between the Nobles and the Commons in Athens and Rome*, by Jonathan Swift.

ed., eds.: edition(s).

FI: earliest printing of Orrery's *Remarks on Swift*, 204-page 12mo by George Faulkner, Dublin.

FIa: 339-page 8vo edition of Orrery's *Remarks on Swift*, by George Faulkner, Dublin.

FIb: 339-page 12mo edition of Orrery's *Remarks on Swift*, by George Faulkner, Dublin.

FII: 339-page 12mo second edition of Orrery's *Remarks on Swift*, by George Faulkner, Dublin.

FIII: 339-page 8vo third edition of Orrery's *Remarks on Swift*, by George Faulkner, Dubin.

FV: 339-page 12mo fifth edition of Orrery's *Remarks on Swift*, by George Faulkner, Dublin.

GT: *Gulliver's Travels*, by Jonathan Swift.

Ham: Hamilton Boyle, Orrery's son and addressee of the Letters in *Remarks on Swift*.

MI: 339-page 8vo first edition of Orrery's *Remarks on Swift*, by Andrew Millar, London.

MII: 214-page 12mo second edition of Orrery's *Remarks on Swift*, by Andrew Millar, London.

MIII: 214-page 12mo third edition of Orrery's *Remarks on Swift*, by Andrew Millar, London.

MIV: 312-page 8vo fourth edition of Orrery's *Remarks on Swift*, by Andrew Millar, London.

MV: 240-page 12mo fifth edition of Orrery's *Remarks on Swift*, by Andrew Millar, Lmndon.

Ms., Mss.: manuscript(s).

Née: maiden name.

O: John Boyle, fifth Earl of Cork and Orrery, author of *Remarks on Swift*.

Remarks: *Remarks on Swift*, by Orrery.

S: Jonathan Swift.

S.P.D.: St. Patrick's Cathedral, Dublin.

sen.: senior.

Stella: Esther (or Hester) Johnson.

T.C.D.: Trinity College, Dublin.

Vanessa: Esther (or Hester) Vanhomrigh.

vol., vols.: volume(s).